Between the Two World Wars: Monetary Disorder, Interventionism, Socialism, and the Great Depression

Ludwig von Mises

Selected Writings of Ludwig von Mises

Between the Two World Wars:
Monetary Disorder, Interventionism,
Socialism, and the Great Depression

Edited and with an Introduction by
Richard M. Ebeling

LIBERTY FUND INDIANAPOLIS

This book is published by Liberty Fund, Inc., a foundation established to encourage study of the ideal of a society of free and responsible individuals.

The cuneiform inscription that serves as our logo and as the design motif for our endpapers is the earliest-known written appearance of the word "freedom" (*amagi*), or "liberty." It is taken from a clay document written about 2300 B.C. in the Sumerian city-state of Lagash.

Frontispiece photograph courtesy of Richard M. Ebeling. Ludwig von Mises, Vienna, 1936. Foto Fayer, A-1010 Wien, Opernring 6.

Printed in the United States of America

06   05   04   03   02   C   5   4   3   2   1

06   05   04   03   02   P   5   4   3   2   1

Library of Congress Cataloging-in-Publication Data

Mises, Ludwig von, 1881–1973.
    Between the two World Wars: monetary disorder, interventionism, socialism, and the Great Depression/edited and with an introduction by Richard M. Ebeling.
        p.   cm.   (Selected writings of Ludwig von Mises; 2)
    Includes bibliographical references and index.
    ISBN 0-86597-384-9
    ISBN 0-86597-385-7 (pbk.)
    1. Von Mises, Ludwig, 1881–1973.   2. Economics.   3. Free enterprise.
4. Liberty.   I. Ebeling, Richard M.   II. Title.
HB101.V66A25   2002
[HB101.V66]
330.15'7 s—dc21
[330.15'7]   2002073029

Liberty Fund, Inc.
8335 Allison Pointe Trail, Suite 300
Indianapolis, Indiana 46250-1684

Contents

Part I Monetary Disorder, Inflation, and Interventionist State (1918–32)

PART VII ECONOMIC CALCULATION UNDER SOCIALISM

Appendix: A Soviet Response to Mises

Acknowledgments

This volume would have been impossible to prepare if not for the assistance and support of the following people. First and foremost were Bettina Bien Greaves, formerly of the Foundation for Economic Education, who provided the permission to bring into print these writings of Ludwig von Mises, Gitta Sereny, the stepdaughter of Ludwig von Mises, and her husband, Don Honeyman, for their kindness and support in pursuing this project. Also invaluable were the Moscow Center for Historical and Documental Collections and its former director, Dr. Mancur Mukhamedjanov, who most generously placed the facilities of the center at the disposal of my wife and myself for the photocopying and microfilming of Mises's "lost papers," and for arranging the Russian permissions that enable these writings to be published.

A most grateful thanks is also due to Mr. and Mrs. Quinten E. Ward, whose generous support enabled my wife, Anna, and me to travel to Moscow in October 1996 and obtain the copies of Mises's "lost papers." In addition, Mrs. Mildred Dunn, Mr. Sheldon Rose, and Dr. John Sheridan have provided significant financial support enabling Hillsdale College to bring this volume to the general public.

Almost all of the articles and essays in this volume had to be translated into English. Dr. Herbert Izzo and Dr. Olga Koutna of Ann Arbor, Michigan, translated more than fifty percent of them. The remaining articles and essays were translated by Dr. Grete Heinz of Monterey, California, Dr. Wolfgang Grassl, professor of marketing at Hillsdale College, and Ms. Elisabeth Garay of Leroy, Michigan. Both Dr. Heinz and Dr. Grassl sometimes worked on tight deadlines with extremely fast turnaround, with no diminishment in the excellence of the finished product. I especially owe a thanks to Wolfgang Grassl for his support, patience, and assistance in sharing his wide and detailed knowledge of the history and institutions of his native Austria, and for the countless times he helped with the nuances of various technical terms and phrases in the German language.

A sincere thanks is also due to Dr. Eberhard Geyer, professor of German at Hillsdale College. He enthusiastically gave of his time and skills in preparing summary translations of a wide selection of Mises's "lost papers" and related documents and material for an exposition and display at the March 1997 Ludwig von Mises Lecture Series on the Hillsdale campus.

At Hillsdale College, my secretary, Carol Kratzer, retyped several of the essays and provided greatly appreciated assistance in getting the manuscript into its finished form.

Preparation of the annotated footnotes for the essays would have been much more difficult if not for the timely and professional assistance of the Hillsdale College library staff, especially Mary "Squeak" Barnett and Judy Leising. They handled numerous interlibrary requests and helped with finding material in the Hillsdale College library collection.

Liberty Fund has enthusiastically supported bringing Mises's papers into publication and been generous with their assistance throughout the process. I owe a special thanks to Christine Ferran and Dan Kirklin for their patience and assistance throughout the preparation of this volume.

Finally, my wife, Anna, remains the point of gravity around which all good things in my life revolve. She has been my patient and enthusiastic supporter and partner in this project, as in everything else I do. Indeed, the success of our work in Moscow is totally due to her efforts and determination. She also kindly translated from Russian the article on "Anti-Marxism" that is the appendix for this volume. To her I owe the most important thanks — for everything.

RICHARD M. EBELING

Ludwig von Mises Professor of Economics
Hillsdale College

October 2001

INTRODUCTION

The "Lost Papers" of Ludwig von Mises

All of the articles and essays contained in this volume were written by Austrian economist Ludwig von Mises during the twenty years between the two world wars, from 1918 to 1938. The common themes running through most of them concern the monetary disorder and inflation that followed the breakup of the Austro-Hungarian Empire at the end of the First World War; the monetary, fiscal, and interventionist problems in Austria and Europe in general in the 1920s and 1930s, including during the Great Depression; and the collectivist policies and ideas that were leading Europe down the road to the Second World War. Also included from this period are articles on the Austrian economists, the methodology of the social sciences, and the problem of economic calculation under socialism.

They all were originally written in German and about a quarter of them have never been published before. Virtually all are taken from the "lost papers" of Ludwig von Mises.

In the years between the two world wars, Ludwig von Mises was one of the most famous and controversial economists on the European continent.[1] Born in Lemberg, Austria-Hungary on September 29, 1881, Mises entered the University of Vienna in 1900 and was awarded a doctoral degree in 1906. In 1909, the Austrian Chamber of Commerce in Vienna hired Mises as one of its economic staff members. In 1913, he was given the title of *Privatdozent*, permitting him the right to teach at the University of Vienna as an unsalaried lecturer, with promotion to the title of Professor Extraordinary in 1918.

---

1 For expositions of Mises's ideas on the rationality of human action, the theory of social order, and the market economy and alternative economic systems, see Richard M. Ebeling, "A Rational Economist in an Irrational Age: Ludwig von Mises," in Richard M. Ebeling, ed., *The Age of Economists: From Adam Smith to Milton Friedman* (Hillsdale, Mich.: Hillsdale College Press, 1999), pp. 69–120; Richard M. Ebeling, "Planning for Freedom: Ludwig von Mises as Political Economist and Policy Analyst," in Richard M. Ebeling, ed., *Competition or Compulsion? The Market Economy versus the New Social Engineering* (Hillsdale, Mich.: Hillsdale College Press, 2001), pp. 1–85; and Israel M. Kirzner, *Ludwig von Mises: The Man and His Economics* (Wilmington, Del.: ISI Books, 2001).

Over the next twenty-seven years, until his emigration to the United States in July 1940, Ludwig von Mises caused firestorms of controversy. In 1912, he published *The Theory of Money and Credit*, in which, besides its many other theoretical contributions, Mises formulated what became known as the Austrian theory of the business cycle. Inflation and depression were not inherent to a capitalist economy, but were the result of government control and mismanagement of the monetary system through manipulation of market rates of interest.[2]

It was an article he published in 1920,[3] and which two years later he expanded into the book-length treatise *Socialism*, that caused the whirlwind of debate that surrounded him for the rest of his life. In this work, Mises demonstrated that the central planners of a socialist state would have no way of knowing how to use the resources of the society at their disposal for least-cost and efficient production. Without market-generated prices, the planners would lack the necessary tools for "economic calculation." The reality of the promised socialist utopia would be poverty, economic imbalance, and social decay. Furthermore, Mises argued that any type of collectivism that was applied comprehensively would result in a terrible tyranny, since the state would monopolize control over everything needed for human existence.[4]

In 1927, Mises published *Liberalism*, in which he presented the clas-

2 Ludwig von Mises, *The Theory of Money and Credit* (Indianapolis: Liberty Fund, 3rd. revised ed., [1924; 1953] 1980). For an exposition of the Austrian theory of money and the business cycle in the context of the Great Depression and in contrast to the Keynesian approach, see Richard M. Ebeling, "The Austrian Economists and the Keynesian Revolution: The Great Depression and the Economics of the Short-Run," in Richard M. Ebeling, ed., *Human Action: A 50-Year Tribute* (Hillsdale, Mich.: Hillsdale College Press, 2000), pp. 15–110. For a comparison of Mises's theory of money and the business cycle with that of the Swedish economists during this period, see Richard M. Ebeling, "Money, Economic Fluctuations, Expectations and Period Analysis: The Austrian and Swedish Economists in the Interwar Period," in Willem Keizer, Bert Tieben, and Rudy van Zip, eds., *Austrian Economics in Debate* (London/New York: Routledge, 1997), pp. 42–74.

3 Ludwig von Mises, "Economic Calculation in the Socialist Commonwealth," [1920] in F. A. Hayek, ed., *Collectivist Economic Planning* (London: Routledge & Sons, 1935), pp. 87–130; reprinted in Israel M. Kirzner, ed., *Classics in Austrian Economics: A Sampling in the History of a Tradition*, Vol. 3: "The Age of Mises and Hayek" (London: William Pickering, 1994), pp. 3–30.

4 Ludwig von Mises, *Socialism* (Indianapolis: Liberty Fund, [1951] 1981). For an exposition of Mises's critique of socialist planning in the context of the critics of socialism who preceded him, see Richard M. Ebeling, "Economic Calculation under Socialism: Ludwig von Mises and His Predecessors," in Jeffrey M. Herbener, ed., *The Meaning of Ludwig von Mises* (Norwell, Mass.: Kluwer Academic Press, 1993), pp. 56–101.

sical liberal vision of the free and prosperous society, one in which individual freedom would be respected, the market economy would be free, open and unregulated, and government would be limited to the primary functions of protecting life, liberty and property.[5] He followed this work with *Critique of Interventionism* in 1929, a collection of essays in which he tried to explain that the interventionist-welfare state was not a "third way" between capitalism and socialism, but a set of contradictory policies that, if fully applied, would eventually lead to socialism through incremental increases in government regulation and control over the economy—and that Germany in the 1920s was heading down a dangerous political road that would lead to the triumph of national socialism.[6]

Not surprisingly, both Marxists and Nazis viewed Ludwig von Mises as a serious intellectual enemy. In fact, in 1925, the Soviet journal *Bolshevik* published an article calling him a "theorist of fascism."[7] What was Mises's "crime" deserving of such a charge? In a 1925 article on "Anti-Marxism," Mises had written that Marxist Russia and a "national socialist" Germany would be natural allies in a war in Eastern Europe—thereby anticipating the infamous Nazi-Soviet Pact of August 1939, which served as the prelude to the beginning of the Second World War.[8]

By the early 1930s, Mises understood that a Nazi victory in Germany would threaten Austria. As a classical liberal and a Jew, he could be sure that after a Nazi takeover of Austria, the Gestapo would come looking for him. So when in March 1934 he was offered a way out by William E. Rappard, cofounder and director of the Graduate Institute of International Studies in Geneva, Switzerland, who offered him a position as Professor of International Economic Relations, Mises readily accepted and moved to Geneva in October 1934.[9]

5 Ludwig von Mises, *Liberalism: The Classical Tradition* (Irvington-on-Hudson, N.Y.: Foundation for Economic Education, [1927] 1996).

6 Ludwig von Mises, *Critique of Interventionism* (Irvington-on-Hudson, N.Y.: Foundation for Economic Education, [1929] 1996). For an exposition of some aspects of the Austrian ideas on interventionism, see Richard M. Ebeling, "The Free Market and the Interventionist State," in Richard M. Ebeling, ed., *Between Power and Liberty: Economics and the Law* (Hillsdale, Mich.: Hillsdale College Press, 1998), pp. 9–46.

7 F. Kapelush, "'Anti-Marxism': Professor Mises as a Theorist of Fascism," *Bolshevik*, No. 15 (August 15, 1925), pp. 82–87. This article has been translated from the Russian and is included as an appendix to the present volume.

8 Ludwig von Mises, "Anti-Marxism," [1925] *Critique of Interventionism*, pp. 71–95.

9 See Richard M. Ebeling, "William E. Rappard: An International Man in an Age of Nationalism," *Ideas on Liberty* (January 2000), pp. 33–41.

Mises kept his apartment in Vienna, where he and his mother had been living since 1911. After she died in April 1937, he returned the apartment to the owner of the building but continued to sublet a room from the new tenant. In this room he stored his papers, manuscripts, family and personal documents, correspondence, and files of his own and other writers' articles, as well as much of his personal library, which included more than two thousand volumes.

On March 12, 1938, the German army crossed the Austrian border. When Adolf Hitler arrived in Vienna on March 15 he announced that his native Austria had been incorporated into Nazi Germany. Over the next several weeks the Gestapo arrested tens of thousands of Viennese. An estimated seventy thousand were soon imprisoned or sent to concentration camps. Among the immediate victims were the Jews of Vienna, who were harassed, beaten up, tortured, murdered, and humiliated by being made to scrub the streets of Vienna on their hands and knees with toothbrushes while being surrounded by tormenting crowds of onlookers.[10] The new Nazi regime soon began a methodical program of appropriating the 33,000 Jewish-owned businesses and enterprises in Vienna.[11] Among those that the Gestapo came looking for soon after the *Anschluss* was Ludwig von Mises.

Towards the end of March 1938, the Gestapo came to Mises's Vienna apartment. He was safe in Switzerland, but the Nazis boxed up everything in his room and carried it away. A year later, on March 4, 1939, Mises sent out a letter of "information" to friends in Europe, explaining what had happened to his possessions:

> From 1911 until the death of my mother, I resided at 24 Wollzeile, Apartment 18 (Vienna, I). Upon her death I returned the apartment to the

---

10 See Joachim C. Fest, *Hitler* (New York: Harcourt Brace Jovanovich, 1973), pp. 549–50; Ian Kershaw, *Hitler, 1936–1945: Nemesis* (New York: W. W. Norton, 2000), pp. 84–85; and Getta Sereny, *The German Trauma: Experiences and Reflections, 1938–2000* (London: Penguin Press, 2000), pp. 6–8. (Getta Sereny, who was a teenager in Vienna at the time of the German occupation, is the stepdaughter of Ludwig von Mises.)

11 See Saul Friedlander, *Nazi Germany and the Jews, Vol. I: The Years of Persecution, 1933–1939* (New York: HarperCollins, 1997), pp. 242–44. For a more detailed account of the events in Austria following the Nazi annexation of the country, see Dieter Wagner and Gerhard Tomkowitz, *Anschluss: The Week Hitler Seized Power* (New York: St. Martin's Press, 1971); and Walter B. Maass, *Country Without a Nation: Austria under Nazi Rule, 1938–1945* (New York: Frederick Unger Publishing Co., 1979).

owner of the building, who rented it out to the physician, Dr. Joseph Reitzes. However, I kept one room in the apartment as his subtenant. In this room I had my library, as well as my personal correspondence, my family papers, diplomas and other important documents. Furthermore, I had there silver tableware, and a considerable number of other silver items—large platters, candelabras, etc. Finally, there was some linen. At the end of March 1938 the Gestapo forcibly entered my locked room and hauled away the contents in twenty-one boxes. Then my room was sealed. In September or October, the rest of the objects in the room were taken away by the Gestapo. Dr. and Mrs. Reitzes have meanwhile left Vienna, and no correspondence from them has reached me. From what I have heard, the Gestapo gave them strict orders not to get in touch with me. In August of last year, I learned from Baron Richthofen that my possessions were in the hands of the Gestapo. When my lawyer, Dr. Rintelen, inquired about what had become of my possessions, he was reportedly given the answer that they could not be found anywhere. My personal library includes about 2,500 books, 1,500 pamphlets and reprints. These works deal with such subjects as economics, economic policy, financial questions, economic conditions in various countries, all varieties of socialism, world and Austrian history, economic history, jurisprudence, philosophy, and *belles-lettres.*

Mises then listed the collections of books, journals and papers that had been among the property taken away by the Gestapo.[12]

Until his death on October 10, 1973, at the age of 92, Mises believed that everything had been destroyed—either by the Nazis or in the chaos of the war. Considering the manner in which the Nazi regime had earlier burned books as a symbolic rejection of ideas opposed to their own, this was, perhaps, a reasonable assumption.[13] However, Mises's papers had not

12 See also Ludwig von Mises, "Bemerkungen über die ideologischen Wurzeln der Währungskatastrophe von 1923" [Remarks on the Ideological Roots of the Monetary Catastrophe of 1923] in *Freunduesgabe zum 12. Oktober 1959 für Albert Hahn* [Friendly Presentations on the Occasion of Albert Hahn's Seventieth Birthday] (Frankfurt am Main: Fritz Knapp, 1959), pp. 54–58. Here Mises remarked that he kept notes of his conversations with members of the *Verein für Sozialpolitik* [Association for Social Policy] on various theoretical and methodological questions, adding "I kept these notes in my apartment in Vienna, which I had maintained after my move to Geneva in 1934. These and other documents disappeared after the Nazis plundered my apartment" (p. 55).

13 That Mises believed that his papers had been destroyed by the Nazis or in the war was told to me in conversation with his widow, Margit, in 1979.

been destroyed. Instead, they had been kept by the Nazis and ended up in Czechoslovakia, along with most of the other documents, papers, and archival collections the Nazis had seized in various German-occupied countries during the war.

During the first days of May 1945, as the war in Europe was reaching its end, the Soviet army, having conquered eastern Germany, began its conquest of the Czech region of Bohemia. Reaching the small town of Halberstadt, the Soviet soldiers began to fan out and occupied the railway station. On a track siding were twenty-four boxcars that the Nazi authorities had been preparing to evacuate to territory still under their control. When Soviet officials opened the boxcars, they found them stuffed with documents, files, dossiers, and personal and professional papers that the Gestapo had looted from France, Belgium, Austria, Holland, Poland, and many other countries, including Germany itself. Among these literally millions of pages of stolen documents were the "lost papers" of Ludwig von Mises.

This massive cache of material was turned over by the Soviet army to the KGB, who reported the find and its apparent content to Stalin. Stalin ordered the boxcars to be transported to Moscow, where a special building was constructed in the early 1950s to store and preserve these papers. They included 20 million documents from twenty countries. From the outside, the building looked like an ordinary residential complex. It had no nameplate on the door, and only the bars on the windows suggested that it was something other than what it appeared. For the next forty-five years the only people allowed access to the documents stored in the building were members of the KGB and the Soviet Ministry of Foreign Affairs. The employees—all KGB archivists—were forbidden to tell even their families where they worked and were restricted from meeting with foreigners, or even eating at restaurants patronized by foreigners in Moscow.

Each of the archival collections had been carefully studied and organized by the KGB. Mises's papers were divided into 196 files containing approximately 8,000 items. In 1951, the KGB prepared an index to his papers, with a one-paragraph description of each file. The entire collection was labeled "Fund # 623—Ludwig Mises."

With the collapse of the Soviet Union in 1991, the documents were declassified and the archive was opened on a limited basis under its new name, the Moscow Center for Historical and Documental Collections. Even foreign researchers could now request to see parts of the collection.

I first heard a rumor that Mises's papers might be in Moscow in the summer of 1993. My wife and I were in Vienna looking for archival material about Mises's life and career. A friend in the Austrian Chamber of Labor, Dr. Gunther Chaloupek, told me that some German diplomats had been in Moscow looking for material about antifascist Germans from the interwar period and had come across a reference to Mises's name among the indexes to captured documents they were permitted to examine.

In 1994, I found Mises's "information" letter from 1939 among Friedrich A. Hayek's papers at the Hoover Institution at Stanford University, so I now had an idea of exactly how and what the Nazis had stolen. It was only in July 1996 that I found out the exact location of Mises's "lost papers." I went to the Holocaust Museum in Washington, D. C., hoping that the researchers there could tell me whether, by chance, a Gestapo file on Mises had survived the war. No one could locate such a file. However, I asked a research staff member whether they could find out if any of Mises's papers were now in Russian hands. She introduced me to a senior researcher, Karl Modek, who specialized in Holocaust material relating to the Soviet Union. Opening a spiral binder containing a full list of the material stored at the Moscow Center for Historical and Documental Collections, he turned to the pages listing the fund numbers and the names of collections in the archive. There it was: "Fund # 623—Ludwig Mises."

Since the archive had been open to researchers since 1991, the question arises as to why the existence of Mises's papers had not come to light earlier, and why hadn't anyone taken the time to examine them and obtain copies? An answer was provided by Kurt Leube, former personal assistant to Friedrich Hayek.

In 1994, Mr. Leube also had heard that Mises's papers appeared to have survived in Russia. He found out that some Austrian researchers, including Gerhard Jagschitz of the University of Vienna and Stefen Karner of the University of Graz, had traveled to Moscow and seen the indexes to Austrian documents captured by the Soviet army. They confirmed that they had seen an index to Mises's papers. Mr. Leube had asked them to examine the files and describe their contents, but they replied that their own research schedule did not permit the time to do so.

In March 1997, Dr. Mansur Mukhamedjanov, then Director of the Moscow Center for Historical and Documental Collections, delivered a speech at Hillsdale College and explained:

> The Ludwig von Mises fund was accessible to researchers. But from the time when the archive has been opened, not one researcher looked into or worked with the materials of this fund. Russian economists who are in-

volved in working out the concept of market reform never showed any interest in Mises's fund. I don't think they even know about its existence.
Foreign researchers were interested in anything but Mises. Some of them
probably saw the index and knew that such a fund existed, but nobody,
I repeat, nobody ever showed any interest or desire to look into the documents. Our careful records show that no researchers ever requested
"Fund # 623—Ludwig Mises."

Mises's Vienna papers remained unexamined until my wife, Anna,
and I traveled to Moscow in October 1996. From October 17 to 27, we
spent every working day examining each of the files. We arranged the
photocopying or microfilming of virtually the entire collection of papers,
manuscripts, articles, correspondence, personal documents, and related
materials. They now have been rearranged and computer-cataloged and
are restored in the Ludwig von Mises Library Room at Hillsdale College.
  The articles and essays in the present volume contain material from
Mises's "lost papers" covering the period from between the two world
wars.[14] They offer a view of a different side of Ludwig von Mises in comparison to many of his other works that have been more readily available
from this period of his life.

The Economist as the Historian of Decline

In the months immediately after he arrived in the United States in the
summer of 1940, Ludwig von Mises set down on paper his reflections on
his life and contributions to the social sciences. It is less an autobiography
and more a restatement of his most strongly held ideas in the context of the
times in which he had lived in Europe. It carries in it a tone of despair
and dismay about the direction in which European civilization seemed to
be moving at the end of the first four decades of the twentieth century. In
clear anguish and frustration, he summarized how he viewed his efforts as
an economist in Europe in general and Austria in particular during those
years between the two world wars:

14 A companion volume will be published by Liberty Fund that contains material from
this collection that relates to Mises's writings before and during the First World War, his
family background, his service in the Austrian army during the First World War, his teaching at the University of Vienna, his private seminar, and his correspondence.

Occasionally I entertained the hope that my writings would bear practical fruit and show the way for policy. Constantly I have been looking for evidence of a change in ideology. But I have never allowed myself to be deceived. I have come to realize that my theories explain the degeneration of a great civilization; they do not prevent it. I set out to be a reformer, but only became the historian of decline.[15]

His activities between 1918 and 1938 were divided into two categories: his scholarly writings, and his work as an economic policy analyst and advocate for the Vienna Chambers of Commerce, Crafts, and Industry. The reader of *The Theory of Money and Credit, Socialism, Liberalism,* and *Critique of Interventionism* easily would have a conception of Mises as primarily a wide-ranging and interdisciplinary economic and social theorist who was especially concerned with advancing various aspects of monetary and general economic theory in the context of critically evaluating the ideological and policy trends of his time.

This view of Mises would also be easily reinforced from reading his economic treatise, *Human Action,* a massive work that represents the capstone of his thinking on a vast number of subjects.[16] He writes on a large canvas that incorporates a theory of human knowledge; the conception of the origin and structure of human society; the foundations and construction of a theory of the competitive market process; the nature of money, interest, capital, and the business cycle; and a detailed critique of the socialist, interventionist, and welfare-statist alternatives to the market order.

Some of the articles and essays included in the present volume show him as a clear and concise expositor of these general and critical ideas. In the context of the Austria of this time, however, they also show Mises as a contemporary policy analyst focusing on a variety of specific political, economic, and monetary problems in the wake of the First World War. In these writings he is an advocate of particular policies, reforms, and institutional changes meant to move his native Austria in the direction of freer markets, a more stable monetary order, and a less distorting fiscal regime.

His efforts in these areas of public policy grew out of his position at the Vienna Chamber of Commerce, where he first worked in October 1909

15 Ludwig von Mises, *Notes and Recollections* (South Holland, Ill.: Libertarian Press, [1940] 1978), p. 115.

16 Ludwig von Mises, *Human Action: A Treatise on Economics* (Irvington-on-Hudson, N.Y.: Foundation for Economic Education, 4th rev. ed., 1996).

as an assistant for the drafting of documents, later becoming a deputy secretary in 1910. Mises was promoted to *Leitenden Kammerssekretärs* (first secretary) of the Vienna Chamber when he returned to his duties after serving as an officer in the Austrian army during the First World War. He was in charge of the Chamber's finance department, which was responsible for banking and insurance questions, currency problems, foreign exchange regulations, and public finance and taxation. He also consulted on issues relating to civil, administrative, and constitutional law. Indeed, because of his wide interests and knowledge, practically every facet of the Chamber's activities concerning public policy and regulation fell within his expertise.[17]

Mises also was assigned special tasks. From November 1918 to September 1919, he was responsible for financial matters relating to foreign affairs at the Chamber. From 1919 to 1921, he was in charge of the section of the Austrian Reparations Commission for the League of Nations concerned with the settling of outstanding prewar debt.[18] After he accepted

---

17 See Alexander Hortlehner, "Ludwig von Mises und die Österreichische Handelskammerorganisation" [Ludwig von Mises and the Austrian Chamber of Commerce], *Wirtschaftspolitische Blätter*, No. 4 (1981), pp. 141–42.

18 The February 1925 issue of *Friedensrecht, Ein Nachrichtenblatt über die Durchführung des Friedenvertrages Enthaltend die Verlautbarungen des Österreichischen Abrechnungsamtes* [The Laws for Peace, A Newsletter for the Execution of the Peace Treaty, Containing Announcements of the Austrian Office for the Settlement of Accounts], pp. 9–10, reported

> the separation of Professor Dr. Mises from the board of directors of the Office of Accounts [for the settlement of prewar debts]. Due to his responsibilities as a deputy director in the offices of the Vienna Chamber of Commerce, Crafts, and Industry, he has had to resign from his activities in the Office of Accounts. As an economic theorist, Professor Mises has made a name for himself in the German-speaking scientific world far beyond the boundaries of Austria. His wide knowledge and his accurate, clear way of thinking are combined with an extraordinary, practical understanding and a detailed knowledge of the economic life in Vienna and Austria. Given Austria's present economic and financial difficulties, that the arranging of the debentures for the settlement of prewar debts has been facilitated under such comparatively favorable conditions we owe to his farseeing and able handiwork. With foresight into the requirements necessary for success, he sketched out the rules for the committee overseeing the settlement of the debentures. And it was his proposals for the issuance of the debentures that were adopted by the consortium of nations. It was just as important and beneficial for the work of the Office of Accounts that Mises applied, in a strictly objective way, his knowledge of the economic situation in the selection of the Office's personnel. Already as a staff member of the Chamber of Commerce, he had won the confidence of wide circles in the business world, and he has kept that confidence in his work with the Office of Accounts.

the appointment as professor of international economic relations at the Geneva Graduate Institute of International Studies, he went on extended leave from the Chamber, though he continued to return to Vienna periodically to consult on various policy matters until February 1938.[19]

At the Chamber, Mises explained, "I created a position for myself." While always having a superior nominally above him, he came to operate on his own with the assistance of a few colleagues. Though he felt that his advice was not often taken, he viewed himself as "the economist of the country" whose efforts were "concentrated on the crucial economic political questions," and as "the economic conscience" of Austria in its postwar period.

Friends often suggested to him that he could have had more of a positive impact on Austrian economic policy if he had been willing to give a little and modify his principled stance on various issues. Yet Mises's only regret, as he looked back on his years at the Chamber, was that he often felt that he compromised too much, though he stated that he had always clearly understood that in politics compromise was inevitable. The challenge was to "give" on the less important issues so as to have a better chance to succeed on the essential ones. This is how he viewed the positions he often took within the Chamber in an effort to get the organization to publicly back policies that he considered crucial at various times during these years.[20]

By the time he left Vienna for Geneva in October 1934, however, Mises believed that he had done little more than fight a series of rearguard actions to delay the decay and destruction of his beloved Austria. "For sixteen years I fought a battle in the Chamber in which I won nothing more than a mere delay of the catastrophe... Even if I had been completely successful, Austria could not have been saved," Mises forlornly admitted. "The enemy who was about to destroy it came from abroad [Hitler's Nazi Germany]. Austria could not for long withstand the onslaught of the National-Socialists who soon were to overrun all of Europe." Still, he had no regrets over the efforts he had made. "I could not act otherwise. I fought because I could do no other."[21]

To appreciate Mises's frustration and sense of failure in having begun, as he expressed it, with the hope of being a reformer and instead ending up in the role of a historian of decline requires an appreciation, however

19 Mises, *Notes and Recollections*, pp. 76 & 91.

20 Ibid., pp. 74–75.

21 Ibid., pp. 91–92.

brief, of the history of Austria between the world wars. Familiarity with this period will also serve to place into their appropriate context most of the articles and essays included in the present volume, writings through which Mises had clearly attempted to influence the course of events in his native land.

Austria Between the Two World Wars[22]

Austria-Hungary under the Habsburg monarchy had been a vast, polyglot empire in Central and Eastern Europe encompassing a territory of approximately 415,000 square miles with a population of 50 million. The two largest linguistic groups in the empire were the German-speaking and Hungarian populations, each numbering about 10 million. The remaining 30 million were made up of Czechs, Slovaks, Poles, Romanians,

22 The following summary of the course of Austrian political and economic history between 1918 and 1938 is taken mostly from the following works: J. van Walre de Bordes, *The Austrian Crown: Its Depreciation and Stabilization* (London: P. S. King and Son, 1924); Otto Bauer, *The Austrian Revolution* (New York: Bert Franklin, [1925] 1970); W. T. Layton and Charles Rist, *The Economic Situation in Austria: Report Presented to the Council of the League of Nations* (Geneva: League of Nations, 1925); *The Financial Reconstruction of Austria: General Survey and Principal Documents* (Geneva: League of Nations, 1926); Carlile A. Macartney, *The Social Revolution in Austria* (Cambridge: Cambridge University Press, 1926); Leo Pasvolsky, *Economic Nationalism of the Danubian States* (New York: Macmillan Co., 1928); John V. Van Sickle, *Direct Taxation in Austria* (Cambridge, Mass.: Harvard University Press, 1931); Malcolm Bullock, *Austria, 1918–1919: A Study in Failure* (London: Macmillan Co., 1939); David F. Strong, *Austria (October 1918–March 1919): Transition from Empire to Republic* (New York: Octagon Books, [1939] 1974); Antonin Basch, *The Danubian Basin and the German Economic Sphere* (New York: Columbia University Press, 1943); Mary MacDonald, *The Republic of Austria, 1918–1934: A Study in the Failure of Democratic Government* (Oxford: Oxford University Press, 1946); Friedrich Hertz, *The Economic Problem of the Danubian States: A Study in Economic Nationalism* (London: Victor Gollancz, 1947); K. W. Rothschild, *Austria's Economic Development Between the Two Wars* (London: Frederick Muller, 1947); Charles A. Gulick, *Austria: From Habsburg to Hitler*, 2 Vols. (Berkeley: University of California Press, 1948); Klemens von Klemperer, *Ignaz Seipel: Christian Statesman in a Time of Crisis* (Princeton, N.J.: Princeton University Press, 1972); Eduard Marz, *Austrian Banking and Financial Policy: Credit-Anstalt at a Turning Point, 1913–1923* (New York: St. Martin's Press, 1984); David Clay Large, *Between Two Fires: Europe's Path in the 1930s* (New York: W. W. Norton, 1990); Helmut Gruber, *Red Vienna: Experiment in Working Class Culture, 1919–1934* (Oxford: Oxford University Press, 1991); and Gordon Brook-Shepherd, *The Austrians: A Thousand-Year Odyssey* (New York: Carroll & Graf Publishers, 1996).

Ruthenians, Croats, Serbs, Slovenes, Italians, and a variety of smaller groups of the Balkan region.

During the last decades of the nineteenth century and the opening decade and a half of the twentieth century, the empire increasingly came under the strain of nationalist sentiments from these various groups, each desiring greater autonomy and some forcefully demanding independence. The First World War brought the 700-year-old Habsburg dynasty to a close.[23] The war had put severe political and economic strains on the country. Power was centralized in the hands of the military command, civil liberties were greatly curtailed, and the economy was controlled and regulated.[24] Yet the more that power was concentrated and the more that the fortunes of war turned against the empire, the more the national groups, most insistently the Hungarians and then the Czechs, Croats, and Poles, demanded self-determination to form their own nation states.[25]

The empire formally began to disintegrate in October 1918, when first the Czechs declared their independence, followed by the Hungarians and the Croats and Slovenes. In early November 1918, the last of the Habsburg emperors, Karl Franz Josef, stepped down from the throne, and on November 12, a provisional national assembly in Vienna proclaimed a republic in German-Austria, as this remnant of the empire was now named. Yet in the second article of the document of independence, it was stated that "German-Austria is an integral part of the German Republic." Thus the new Austria was born—reduced to 52,000 square miles with a population of 6.5 million inhabitants, one-third of whom resided in Vienna—with a significant portion of the population not wishing their country to be independent but unified (an *Anschluss*) with the new republican Germany.

For almost five months after the empire had politically broken apart, the Austro-Hungarian National Bank continued to operate as the note-issuing central bank within German-Austria, Czechoslovakia, and Hungary. The Czechs, however, increasingly protested that the Bank was expanding the money supply to cover the expenses and food subsidies of the German-Austrian government in Vienna. In January 1919, the new

23 See Edmond Taylor, *The Fall of the Dynasties: The Collapse of the Old Order, 1905–1922* (New York: Doubleday, 1963), pp. 69–96 & 337–56.

24 See Joseph Redlich, *Austrian War Government* (New Haven, Conn.: Yale University Press, 1929).

25 On the nationalist currents in Austria-Hungary, see Oscar Jaszi, *The Dissolution of the Habsburg Monarchy* (Chicago: University of Chicago Press, 1929).

Yugoslavian government declared that all notes of the Austro-Hungarian Bank on their territory would be stamped with a national mark, and only such stamped money would then be legal tender. The Czech government announced the same in late February 1919. The Czech border was sealed to prevent smuggling of notes into the country, and the notes within Czechoslovakian territory were stamped between March 3 and 10. Soon after, both Yugoslavia and Czechoslovakia began to issue their own national currencies and exchange the stamped Austrian notes for their new monetary units.

In Hungary the situation was more chaotic. In March 1919, a Bolshevik government took power in Budapest and began printing huge quantities of small-denomination notes with Austro-Hungarian Bank plates in their possession, as well as larger notes of their own design, causing a severe inflation. The Bolshevik government was overthrown in August 1919 by invading Romanian armies. The Austrian Bank notes were not embossed with a national stamp until March 1920, and a separate national currency was introduced in Hungary in May 1921.

The Austrian government, in response to the monetary decisions of the Yugoslavians and Czechs, began their own official stamping of Austro-Hungarian Bank notes within its territory between March 12 and 24, 1919.[26] However, the limiting of notes considered legal tender in the new Austria did not end the problem of monetary inflation. In a matter of weeks after the declaration of the Austrian Republic, the coalition government made up of the Social Democrats, the Christian Socialists, and the Pan-German Nationalists began the introduction of a vast array of social welfare programs. They included a mandatory eight-hour work day, a guaranteed minimum one- to two-week holiday for industrial employees, a continuation and reinforcement of the wartime system of rent controls in Vienna, centrally funded unemployment and welfare payments, and price controls on food supplies that were supplemented with government rationing and subsidies.[27] The cost for these latter programs was huge and kept growing.

26 On the introductions of separate currencies within the successor states of the former Austro-Hungarian Empire, see John Parke Young, *European Currency and Finance*, Vol. II (Washington, D. C.: Government Printing Office, 1925), on Austria, pp. 9–25; Czechoslovakia, pp. 55–77; and Hungary, pp. 103–24.

27 Eduard Marz, *Austrian Banking and Financial Policy: Creditanstalt at a Turning Point, 1913–1923*, pp. 290–317. On the effects of rent controls in Vienna in the 1920s, see F.A. Hayek, "The Repercussions of Rent Restrictions," [1930] in *Rent Control, A Popular Paradox* (Vancouver: Fraser Institute, 1975), pp. 67–83.

In 1921, half of the Austrian government's budget deficit was caused by the food subsidies.[28]

To cover these expenditures, the Austrian government resorted to the printing press.[29] Between March and December 1919, the paper money of the Austrian Republic increased from 831.6 million crowns to 12.1 billion crowns. By December 1920, it had increased to 30.6 billion crowns; by December 1921, to 174.1 billion crowns; by December 1922, to 4 trillion crowns; and to 7.1 trillion crowns by the end of 1923. Prices rose dramatically through this period. A cost-of-living index, excluding housing (with July 1914 = 1), stood at 28.37 in January 1919; by January 1920, it had risen to 49.22; by January 1921, it had gone up to 99.56; in January 1922, it stood at 830; by January 1923, it had shot up to 11,836; and in April 1924, it was at 14,850.

The foreign-exchange value of the Austrian crown also dramatically fell during this period. In January 1919, one dollar could buy 16.1 crowns on the Vienna foreign-exchange market; by May of 1923, a dollar traded for 70,800 crowns.[30]

Adding to the monetary and financial chaos was the virtual political disintegration of what remained of Austria. Immediately after the declaration of the Austrian Republic, political power devolved to the provinces

---

28 Budget deficits in nominal terms grew from 2.7 billion crowns in 1919 to 137.7 billion crowns in 1922. The deficits averaged between 40 and 67 percent, as a fraction of total federal government expenditure in Austria during this period of time. See Kurt W. Rothschild, *Austria's Economic Development Between the Two Wars*, p. 24.

29 In 1925, at a meeting of the *Verein für Sozialpolitik* [Society for Social Policy], Mises told the following story: "Three years ago a colleague from the German Reich, who is here in this hall today, visited Vienna and participated in a discussion with some Viennese economists. Everyone was in complete agreement concerning the destructiveness of inflationist policy. Later, as we went home through the still of the night, we heard in the *Herrengasse* [a main street in the center of Vienna] the heavy drone of the Austro-Hungarian Bank's printing presses that were running incessantly, day and night, to produce new bank notes. Throughout the land, a large number of industrial enterprises were idle; others were working part-time; only the printing presses stamping out notes were operating at full speed. Let us hope that industry in Germany and Austria will once more regain its prewar volume and that the war- and inflation-related industries, devoted specifically to the printing of notes, will give way to more useful activities." See Bettina Bien Greaves and Robert W. McGee, eds., *Mises: An Annotated Bibliography* (Irvington-on-Hudson, N.Y.: Foundation for Economic Education, 1993), p. 35.

30 J. van Walre de Bordes, *The Austrian Crown: Its Depreciation and Stabilization*, pp. 48–50, 83, 115–39.

and the local communities, which showed little loyalty to the new national government and great animosity towards the capital city of Vienna. They soon blocked the provincial borders, imposing passport and visa restrictions for entering and exiting their territories. Some of the provinces in 1919 even entered into independent negotiations with Switzerland and Bavaria about possible political incorporation into these neighboring countries. A primary motivation for this provincial "nationalism" or "particularism," however, was the food and raw materials crisis.

The imperial government had forcefully requisitioned food from the agricultural areas of German-Austria during the war. The new republican government in Vienna continued the practice of forced requisition at artificially low prices, using a newly formed *Volkswehr* [People's Defense Force] to seize the food supplies sold in Vienna at controlled prices for ration tickets. The provincial governments used their local power to prevent the export of their agricultural products to Vienna at these below-market prices. Vienna, however, received food from the countryside through a vast black-market network that operated throughout the country.

The food crisis was reinforced by an economic blockade, one that was continued for a brief time after the armistice by the Allied powers but mostly imposed by the Czechs, Hungarians, and Yugoslavians. Coal supplies throughout 1919 and early 1920 were hard to come by. The Czechs and Hungarians refused to supply coal unless they received actual manufactured goods as payment in trade. The inability to acquire coal and other essential raw materials resulted in Austrian and especially Viennese industry grinding to a halt, with no way to produce the goods necessary to pay for the resources required for production. Throughout 1919 and part of 1920, Vienna was on the verge of mass starvation, with food and milk rations almost nonexistent except for the very young. Only relief supplies provided by both the Allied powers and private charities saved thousands of lives in the city.[31]

In October 1920, a new constitution was promulgated as the law of the land. Written primarily by the Austrian legal philosopher Hans Kelsen, it defined the lines of authority between the central government and the

31 See Lord Parmoor, et al., *The Famine in Europe: The Facts and Suggested Remedies* (London: Swarthmore Press, 1920), especially the contributions about the situation in Austria by Friedrich Hertz, "What the Famine Means in Austria," pp. 17–26; Dr. Ellenbogen, "The Plight of German Austria," pp. 39–48; and Friedrich von Wieser, "The Fight Against the Famine in Austria," pp. 49–56.

provinces. The provinces were given wide powers at the local and regional level, but the supremacy of the federal authority over essential political and economic matters that the constitution established ended the provincial nationalism and "particularism."

One new element resulting from the constitution was that the city of Vienna was now administratively recognized as having a separate "provincial" status. Thus, neither the surrounding province of Lower Austria nor the federal government located in Vienna had jurisdiction over the affairs of the city. From 1920 until 1934, the city became known as "Red Vienna." Throughout the interwar period, Austrian politics were dominated by the battle between the Social Democrats and the Christian Socialists. The Social Democrats, while rejecting the Bolshevik tactic of dictatorship to achieve their ends, were dedicated to the ideal of marching to a bright socialist future. But outside of Vienna (where they consistently won a large electoral majority) they were thwarted in this mission by the Christian Socialists, who held the majority in the Alpine provinces of Austria and therefore in the National Assembly that governed the country as a whole. The Christian Socialists based their support in the agricultural regions of the country where there was a suspicion and dislike for socialist radicalism. The Christian Socialists, however, were willing to use, in turn, domestic regulations, trade restrictions, and income transfer programs to benefit segments of the rural population at the expense of the larger municipalities, and especially Vienna.

The battle between these two parties had first been fought out in 1921 and 1922, when government expenditures and the mounting increases in the money supply to pay for them were threatening runaway inflation and a financial and economic collapse. After several appeals to the Allied powers, the League of Nations extended a loan to the Austrian government to repay outstanding debts left over from the war and temporarily to cover current expenditures. In return the League supervised a demanding austerity plan that required sizable cuts in government spending, including the ending of the expensive food subsidies for the urban population and the firing of 80,000 civil servants. In addition, the League assisted in the construction of a new Austrian National Bank, for which Mises played a central role in the writing of the charter and bylaws.

In Vienna the Social Democrats remained determined to press on with creating a model socialist community. Huge sums of money were spent in the 1920s on building dozens of schools, kindergartens, libraries, and hospitals in the "working class" districts of the city. They also constructed vast new housing complexes, sometimes built literally like fortresses ready to be defended against any counterrevolutionary attacks; one of the most famous of these complexes was Karl Marx Hof. In other parts of the city rent controls kept the cost of apartment housing artificially low at the expense of the landlords. Municipal social and medical insurance programs provided cradle-to-grave protection—including free burials —for the constituents of the Social Democratic Party in Vienna.

To pay for these programs and projects, the Social Democrats imposed a "soak the rich" tax system. Various progressive tax devices were introduced on income, consumption, "entertainment," and "luxury" expenditures, as well as on rents, business enterprises, and capital assets within the boundaries of the city's jurisdiction. One newspaper referred to the city's fiscal system as "the success of the tax vampires," especially since to cover these municipal expenditures the tax base and rates soon enveloped a large portion of Vienna's middle class as well as "the rich."

Parallel to the electoral combat between Social Democrats and the Christian Socialists were paramilitary battles around the country as well. In 1919 and 1920, under the threat of foreign invasion—especially by Yugoslavian armed forces along Austria's ill-defined southern border—and the plundering expeditions of private gangs and the government's *Volkswehr* attempting to forcibly seize food supplies from the rural population, the farming communities created a *Heimwehr* [Home Defense Force]. It soon became the paramilitary army of the Christian Socialists. In turn, the Social Democrats created the *Schutzbund* [Protection League] as their private armed force. Armed with war surplus and other weaponry, they both had training camps, parades, and military drills, and held maneuvers in the countryside during which they would sometimes clash in actual combat.

One of the most serious of these clashes occurred in January 1927, in a town near the Hungarian border southeast of Vienna. In the fighting several people were killed, including a small child. In July 1927, three members of the local *Heimwehr* where the combat occurred were put on trial in Vienna but soon were acquitted. Mobs from the "working class" districts of the city, who were led by known communists, rampaged through parts of the center of Vienna; they burned down the federal palace of justice, requiring the police to use deadly force to put down the violence. In response, the Social Democratic mayor of the city declared the police incompetent and set up a new parallel police force, the *Wiener Gemeindewache* [Vienna Municipal Guard], manned mostly by recruits from the Social Democrats' *Schutzbund*, and all at the taxpayers' extra expense.

Throughout the 1920s, Austria lived a precarious economic existence. Heavy taxes and domestic regulations hampered private investment in the country with both the private sector and the municipal authorities dependent upon foreign lenders and domestic credit expansion for financing many of their activities. Indeed, the burden of rising taxes and social insurance costs, increasing wage demands by labor unions, and tariff regulations actually resulted in *capital consumption* in the Austrian economy through the 1920s.[32] In a report for the Austrian government that Ludwig von Mises had coauthored in 1931, it was shown that between 1925 and 1929 taxes had risen by 32 percent, social insurance by 50 percent, industrial wages by 24 percent, agricultural wages by 13 percent, and transportation costs by 15 percent—while an index of the prices of manufactured goods bearing these costs had increased only 4.74 percent between 1925 and early 1930.[33]

This was the political and economic situation in the country as Austria entered the Great Depression in 1929. Austria's crises in the early

32 See Mises, *Socialism*, p. 414: "Capital consumption can be detected statistically and can be conceived intellectually, but it is not obvious to everyone. To see the weakness of a policy which raises the consumption of the masses at the cost of existing capital wealth, and thus sacrifices the future to the present, and to recognize the nature of this policy, requires deeper insight than that vouchsafed to statesmen and politicians or to the masses who have put them in power. As long as the walls of the factory building stand, and the trains continue to run, it is supposed that all is well with the world. The increased difficulties of maintaining the higher standard of living are ascribed to various causes, but never to the fact that a policy of capital consumption is being followed." On the theory of capital consumption, see F. A. Hayek, "Capital Consumption," [1932] in *Money, Capital, and Fluctuations: Early Essays* (Chicago: University of Chicago Press, 1984), pp. 136–58.

33 *Bericht über die Ursachen der Wirtschaftsschwierigkeiten Österreichs* [A Report on the Causes of the Economic Difficulties in Austria] (Vienna: 1931): For a summary of some of the report's conclusions and related data on capital consumption and the shortage of capital in Austria during this time, see Friedrich Hertz, *The Economic Problem of the Danubian States*, pp. 145–68; Nicholas Kaldor, "The Economic Situation in Austria," *Harvard Business Review* (October 1932), pp. 23–34; and Fritz Machlup, "The Consumption of Capital in Austria," *The Review of Economic Statistics* (January 15, 1935), pp. 13–19, especially p. 13, n. 2: "Professor Ludwig v. Mises was the first, as far as I know, to point to the phenomenon of consumption of capital. As a member of a committee appointed by the Austrian government . . . he also emphasized comprehensive factual information." The process of capital consumption due to economic miscalculation under inflation was explained by Mises immediately after the war in his work *Nation, State and Economy: Contributions to the Politics and History of Our Time* (New York: New York University Press, [1919] 1983), pp. 161–63; and also in his *The Theory of Money and Credit*, pp. 234–37.

1930s were both political and economic. Between 1929 and 1932, Austria had four changes in the government, with finally Engelbert Dollfuss becoming chancellor in May 1932. The economic crisis became especially severe in May 1931. One of Austria's old imperial-era banks, the Credit-Anstalt, had taken over the Boden-KreditAnstalt in October 1929. The latter bank had branches throughout central Europe and suffered heavy financial losses through most of 1929 into 1930. To sustain the Boden-KreditAnstalt and its own financial position, CreditAnstalt borrowed heavily in the short-term market. In May 1931, panic set in that CreditAnstalt would not be able to meet its financial obligations, precipitating a run on the bank. At the same time, there was a rush to exchange Austrian schillings for foreign currencies and gold.

The Austrian government responded by passing a series of emergency measures between May and December 1931. Concerned about continuing losses of hard-currency reserves, the Austrian government instituted foreign-exchange controls. Distortions, imbalances, and corruption resulting from that law led to three revisions during the first year, each one loosening the controls a little more. The controls were phased out by 1934, after the Austrian government received loans from a group of foreign sources.[34]

In June 1931, Austria had appealed for financial assistance to provide funds needed to stem the massive loss of gold and foreign exchange.[35] The Bank of England and the Bank for International Settlements in Basil, Switzerland, extended credits to the Austrian National Bank. In August 1931, the Austrian government appealed to the League of Nations for a loan, as it had in 1922. The loan agreement was finally signed almost a year later in July 1932. It supplied funds to repay the credits extended by the Bank of England and the Bank for International Settlements. Refinancing of the loan a short time later at a lower rate of interest significantly reduced Austria's total foreign debt.

But the events that were to seal Austria's fate were being played out in

---

34 For accounts of Austria's experience with foreign-exchange controls between 1931 and 1934, see Howard S. Ellis, *Exchange Control in Central Europe* (Cambridge, Mass.: Harvard University Press, 1941), pp. 27–73; and Oskar Morgenstern, "The Removal of Exchange Control: The Example of Austria," *International Conciliation*, No. 333 (October 1937), pp. 678–89.

35 For a summary of the economic events in Austria in 1931 and 1932, see Vera Micheles Dean, "Austria: A Nation Paralyzed," *Current History* (December 1932), pp. 303–7.

the political arena. The League loan, like the one in 1922, required a League representative to supervise the allocation and use of the funds and insisted upon austerity measures to reduce the government expenditures, in addition to a renewal of the pledge against an *Anschluss* with Germany.[36] The Social Democrats and Pan-German Nationalists in the Austrian Parliament unsuccessfully attempted to block passage of the loan bill, an action which left a bitter and tense relationship between these two parties and Dollfuss's Christian Socialists.

In March 1933, a procedural argument arose during a parliamentary vote and the leading members of each of the major parties stepped down from the rostrum, bringing the proceedings to a halt. The next day, Chancellor Dollfuss used this as an excuse to suspend the parliament and announce that he was going to rule by decree. Tensions continued to mount for the next year until finally the situation exploded into civil war. Based on information that units of the *Schutzbund,* the paramilitary arm of the Social Democratic party, were going to initiate a coup attempt, the Christian Socialists' *Heimwehr* attempted to disarm them in several cities around the country, including Linz. When fighting broke out, the Austrian army was called into action to put down the combat.

In Vienna, the Social Democrats called for armed insurrection in "self-defense" against the "reactionary" forces of the Austrian army and the *Heimwehr.* For four days, deadly and destructive fighting went on in the outer districts of Vienna, with hundreds either killed or wounded and the government forces using artillery pieces to bombard Social Democratic strongholds. When the fighting ended, the Social Democratic forces were completely defeated. Most of the party's leadership fled the country, and the party was declared illegal.

Then in July 1934, a group of Austrian Nazis, inspired by Hitler's rise to power in Germany the preceding year, attempted a coup. They seized the Chancellery building, captured and killed Dollfuss, and proclaimed a National Socialist government. They were swiftly defeated by forces loyal to the Austrian government, as was another Nazi-led uprising in the region

---

36 In March 1931, the German and Austrian governments signed a protocol for the establishment of an Austro-German customs union. Under opposition from the governments of Great Britain, France, Italy, and Czechoslovakia, the customs union was prevented from operating after the World Court at the Hague found it to be inconsistent with the international agreements that Austria had signed in 1922. See Mary Margaret Ball, *Postwar German-Austrian Relations: The Anschluss Movement, 1918–1936* (London: Oxford University Press, 1937), pp. 100–185.

of Styria at the same time. When Mussolini declared Italy's intention to preserve Austria's independence by sending military forces to the Brenner Pass at the Italian-Austrian border, Hitler repudiated his Austrian followers (for the time being).

Kurt von Schuschnigg became chancellor following Dollfuss's death, a position he held until March 1938, when Nazi Germany annexed Austria. Thus ended Austria's tragic twenty-year history between the two world wars.

Monetary Disorder, Inflation, and Interventionist State (1918–32)

The first three chapters in this volume were written in 1918, before the end of the First World War. At this time, Mises was serving as an economic consultant to the Austrian General Staff in Vienna. The chapters look forward to a return to peace, but they contain nothing suggesting the actual cataclysm of events that were to follow. In his article, "The Quantity Theory," Mises restated the basic principles behind the quantity theory of money and emphasized that it had been the abuse of the printing press that had caused the wartime inflation. The task ahead would be to end the inflation and restore the soundness and stability of the Austrian currency when the fighting stopped.

In response to questions raised by two commentators, Mises made clear in "On the Currency Question" that monetary theory as a social-scientific endeavor offered no answer to the question as to which policy was best to follow in the postwar period. One option would be to end the printing of bank notes and allow the value of the Austrian crown to stabilize in terms of its then-current depreciated market value in exchange for gold and foreign currencies. A new fixed rate of exchange could be established, Mises suggested, say, one year from the day the war ended. If, on the other hand, there were a strong preference to return to the status before the war began in 1914, including a restoration of the prewar foreign-exchange value of the Austrian crown, it would be necessary for the government to run a budget surplus and pay off its debt to the Austro-Hungarian Bank, which would then take the bank notes out of circulation. The monetary contraction would have to continue until the value of the crown had once again risen to its prewar parity.

Mises emphasized that such a monetary deflation would have various disruptive social consequences in the transition to the higher foreign-exchange rate for the crown. Whether to contract the money supply or stabilize the value of the crown at its depreciated value was a political question that economic theory could not answer, other than to explain the consequences that were likely to follow from either course of action.[37]

In the spring of 1918, following the Treaty of Brest-Litovsk that ended the war on the eastern front that imperial Germany and Austria-Hungary had waged with the new Bolshevik government in Russia, Mises served as the officer in charge of currency control in Austrian-occupied Ukraine, with his headquarters in Odessa. An independent Ukraine had been declared in Kiev during this time, and in "Remarks Concerning the Establishment of a Ukrainian Note-Issuing Bank," Mises outlined the institutional rules that should be followed by a Ukrainian central bank. All bank notes issued and outstanding should be at all times covered with gold or foreign exchange redeemable in gold equal to one-third of the bank's liabilities. Bank assets in the form of secure, short-term loans should back the remaining two-thirds of the notes in circulation. Mises admitted that there were particular institutional and historical circumstances that would have to be taken into consideration in setting the conditions under which certain types of borrowers might have access to the lending facilities of the Ukrainian central bank. But what was crucial for Ukraine to have a sound monetary system were ample reserves for redemption of bank notes on demand and limits on the term-structure of the loans made by the bank.

These first essays have an almost surrealistic quality to them in suggesting a postwar period in which there would be a calm, stable, and relatively smooth transition to a restructured monetary system as a complement to the return to a tranquil peacetime economy. Instead, the problems that Mises attempted to grapple with in the essays that followed

---

37 See Mises, *Notes and Recollections*, p. 66: "Toward the end of the war, I published a short essay on the quantity theory in the journal of the Association of Banks and Bankers, a publication not addressed to the public. The censor did not approve my treatment of the inflation problem. My tame academic essay was rejected. I had to revise it before it could be published. The next issue immediately carried critical responses, one of which, as far as I can remember, came from bank director Rosenbaum."

concerned an actual situation of monetary disintegration, high inflation, political disorder, and general economic chaos.

The next three essays, "The Austrian Currency Problem Prior to the Peace Conference," "On the Actions to Be Taken in the Face of Progressive Currency Depreciation," and "The Reentry of German-Austria into the German Reich and the Currency Question," were all written in the first half of 1919. They deal, respectively, with distinct but interrelated questions: how shall a previously unified monetary system be separated into different national currencies; how might the private banking sector create a transition to a new currency after government mismanagement of the monetary system will have brought about a sudden inflationary collapse of the currency; and how shall two separate national currency systems be unified or reunified into a single monetary regime?

In "The Austrian Currency Problem Prior to the Peace Conference," Mises outlined alternative possibilities that might be followed in establishing a new monetary order in the wake of the collapse of the Austro-Hungarian empire and its unified currency system. He discussed the possibilities of maintaining a common single-currency area with a single central bank, or a monetary union with independent central banks, or completely independent national currencies issued and managed by separate central banks. Mises assumed that none of the newly independent "successor states" would opt for the first alternative. Thus the issue at hand was how all the people presently holding notes issued by the Austro-Hungarian National Bank would convert them into units of the respective new national currencies. He suggested that those residing in the respective successor states should have the freedom of converting their old notes into either the national currency of the new country in which they resided or into the currency of any other of the successor states, as they found most convenient and useful. The same free choice of currency conversion also should be available to those holding quantities of the old notes in countries outside the territory of the former empire. The additional problem to which the currency conversion would be tied was the distribution of the Austro-Hungarian prewar and wartime debt among the successor states. Mises offered a detailed formula of how the distribution of this debt and the conversion of the old notes into new currencies might be reasonably balanced without an undue financial burden on any one of the new countries.

But in the spring of 1919, a far greater problem that confronted the new Austria was the danger of runaway or hyperinflation. With state spending seemingly out of control because of the welfare-redistributive programs introduced by the Social Democratic and Christian Socialist coalition government, and especially because of the cost of subsidized food for the urban populations, the monetary system seemed headed for a collapse. Mises was cautious to say that it was neither certain nor inevitable that such a currency collapse had to occur. But if it did, Austria—and particularly Vienna, with its large urban population—could be faced with social disintegration, food riots, and mass destruction and theft of property as the value of the medium of exchange fell to zero. Government would have lost all legitimacy and trust in relation to monetary matters. It was to solve this problem that Mises presented his proposal, "On the Actions to Be Taken in the Face of Progressive Currency Depreciation."

It would fall on the shoulders of the private sector—banks and businesses—to devise the mechanism to bridge the gap between any dramatic and rapid collapse of the old currency and the spontaneous shift to the use of alternative monies by the citizens of the society. Thus, Mises presented a plan for these elements in the private sector to use export revenues and sales of assets to accumulate cash reserves of small-denomination units of Swiss money to use as the temporary, emergency medium of exchange. It would be used to pay salaries and pensions and to loan to the government and other employers in the market so that the population would have access to a medium of exchange they could have confidence in accepting and using for survival. This only would be necessary until normal export sales and capital transfers supplied over time the required quantities of gold or foreign currencies to be used as the permanent substitute monies in a postinflationary Austrian economy. Mises also explained the process by which private banks could form an informal consortium to jointly cover the costs and clearings of providing this emergency alternative currency.

While Mises alluded to the possibility of a private monetary order without a central bank in the wake of a currency collapse, realistically central banking was and would remain the prevailing monetary regime. The question then arose as to whether the new Austria should have its own independent central bank and national currency or instead should be integrated into a common currency area with the new Germany. This also related, in the long run, to whether or not there should be political unification, *Anschluss*, between Germany and Austria, which is the theme of

"The Reentry of German-Austria into the German Reich and the Currency Question."[38]

If Austria were to be integrated into a common monetary system with Germany, certain preconditions were essential for the unification. First and foremost, both countries would have to renounce inflationary monetary policies if there were to be a stabilization of their respective currency's value for purposes of conversion and unification. But this was not likely to be possible until and unless both countries brought an end to deficit spending, which usually was the impetus for monetary expansion to cover the government's spending in excess of tax revenues. Therefore, also essential for currency unification would be the establishment of parallel sets of fiscal-policy rules to govern taxing and spending in the two countries.

For the transition to a common currency, Mises suggested the German mark could first be introduced as a "core" or reserve currency in Austria, with a specified ratio of exchange at which the Austrian bank would be obliged to redeem Austrian notes for German marks, and vice versa. Increases and decreases in the number of units of Austrian currency in circulation would be dependent upon deposits or withdrawals of marks from the Austrian banking system. The Austrian National Bank would no longer be an independent authority that determined the quantity of money in the country (similar to the currency boards in a number of countries around the world). Final unification would then come through the German central bank redeeming all Austrian bank notes for marks at a specified ratio of conversion, after which there only would be one monetary system and one currency in use in both countries.

At the same time Mises was considering the currency question, he was working through the Chamber of Commerce to eliminate a major stumbling block to Austrian economic recovery through international trade. In "Foreign-Exchange Control Must Be Abolished," he argued that exchange

---

38 When he looked back at this period immediately after the First World War in his 1940 *Notes and Recollections*, Mises wrote on the issue of Austrian unification with Germany: "The situation [of Austria's apparently paralyzed political and economic situation after the First World War] sometimes made me vacillate in my position on the annexation program. I was not blind regarding the danger to Austrian culture in a union with the German Reich. But there were moments in which I asked myself whether the annexation was not a lesser evil than the continuation of a policy that inescapably had to lead to catastrophe" (p. 87). Yet in certain passages of his essays written in 1919, it is clear that at the time Mises was persuaded that unification with Germany was a "political and moral necessity."

control limited the ability of importers to acquire required raw materials and goods for the production of manufactured exports and placed insufferable delays and hurdles in the way of entrepreneurial adjustment to changing market opportunities.

This problem was matched by the economic disintegration of trade between the provinces and regions making up the new Austria, a theme that Mises took up in his essay, "Vienna's Political Relationship with the Provinces in Light of Economics." The cause, he argued, was preferential abuse of the fiscal structure through the system of differential tax incidence borne by the rural areas in comparison to the urban population, and Vienna in particular. The price controls on food supplies and the government's subsidies for Vienna residents at the financial expense of the farmers reinforced the tension. Far worse, considering that Vienna was on the verge of mass starvation, was the loss of the bourgeois spirit of enterprise and work that is both the hallmark and the necessity of city life. Attempting to live off the output of the rural areas by means of either begging or the use of arms would only drive a deeper wedge between the regions of Austria, threatening a further political breakup of what remained of the country. Free trade and division of labor on the basis of market prices was the only path to salvation if the new Austria were to survive.

Mises discussed the fiscal problems of Austria further in his two articles, "Direct Taxation in City and Country" and "Viennese Industry and the Tax on Luxury Goods." Both during and after the war, the tax burden had been shifted from the agricultural sectors to the urban industrial and commercial centers of the country; consequently, the manufacturing capital of the society was being consumed, which was seriously reducing Austria's productive capability. In Vienna, the socialist city government had imposed heavy taxes on "luxury goods." Mises warned that these taxes threatened the income-earning capacity of the city, particularly in relation to the tourist industry and the specialized goods for which Austria had built up an international reputation in its export trade.

Yet the greatest threat facing Austria, Germany, and many other countries over the next three years was worsening inflation, as Mises described in "A Serious Decline in the Value of the Currency," "The Abolition of Money in Russia," and "Inflation and the Shortage of Money." In the latter essay, Mises emphasized that as inflation accelerates people start anticipating future declines in the value of money and rush to reduce their cash holdings before money's value falls even more. Prices start rising faster than the increase in the quantity of money, creating the illusion of a "short-age of money." If the monetary authority tries to compensate for this by expanding the money supply at an even faster rate, this will only succeed in reinforcing popular inflationary expectations and speed up the currency's race to its collapse.[39]

With the currency reform in Austria in 1922 and the monetary reconstruction in Germany after the inflationary destruction of the mark in 1923, plus the end to inflation in a number of other countries, Europe turned once more to a gold standard. Yet, as Mises argued in his 1924 essay, "The Return to the Gold Standard," the battle to end inflation now was replaced with a debate over the most appropriate monetary system. Mises explained the merits of a gold standard, most especially the fact that a gold-based currency removed direct control of the printing press from the grasping hand of government. He also critically evaluated the counter-proposals of Irving Fisher and John Maynard Keynes for "managed currencies," the value of which would be manipulated by government to stabilize the price level or assure a desired level of employment and output.

Equally worrisome, Mises argued in his essays, "Restoring Europe's State Finances," "Changes in American Economic Policy," and "Commercial and Bureaucratic Business Management," was the direction of government spending, regulation, and nationalization of enterprises. The governments of Europe threatened the longer-term prosperity of their countries with burdensome levels of taxation and spending to finance income-transfer programs and to subsidize bankrupt state enterprises that should, in fact, either be privatized or shut down. Even in America, the bastion of free enterprise, political currents were moving in the direction of increasing government intervention and regulation. Those who hoped that state enterprises could be made profitable by introducing business-management styles into their operation failed to see fully the difference between an enterprise guided by the profit motive and one designed to pursue costly and inefficient "social" ends.

---

39 For Mises's detailed analysis of the hyperinflation in Germany and the methods to end it, see Ludwig von Mises, "Stabilization of the Monetary Unit—From the Viewpoint of Theory," [1923] in Percy L. Greaves, ed., *On the Manipulation of Money and Credit* (Dobbs Ferry, N.Y.: Free Market Books, 1978), pp. 1–49; and Mises, "The Great German Inflation," [1932] in Richard M. Ebeling, ed., *Money, Method and the Market Process: Essays by Ludwig von Mises* (Norwell, Mass.: Kluwer Academic Press, 1990), pp. 96–103.

The Political Economy of the
Great Depression (1931–36)

This continuing drift toward government intervention, regulation, and planning was accelerated and intensified with the start of the Great Depression in 1929. In an ideological environment dominated by socialist and interventionist leanings, Mises tried hard to defend the market order in a series of articles on "The Economic Crisis and Capitalism," "The Gold Standard and Its Opponents," "The Myth of the Failure of Capitalism," "Interventionism as the Cause of the Economic Crisis," "Planned Economy and Socialism," and "The Return to Freedom of Exchange," as well as in "Two Memoranda on the Problems of Monetary Stabilization and Foreign-Exchange Rates."[40]

The economic crisis through which the world was passing, Mises explained, was not caused by the market economy but was due to the monetary and credit-expansion policies of the previous years that had brought about a misdirection of resources and a malinvestment of capital. An economic adjustment was unavoidable once the inflationary policies had come to an end, but the severity and duration of the economic crisis was being caused by interventionist policies that prevented the necessary changes in the structure of relative prices and wages to bring the economy back into balance. Instead, governments supported inefficient industries and fostered trade-union resistance to cuts in the level of money wages. The result was idle resources and unemployment. Perversely, all of the disastrous effects resulting from these interventionist policies were being used to claim that it was capitalism that had failed. The new ideal of "planning" that was being advocated in place of the market economy was merely a new name for socialism, and government direction of a society's economic activities would merely lead to worse economic consequences.

The gold standard, Mises said, was being opposed and overthrown as a complement to the regime of interventionism so governments could have a free hand to manipulate the value of money; he attempted, at the same time, to refute many of the arguments against the gold standard. Through devaluation and monetary depreciation, the goal was to restore

---

40 Mises also presented an analysis of the causes and duration of the Great Depression and the policies needed to overcome the economic crisis in his monograph, "The Causes of the Economic Crisis: An Address," [1931] in Percy L. Greaves, ed., *On the Manipulation of Money and Credit*, pp. 173–203.

full employment by lowering workers' real wages by increasing the prices of goods and services while trying to keep money wages at their initial level or at least not rising as fast as prices were going up. At the end of the day, Mises argued, such a policy would fail. Nor could national prosperity and balance be restored through the introduction of foreign-exchange control. Artificially fixing the price at which a currency might be bought and sold, and putting control over the allocation of foreign exchange in the hands of the government, only intensified the distortions and imbalances in both the domestic and international markets.

Austrian Economic Policy and the Great Depression (1927–35)

In his native Austria, Mises considered that economic policy was continuing to follow the wrong direction even before the Great Depression set in. In "The Balance Sheet of Economic Policies Hostile to Property" and "Adjusting Public Expenditures to the Economy's Financial Capacity," he emphasized that taxes and government expenditures were strangling the Austrian economy. One indication of this was that the trade balance was in deficit because of foreign borrowing to compensate for capital consumption in the country. At the heart of the country's problems was a wrongheaded conception that said that, while in the private individual's budget expenses must be restrained by income, on the government balance sheet taxes should be adjusted to cover any level of expenditures considered desirable. This was a road to ruin, Mises warned, because there were always rationales for government to spend more money and never reduce any existing spending. This attitude had to be turned around to the view that it is the amount of taxes collectable without threatening the capital, standard of living, and growth of the economy to which government spending needed to conform.

Another element in Austria's policy irrationalities, Mises explained, was its labyrinth of layered and redundant government bureaucracies and regulations at the municipal, provincial, and federal levels. Government administration and regulation needed to be streamlined, simplified, and reduced. This in itself would not only make the economy more flexible and competitive, but also reduce the size and cost of government.

With the start of the Great Depression and the collapse of the

CreditAnstalt Bank in Vienna in May 1931, Mises's focus became the financial and economic crisis into which Austria had now fallen. He offered his policy prescriptions in five papers written in 1932 that he prepared for meetings of the Vienna Chamber of Commerce: "Foreign-Exchange Control and Some of Its Consequences," "An Agenda for Alleviating the Economic Crisis," "An International Loan as the 'Breathing Room' for Austrian Economic Reform," "On Limiting the Adverse Effects of a Proposed Increase in the Value-Added Tax," and "Foreign-Exchange Policy."

To try to save the CreditAnstalt, the Austrian National Bank had extended credits for which there was no gold backing as required by the bank's reserve requirements; to stop the run on its reserves, the bank had ended redemption on demand. The value of the Austrian schilling fell on the foreign-exchange markets. The government's response was to institute foreign-exchange control pegged at the former gold-parity rate. Mises explained that this would not bring about recovery in the market or restore balance in the international trade accounts. Instead, it would artificially induce even more imports and stymie the sale of exports—the exact opposite of what the government said it wished to do in terms of the country's balance of trade. The inconsistencies and contradictions in the foreign-exchange control system manifested itself in the fact that, as the year went on, the government was forced to loosen the restrictions on the sale and purchase of foreign currencies and allow more market-based allocation and pricing of foreign exchange. The only lasting cure, Mises insisted, was to immediately abolish the entire network of controls and return to a free market in foreign-exchange dealings.

The fundamental cure for Austria's problems in the world economic crisis required, among other things, the restoration of redemption of the Austrian currency at the legal gold parity. To do so, the Austrian National Bank had to reverse the monetary and credit expansion it had been following. Mises clearly stated that this monetary deflation had to be instituted as quickly as possible before the entire structure of prices and wages in the country had fully adjusted to the depreciated value of the schilling. At that point, returning to the legal gold parity would necessitate a wrenching adjustment of prices and wages downwards that might not be possible.

Equally crucial to a return to economic balance and the path to prosperity were reductions in government spending to alleviate the strain on the private sector from a state budget that was pushing the country to live beyond its means. It was government spending that was creating the pressure for tax increases, which Mises considered a serious danger to Austrian business. If certain taxes were raised, he maintained, they should at least be imposed in a way that did not unduly discriminate against some sectors of the economy for the benefit of others.

When the Austrian government applied for and received an international loan from the League of Nations to facilitate a solution to its financial difficulties, Mises endorsed it, but only if it was understood and used as a "breathing space" for actual and real institutional reform in the government's taxing and spending practices. Otherwise, Austria would be merely digging its financial grave even deeper.

At the end of 1934, as Mises was departing for Geneva, Switzerland, to take up his teaching appointment at the Graduate Institute of Economic Studies, he wrote "The Direction of Austrian Financial Policy: A Retrospective and Prospective View." Democratic government had ended in Austria, a brief civil war had been fought and had crushed the Social Democrats, and now Mises hoped that a new calm in the country could serve as the backdrop for returning to the path of economic reform and recovery. He reviewed the course of Austrian economic policy during the preceding fifteen years since the end of the First World War, and emphasized that what the country still needed was less government spending and taxing, more flexibility in the country's price and wage structure, a stable currency, and acceptance that as a small nation in a large global economy Austria had to adjust to the international conditions of supply and demand. Sadly, in under four years, Austria's fate would be sealed for the duration of the Second World War.

The Political Economy of Irrationalism, Autarky, and Collective Security on the Road to War (1935–38)

From his new vantagepoint in Geneva at the Graduate Institute, Mises was freed from the everyday affairs of Austrian economic policy that had been the focus of his attention at the Vienna Chamber of Commerce.[41] As he wrote in the foreword to the first edition of *Human Action*, "In the serene atmosphere of this seat of learning... I set about executing an old plan of mine, to write a comprehensive treatise on economics."[42]

41 Mises, *Notes and Recollections*, p. 137: "For me it was a liberation to be removed from the political tasks I could not have escaped in Vienna, and from the daily routine in the

Still, he devoted his attention to the political, ideological, and economic currents in Europe and periodically commented on them. In "The Cult of the Irrational," prepared for a Hungarian publication, Mises challenged those who argued against the liberal market economy and for nationalism and protectionism on the basis that there is more to public policy than logic and reason. Humanity's only tool for evaluating the reasonableness of any course of action is rationality, Mises insisted, otherwise it is blind in deciding what alternatives are more likely to yield the ends desired. Furthermore, if people were, in fact, driven by irrational forces of national "belonging" to prefer those goods that were domestically manufactured, then why did governments need to use their power to prevent their citizens from purchasing foreign commodities?[43]

This led Mises to warn of "Autarky: The Road to Misery." Self-sufficiency neither guaranteed security nor provided prosperity. European civilization was based and dependent upon the international division of labor. Abandoning it would only lead to societal decay and destruction.[44] In "The League of Nations and the Raw-Materials Problem," Mises explained that a country's prosperity did not require "ownership" of mines and raw materials and land in other parts of the world. The market economy brought all of the means of production around the globe to everyone's service through trade. If the League of Nations was to prove its worth as a force for peace, then it had to challenge the argument that wars were inevitable among nations for control of the resources of the world.

Chamber. Finally, I could devote myself completely and almost exclusively to scientific problems."

42 Ludwig von Mises, *Human Action: A Treatise on Economics* (New Haven, Conn.: Yale University Press, 1949), p. iii. This first edition of *Human Action* was handsomely reprinted in 1998 by the Ludwig von Mises Institute of Auburn, Alabama, with an introduction by Jeffrey M. Herbener, Hans-Hermann Hoppe, and Joseph T. Salerno that tells the history of how the volume came to be published in the United States. In Geneva, between 1934 and 1940, Mises had written the German-language forerunner to *Human Action*, entitled *Nationalökonomie: Theorie des Handelns und Wirtschaftens* (Munich: Philosophia Verlag, [1940] 1980).

43 Mises later was to call this cult of the irrational the twentieth-century "revolt against reason." See *Human Action*, pp. 72–91; and Ludwig von Mises, *Omnipotent Government: The Rise of the Total State and Total War* (Spring Mills, Pa.: Libertarian Press, [1944] 1985), pp. 112–16.

44 See also Mises's "The Disintegration of the International Division of Labor," [1938] in Richard M. Ebeling, ed., *Money, Method and the Market Process*, pp. 113–36.

Finally, in "Guidelines for a New Order of Relationships in the Danube Region," Mises explained that the nations of Eastern Europe had no hope of avoiding being the plundered pawns of their larger, stronger, and aggressive neighbors unless they turned away from their respective policies of political and economic nationalism. They needed to form a political and economic union that would guard their freedom from external enemies and finally secure liberty and prosperity within their territories.[45]

Austrian Economics

In two essays that he wrote in the 1930s and 1920s, respectively, Mises briefly summarized what he considered to be some of the more important contributions and insights of the Austrian economists, including the theory of marginal utility and the formation of prices for both final goods and the factors of production. He also stated that the ideas of the Austrians still contained insights that could be useful in public policy. At the University of Vienna, Mises had attended the seminar of Eugen von Böhm-Bawerk, who was one of the most famous of the Austrian economists. Mises's short memorial piece on the tenth anniversary of Böhm-Bawerk's death shows just how much he considered his old teacher to have contributed to both economic theory and policy.[46]

---

45 Mises developed the idea of an Eastern European Democratic Union after he came to the United States. See "An Eastern Democratic Union: A Proposal for the Establishment of a Durable Peace in Eastern Europe," [1941] in Richard M. Ebeling, ed., *Selected Writings of Ludwig von Mises, Vol. 3: The Political Economy of International Reform and Reconstruction* (Indianapolis: Liberty Fund, 2000), pp. 169–201.

46 For an overview of the ideas and historical significance of the Austrian School of economics, see Ludwig von Mises, "The Historical Setting of the Austrian School of Economics," [1969] reprinted in Bettina Bien Greaves, ed., *Austrian Economics: An Anthology* (Irvington-on-Hudson, N.Y.: Foundation for Economic Education, 1996), pp. 53–76; Ludwig M. Lachmann, "The Significance of the Austrian School of Economics in the History of Ideas," [1966] in Richard M. Ebeling, ed., *Austrian Economics: A Reader*, Champions of Freedom Series, Vol. 18 (Hillsdale, Mich.: Hillsdale College Press, 1991), pp. 17–39; and Richard M. Ebeling, "The Significance of Austrian Economics in 20th Century Economic Thought," in Richard M. Ebeling, ed., *Austrian Economics: Perspectives on the Past and Prospects for the Future*, Champions of Freedom Series, Vol. 17 (Hillsdale, Mich.: Hillsdale College Press, 1991), pp. 1–40.

Methodology of the Social Sciences

In the spring of 1933, Ludwig von Mises published a collection of essays, *Epistemological Problems of Economics,* devoted to questions of methodology in economics and the social sciences in general.[47] They dealt with the issue of whether economics is an *a priori* and deductive science that is able to derive qualitative and logical laws of human action and market relationships, or a discipline constructed on the basis of empirical observation, historical induction, and quantitative analysis.

Mises's position was that economics is inherently an axiomatic-deductive science that derives its insight through introspective reflection, on the basis of which it is able to formulate the logic of action and choice. History is the study of actual actions undertaken and their intended and unintended consequences. However, to do history there first must be a theory of what it means for man to choose: to weigh alternatives, compare costs and benefits, to make evaluations at "the margin," and to act once a goal in mind has been decided upon. But insight into the logic of action and choice cannot be derived from empirical experience. We discover them, their meaning, and their logical implications, by looking inside ourselves and asking what it means for a person to "act."

In June 1933, Mises had been asked to contribute a short essay for a volume in honor of the German scholar, Christian Eckert, on "The Logical Problem of Economics." The volume never appeared because of the "new environment" under the Nazi regime. The unpublished essay, among Mises's "lost papers," explored the similarities between positivism and historicism, in spite of their apparent antagonism toward each other. The crucial element, Mises argued, is to understand the difference between the logic of economic theory and the logic of historical analysis—and that, while they are distinct, they are not in conflict with one another.

In June 1937, Mises delivered a lecture at a philosophy conference in Paris on "The Logical Character of the Science of Human Action." In a nutshell Mises stated his general position on the nature of the social sciences. He emphasized that knowledge in the human sciences is derived from a fundamentally different source—introspection and reflection on the meaning and implications of "action"—from the basis of knowledge in the natural sciences, which comes from empirical investigation and

---

47 Ludwig von Mises, *Epistemological Problems of Economics* (New York: New York University Press, [1933] 1981).

laboratory experimentation. Inanimate matter does not assign meanings to its movements or to the other objects around it. A person most certainly does do these things, and this is what makes one's movements and doings "actions," which can only be formally comprehended through introspective reflection.

Economic Calculation under Socialism

After the appearance of Mises's treatise on *Socialism* in 1922, a large number of works were written by socialists and others who challenged or questioned his argument that the abolition of private property, market competition, and money prices for the factors of production under central planning made impossible any rational economic calculation for an efficient allocation and use of the resources of society. In the 1932 revised edition of *Socialism*, Mises added comments and replies to some of his critics. *Human Action* contains a refined restatement of his critique of socialist planning in the context of criticisms that had been made since that revised edition of *Socialism*.

In addition, he wrote two articles in the 1920s in direct response to his critics, "New Contributions to the Problem of Socialist Economic Calculation" (1923) and "Recent Writings Concerning the Problem of Economic Calculation under Socialism" (1928), neither of which has been previously published in English. In the first and longer article, Mises pointed out that those who challenged his argument either in fact ended up conceding his main thesis or were confused and misunderstood what the debate was about. He devoted the most attention to writings of the economic anthropologist Karl Polanyi and the Christian socialist Eduard Heimann, as well as to the arguments of a group of Soviet economists and German socialists, including Karl Kautsky and Otto Leichter.

In the 1928 article, Mises discusses the writings of Jacob Marschak, Otto Neurath, and the Russian economist Boris Brutzkus. In Brutzkus's work Mises finds a reinforcement of his own argument against socialism in the context of the failure of the Soviet experiment with planning during the period of War Communism in Russia between 1918 and 1922.[48]

48 Boris Brutzkus, *Die Lehren des Marxismus im Lichte der russischen Revolution* [Marxian Theories in the Light of the Russian Revolution] (Berlin: Hermann Sack, 1928). This work is included as the first part of Brutzkus's volume, *Economic Planning in Soviet Russia* (London: George Routledge, 1935), pp. 1–94. It has been reprinted in Peter J. Boettke, ed., *Socialism and the Market, Vol. III: The Socialist Calculation Debate Revisited* (London/New York: Routledge, 2000).

Also among Mises's "lost papers" was an unpublished manuscript on "Economic Calculation under Commercial Management and Bureaucratic Administration." It was written in longhand on the back of the pages of one of his reports for the Chamber of Commerce presented in July 1932. Mises explained that only where there is private property in the means of production and a goal of profit maximization by the enterprise can there be fully rational economic calculation. The very nature of bureaucratic administration is that among its chief goals are management of the public enterprise for purposes other than profit maximization. As a consequence, to restrain expenditures and prevent any arbitrary discretion on the part of the bureaucratic personnel, the public enterprise must be made to follow precisely defined and delimiting rules and regulations concerning all facets of its activities. In other words, there is no escape from it being managed "bureaucratically." The more government imposes regulations that steer private enterprises away from their market tasks of satisfying consumer demand in the pursuit of profits, the greater becomes the bureaucratic element in all economic activities. Thus, the choice society faces is profit-oriented businesses or bureaucratically directed enterprises. There is no sustainable alternative in between.[49]

The final piece in the present volume, included as an appendix, is the 1925 article by Soviet economist F. Kapelush on "'Anti-Marxism': Professor Mises as a Theorist of Fascism," which appeared in the Soviet journal *Bolshevik*. It provides a taste of the tone, style, and mode of argumentation by many Soviet scholars in response to antisocialist writings during this time. Readers may draw their own conclusions about the intellectual caliber of some of Mises's opponents in the Soviet Union.[50]

---

49 Mises later further developed this theme of management under private enterprise in the market economy and state management of public enterprises in the interventionist economy and under socialism in his book, *Bureaucracy* (Spring Mills, Pa.: Libertarian Press, [1944] 1983).

50 The same year Kapelush's article appeared, *Bolshevik* carried another article touching on Mises's criticisms of socialism. See Nikolai Bukharin, "Concerning the New Economic Policy and Our Tasks," *Bolshevik*, No. 8–9/10 (April 30–June 1, 1925); reprinted in Peter J. Boettke, ed., *Socialism and the Market: The Socialist Calculation Debate Revisited, Vol. I: The Natural Economy* (London/New York: Routledge, 2000), pp. 588–613). Bukharin wrote:

> Although bourgeois critics of the policy of the proletarian dictatorship in Russia have offered mainly nonsense and foolishness some of their comments were not so stupid and contained a relative truth. One of the most learned critics of communism, the Austrian Professor Mises, presented the following propositions in a

Conclusion

The essays in this volume, and his other writings from the period between the two world wars, closed off a chapter in the life of Ludwig von Mises. After 1940, when he was living in America, Mises wrote with a different purpose in mind than had been the case to a great extent during the 1920s and 1930s. In America he was not concerned with unraveling and critically arguing against particular policies or offering in their place specific policy prescriptions in the constantly changing currents of political life. He was

---

book on socialism written in 1921–22. In agreement with Marxist socialists he declared that one must brush aside all sentimental nonsense and accept the fact that the best economic system is the one that develops productive forces most successfully. But the so-called "destructive" socialism of communism leads to the collapse of productive forces rather than their development. The collapse occurs mainly because the communists forgot the enormous role of private individualistic incentives and private initiative. True, capitalism suffers from certain defects. But capitalist competition leads to growth of productive forces and drives capitalist development forward. As a result of the growth in society's productive forces, the lot of the proletariat improves as well. So long as the communists attempted to arrange production by commands, with a stick, their policy would lead, and already was leading, to an inevitable collapse. There is no doubt that the system of War Communism, viewed in terms of its economic essence, somewhat resembled this caricature of socialism whose destruction was predicted by all the learned economists of the bourgeoisie. Thus, when we began to reject this system and shift to a rational economic policy, bourgeois ideologists began to cry: Now you are retreating from communist ideas, they are surrendering their positions, they have lost the game, and are returning to time-honored capitalism. That is how they summarized the question. But in fact they were the ones who lost, not we....When we crossed over to the NEP [New Economic Policy] we began to overcome in practice the above-mentioned bourgeois case against socialism. Why? Because the meaning of the NEP lies in the fact that by using the economic initiative of the peasants, of the small producers, and even of the bourgeoisie, and by allowing private accumulation, we also placed these people objectively in the service of socialist state industry and of the economy as a whole....We control the main commanding heights [heavy industry, banking, and foreign trade] we organize what is *essential*: then our state economy, by different means, sometimes even by competing with the remnants of private capital through market relationships, gradually increases its economic might and, in diverse ways, draws the backward economic units into its own organization, doing so, as a rule, *through the market*" (pp. 593–94) [emphasis in the original].

Bukharin avoided Mises's main argument on the question of rational economic calculation and made Mises appear to have focused attention only on the issue of "incentives" under a socialist regime, while at the same time making a roundabout concession of the most important point by saying that the regime in Russia had now shifted to "market relationships," in comparison to the earlier phase of War Communism during which private property, money, and competition had been officially abolished.

not obliged to speak as a representative of a coalition of interests, as he had at the Vienna Chamber of Commerce, sometimes having to temper his arguments in the name of winning the endorsement of the Chamber members so he could advance what he considered "sound policy."

That "liberation," as Mises called it, had already begun for him when he moved to Geneva in the autumn of 1934. He was free to address himself to wider and more fundamental issues that he had certainly dealt with in many of his writings in the earlier years, but which he had not had the time or the intellectual autonomy to write about without distraction. The majority of his writings, especially after his arrival in America, tend to be written against the backdrop and in the context of fundamentals and first principles. Even his writings touching on various policy problems of the day, such as inflation or price controls, always focus the discussion on general principles or broad historical examples and lessons to be learned from the human experiences of the past.

By contrast, in most of the essays in the present volume, what is offered is Mises having to apply these general principles and historical lessons to questions concerning what is to be done now, in the practical circumstances of the time. They represent, in many instances, examples of "applied" Austrian economics by the person who, besides Friedrich Hayek, is usually considered the twentieth-century exemplification of "the Austrian approach."

A monetary order is disintegrating. How do you disentangle one monetary regime into several? A country is faced with a monetary collapse due to hyperinflation. How do you prepare for the transition to a substitute currency? Two monetary systems may be combined into one. What are the specific policy and institutional prerequisites for the change to a unified monetary system? Tax incidence and price controls are bringing about the breakup of a country into separate regions. What economic policies would reintegrate them? Layers of bureaucracy and divided political authority burden a society with excessive government expenses and regulations. How do you streamline the administrative structures to reduce both? State-run enterprises are run along costly and bureaucratically inefficient lines. What would have to be done to make them profitable, efficient, and flexible to economic circumstances, and what methods will not work in bringing this about? An economic crisis results in currency devaluation and the imposition of foreign-exchange control. Do you reverse the devaluation, and if so in what time frame should it be introduced? What are the consequences of the exchange-control system, and what are the prerequisites for a full restoration of stability in the foreign-exchange market?

These were the questions, besides others, that Mises was called upon to discuss and solve in terms of policy prescriptions in those years in Vienna between the two world wars.

We saw that Mises, in clear frustration in the months after he arrived in America, lamented that in Austria he had started out hoping to be a reformer but instead ended up being a historian of decline. But precisely because of this, these essays offer us a clearer understanding of precisely why it was that in the countries of Europe between 1918 and 1938, inflation, interventionism, socialism, and economic nationalism led to stagnation, social disruption, a Great Depression, and finally to a new world war.

In spite of his pessimism, Mises was not a fatalist. He said more than once in his writings that trends can change, that they had changed in the past and could change again in the future.[51] With this in mind, after coming to the United States he devoted a sizable amount of time to working out the political and economic policies and reforms that could bring about a rebirth of freedom and prosperity in Europe after the Second World War.[52]

Likewise, from the perspective of these first days of the twenty-first century, Mises's writings from his earlier period offer important instructions for the present and the future. Within each of these articles and essays criticizing the direction of economic and social policy are also ideas and prescriptions for free-market oriented alternatives in the areas of monetary and fiscal policy, government regulation and planning, and the social institutional order, ideas which would move a society along the path that leads to freedom and prosperity. I would suggest that is precisely how Mises would want the modern reader to view these writings. He stated this very clearly in the preface he prepared for the 1932 second edition of *Socialism*:

> I know only too well how hopeless it seems to convince impassioned supporters of the Socialist Idea by logical demonstration that their views are preposterous and absurd. I know too well that they do not want to hear, to see, and above all to think, and they are open to no argument. But new generations grow up with clear eyes and open minds. And they will approach things from a disinterested, unprejudiced standpoint, they will

51 Ludwig von Mises, "Trends Can Change" [1951] and "The Political Chances for Genuine Liberalism," [1951] in *Planning for Freedom* (South Holland, Ill.: Libertarian Press, 1980), pp. 173–84.

52 That is precisely the theme and purpose of the essays that he wrote in the early 1940s. See Richard M. Ebeling, ed., *Selected Writings of Ludwig von Mises, Vol. 3: The Political Economy of International Reform and Reconstruction*.

weigh and examine, will think and act with forethought. It is for them that this book is written.[53]

These articles and essays, originally penned for audiences more than sixty and seventy years ago in the context of the policy controversies of those times, were, therefore, also written for us. They are warning signs and guideposts left behind by one of the greatest economists of the twentieth century to assist us in thinking about and designing better policies for our own times.

RICHARD M. EBELING

Ludwig von Mises Professor of Economics
Hillsdale College

October 2001

---

53 Mises, *Socialism*, p. 13.

PART I

Monetary Disorder, Inflation, and Interventionist State (1918–32)

CHAPTER 1

The Quantity Theory[1]

The quantity theory is the application of the doctrine of supply and demand to money. In two respects, the law of supply and demand does not provide a complete explanation of the structure of exchange relationships between goods. It gives no information at all about how exchange relationships arise; instead, it is satisfied merely to indicate the direction in which a given exchange relationship is shifted when there are changes in supply and demand. The second inherent defect is that it regards supply and demand as given quantities and fails to investigate the motives that determine people's decisions in their buying and selling. Modern economics works with infinitely more refined and thorough methods. Starting from the law of marginal utility it has constructed a theory of value and price that can no longer be reproached as having the same defects as the older doctrine of supply and demand. Only with its assistance can the importance of supply and demand for price formation be fully grasped.

The simple quantity theory was no longer satisfactory for an explanation of the value of money. So in recent years theories have been developed with the aim to replace the older, inadequate quantity theory with an approach consistent with the standards of modern economic science. In reconstructing the quantity theory the difficulties to be overcome were the same as those in the general theory of value. As a logically consistent explanation of all problems relating to the value of money, the modern, scientific theory of money has now been perfectly integrated into the general theory of value and price.

Just as the general theory of value has not overthrown or rejected as

1 [This article originally appeared in German in *Mitteilungen des Verbandes österreichischer Banken und Bankiers*, Vol. 1, No. 3/4 (1918).—Ed.]

false the basic laws of supply and demand, but instead has enriched and developed them further, so too the modern theory of the value of money has taken up and improved the quantity theory. No theory can thoughtlessly ignore the fact that a close connection exists between changes in the purchasing power of money and changes in the relationship existing between the supply of money and the demand for money.

The quantity theory specifies that when there is an increase in the quantity of money, other things being equal, the value of the monetary unit will decrease, and when there is a decrease in the quantity of money the value of the monetary unit will increase. However, it must not be presumed that, in a situation in which the demand for money stays the same, any given change in the supply of money must cause an inversely proportional change in the purchasing power of the monetary unit; e.g., that a doubling of the quantity of money must lead to a decrease in the purchasing power of the monetary unit by one half. It is not necessary to enter here into the controversy about whether under certain hypothetical preconditions such inversely proportional changes in the value of money would have to take place or not. There can be no doubt that those hypothetical preconditions under which such inversely proportional changes would have to occur never exist in the real world. It has been amply shown that changes in the value of money will not be quantitatively equivalent to changes in the supply of money. Economic theory only makes use of this special case as a mental tool.

There is an even more important insight that has deepened our understanding of the process by which changes occur in the value of money. The rise in the prices for goods in general caused by an increase in the supply of money does not happen in one stroke across the entire economy. Additions to the quantity of money only gradually spread throughout the economy. At first, the new money enters into certain sectors and branches of production; at first, it only increases the demand for certain goods, not for all of them at once; only later do the prices for other goods start to rise. "During the issue of notes," say Auspitz and Lieben, "the increase in currency will be concentrated in the hands of a small fraction of the population, e.g., of the suppliers and producers of war materials. As a result of this, these people's demands for various articles will increase; and thus the prices and also the sales of the latter will rise, especially the prices for luxury items. Consequently, the situation of the producers of all these articles improve; their demands for other goods will also increase; the rise in prices and sales will therefore progress even further and spread to a larger and larger number of articles, and finally to all of them."[2]

This insight is very important; it is one of the two roots of the social consequences that always accompany changes in the value of money.[3] If monetary depreciation occurred in relation to all goods at one stroke and in the same proportion throughout the entire economy, then economic booms would not appear and it would not bring about shifts in the distribution of income and wealth. In reality, monetary depreciation brings an advantage for those whose money prices and money wages rise first, and it brings a disadvantage for all of those who sell goods and services whose money prices lag behind closer to their original levels.

These remarks will be misunderstood if in thinking about the "demand for and supply of money" they are thought about in terms of the "needs of trade" as relating to the demand for loan capital in the form of money. The language of commerce understands by "money" not only the medium of exchange but also loan capital in the form of money that is sought for short-term investments and other uses. Thus, references are made to the money market, to the cheapness or dearness of money, to the tightness or looseness of the situation on the money market, and to the rate of interest as the price for money. Monetary theory uses the expressions the "demand for money" and the "supply of money" in a different sense. Money is always just the medium of exchange. An individual's supply of money refers to that amount of the general medium of exchange that he has on hand as his ready cash in his till. The individual's demand for money is that amount of money that he wishes to have on hand in the cash box under given conditions. The supply of money and the demand for money in the economy as a whole is the sum of the money supplies and money demands of the individuals in that economy. Supply and demand always coincide in their amount. Price changes in the market have as their purpose to bring about shifts in the general level of prices until the supply of and demand for money do coincide.

In explaining the present rise in prices, it is not completely true to say

2 [Rudolf Auspitz and Richard Lieben, *Untersuchungen über die Theorie des Preises* [Investigations into the Theory of Prices] (Leipzig: Duncker & Humblot, 1889), p. 64. — Ed.]

3 The other root of these accompanying consequences is to be found in the relationship between debtor and creditor. The lowering of the value of money favors the debtor and harms the creditor.

that there is more money in circulation than corresponds to the "needs of business." Today there are more bank notes than corresponded to the "need for money" at the older and lower level of prices. At the new, higher level of prices the larger quantity of money is needed to satisfy the demand for money in the economy as a whole. If the former viewpoint were correct, then somewhere in the economy an excess of money would have to be present, which, as we have said, is not to be confused with an excess supply of loan capital in money terms. But that is by no means the case. Every individual today has in his till more money on hand in the form of cash than earlier, and this has completely absorbed the greater quantity of money. This has happened, however, only because of the general rise in prices.

In reference to the rise in prices mention is often made to the reductions in production and imports from abroad that have been caused by the war. That, however, explains only a part of the increase in the prices of goods. The prices of various goods have increased even when their production has not declined relative to the demand for them. The inflation of bank notes would have led to an increase in the money prices of goods even if there had not appeared any factors pushing up prices from the goods-side of the market. A *general* rise in the money prices for all goods can only be explained by factors on the money-side of the market, never by a shortage in the supply of all goods alone. If the decrease in supply were restricted to one or a few commodities, then it would, of course, lead to an increase in the prices for these commodities, but this would have to be balanced by a decrease in the prices of other commodities. If grain becomes scarcer and grain prices rise, other articles of mass consumption must decline in price because the population's ability to consume is limited by its overall money income.

But if all goods become scarcer while the amount of money in circulation remains constant, then all goods cannot rise in price. The price increases for one group of goods must be matched by price decreases for other goods. Among the goods that are falling in price there will also be those whose supply has declined, unless this decrease in the supply occurs faster than the decline in its demand resulting from shifts in consumption. Therefore price increases for some goods would be matched by price decreases for others; the average price level would remain unchanged.

The situation in which we find ourselves at present is a different one. The decrease in the supply of goods is going on hand-in-hand with an enormous increase in the supply of money. The shift in relative prices for different goods is to be attributed to the former and the general rise of the overall price level is due to the latter. The former—the decrease in the supply of goods—is the cause of the deficiencies under which we are suffering and will suffer as long as it persists; the latter—the increase in the supply of money—is the cause of the rise in the general price level. The general rise in prices is viewed as undesirable not because prices have gone up absolutely, but because of the social consequences that accompany it. When the blockade is lifted and the labor force, which today is tied up in war service, is free, prices will decline. But as long as a restriction in the supply of the bank notes in circulation has not taken place, prices will not decline back to the old level; instead, they will remain considerably higher.

There is an opinion that was widely held in literary circles in Germany and that has acquired special importance because it obviously is the basis for certain government measures that aim at improving the foreign exchange rate of our currency. It distinguishes between a devaluation of the currency, i.e., a decrease in its value on the international exchange market, and depreciation, i.e., a decrease in its domestic purchasing power. It is alleged that there is only a loose connection between the two—or, as some maintain, no connection at all. The amount of money in circulation is supposedly irrelevant in terms of both its purchasing power with respect to goods and for the formation of the foreign-exchange rate. The former, it is claimed, is completely determined by the availability of goods; the latter is a result of the monetary situation of the balance of payments. This view is refuted in the clearest way by historical experience, which teaches that price increases at home and increases in the foreign-exchange rate have always gone hand-in-hand. Just a bit of simple reflection shows that a close connection must exist between the two phenomena, and that one without the other is inconceivable. Imagine, for example, that the ruble declines vis-à-vis the German mark without a rise in price of goods and resources taking place on the Russian markets at the same time. Then it would become especially profitable to export goods and securities from Russia to Germany; but such exportation of goods and securities would immediately change an unfavorable balance of trade for Russia into its opposite. A divergence between foreign-exchange rates and the prices of goods could occur only temporarily; it would always have automatically to disappear. Even the obstructions in the way of international trade caused by the war can only hinder and delay this automatic balancing process; it cannot prevent it since the movement of securities alone would suffice to bring it about.

If a narrow circle of German and Austrian writers is disregarded, then it can be stated that the quantity theory, in the sense in which it has been presented here, is hardly questioned anywhere today. For the issues dealt with here, the differences of opinion that arise concerning certain problems relating to the quantity theory are of little importance, however meaningful they may be for other questions relating to monetary theory.

In general, then, the correctness of the quantity theory is no longer contested, though its practical importance is questioned. The present-day organization of the money, payment, and credit system allegedly has a tendency to automatically balance changes in the quantitative relationships between the supply of and demand for money. The "elasticity" of the circulation of the currency created under the modern structure of the banking system is supposed to have now made movements in prices independent of changes in the quantity of money. Elsewhere I have explained that this widely held view—and in Germany, it is in general the reigning view—is completely incorrect.[4] However, for purposes of discussing the causes of the present rise in prices this question has no importance. Even the most extreme proponents of this doctrine have assigned "elasticity" only to a circulation of bank notes based on short-term commercial transactions, not to an expansion of bank notes resulting from government borrowing.

The quantity theory shows us how to recognize the causes behind a worsening of the value of our currency and also shows us the way that leads back to the conditions of an orderly currency. If we really want to continue to suffer the disadvantages of a currency fluctuating in its value then we can retain the present system and even come to the aid of the state's finances from time to time by a new inflation of the currency. But if we wish to achieve a monetary system that is as stable as possible, then we can follow one of two paths. We can simply limit ourselves to stabilizing the value of the Austrian crown at its reduced purchasing power. For that it would be enough if we halted any further running of the monetary printing presses and resumed cash payments either *de jure* or even only *de facto* in the way it was before the war on the basis of a fixed rate of foreign exchange. For example, the foreign-exchange rate could be fixed at its market quotation one year from the day that the war ends. It is clear that this solution would be in contradiction with the principles behind the cur-

---

4 Ludwig von Mises, *The Theory of Money and Credit* (Indianapolis: Liberty Fund, 3rd rev. ed., [1924, 1953] 1980), pp. 331 ff.

rency policy that was adhered to for the last two generations, and will be rejected by many of our leading financial policymakers. That means that only a second way seems viable. A real effort would have to be made to increase the gold price of the crown back to the value established for it by the laws of August 2, 1892.[5] To do this the debts of both nations [Austria and Hungary] will have to be paid back to the central bank so that the central bank will be in a position to correspondingly reduce the quantity of bank notes in circulation.

5 [This refers to the Austro-Hungarian government's currency reform of August 2, 1892, which enacted an exchange rate of one guilder to two crowns to 2.10027 French francs and called for gold redemption of bank notes by 1896 or 1897. — Ed.]

CHAPTER 2

On the Currency Question

In Reference to the Essay by Prof. Dr. Ludwig
v. Mises on "The Quantity Theory"[1]

I   *Letter from Siegfried Rosenbaum,*
       Director of the Anglo-Austrian Bank

Professor Ludwig von Mises's published presentation leaves—at least for me—some unanswered questions. The importance and the extraordinary urgency of the measures set forth for discussion make it seem justified if questions are posed and debated from the circles of those bankers to whom Dr. von Mises has informatively spoken. Dr. von Mises's exposition concludes as follows:

> The quantity theory shows us how to recognize the causes behind a worsening of the value of our currency and also shows us the way that leads back to the conditions of an orderly currency. If we really want to continue to suffer the disadvantages of a currency fluctuating in its value then we can retain the present system and even come to the aid of the state's finances from time to time by a new inflation of the currency. But if we wish to achieve a monetary system that is as stable as possible, then we can follow one of two paths. We can simply limit ourselves to stabilizing the value of the Austrian crown at its reduced purchasing power. For that it would be enough if we halted any further running of the monetary printing presses and resumed cash payments either *de jure* or even only *de facto* in the way it was before the war on the basis of a fixed rate

1 [The contributions in this chapter originally appeared in German in the *Mitteilungen des Verbandes österreichische Banken und Bankiers* Vol. 1, No. 5/6 (1918). They include two responses to Mises's article on "The Quantity Theory" and his replies to the commentators. —Ed.]

of foreign exchange. For example, the foreign-exchange rate could be fixed at its market quotation one year from the day that the war ends. It is clear that this solution would be in contradiction with the principles behind the currency policy that was adhered to for the last two generations, and will be rejected by many of our leading financial policymakers. That means that only a second way seems viable. A real effort would have to be made to increase the gold price of the crown back to the value established for it by the laws of August 2, 1892. To do this the debts of both nations [Austria and Hungary] will have to be paid back to the central bank so that the central bank will be in a position to correspondingly reduce the quantity of bank notes in circulation.

These are the final results of the quantity theory. I personally wish to avoid here any argument about which one of the different theories I consider correct out of those that are now seeking adherents more strongly than ever before. It is not possible for me and for many others, who are engaged in the actual practice of business, to take notice of all arguments regarding these matters, much less analyze them minutely. Many of the champions parading on the various pages are not known to me, so I must accept it without any quantitative proof when Dr. von Mises says, by way of example, that according to his view and the view of his like-minded colleagues the generally "reigning view" in Germany is "completely incorrect." I do not wish to meddle here in this controversy in an abstract way. I should only like to ask for the answer to the question: In light of the quantity theory, how should what Dr. von Mises demands be carried out? I assume that he desires a practical solution, I assume that he desires it (even if it were only a matter of preparatory measures) as quickly as possible (for we are indeed in the midst of experiencing the grave damages of a disorganized currency situation), and I believe, finally, to have deduced from what I have read that banking measures should have an important share in bringing about a recovery. But if it is a question of banking actions whose execution is demanded for the immediate present or right after the end of the war, then they will have to be measures that appear feasible and at least possibly effective to the practicing banker, whatever theories he may otherwise prefer. If they should not appear so at first sight, it would be the duty of the advocate to demonstrate their feasibility and sufficiently prospective efficacy to those bankers who would be entrusted with their execution or who would have to live with the consequences.

So in this sense I ask more specifically: *Should the measures that arise from the principles of the quantity theory be put into practice partly at once, or partly at the end of the war? And which measures should be undertaken immediately? What role will the bank transactions that are to be carried out immediately have in the recovery measures, and what role in those to be undertaken later?* A precise presentation of these required bank transactions would be extremely desirable so that their probable effect can be discussed.

In connection with these questions I should like to ask a few others which emerge from the discussions in the daily press.

Are new large issuances of notes really going to come to the aid of government finances? Is it to be assumed that a steep rise in war-bond subscriptions will decrease the circulation of notes in a numerically corresponding degree? Will it agree with the claims of the quantity theory if the finance ministers henceforth stop all further indebtedness to the note-issuing central bank? How are the finance ministers supposed to do this? Will the circulation of bank notes decrease if the finance minister transfers treasury bonds to the banks? Will our currency situation improve if the Austro-Hungarian Bank issues cash certificates?

The answer to these questions seems so important to me because I believe it is necessary at this point in time that support for a practical viewpoint should immediately be merged with theoretical directives. The best theory would turn out to be worthless without such instructions. It is, of course, not fair to demand a procedure that, following a specific prescription, carries with it the assurance that the blessed result will appear by itself in the form of a previously unattested miracle. After four years of war the judgement of the possible effects of certain measures has surely been able to be debated fairly reliably in most branches of practical activity by those who have no connection with the theory. I think therefore that it is right if today bankers ask the representatives of the quantity theory: what do you expect to happen, and what should we do about it?

II   *Reply by Prof. Dr. Ludwig v. Mises*

I believe one must be grateful to Director Rosenbaum for having expressed in a clear and precise way the doubts and reservations that my exposition has aroused in him. Only through a free and complete discussion can views about the currency problem be clarified. Perhaps I shall succeed in contributing a little bit to this by answering the questions he poses.

First it must be stated that the quantity theory is nothing more than a scientific statement about a causal relationship. It indicates what consequences, other things being equal, will be brought about by an increase or a decrease in the quantity of money in circulation. That is all. The quantity theory is not an economic policy program. It does not set up any demand, no sort of "practical directive" arises from it. For a theorem of science can never give clarification about whether the achievement of a specific goal is *per se* desirable or not. That is a matter of will and not of knowledge. That we have recognized the quantity theory essentially to be correct and have formed by means of it an opinion about the causes of our currency situation does not in any way signify that we have committed ourselves to a specific point of view regarding questions of currency policy.

The question of whether we should return to the old gold relationship of the laws of 1892 or to stabilize the present level of the gold premium or indeed to continue inflation by the issuing of more notes is something only the politician can decide. The theory can help him in this only insofar as it shows him the ways by which each one of these three alternatives can be achieved and explains to him the consequences that are inevitably connected with each alternative. The same considerations that for some constitute a recommendation for the return to the old currency relationship can induce others to assume the opposite point of view. It depends precisely upon the evaluation made in the eyes of individuals and parties according to their overall worldview, their interests, and their general political position concerning the social consequences that accompany changes in the value of money.

But I believe that I can conclude from his remarks that Mr. Rosenbaum takes the view that we should go back to the old currency situation, and that he raises the question of what must be done to reach this goal in light of the logic that follows from the quantity theory. The answer to this question is that the quantity of bank notes must be reduced. That is, the two governments [of Austria and Hungary] must pay back the states' debt to the central bank. Whether they should do this by the issuing of a consolidated loan or by way of taxation is a question all by itself. In any case, notes would have to flow to the state treasuries, and by the transfer of these notes to the coffers of the Austro-Hungarian Bank the debt of the two states would have to be paid off. I repeat once more that I know perfectly well that this will have to result in certain economic and social consequences as part of the bargain. Which of the two alternatives—a restoration or a stabilization of the currency's value (the third alternative, a continuation of inflation, I can reasonably set aside)—is the lesser evil, that is a preliminary question that will have to be decided before the discussion of the technical carrying out of the restriction begins.

The question of the foreign-exchange rate is for the moment not a specifically Austro-Hungarian question. Many other nations are in the same situation even if the quantitative importance of the problem is different in the individual countries. (And precisely this quantitative difference may tip the balance for the decision of the politician.) It can be assumed that the solution will not occur in the same way in all countries. In some states it will be restriction, in others stabilization. In one or another country perhaps inflation will even continue until the problem is solved when the zero point of a currency's value is reached. For this too is a solution. History has known examples of this, and an Eastern state seems well on its way to becoming a new example.[2]

In Austria itself the foreign-exchange rate question is not a problem that has never existed before. In 1811 it was solved by stabilization, in 1854 to 1858 by restoration. In 1863 to 1865 the attempt was made again to solve it through restoration by way of restriction, and the goal that was set also would have been achieved that time if the war events of the year 1866 had not caused a new inflation.[3] It is not without interest to go briefly into this last Austrian attempt at restoration of the currency's value.

Austria had defrayed the costs of the war with France in 1859 largely by the assumption of loans with the National Bank.[4] An imperial decree of April 29, 1859, provided for state loans from the bank while at the same time it released the bank from the duty of redeeming its notes in cash and

---

2 [Mises is referring to Bolshevik Russia. In October 1917, shortly before the Bolshevik coup in Petrograd, the money supply in Russia was 18.5 billion rubles. In June 1918, approximately the time when Mises's article was published, the Russian money supply had increased to 40.7 billion rubles. In June 1919 it had grown to 92.4 billion rubles, in June 1920 to 450.6 billion rubles, and by December 1921 to 9.845 trillion rubles.—Ed.]

3 [This refers to the Austro-Prussian War of 1866, also known as the Seven Weeks' War, between Prussia on one side and Austria, Bavaria, Hanover, and a number of other smaller German states on the other. The Prussian victory at the Battle of Königgrätz (or Sadowá) is considered to have been the turning point of the war, which resulted in Austria being excluded from the German Confederation that was then dominated by Prussia.—Ed.]

4 [This refers to the Austro-Italian War of 1859, in which the Austrians were defeated by the Kingdom of Sardinia with the assistance of the French army sent into Italy by Napoleon III. Austria ceded Lombardy and though retaining Venetia as part of the peace settlement lost most of its influence over the development of political events on the Italian peninsula. —Ed.]

authorized it to issue five gulden notes with a legally established rate of exchange. Altogether in the course of 1859 the state received 153 million gulden in loans from the bank. The inflation of bank notes led to an increase in prices for goods and the rate of exchange. The metal premium on the Vienna stock exchange temporarily rose as high as 53.2 percent. Immediately after the end of the war the government undertook reform of the currency system in earnest; all of its measures were directed toward the reinstitution of the currency relationship of the German-Austrian monetary convention of 1857 through the reduction of bank notes in circulation not backed by metal.

During 1860, a part of the debt was repaid to the bank. By means of the Plener Bank Act of December 17, 1862, which is patterned on the Peel Bank Act,[5] the sum of the notes not backed by metal was firmly and inalterably fixed at 200 million gulden. By a gradual decrease of the notes in circulation this prescription was supposed to be satisfied by the end of 1866. In fact, the previously undertaken withdrawal of the excessive quantity of notes was then continued. From the end of 1862 to the end of 1865, the notes in circulation fell from 426.8 million gulden to 351.1 million gulden; in 1866, a further decrease in circulation of not quite 30 million gulden should have occurred. The metal premium, which had averaged 41.25 percent in 1861, fell to an average of 8.32 percent in 1865, and at the beginning of 1866 it had almost disappeared. So then, the currency policy would no doubt have achieved its goal if the new war had not occasioned a breach of the Bank Act and a new inflation.

That is *one* historical example of the restoration of a currency by decreasing the amount of money in circulation; many others could be added. The proportions with which we have to reckon today are much greater. But that changes the problem only quantitatively, not qualitatively. And I repeat here once again that precisely the consideration of the quantitative element may settle the decision about what goal the reform should strive for.

I will now answer the questions of Director Rosenbaum in detail as briefly as possible.

---

5 [Peel's Bank Act of July 1844 divided the Bank of England into two parts, a Note Issuing Department and a Banking Department. The Issuing Department was restricted in the quantity of bank notes it could issue on the basis of the government debt (a maximum of fourteen hundred pounds), and notes issued beyond this had to be covered fully on the basis of additional deposits of gold coin or gold or silver bullion. —Ed.]

If we want to stop a further rise of prices and wages, to the extent this is not caused by the well-known difficulties of production and trade, and the further deterioration of the foreign exchange rate, we must avoid any further increases in the circulation of notes.

If we wish to go back to the old currency relationship of the 1892 laws, then we must decrease the number of notes in circulation until parity has been reached. That can only happen if the two states—either through taxation or by a loan in the form of treasury certificates or bonds—provide themselves with the means to repay their debts to the note-issuing central bank. In this way the question of the necessary bank transactions is also settled. That restriction brings along with it very definite economic and social consequences; that these consequences will be designated as harmful by some, or at best the lesser evil by others, has already been said. That new issuances of bank notes relieve the states' finances of *momentary* difficulties hardly anyone can dispute.

The war-loan subscriptions cannot in themselves diminish the note circulation. But if the state clears its debt with the bank by the proceeds of bond loans they can indirectly contribute to the process. Therefore a good result for the war-loan subscriptions is the first step on the way toward lifting the foreign-exchange rate. If in the future all further indebtedness to the bank is to cease, then the necessary means must come to the state treasury through taxes or by bonds and treasury-certificate loans, which will be designated as without claim by the public on the note-issuing bank. The success of the war-loan subscription—not counting extra economic possibilities—can be increased only by the amelioration of conditions for creditors. The endeavor to maintain a low interest rate, as befits the general economic situation, must always be unsuccessful. The only thing that can be achieved in this way is inflation and currency debasement.

If the finance minister transfers treasury bills to the banks and these raise the necessary funds without recourse to the note-issuing bank, then the note circulation will indeed not be decreased, but neither will it be increased. If the Austro-Hungarian Bank issues cash certificates, and the public hands over as their equivalent bank notes that they otherwise would have kept in their cash boxes, then the number of notes in circulation is decreased by this amount. In conclusion, I can only emphasize once again that the question of what goal our currency policy should strive to attain cannot be answered by science but only by politics. Science can offer to the politician only the possibility of assessing the consequences of his decision in advance. Every patriot must wish that in making the decision—

however it may turn out—only consideration of these expected conse-quences will be decisive, and not any regard for false slogans, momentary political successes, and the convenience of the administration.

III   *Letter from a banking specialist*

The literature concerning the problems that the war has posed for mone-tary theorists is already immense. One could well speak of an inflation of the book market. Unfortunately, the voices of those who actually work in the area are almost imperceptible, and yet their opinions would be ex-tremely valuable and desirable. Perhaps a future currency investigation, which is proving more and more to be an urgent necessity, will provide the opportunity for it. I do not believe, like Prof. von Mises does, that the quan-tity theory already shows the way "that leads back to the conditions of an orderly currency." Unfortunately, he does not say how is to be achieved "that increase in the gold price of the crown back to the value established for it by the laws of August 2, 1892." This problem, unfortunately, will not be solved by theories. But some modest doubts must also be expressed from a purely theoretical point of view. Prof. v. Mises says: "The inflation of bank notes would have led to an increase in the money prices of goods even if there had not appeared any factors pushing up prices from the goods-side of the market."

That approximately coincides with the theory of Irving Fisher, who constructs a direct effect between an increase in the quantity of money in circulation and higher prices, and in addition with the fairly general view that the inflation of bank notes is the cause of the high cost of living, of the upward trend of the stock market, etc.

This belief was not always the prevailing one. In 1867, after the war, a very significant inflation occurred, the likes of which had never been seen before. Nevertheless, in the course of that year the exchange pre-mium receded by about 10 percent, prices were completely normal, and the flourishing of businesses was attributed to the *beneficial increase of the circulating media* (instead of to the extraordinarily favorable harvest, which made large exports possible). Today, like fifty years ago, we see two events taking place at the same time, and we are naturally inclined to see a connection between them. Fifty years ago, there was inflation—with a falling exchange premium and rising prosperity. At that time the theory was promulgated that saw the panacea for all social ills in the increase of bank notes. Now, there is inflation—with an exchange premium and rising prices for goods; and just as we take smoke for the result of fire, we consider inflation to be the cause of the high cost of living.

But prices of goods can never be explained from the money-side, only and always from the side of goods. That the prices of all goods have risen cannot cause any astonishment when there prevails a scarcity of all goods. No doubt a connection exists between commodity prices and inflation, but it is an inverted one. High prices obviously have brought about a greatly increased circulation of bank notes as their consequence. It would not be difficult to investigate the whereabouts of the notes, whether it is 20 or 21 billion. If one considers that prices have risen about 500 percent, then 500 percent of the earlier note circulation is necessary to satisfy the need for cash; that extension of credit by sellers has completely ceased, so that every individual needs a larger stock of cash in hand; and if one takes into consideration the billions of notes that the army and of all central military treasuries have, as well as all the hoarded bank notes, then the seemingly high figures will not appear excessive.

Hoarding is especially designated as the most dangerous kind of inflation, and yet no matter how much I think about it, I am unable to explain how hoarded notes can bring about an increase in prices. Rather to the contrary, since they clearly do not appear on the market as competitors for the constricted supply of goods. The other great detriments of inflation, the severe ills of hoarding, especially for the consolidation of the national debt, certainly cannot be left out of consideration; but it seems to me that inflation has no influence on the prices of goods.

Goods have become rarities—they have curiosity value. Does it occur to anyone to explain the huge prices that some painting fetches, and moreover, also fetched before the war, by the inflation? Let us imagine, as difficult as it is, an excess of some commodity, say, for example, if, like once upon a time, it were to rain manna for forty years—don't the theorists believe that the price of manna would decline in spite of all inflation?

The slogan of the devaluation of money has been the foundation of much misfortune. Devaluation of the currency and the rise in the prices of goods is simply one and the same thing. We have been living on our reserve supplies for four years; are any profound explanations needed for the fact that the scanty remnants of goods bear fantastic prices? All goods have been converted into money; the reverse conversion process is not possible at this time, and thus the anxious possessor of the means of payment seeks to get possession of the deeply longed-for commodity at any price.

So as not to be misunderstood, a restriction of the number of notes in circulation would be of great value. But the way for it can and will be prepared for exclusively by a reduction of prices. After the disastrous war of 1859 we had an exchange premium of 505 percent; by the beginning of 1866 it had been reduced to 2 percent. If it is permitted to cite a great thinker, even though he was by no means a financial expert, Fedor Dostoevsky: "To achieve good finances in a state, when these finances have suffered certain shocks, one must not give too much thought to the needs of the present, as urgent as they might be, but first about the resaturating of the roots; and finances will improve by themselves. The roots would be healed if we could at least forget the present by half: all present-day questions, the crying needs of our budget, the interest on foreign loans, the deficits, the ruble [we shall say: the crown], even bankruptcy—that, however, will never happen in our country, no matter how much our malicious foreign enemies may prophesy it—; in a word, if we were to forget the present entirely and work for the root until we could really harvest a rich and sound fruit." Do these words not sound as if they had been written today and not forty years ago?

And these roots are the same as they once were: frugality and increasing production.

IV   Reply by Prof. Dr. v. Mises

If I feel myself obliged to take a position against the foregoing comments, I must first explain, in order to forestall any misunderstanding, that this polemic is not directed against the final sentence, in which the respected author recommends thrift and the increasing of production. On the contrary, I am also convinced that there is no other way to repair the damages of war. But I believe that the author is mistaken if he thinks that with this exhortation to frugality and work or by citing the words of Dostoevsky he can contribute anything to the clarification of the foreign-exchange problem, with which we are exclusively concerned here.

My remarks concerning the currency problem are only those of a theorist. Not only have I never contested this, I have always emphatically stressed it. But anyone who seeks to explain specific events is a theoretician. Only he who acts is a practitioner. Whoever writes essays about currency problems that are supposed to reveal causal connections is a theoretician no matter what profession he may otherwise follow. He too advances "theories." And then, who is a practitioner in the area of currency? If one does not wish to declare everyone who buys or sells for money a practitioner in this field, then one can grant this designation only to the makers of currency policy. This would be the ministers who directly determine notebank policy, and the party leaders, agitators, journalists, and writers on currency policy, who work with the intention of influencing this policy indirectly. And of course underlying every practical program—whether it is carried out or forever remains a program—is a specific theory. The rulers who once sought to confront the deterioration of the Austrian currency by police measures were "practitioners." Their actions were based on a particular theory about the causes of the monetary depreciation (they attributed it to the activities of speculation); one can consider this theory false —as I do—but one cannot deny that it was also a theory.

Theories can never solve a political problem. Action can. And a theory can only explain what consequences certain actions bring. In this the theories of the author do not differ in the slightest from my theories, however much the two may differ in content. For he, too, as long as he is writing about currency questions, is a theoretician, a well-informed and sagacious theoretician, but still a theoretician.

The author briefly mentions the events in Austria in 1867. I will not enter into a detailed analysis of those events, which would require considerable space, because I believe I discern the core of his comments not in the significance of those events but in the assertions about the theory of inflation. And there I must emphatically contradict him. If one disregards the already mentioned "speculation theory" of the absolutist bureaucracy, the fact is that in Austria at that time there were various views about the effects of inflation of prices. Inflationists and sound-money proponents were both of the opinion that inflation must lead to higher prices. But the former saw precisely in the rise in prices the special advantage of inflation. They championed the increase of money because they wanted higher prices, since they considered higher prices and prosperity to be identical. For this reason they fought for paper money, for "the cheap money of the poor," and they fought against the gold standard, "the money of the rich." That is true not only of the older Austrian inflationists and of those whose leaders around 1892 were Lueger,[6] Liechtenstein,[7] and Schlesinger,[8] but also of those in all other countries. The opponents of the inflationists also based their arguments on the quantity theory. But they were of the opinion that price increases and the increase in prosperity were not identical, and that inflation was not the sign of a heyday but only simulated the appearance of well-being. They were precisely of the view, in which I concur with the respected author, that prosperity can be increased only by thrift and increased production.

It is true that the need for money has risen immensely because of wartime circumstances—the most important reasons being the establishment of the numerous army pay offices, the extension of the circulation of our currency to the occupied regions, and hoarding.[9] But there is no doubt that the increase in the quantity of notes has far, far exceeded the degree to which it could have been acceptable to meet the increased need for notes in circulation without bringing about increases in prices.

If the author declares it to be obvious that the high prices for goods have, as their consequence, sharply increased the number of notes in circulation, then one must ask how these allegedly obvious connections are established. These consequences are certainly not produced spontaneously, because even if prices rise ever so much, no notes can get into circulation by themselves. They could only come into circulation because the law restricting the issuance of notes by the central bank was suspended,

6 [Karl Lueger (1844–1910) was the mayor of Vienna from 1897 to 1910. He condemned international capitalism as a Jewish plot. He advocated municipal socialism on the rationale that small shopkeepers needed to be protected from large private enterprises. He municipalized the gasworks (1899) and the electric trolleys (1902). He once said that, in reference to anti-Semitic discrimination, "who is a Jew is for me to decide."—Ed.]

7 [Prince Alois von Liechtenstein (1846–1920) was a proponent of a return to a medieval-type hierarchical society that resembled what later in the twentieth century came to be known as the corporativist model of fascism.—Ed.]

8 [Josef Schlesinger (1830–1901) was a professor of mathematics and natural philosophy and president of the University of Agronomy and Soil Sciences in Vienna. He also served as deputy to the Vienna City Council and the Austrian Parliament for the Christian Socialist party. In 1892, he charged that the Jews were the primary dealers in white slavery in the Austrian capital.—Ed.]

9 Those who hoard bank notes do not act wisely from the point of view of their own interests. But who can hold it against them? Certainly not the finance minister. Rather it is those who have an interest in still higher prices. For if all the hoarded amounts were to come back on the market, prices would rise still more.

because the government ordered the issuing of new notes. And the question arises, what would have happened if twenty or more billion notes had not been put into circulation? If the respected author admits that the additional quantity of notes corresponds to the increased need for money caused by the rises in prices, then he has thereby also conceded that the general price level could not have risen if no new notes had been printed.

If it rains manna for forty years, other things being equal, the price of manna must go down. It has now been raining notes for four years; shouldn't the price of notes go down?

What are supposed to be the other great disadvantages of inflation, of which the author speaks, if inflation has no influence on prices? I should not be able to name any others. If the expansion of the note circulation is not the cause of the high price level, then wherein lies the great value that he attributes to the restriction of the number of notes in circulation? He who is of the opinion that the fall in the purchasing power of money is not caused by the increase of notes has no reason to argue for the reduction of the quantity of notes in circulation. How could he object to the proposal not to take up a national loan but to satisfy the entire credit requirement of the nation by indebtedness to the Austro-Hungarian Bank that can grant the state the cheapest credit?

CHAPTER 3

Remarks Concerning the Establishment of a Ukrainian Note-Issuing Bank[1]

As far as the matter can be seen from here, the establishment of the planned Ukrainian State Bank would find an appropriate model in the Russian Imperial Bank.[2] The Ukrainian bank, like the Russian Imperial Bank, is supposed to become a purely state institution. By and large the Russian Bank has worked well, and Ukrainian businessmen are accustomed to dealing with its branch offices situated in the Ukraine. Of course, the statutes of the Russian Imperial Bank will require revision in several respects in view of the situation brought about by the war and in considera-

1 [This paper was written in the summer of 1918, while Ludwig von Mises was serving as an economics advisor to the General Staff of the Austrian army in Vienna, after having served as the officer in charge of currency control in Austrian-occupied Ukraine through most of the spring of 1918. It has not been previously published.—Ed.]

2 [In January 1918, the Ukrainian National Republic was declared an independent state. In March 1918, Lenin's Bolshevik government signed the Treaty of Brest-Litovsk, ending the state of war between Russia and the Central Powers (imperial Germany, Austria-Hungary, Romania, Bulgaria, and the Turkish empire). As part of the treaty, Soviet Russia ceded the Ukraine to the Central Powers. The Germans occupied northern and eastern Ukraine, including the cities of Kiev, Kharkov, and Rostov, as well as the Crimea. The Austrians occupied western and central Ukraine, with their headquarters in the city of Odessa. The Romanians occupied and annexed the region of Bessarabia. Following the armistice of November 11, 1918, which ended the fighting between the Central Powers and the Entente (the Allied powers of Great Britain, France, Italy, and the United States), the Germans and Austrians withdrew from the Ukraine. For the next year and a half, the Ukraine was one of the central and most bloody battlegrounds of the Russian Civil War between the Soviet Red Army and the antiCommunist White Armies, at the end of which the Ukraine was incorporated into Soviet Russia. Ukraine regained its independence in 1991, with the formal end of the Union of Soviet Socialist Republics.—Ed.]

tion of the conditions that are of special importance for the establishment of the Ukrainian State Bank.[3] In our opinion the following points of view are chiefly to be taken into consideration.

I   Capital Stock

Of course, the capital stock does not have as great an importance for a note-issuing central bank as for a private institution, since the means for the operation of its activities essentially arise from the issuing of notes. Nevertheless, it remains of considerable importance; it serves as a surety fund, forms the foundation for its original establishment, and provides the operating resources for the branches of its business that are not connected with the privilege of issuing notes. It is not recommended to look upon the general wealth of the government as the capital stock standing behind the note-issuing bank. By being equipped with a fixed amount of capital, the credit of the institution is strengthened and well-ordered management in accordance with commercial principles is assured.

The existing imperial Russian government bank notes were all backed with a capital stock. The capital stock of the Russian Imperial Bank comes

---

3 [The State Bank of Imperial Russia was reorganized through the monetary and banking reforms of 1895–1897, on the basis of which Russia was formally placed on a gold standard. The working of the Imperial Russian Bank is briefly explained by L. N. Yurovsky, *Currency Problems and Policy of the Soviet Union* (London: Leonard Parsons, 1925), p. 11:

> State credit notes constituted a liability of the State Bank and took the place of what is commonly known as bank notes. The nature of this liability consisted in the Bank being compelled to pay on demand for each ruble in credit notes presented to it, 17.424 dolyas pure gold [11.94792 grains of fine gold]. Whilst entitled to issue credit notes to an unlimited amount, the Statutes of the Bank compelled it to keep a sufficient metal reserve to ensure unrestricted convertibility. In this respect its Statutes were particularly stringent, the legal minimum cover of its issues being higher than that of all other central banks, with the exception of the Bank of England. The sum of gold held as cover was not allowed to fall below 50 percent of the aggregate figure of credit notes in circulation, whilst every note issued over and above 600 million rubles had to be fully backed by a corresponding quantity of gold [ruble for ruble]. The reason for these rigorous restrictions lay...in the desire to promote the largest possible measure of confidence in the circulation.

See also Arthur Z. Arnold, *Banks, Credit and Money in Soviet Russia* (New York: Columbia University Press, 1937), pp. 10–26. — Ed.]

to 50 million rubles. For the new Ukrainian State Bank the sum of 20 million Karbovanits [the Ukrainian monetary unit] should be required. If such an amount could not be made available, then the only thing to do would be first to use any profits for the formation of the capital stock. Beside the capital stock, consideration should be given to the creation of an adequate reserve, say, in the amount of up to half of the capital stock.

II   *Allowable Transactions*

Since the duty of a note-issuing institute is to provide business with *Zahlungsmitteln* [legal tender], it must necessarily restrict to a narrow circle the businesses to which it will be allowed to extend loans. Only secure and liquid investments are suitable for a note-issuing bank. Speculative undertakings, as engaged in by credit banks, are ruled out in advance for a note-issuing bank. They are inevitably connected with great risk, and the possibility of losses would severely endanger confidence in the notes, upon which the entire economic life of the state rests.

It is inappropriate for a note-issuing bank to extend loans to certain commercial sectors that tie up capital for long periods of time, such as the mortgage business. Long-term investments are not readily available for repayment, and therefore are not suitable for a note-issuing bank that is meant to assure redemption of notes on demand under normal circumstances. Experience has taught that a deviation from these principles always exacts a heavy penalty.

In general, the types of companies that are permitted access to the Russian Imperial Bank can also be allowed access to the Ukrainian State Bank. The pertinent regulations in the statutes of the Russian Imperial Bank, of course, go beyond the framework followed by other note-issuing central banks, in particular in comparison to the companies that are allowed access to the German Reichsbank. The Russian Imperial Bank permits access not only for the discounting of bills of exchanges with at least two good signatures, to goods- and securities-backed collateral loans, to buying and selling securities certificates that are eligible as collateral, to security trading and collections, to the acceptance of interest-bearing and non-interest-bearing deposits, and to the safekeeping of valuables. But, in the interest of promoting industry, agriculture, handicrafts, and retail business, it also allows the concession of loans against promissory notes with only one signature as well as the granting of unbacked loans to credit organizations and to municipalities.

It is obvious that, from the standpoint of a prudent policy for a note-issuing bank, doubts should be raised about this accessibility. On the other hand, however, it cannot be ignored that credit conditions in Russia are essentially different from those in Germany. The extended availability of credit from the note-issuing bank has its origin in the special needs of the Russian national economy, and it will be difficult to eliminate this as long as these needs continue to exist. We may therefore conclude that the contents of articles 72 to 177 in the statutes of the Russian Imperial Bank can be transferred in substance to the statutes of the Ukrainian State Bank.

Nevertheless, the regulations concerning the goods- and securities-backed collateral loans, as well as concerning guarantees by the pledging of goods, need modification insofar as the statutes only allow the granting of a collateral-backed loan against the pledge of domestic securities and of domestically produced goods, and only admits such goods for the purposes of safekeeping. The provision would appropriately be expanded to include reliable foreign securities that must, of course, be selected with great caution, as well as goods of foreign origin. Given the Ukraine's massive need to import manufactured products from abroad, namely agricultural machines and implements, it would hardly be justified to exclude these objects from admissibility as collateral for the purpose of obtaining a loan.

III   Backing of Notes

Questions concerning the backing of the notes are of critical importance. If backing for the notes is not regulated in a satisfactory way that corresponds to the principles of a sound note-issuing banking policy, then in the long run the notes will not acquire confidence and trust either at home or abroad. The absolutely necessary conditions for the orderly functioning of the note-issuing bank would disappear. From then on, the possibility of strengthening the currency of the country and of maintaining a well-ordered circulation of money also dissolves away at the same time.

Reference to the national wealth of the country or the stipulation that the entire assets of the state stand behind the note holder cannot be considered as a substitute for an insufficient covering of the notes; it offers the note holder no real, tangible assurance; and it in no way prevents an unlimited and, finally, complete devaluation of the notes by the primary issuer of notes. The history of the French *assignats,* which were "covered" by the collateral of the entire domain of the government, serves as a cautionary example in this regard.[4]

Until the beginning of the war the notes of the Russian Imperial Bank had to be covered by gold to the extent that they exceeded the amount of 600 million rubles. Foreign bank notes, bills of exchange in gold currency of foreign countries, as well as assets with foreign banking houses were included in the gold coverage. For the Ukrainian State Bank this regulation for covering notes, which was effectively made null and void by the enormous increase of the uncovered portion (16 billion rubles by November of last year), could hardly be considered applicable. The note-covering regulation of the German Imperial Bank specifies that notes must be one-third covered by gold: German money presently in circulation, national-bank or loan-bank certificates (the so-called one-third coverage); and, with respect to the rest, by secure short-term bills of exchanges or checks and exchequer bonds of the Reich (the banking coverage). These restrictions are not readily transferable to the Ukrainian State Bank without essential modifications; but it seems to us that it does form an appropriate foundation for a regulatory system corresponding to Ukrainian conditions.

In connection with this regulation we should like to recommend a qualification, according to which the notes of the Ukrainian State Bank must be covered up to at least one third by assets that make possible the immediate redemption of the notes under normal circumstances or that are secured in foreign exchange held abroad. The rest of the notes would be covered in normal banking fashion, that is, secured by safe fixed assets.

For the one-third coverage the following would come into consideration:

1. Circulating Ukrainian metallic money taken at its face value. Russian silver rubles would fall under this heading so long as they are legal tender in the Ukraine.

---

4 [During the French Revolution, the revolutionary government issued *assignats,* a form of paper money that soon generated a high inflation, resulting in the imposition of price and wage controls. In 1795, they were exchanged for *mandats territoriaux* at the rate of thirty to one. The *mandats* were scrip representing claims to land titles. The *mandats* were soon increased in such quantities that another inflationary process was set in motion. In 1797, the engraving plates for printing *mandats* were destroyed. See Andrew Dickson White, *Fiat Money Inflation in France* (Washington, D.C.: Cato Institute, [1913] 1980); Edwin W. Kemmerer, *Money: The Principles of Money and Their Exemplification in Outstanding Chapters of Monetary History* (New York: Macmillan Co., 1935), pp. 173–97. —Ed.]

2. Gold in ingots and foreign coins calculated according to the relative value that results from the gold content of Ukrainian gold coins.

3. Silver ingots according to their market value and foreign silver coins according to their exchange value.

4. Foreign bank notes and foreign governmental paper money, as well as foreign loan-bank certificates according to their exchange value. Russian notes, as long as they are legal tender in the Ukraine, would be calculated according to their face value.

5. Drafts on foreign countries in gold currency and credits with foreign note-issuing central banks, other banks, and other institutions of unconditional reliability according to their exchange value. (Among the institutions of unquestionable reliability would be, for example, the German Central Purchasing Association, the Austrian War Grain-Trading Institute, and the Hungarian War Production Joint-Stock Company.)

The covering of notes by credit balances abroad—namely, in Berlin and Vienna—will be, in accordance with all prudence, of very special practical importance. The credits will be provided without difficulty in connection with exports. Their provision will considerably facilitate the financing of exports, and their availability would most effectively support the Ukrainian currency abroad.

Insofar as the notes find no covering under the items 1 through 5 cited above, they would be covered by bills of exchange, by six-month treasury bonds of foreign countries at face value, and by secured-loan investments.

The unsecured loans that the note-issuing bank would be authorized to grant under certain conditions would not come into consideration as a covering for notes. The means used for the granting of such loans could therefore not be provided by the issuance of notes; it would have to be taken out of the capital stock and the reserves or possibly out of deposits.

IV   Administration

At the head of the administration of the German Reichsbank is the Reichsbank board of directors that, as a committee, deals with matters of administration. This collaborative structure has so far proven to be a good system in every respect. It assures the independence of the administration and guarantees it continuity. Our only advice, therefore, would be also to place a collaborative authority at the head of the Ukrainian State Bank. This authority would, of course, be subject to the jurisdiction of the government.

A note-issuing central bank should not be managed in accordance with the fiscal requirements of the State but instead from the point of view of the economy as a whole. Perhaps it should be recommended, therefore, that at the highest level the direction of the State Bank should not be assigned to the head of the Department of Finance but to the prime minister or the minister of commerce. In the same way, the German Reichsbank is under the control of the imperial chancellor and, on his behalf, of the state secretary of the Imperial Bureau of Economics.

V   Publications

A great importance is to be placed upon the publication of the annual balance sheet and its [the bank's] regular publications. The Russian Imperial Bank dated its weekly statements — until the discontinuation of publications in November of last year [1917] — on the 1st, 8th, 16th, and 23rd (according to the old-style Russian calendar). German bank law establishes the 7th, the 15th, the 23rd, and the last of each month as the dates for publication. The one as well as the other procedure allows for clear estimate of the demand for money, which is conditioned by activity at the end of the month and especially at the end of each quarter and as well as at the end of the year. It deserves preference over the procedure of the Bank of France and the Bank of England, which always prepare their weekly statements according to the situation on Wednesday evening.

VI   Distribution of Profits

Out of the earnings that may show themselves on the annual balance sheet, at least 50 percent would at first be used for the formation of the capital stock, if the latter cannot be transferred in advance to the State Bank. If the capital stock has reached the amount of 20 million Karbovanits, about 10 percent would be set aside for the formation of a reserve until it has reached at least half of the capital stock. Any losses would be covered first from the reserve and, in case this should not be sufficient, from the capital stock. Of course, then the capital stock and the reserve would have to be replenished in the following years by transfers out of earnings. For the rest, the profit would fall to the national treasury, which is also responsible for losses not covered by the capital stock and the reserve.

CHAPTER 4

The Austrian Currency Problem Prior to the Peace Conference[1]

The liquidation of a common monetary standard constitutes an internal problem for the successor states of the former Austrian monarchy.[2] The new successor states have adopted unilateral and in many instances even antagonistic monetary policies, and have resisted attempts on the part of the government of German-Austria[3] to find a consensual solution to cur-

1 [This paper was written in German in April 1919, shortly before a delegation for the Austrian government met with the representatives of the victorious Allied powers near Saint-Germain, France, in June 1919 to receive the terms for peace. It has not been previously published. Mises had been assigned responsibility in the Vienna Chamber of Commerce for all financial matters relating to foreign affairs from the time of the Armistice of November 1918, which ended the fighting between Austria and the Allied powers, through September 1919, when the Austrian Parliament's ratification of the Treaty of Saint-Germain officially ended the state of war.—Ed.]

2 [With the end of the war, the Austro-Hungarian empire disintegrated. Bohemia, Moravia, and Slovakia were joined as the new, independent state of Czechoslovakia. Hungary declared its separate independence from Austria. The Balkan territories of the empire—Slovenia, Croatia, and Bosnia-Herzegovina—were unified with Serbia as the new state of Yugoslavia. Transylvania, which had been under the jurisdiction of the Hungarian part of the empire, was incorporated into Romania. Galicia, which had been part of the Austrian Crownlands of the empire, was added to the new state of Poland; and Italy occupied the area around the Adriatic port of Trieste and the southern Tyrol. The new countries that emerged out of this political disintegration of the Austro-Hungarian empire were referred to as the "successor states."—Ed.]

3 [The remnant of the Austrian part of the empire was declared to be an independent state as the other components were breaking away, and was proclaimed on November 12, 1918, to be the democratic *Deutschösterreich*—German-Austria—with the stated intention of leaving the door open to being unified with the new German Republic. But at the peace negotiations at Saint-Germain the Allied powers, especially the French, prohibited any Austrian unification (*Anschluss*) with Germany, and insisted that the official name of the country be "the Austrian Republic."—Ed.]

rency questions. Thus it seems likely that only the intervention of the peace conference will produce a generally acceptable solution. This is reason enough to try to raise the currency question at the Paris Peace Conference. The Entente,[4] as well as the neutral states, moreover, have a stake of their own in a sensible reorganization of our monetary system. The value of uncertified bank notes held in other countries hinges on such a successful resolution, as does the fate of accounts and claims in crowns held by other countries against the successor states of the former monarchy.

Before we attempt to approach the whole currency question on a practical level, let us first disregard all practical complications and attempt to work out an ideal theoretical solution. Let us for the moment forget that the successor states have disrupted the bond of a common currency by their unilateral monetary measures, which have not only wreaked havoc on the monetary system of the individual nation states but have also seriously threatened the whole network of the former monarchy's liabilities to other countries.[5]

The first question to be raised is the manner in which bank-note circulation and related legal provisions should have been altered, presupposing that the successor states had refrained from any unilateral intervention in the common bank-note system.

Let us begin with a few preliminary remarks about the legal and economic character of bank notes as it relates to the problem of state debts.

From a legal point of view, bank notes represent a claim against the Austro-Hungarian Bank for a specified amount of gold that has been certified by the state, a claim that is held by the owners of the bank notes. It is true that Article 111 of the statutes indefinitely suspended this gold payment. Thus, even before the war, the free circulation of bank notes relied less on the note holders' conviction that the notes represented a specified amount of precious metal to be paid out by the Austro-Hungarian Bank than on the realization that the notes were valid as legal tender in the en-

4 [The Entente refers to the coalition of Allied powers in the First World War, especially Great Britain, France, Italy, and the United States. — Ed.]

5 [On January 8, 1919, the Yugoslavian government began monetary separation from Austria with an order that all Austro-Hungarian bank notes on Yugoslavian territory were to be stamped with a national mark. On February 25, 1919, the Czechoslovakian government did the same. The Czechoslovakian border was placed under military guard to prevent the smuggling of bank notes. The actual stamping of bank notes occurred between March 3 and 9. At the same time, the government took over all branches of the Austro-Hungarian Bank on Czechoslovakian territory. A separate currency began to be introduced shortly after a law to that effect was passed on April 10, 1919. — Ed.]

tire monarchy thanks to the Austro-Hungarian Bank's privileged position. The emission of bank notes was vastly increased in all the belligerent countries, not just in Austria, because of the pressure of military expenses. As early as 1914, the Austrian government had already had to suspend statutory regulations covering the gold backing of these notes. At the present time over 39 billion bank notes have been issued, to which should be added bills of exchange and other current liabilities of about 6.5 billion. A further 6.75 billion in the form of treasury notes—which must be repaid in the foreseeable future—should also be included. This total is presently backed—to the tune of 33 billion crowns—by the debt owed respectively by the former imperial Austrian and the former royal Hungarian government in equivalent treasury bonds. Another 9.2 billion are backed by Lombard credits, specifically in the form of war savings bonds. Ninety-four percent of all bank notes in circulation, treasury notes, and bills of exchange are indirectly or directly based on the state's obligation to repay its debts. For this reason, the notes would have only minimal backing in terms of their face value, should the state go bankrupt. There would be other claims against the remaining bank assets, which might otherwise provide partial backing for the notes.

On the strength of this short introduction, it is clear that any discussion of the currency problem must strictly distinguish between the following issues:

I. The allocation of the debt incurred by the Austro-Hungarian Bank among various successor states' governments.

II. The legal and economic status of entitlement incorporated in each individual bank note and in each bill-of-exchange.

III. The redemption of certain quantities of notes by the individual successor states and the resulting monetary effects.

IV. The liquidation of the Austro-Hungarian Bank.

Regarding each state's indebtedness to the note-issuing bank, our petition to the peace conference should request that an allocation scheme be devised to divide this debt, as well as other categories of state debt, among the successor states. As to the question of the legal and economic status of the bank notes, we must take the position that the owners of uncertified bank notes originally acquired a form of money that was legal tender at a fixed value in the entire monarchy before its collapse.

It is undeniable that each sovereign state is entitled to regulate as it sees fit the legal and economic relations between persons over whom it exercises its sovereignty, and this holds true as well for the successor states that arose on the soil of the former monarchy. This right, however, is constrained by the rights of foreign nationals, a fact that each of the individual successor states must keep in mind in its dealings with subjects of other successor states as well as in their dealings with countries that were never a part of the monarchy. We shall first concern ourselves with the latter.

The same considerations that apply to foreign owners of bank notes must also apply to foreigners who have accounts or claims against persons or firms in the territory of the former monarchy. There are several ways in which the rights of note owners or creditors residing in foreign countries can be guaranteed in settling the currency question. The first is to say that bank notes in the hands of foreigners shall remain legal tender in all the successor states of the former monarchy. The second is to allow foreigners to exchange the old bank notes against a currency unit that they can use for payments in all the successor states, without loss in the exchange value of the notes. The last approach is to say that they can exchange their bank notes for whatever national currencies they need for use in any specific successor state, again without loss in exchange value of the notes. The first of these solutions (solution A-1) implies the rescinding, with retroactive validity, of any measures taken by the successor states against the common currency, a sort of *restitutio in integrum* of the old currency. It is also conceivable that the successor states might maintain their own currency but at the same time assume the obligation to accept uncertified crowns as legal tender along with their own currency, at a fixed exchange value (solution A-2).

The second solution (solution B) involves the exchange of the old bank notes against a new monetary unit, which becomes legal tender in an identical manner in all the successor states. This solution can be interpreted in two ways.

1. The old crown currency is eliminated, but it is replaced in *all* successor states by a *formal* common currency with a single common note-issuing central bank. The difference between this approach and the preservation of the old crown currency lies in the possibility that the value of the new currency will now correspond to the reduced purchasing power of the new currency. It also allows the possibility of a merger with another currency system.

2. Each successor state is endowed with its own national currency and its own note-issuing bank, but each of these currencies is based on the same monetary standard, each of the note-issuing banks follows the same regulation concerning backing of notes, and the banks may form a cartel

(a closer or looser monetary union). This solution makes greater allowance for the successor states' desire to enhance their prestige. At the same time, it is more expensive and more complicated than solution B-1 because of the coexistence of several note-issuing banks.

The final possibility (solution C) is undoubtedly the most imperfect, but it requires none of the above-mentioned preconditions for its implementation. In this case each successor state maintains its own completely independent currency, without regard for the other states; it takes on the obligation, however, to exchange notes held by foreigners into notes issued by its own banking system, without giving a special premium to this or that note. The exchange rate would be solely determined by the gold parity of the newly created individual currencies.

It will depend, first of all, on wide constellation of political circumstances within the former monarchy as to whether solutions A-1 and A-2 and B-1 and B-2 are feasible. These solutions would in any case be complicated by the fact that segments of the monarchy's territory were incorporated into states with pre-existing and unrelated currencies (e.g., Italy and Serbia), a difficulty that might be surmounted by a currency union. It would become impossible to allow the concurrent circulation of uncertified crowns with the regular currency once the joint note-issuing bank [the Austro-Hungarian Bank] has been liquidated, since the uncertified notes would immediately lose their nominal backing and would at best circulate as a sort of state-sanctioned paper money. Under solutions A and B-1 the currency would maintain its unity, so that the question of their technical implementation would not arise; but in the case of either a currency union or completely independent currency systems, these technical questions assume a major role.

If we continue to assume that no actual steps with respect to note certifications have been taken by the individual successor states, we can visualize the following procedure for the exchange of notes. The successor states would issue uniform proclamations according to which a certain deadline would be set for all bank notes to be recalled and exchanged against the new, national notes. This deadline would have to take geographic and transportation factors into consideration, just as do the legal regulations for bills of exchange. Beyond the deadline, the old bank notes would lose their status as legal tender in all the successor states. The recall of bank notes would apply both to those held within the individual successor states as well as in other countries.

Subsequent handling of the notes would be different for those circulating within the various successor states and those circulating in other countries. As to the notes circulating within its own territory, each successor state would undoubtedly have the right to replace them by notes of its own issue (bank or state notes). Such a measure is well within the scope governments can take on their own territory. On the other hand, as we pointed out earlier, such a forced nationalization would violate international law if it involved other countries, since it would make them suffer from the splitting of the former monarchy into separate currency systems.

In case foreign holders of crowns were to receive payments in currency that could not be used in all the successor states—though that would be alleviated to a large extent if there were a currency union—at the very least they should have the right to decide for which national currency they would want to exchange their uncertified bank notes, depending on where they intended to spend the money or what was most convenient to them. Thus, after the deadline for turning in the bank notes, there would exist only national notes. However, for notes held internally, the territorial principle would hold in the successor states; but for notes held outside the country, the only criterion would be the wish of the note owners.

After the completion of this operation, there would undoubtedly be a discrepancy between the notes exchanged by the successor states and the allocation of the state debt. This would require some readjustment, such as compensation through other types of state debt, first and foremost short-term liabilities such as the central government's current account debts to the banks or debts of the Ministry of War to weapons suppliers. But even this approach runs into insurmountable obstacles on closer inspection. A large Viennese bank, for instance, can hardly be expected to accept settlement of its entire claims in the form of Hungarian or Ukrainian notes, just to establish a balance between notes exchanged and the debt allocation. On the contrary, some banks that had become creditors to the state would have a kind of *sujet mixte*[6] due to extensive commercial activity throughout the entire former monarchy. They would undoubtedly insist, in case national currencies were created, that they be paid in the various national currencies in amounts determined by the allocation of the state debt. One might conceive a solution along territorial lines, so that a purely Czech creditor would receive his entire claim in Czech crowns and a purely Austrian creditor in Austrian crowns. As to the *sujets mixtes*, such as

---

6 [The French expression *sujet mixte* means a mixed amount or combination.—Ed.]

with banks, the category that would include the majority of the state creditors, would require payments based on the debt allocation.

Let us now imagine that one tried to compensate for any excess over
the allocated state debt in the bank notes that were exchanged by reducing the banks' burden of payments for annuities or war loans. This too
would create considerable difficulties. In the first place, there is no way to
find a common denominator for the burden on the state created by the
issue of treasury notes and the burden created by an interest-paying loan.
There is an even greater economic difference between these two types of
transactions. When a particular successor state is overwhelmed with bank
notes far in excess of its need for notes in circulation, this represents a
much more severe economic burden than the obligation to make interest
payments on a war loan. A fair way to even things out might be to shift the
quantity of bank notes that a successor state must trade in over and above
its allocated debt to whichever successor state had to trade in fewer bank
notes than its allocated debt. The latter state would compensate the state
that had to trade in a surplus of bank notes by backing the surplus with
state obligations. These state obligations should be in the currency not of
the debtor state but in the currency of the state that had to increase its
note issue by an excessive number of bank notes. This would also significantly reduce differences in the exchange rates that might arise between
the individual successor states.

Let us take a concrete example. Let us say that the grand total of bank
notes circulating in German-Austria, Czechoslovakia, and in other countries came to 10 billion. Let us further assume that on the basis of the allocated debt, German-Austria and Czechoslovakia each had to assume 50
percent of the bank notes, that is, 5 billion bank notes. Czechoslovakia
has 4.5 billion notes in circulation, Austria only 3.5 billion. These notes
would have to be traded in for national bank notes in each state. The remaining 2 billion would be held in other countries. Let us assume that all
the foreign owners decided to exchange their uncertified notes into Czech
money. That would raise the share of the Czech state to 6.5 billion. The
3.5 billion raised by Austria must be backed in Austria on the basis of the
future currency law. Similarly, the Czech state must back 5 billion notes,
the full amount of its allocated debt, according to its own currency law.
The 1.5 billion notes that the Czech state must take in over and above its
share will be covered by treasury bonds of the Austrian state, expressed in
Czech currency. An agreement as to interest payments would be concluded between the two nation-states. A provision would be included in

the currency laws of the individual nation-states that such treasury bills of exchange of another nation-state could be included as backing for a certain percentage of bank notes. The date the treasury bills of exchange would fall due would have to take concrete economic conditions into account, so that the debtor state could be reasonably expected to repay its debt in this time span through the export of goods or capital.

The uncertified bank notes traded in by the successor states would then have to be turned over to the Austro-Hungarian Bank to wipe out the debt incurred on the loan.

As we have seen, differences in the amount of money in circulation in the various successor states will inevitably produce discrepancies between the bank notes exchanged in their own territory (on the basis of the territorial principle), and the allocated state debt. Whether this discrepancy will be eased or aggravated by the ways in which foreigners will decide to exchange their notes is as yet unpredictable. All that is certain is that the discrepancy will persist.

The only remaining point is the handling of debts and claims. Claims that fall due before the deadline for exchanging the old bank notes would be paid in uncertified crown notes, while claims falling due after the deadline would be paid in the currency of the successor state that is the site where the claim must be settled. This is in line with a generally recognized norm of international civil law. Since the exchange of uncertified notes must be made on the basis of the nominal parity in the currency of each successor state, it would make no difference whether the claim falls due before or after the deadline, unless later on significant differences in exchange rates develop between the various currencies.

The matter of debts is somewhat more difficult to resolve. It must be assumed that the owner of short-term debt is entitled to convert it to uncertified crown notes. When the owner is a foreigner, in our view he should be able to exchange the debt into uncertified bank notes in any of the successor states. It might, however, be reasonable to say that beyond the deadline for the exchange, if the debt is not converted into notes, the owner has tacitly agreed to be repaid in the currency of the place where the debt is held. The same would apply to owners who are citizens of one of the successor states. In their case, too, the debt would have to be exchanged for uncertified bank notes prior to the deadline (since no other notes exist at that point under our construct). But after the deadline it would have to be paid out in the currency of the place where the debt is held. This solution presents an undeniable danger for Austria: As it was the former financial center of the whole monarchy and therefore the place where most debts were located, the exchange burden would be especially heavy. The overall situation will become clear once we have a quantitative survey of bank debts and other obligations between the individual successor states. Any other solution, which in view of the above consideration might improve our exchange situation, would greatly damage our credit position. It would irremediably compromise Vienna's status as a financial metropolis, which might otherwise be partly continued from force of habit.

So far we have worked out a theoretically correct solution to the currency problems and disregarded the currency measures that have already been put into effect. We shall now ascertain what modifications are required when we take into account the legal situation that has developed in the individual successor states.

In those states where the certification of bank notes was decreed and implemented (Yugoslavia, the Czech Republic, and German-Austria), only certified bank notes can serve as legal tender, with a few exceptions to be discussed later. In Hungary, certification is required by law but has not yet been implemented as a result of the political turmoil.[7] In the territories occupied by the Italians, certification has not yet taken place, but crowns must be exchanged for lire notes at the rate of 1 crown for 40 centesimi. Insufficient information is available about the measures taken by the Polish, Ukrainian, and Romanian governments. Even in the states that have in principle carried through the nationalization of bank notes, one- and two-crown notes have been exempted from certification and retain their role as legal tender in all the successor states. In addition, there remain a substantial number of uncertified notes in the Entente and in neutral countries, in all those successor states that have not yet implemented the certification (Hungary and parts of the monarchy that now belong to Romania, the Ukraine, and Poland), and also in wartime enemy territory

---

7 [At the time when Mises wrote this paper in April 1919, Hungary was in the midst of a Communist revolution. On March 20, 1919, the Marxist revolutionary, Béla Kun, had acquired a dominant position in the Communist-Social Democratic coalition government. He soon was able to eliminate the more moderate elements in the government through a reign of Red terror. His Soviet-style government finally collapsed on August 1, 1919, after his attempt to nationalize the large landed estates alienated the peasantry, who wanted the land divided among themselves. They refused to supply food to the towns and cities, and the Red Army that Kun had created refused to fight. Béla Kun's short-lived Soviet Republic was replaced by a nationalist government headed by Admiral Miklós von Horthy, who served as regent heading the government of Hungary.—Ed.]

that had been temporarily occupied by Austrian troops. Last but not least, even in the states where certification was decreed and implemented, there are of course considerable quantities of uncertified notes that their owners have failed to turn in, either out of negligence or for speculative purposes, or, finally, for tax evasion. In the following paragraphs we shall review the essence of the major currency provisions enacted by the successor states, to the extent that they are known here.

According to the Czech decree issued February 25, 1919, paragraph 2, all bank notes must be certified and only certified bank notes serve as legal tender in the territory of the Czech state. The minister of finance is empowered, however, to permit certain types of uncertified bank notes to continue to serve as legal tender, a provision that has been applied by him to one- and two-crown notes.

The Czech decree of February 25, 1919, paragraph 8 (*Laws and Decrees*, no. 86) expressly states that from March 10, 1919, on, uncertified crowns no longer can serve as legal tender in the territory of the Czech state. In this territory, obligations incurred prior to compulsory certification and payable in crowns are now to be paid in certified crowns. Legal transactions concluded beginning with March 10, 1919, and in which payment is to be in uncertified bank notes are valid only if this mode of payment has been specified.

In response to these measures taken by the Czech government, an Austrian executive order was issued in turn on March 25, 1919 (No. 191). It provides that, immediately following the executive order, only certified notes of the Austro-Hungarian Bank will be considered legal tender, with exceptions to be discussed later. To mitigate the harshness of this decree, the state secretary for finances is permitted to accept notes certified in other successor states when presented at government or other pay-offices. He may also, under special circumstances, allow uncertified notes to be accepted at these pay-offices. In especially deserving cases, he may even permit uncertified notes to be certified with the Austrian stamp. According to paragraph 4 of the decree, all obligations that are to be repaid in crowns are payable in Austrian certified bank notes in the amount specified in crowns at a one-to-one ratio, with the exception of certain cases we will discuss later.

The recent Czech law of April 10, 1919, No. 187, which covers the circulation and management of money, is much more comprehensive than the Austrian executive order. Paragraph 1 of this law provides that only the Czech state is entitled to issue notes and mint coins in its territory. As the Czech state does not yet have a note-issuing bank, this means that the Czech Republic will rely on state paper money. The monetary unit that will be used for this state paper money is identified in paragraph 5 of the law as the Czech crown. Uncertified bank notes of the Austro-Hungarian Bank no longer serve as legal tender, according to paragraph 3. The Czech government reserves the exclusive right, according to paragraph 4, to present claims to the Austro-Hungarian Bank with the certified notes in its possession. Paragraph 6 states furthermore that former obligations specified as payable in Austro-Hungarian currency are to be paid in Czech crowns at a one-to-one rate, as long as the payment is to be made in the Czech state. Finally, according to paragraph 9, the new Czech crown notes will constitute part of the financial obligations of the Czech state, since they are state notes, and they will at the same time be considered legal tender.

Our information is very sketchy for the other territorial states. We do know that in the territory occupied by the Italians there exists a decree from the High Command stating that from April 10, 1919, on, Italian money will be legal tender in the Trentino and in Giulia Venzia.[8] Whatever Austro-Hungarian money is still in circulation can be exchanged into Italian money at the owner's request at the following rate: Crown notes of the Austro-Hungarian Bank issued on the basis of legal provisions prior to October 27, 1918, will be exchanged for 0.40 lire per crown, and Austrian silver coins at the rate of 0.80 Italian paper money per silver coin. This exchange will take place between April 10 and April 19, 1919.

After April 1919, the Austro-Hungarian money ceases to be legal tender. Austro-Hungarian silver coins will continue to remain in circulation. The value will be fixed at the rate of 1/100 lire for each 1/100 crown.

Let us now examine how well our initial construct applies to the legal situation described above.

SOLUTION A-1   Letting the old crown notes continue to serve their prior function. This implies a *restitutio in integrum* and thus assumes an annulment of all prior currency measures, which is politically almost inconceivable.

---

8 [Trentino refers to the southern portion of the Austrian Tyrol that the Italian government occupied and annexed, following the First World War. Giulia Venzia refers to the Austrian region bordering on the Adriatic coast, including the port city of Trieste, which was occupied and annexed by Italy after the war.—Ed.]

SOLUTION A-2   Letting old crown notes continue to serve as a secondary currency wherever it was valid before, alongside the individual national currencies. This arrangement is fully compatible with the existing state of affairs. Problems arise here, as mentioned earlier, with respect to the liquidation of the Austro-Hungarian Bank.

SOLUTION B-1   The creation of a new common currency for all of the successor states. Formally, this arrangement would run counter to the latest Czech currency law. Practically speaking, however, no steps have yet been taken that exclude this approach, with the exception of the compulsory exchange of crowns into lire decreed in the territory under Italian rule. Since Italy would under no circumstances be included in the common currency, this exception is of little practical significance, even though it may present some special formal problems.

SOLUTION B-2   The creation of a currency union. The same considerations hold for this solution.

SOLUTION C   The creation of completely independent currency systems. No measures taken run counter to this solution.

Although we have examined our proposals in the light of the current monetary measures of the successor states, we have not examined these laws in any detail. When one looks at the finer points, numerous incompatibilities in these finer points will certainly stand in the way of the requisite legal uniformity in the individual successor states. We cannot deal with them in this discussion, nor does it serve any useful purpose to do so until it is determined which of the proposed solutions is accepted by the peace conference.[9] From a technical point of view, Solutions B-2 and C would require that certification is implemented by a certain deadline even in those successor states where it has not yet been decreed.

An undeniable problem facing the negotiators will be how to deal with

---

9 The Treaty of Saint-Germain, which ended the war between Austria and the Allies, and the Treaty of Trianon, which ended the war between Hungary and the Allies, basically accepted the monetary separation among the successor states that had begun as described in Mises's paper. The treaties specified that the liquidation of the Austro-Hungarian Bank would begin the day after the treaties were ratified. However, because of the delay in Hungary's signing of its treaty until June 4, 1920, the liquidation process did not begin until September 1, 1920. The process took four years, until July 31, 1924, when the Austro-Hungarian Bank officially ceased to exist. — Ed.]

the premium on Czech notes that has arisen since the unity of the currency was torn asunder by the Czech Republic. It is perfectly obvious that when a foreigner who owns uncertified bank notes is given the choice in which successor state to exchange his notes, he will opt for the Czech currency, in view of the premium it offers. He would do so even if he had to make payments in German-Austria, since he could in any case procure Austrian crowns by selling his Czech crowns at a considerable gain. It is to be assumed under these conditions that if solution C were adopted, all notes held in foreign countries would find their way into the Czech Republic, where the most advantageous terms were offered. This would undoubtedly increase the share of notes to be exchanged by the Czech state compared to the Czech share of the state debt. This is a result that the government in Prague will oppose vigorously, since it is likely to have a significant negative impact on the premium of the Czech currency in relation to the currencies of the other successor states. Conversely, this solution is desirable for German-Austria from the monetary point of view, and for that very reason the Czechs will probably contest it. (It should be kept in mind that this solution would, for the same reason, impose a burden on us in view of the desperate Hungarian situation.)

But for us too this will create problems, inasmuch as we will have to fund the surplus of Czech notes with promissory notes of the Austrian government in Czech currency. Despite the reduction in the premium on Czech notes, German-Austria would suffer a greater burden than if part of these foreign-held notes had been exchanged in German-Austria and had to be backed only in its own currency. In any case, should formula C be adopted in principle, we would do well tactically speaking to make this demand from the very start. The objections of the Czechs could justly be countered by blaming the negative consequences entirely on the Czech state for its unilateral and illegal currency measures. It would be even more expedient, tactically, to induce the neutral states, which are large holders of uncertified notes and have a big stake in the proposed solution, to present this demand at the peace conference. The fact that the Swiss government has already taken this stand in its intervention with the Foreign Ministry in charge of liquidation should facilitate this approach. On this occasion the neutral states established the principle that all the successor states were to be held jointly responsible for bank notes held abroad.

The proper legal way of handling debts held by persons or firms residing or permanently settled in other countries is to pay them in uncertified bank notes, in line with the principles enunciated earlier. All the successor states must then commit themselves to exchanging the uncertified notes for money that is considered legal tender in their own territory. At the option of the owner, the redemption should be either at face value or at the legal exchange rate. As to settlement of *claims*, the procedure established in the Austrian Executive Order No. 191 for claims in German-Austria has much in its favor. It specifies that whatever claims can possibly be settled in crowns, with a few minor exceptions, are to be paid in Austrian certified notes at face value, irrespective of the date at which the obligation falls due. The fact that the Czech law of April 10, 1919, No. 187 has an identical provision for the Czech Republic makes this procedure all the more likely to be accepted.

We have already mentioned earlier in our theoretical discussion that this principle of obligations being payable at the previously agreed-upon site may place an undue strain on Austrian currency. However, it would be difficult to have any other procedure accepted, in view of the international civil-law provision according to which the agreed-upon site determines where payments must be made. It should also be kept in mind that any other arrangement would seriously damage Austria's credit status, a negative effect that would greatly outweigh the monetary drawbacks of the proposed solution.

The formula proposed here must be viewed as nothing more than a first line of defense. For this reason we must be ready with an alternate approach, in case the above formula is turned down. For this eventuality, the Commission for the Preparation of the Financial Peace Settlements proposes the following, applicable to both bank notes and short-term debts: that the principle of proportional allocation be applied. According to this principle, owners of either uncertified bank notes or crown debts in any of the successor states of the former monarchy are entitled to exchange their uncertified notes into the bank notes of the various successor states in the same ratio that the peace conference will have established for the allocation of the state debts. For *claims* by foreigners, however, the principle still applies that repayment must be made at the previously agreed site.

We have already set forth the proper procedure for bank notes within the individual successor states, namely, that they be redeemed on purely territorial principles. We must still make some further observations about debts held by nationals of one successor state in the territory of another successor state and the reciprocal settlement of claims between nationals of different successor states. Here, from a tactical point of view, our position is much more difficult, as we cannot marshal the clear self-interest of foreign countries in defense of our point of view. As to claims between nationals of the different successor states, here too the rule of international civil law (that the agreed-upon site for repayment is decisive) will almost certainly prevail. Several different solutions are conceivable with respect to debts. The peace treaty may establish the rule that each creditor, no matter to which successor state he belongs, is entitled to be paid by the debtor in the currency of the successor state of the creditor's choice. Such a rule would be based on the fact that uncertified bank notes served as legal tender in the territory of the entire former monarchy. In this case, nationals of successor states would be treated like nationals of countries that were never part of the monarchy. Another possibility might be—our second line of defense—that debtors have to make repayments in the currencies of the individual successor states in proportion to the allocation of the state debts. A third possibility would be to drop the distinction between debts and claims and to declare that even for debts payment should be made in the currency of the agreed-upon site.

It is impossible to predict which of these solutions is most favorable for us without an exact knowledge of the balance of payments of the individual successor states. We would have to take into account, furthermore, how that balance would shift after a large number of enterprises have moved their headquarters from Vienna to the territory of other successor states. We would also have to know the impact of the possible nationalization of branch offices located in the successor states. But even if we disposed of all this information, we would still be none the wiser about what is the best solution from our point of view. A crucial factor would still be the exchange rate of the national currencies of the individual successor states, which remains uncertain.

A few remarks seem appropriate about what constitutes a foreign country and what must be regarded as a successor state from the point of view of currency relations. Any solution that favors foreign countries in relation to the successor states must lead to a migration of uncertified notes to that foreign country. This drawback can be only partially mitigated by requiring the submission of an affidavit. The situation becomes even more complicated when a foreign country annexes a territory of the former monarchy. This is exemplified by Poland's annexation of Western Galicia, the Ukraine's annexation of Eastern Galicia, Romania's annexation of Bukovina, Serbia's annexation of Croatia, Carinthia, the Krain, and Steiermark, and lastly Italy's annexation of South Tyrol and littoral areas formerly part of the monarchy. Since it is impossible to differentiate between the foreign country and the annexed Austrian territories, which in this respect must be treated as successor states, all these states should be treated as successor states and not as foreign countries from the point of view of currency relations. Countries that have annexed territories of the former monarchy should thus not be counted in this respect as foreign countries.

And, finally, a few remarks about tactical and more formal aspects of these questions seem in order. It is undeniable that the resolution of the currency problem is intimately tied to the question of how the state debts will be allocated. On the other hand, we must assume that any definitive allocation of the debts will be the result of protracted negotiations. Since the currency question must be resolved at least provisionally to allow the resumption of economic activity in our country, we will have to distinguish between a provisional stage and a final settlement. We might suggest the allocation of the state debt in proportion to the number of inhabitants, which could easily be ascertained in a matter of days once territorial borders are determined. The final clearing between the share of bank notes and the allocated state debts could then be determined on the basis of the definitive debt allocation.[10]

In view of the tangled nature of the currency problem and of the great conflict of interests between the individual successor states, international arbitration alone can lead the way to a settlement. But even such a settlement will only provide an international legal framework, without eliminating the large number of practical difficulties that will arise within the national legal systems. The successor states will have to assume the obli-

---

10 [The peace treaties divided the Austro-Hungarian prewar debts into two categories, secured and unsecured. Secured debts, such as railroads against which the property had been secured for the loan, were charged to the country in whose territory the property was now located. If the property was located across more than one of the successor states, each country was responsible for the portion of the debt corresponding to the amount of the secured property under its jurisdiction. Unsecured debt was distributed among the successor states on the basis of the fraction of the tax revenue its territory had supplied to the Austro-Hungarian monarchy. For a more detailed summary of the debt-allocation process following the signing of the peace treaties, see Leo Pasvolsky, *Economic Nationalism of the Danubian States* (New York: Macmillan Co., 1928), pp. 42–47. In 1919–1920, Ludwig von Mises was the director of the Austrian Reparations Commission for the League of Nations that was responsible for the settling of prewar debts and claims.—Ed.]

gation to incorporate the solution resulting from arbitration as the basis of their own currency legislation. Moreover, private international law will have to expand its meager rules in this area and will have to provide means of legal redress to secure uniformity in the internal adjudication of currency questions in the successor states. Only thus can the arbitrary handling of civil-law disputes resulting from the dissolution of the currency be avoided.

CHAPTER 5

On the Actions to Be Taken in the Face of Progressive Currency Depreciation[1]

I

We are going down a road that leads to the collapse of our currency. Our financial policy has been reduced to *one* remedy: printing more and more paper money. There is almost no prospect that things will change in this respect. It is unreasonable to expect that the Social Democratic party will suddenly admit the inner collapse of its socialist ideas or openly recognize the falsity of all that it has proclaimed for decades. We cannot expect better things from the Christian Socialist party, whose economic ideal is the survival of autarchic farmers and of small craftsmen mainly concerned about their daily bread. For decades the Christian Socialist party has advocated restrictive competency certificates and high protective tariffs; it has defended Prince Liechtenstein's[2] program for "Austria without factories" and fought alongside with Lueger[3] and Schlesinger[4] for *Gulden der Väter*[5] and *Volksgeld*.[6] How could it now suddenly become a proponent of

---

1 [This essay was written in German, most probably in May or June of 1919. It has not been previously published. Typed at the top of the first page was the word "Confidential." It was most likely prepared for Austrian bankers and businessmen affiliated with the Vienna Chamber of Commerce, whom Mises wished to enlist in devising a private-sector plan for confronting the monetary problems that would exist if the inflation in Austria reached the point of a complete collapse of the currency.—Ed.]

2 [See Chapter 2, "On the Currency Question," footnote 7.—Ed.]

3 [See Chapter 2, footnote 6.—Ed.]

4 [See Chapter 2, footnote 8.—Ed.]

5 [*Gulden der Väter* means the "money of our forefathers."—Ed.]

6 [*Volksgeld* means the "people's money."—Ed.]

free trade and liberalism? And when it comes to the German Nationalists, they have always tried to outdo the other parties by their social-reformist radicalism and are currently the special advocates for the large sector of public employees, whose syndicalism has dealt the final blow to our financial situation.[7] As to foreign policy, they have learned nothing from the terrible military defeat, nor have they forgotten anything. How could experience possibly have taught them economic and financial wisdom? It is our country's misfortune that its survival depends on the export of industrial goods, while modern economic thinking has remained alien to its population. Our entire political life is impregnated with imperialist, mercantilist, and socialist thinking, and with the fantasies of "economic nationalism."

It is impossible to rationally refute political ideas that have held sway for decades, to the exclusion of all others. These ideas cannot fail to exert their influence in real life and will only succumb in the face of great catastrophes.

We require free trade in both our foreign and domestic economic transactions. Yet all our political parties are dedicated to the implementation of a more or less consistently applied system of interventionism. We have succeeded in avoiding the naked Bolshevism that has sprung up in Russia, Hungary, and Munich.[8] The only difference between the system

7 [In February 1919, an election was held for the formation of a constituent assembly that would govern the country and prepare a new constitution. The Social Democrats won 69 seats, the Christian Socialists gained 63 seats, and the Nationalists filled 24 seats. In March 1919, a couple of months before Mises prepared this essay, the Social Democrats and the Christian Socialists formed a coalition government, with the head of the Social Democrats, Karl Renner, serving as chancellor. The coalition governments continued until November 1920, when the Christian Socialists won an election and formed a government.—Ed.]

8 [In November 1917, Lenin and the Bolsheviks had seized power in Petrograd (later Leningrad and now renamed St. Petersburg) with the goal of establishing a socialist society and a planned economy in Russia. They instituted a policy of "War Communism" in 1918, as part of the leap into Communism—with the abolition of private ownership of the means of production, prices, money, and the market—and as a method for regimenting the portions of Russia under their control during the Russian Civil War that continued until 1920, with their victory over the "White Armies." From March to August 1919, a short-lived Soviet-type regime was imposed in Hungary under the Marxist revolutionary, Béla Kun, who implemented a Red reign of terror along the lines of Lenin in Russia. Between March and May 1919, there was a brief Soviet Republic established in Munich, Bavaria under the leadership of a group of German and Russian Marxist revolutionaries, who also imposed a brutal Red reign of terror.—Ed.]

of government under which we live, or, more precisely, under which we vegetate, and the Bolshevik system lies in our avoidance of open and bloody acts of violence. In terms of economic policy, however, our system, like that of the Bolsheviks, promotes an undisguised onslaught on private property, not only of the means of production but of consumption goods as well. And like Bolshevism, it survives only by using up the capital that has been accumulated over several generations under a freer economy. Movable and fixed equipment in public enterprises is not replaced as it gets worn out, and devious taxation and trade policies combine to hinder private enterprises in renovating their technical equipment. Food supplies are imported from other countries, and their counterpart is generated not by the export of domestically produced goods but by increasing indebtedness, the piecemeal sale of domestic productive capital—sale of shares, decimation of timber supplies—and an equally undesirable reduction of the domestic stock of consumption goods.

All this has historical precedents. All imperialist or socialist periods have had these same characteristics. The historian, René Stourm, revealed equivalent features in tracing out the financial conditions under the French Revolution. He has this to say about the policy of the Jacobins: "The attitude of the Jacobins about finances can be quite simply stated as an utter exhaustion of the present at the expense of the future. They never worried about the morrow, handling all their affairs as though each day were the last. That approach distinguished all actions undertaken during the Revolution. What permitted it to survive as long as it did was the fact that the day-by-day depletion of the resources accumulated by a rich and powerful nation allowed unexpectedly large resources to come to surface. The *assignats*, as long as they had any value at all, little as it might be, flooded the country in ever increasing quantities. The prospects of impending bankruptcy never stopped their being issued even for a moment. Only when the public absolutely refused to accept paper money of any kind, at no matter how low a value, did the issue of new notes come to a halt."[9]

The catastrophic depreciation of our currency must be accepted as

9 [René Stourm, *Les Finances de l'Ancien Régime et de la Révolution* [The Finances of the Old Regime and the Revolution], 2 Vols. (Paris: Guillaumin et Cie, 1885). For a brief account of the economic policies during the French Revolution, see Richard M. Ebeling, "Inflation and Controls in Revolutionary France: The Political Economy of the French Revolution," in Stephen Tonsor, ed., *Reflections of the French Revolution* (Washington, D. C.: Regnery/Gateway, 1990), pp. 138–56.—Ed.]

our inescapable fate. Imperialist and militarist policies are inevitably linked with inflationism. A consistent implementation of socialization necessarily leads to the total collapse of the monetary system. This fact is corroborated not only by the history of the French Revolution but by what is happening in Russia under Bolshevism and in a series of other countries that have more or less closely followed the Russian example, but where less bloody methods have replaced the appalling brutality of the Jacobins and the Bolsheviks. No matter how disastrous a collapse may be, it does at least have a salutary effect in that it annihilates the system that brought it into being. The collapse of the *assignats* dealt a deathblow to the policies of the Jacobins. After the collapse, new policies were pursued. In our case, too, the collapse of the currency will give us a fresh start in our economic policy.

Unless the further multiplication of bank notes is stopped instantly, the fate of our currency is sealed. It would be a serious error to believe that crowns can become valueless externally without the simultaneous loss of their domestic purchasing power, even if their exchange rate is no longer quoted on the foreign-exchange markets. In the last analysis, exchange rates are determined exclusively by the purchasing power of money in relation to commodities. For this reason, the much-discussed lag in the rise of commodity prices as compared to the rise in the foreign-exchange rate has proven to be a purely temporary phenomenon, a fact that the movement in prices in the last few weeks has again brought to the fore. Moreover, the psychological significance of a complete depreciation of the crown on foreign-exchange markets should not be underestimated. The crown has already lost a lot of ground in the wholesale and real-estate markets, and it is becoming more and more common to buy and sell with foreign currencies, even in the retail market. As the value of the crown falls close to zero in foreign-exchange markets, this tendency will become all the more pronounced and will assume catastrophic proportions as soon as the crown becomes valueless in Zurich and Amsterdam. It is obvious that it will become impossible to sell imported commodities in crowns. As soon as the "black marketers" — on whom the urban population in German-Austria is entirely dependent for its food supply — refuse to accept crowns, they will be completely displaced from the domestic markets. Crowns will still be accepted for taxes, for the payment of rent, and for rationed food supplies, but they will no longer be usable on the unregulated markets.

Our politicians, blinded by their *Étatist*[10] illusions, believe that the urban population is entirely dependent upon whatever is supplied to them by the state sector. That may be true for public employees without a second income and for many pensioners, to the extent that they are not supported by food supplements provided by relatives in the countryside. It is completely erroneous as far as the majority of the population is concerned. Rationed food items do not supply enough nutrition to sustain bodily functions in an adult at rest. Anyone who must restrict himself to what the government provides and what is offered in public food kitchens is doomed to a slow death from starvation. Expenses for rationed food items and prepared meals in war kitchens do not at this point use up the entire income of the workers. Any money left over finds its way into the black market. The masses live on what their black market purchases provide, and as soon as they can no longer obtain food supplies from the black market with crowns, they will be faced with a very difficult situation.[11]

10 ["Étatism" is from the French word *état*, or the state. Mises later explained that he preferred it to the English word "statism." He defined his use of the term in his *Omnipotent Government: The Rise of the Total State and Total War* (Spring Hills, Pa.: Libertarian Press, [1944] 1985), pp. 5 & 46: "Étatism appears in two forms: socialism and interventionism. Both have in common the goal of subordinating the individual unconditionally to the state, the social apparatus of compulsion and coercion. . . . Étatism assigns to the state the task of guiding the citizens and of holding them in tutelage. It aims at restricting the individual's freedom to act. It seeks to mold his destiny and to vest all initiative in the government alone."—Ed.]

11 [Following the collapse of the Austro-Hungarian Empire and the declaration of German-Austria as an independent republic in November 1918, the provincial authorities took increasing power over political and economic affairs in their jurisdictions, including restrictions on the sale and shipment of food supplies out of their areas to Vienna, leading to near-starvation conditions in the capital city through all of 1919 and into 1920. See Chapter 9, "Vienna's Political Relationship with the Provinces in Light of Economics." The black market became the only avenue for many in Vienna to acquire many of the essential items of life; see Charles A. Gulick, *Austria: From Habsburg to Hitler*, Vol. I (Berkeley: University of California Press, 1948), pp. 90–92:

Closely connected with the problem of state particularism [provincial political and economic nationalism] were the important *Schleichhandel* or black market difficulties; indeed, the restrictive policies of the [provinces] rendered that trade possible. And because of the desperate food shortage it became the most thriving "business enterprise" of Austria. The number of persons engaged in it, in defiance of law and decrees both of central and [provincial] governments, was naturally never statistically ascertained, but must have amounted to many thousands. . . . Despite their support for laws and ordinances on the matter, the

Given the mental disposition of the population, nasty riots must be anticipated; retail stores will be looted first, with the looting extended to public buildings, banking establishments, and private apartments. The last shreds of governmental authority will disappear. Armed bands will attempt to requisition food in the countryside, an undertaking that may perhaps succeed in the immediate vicinity of large industrial centers, but is doomed to bloody defeat elsewhere in the face of an armed rural population supported by a well-armed and disciplined local police force.

This internal anarchy will be exacerbated by serious external dangers. Popular excesses can easily result in the injury of foreign citizens and provide a pretext for intervention by foreign troops. The Entente for the most part pays little attention to conditions in our country. Moreover, in view of its current military weakness, it will not be inclined to intervene. The situation is different in Hungary and Czechoslovakia. Both states have a strong and well-trained army and may be inclined, for political reasons and for the sake of chauvinistic prestige, to occupy parts of German-Austria, and Vienna in particular. The Czechs are humiliated by the fact that their independence was attained without glorious military exploits. Czech militarists are understandably ashamed of the Czech army's cowardly retreat before the Hungarian Bolshevist troops. They would like to erase this shame. Hungarian troops, in turn, thirst for a "national" claim to glory, an expedition worthy of Kurdish marauding raids. Both the Czechs and the Hungarians would be only too happy to loot Vienna and will seize any opportunity to settle scores for some alleged injury done to them by "Vienna."[12] The truth of the matter is that the Czechs want to

---

Socialists soon recognized that a major result of punitive measures against the black market was an increase in the profits from it. The consumer needed commodities so badly that he had to buy them at almost any price; consequently, he was generally prepared to pay for the greater risks of the profiteer and his higher costs, that is, bribes, entailed by the prohibitive measures.... Specifically, the black market became a source of income for many official circles in the [provinces], for the bribes willingly paid by the profiteer were a welcomed addition to the lean wages of the civil servants. Thus the state bureaucracy had a special reason for supporting the system of trade restrictions which, as already noted, rendered the illicit trade possible.

—Ed.]

12 [This dramatic image of a Vienna pillaged by either Czech or Hungarian armies, though it never happened, need not have seemed impossible in 1919. Along what would

make up for the great disappointments that they have suffered from the young Czech state and the Hungarians want to get even for the plundering inflicted on them by the Romanians.

Today we have no army that could keep marauders from our borders. We would be defenseless in the face of an armed incursion. Our only hope would be from the German Reich. Germany will surely not leave us to our fate, but it is doubtful whether the Entente would agree to a German intervention. A few days' delay might already seal our fate. Once the robbers have completed their looting and safely removed their booty, it will do little good to chase them away.

Domestic anarchy, a possible Communist-Bolshevik uprising, and enemy occupation, these are all conceivable consequences resulting from the collapse of our currency. If we wish to avoid all these eventualities, we must prepare for the day of the catastrophe. We can hardly expect the government to be of any help. For five years the Ministry of Finance has not only pursued a disastrous inflationary course but has repeatedly tried to defend it. Beyond that, it has accelerated the depreciation of the crown by misguided measures that stemmed from its complete blindness to the single true cause of the monetary depreciation. It can hardly be assumed that it will now suddenly see the light. Even those influential financial policymakers who have an insight into the economic nexus have not been able to swim against the tide of prevailing ideas. It is up to us citizens to try to do on our own what the government is failing to do for us. All we can hope for from the government is that it will not stymie the endeavors of its private citizens. In their own interest and in the interest of the community, banks as well as large industrial and commercial enterprises must take the necessary preparatory steps to avert the catastrophic consequences that will follow from the collapse of the currency.

---

eventually become the border between Austria and Yugoslavia, heavy fighting went on for months with Yugoslavian forces occupying part of the Austrian province of Styria and nearly capturing Klagenfurt, the capital of the province of Carinthia, at the cost in lives of three hundred dead and eight hundred wounded among the Austrian defenders. To the north of Vienna, the freshly organized Czech forces had rapidly occupied the Sudetenland along the western fringe of Bohemia, with Austrian soldiers sent into retreat after their failed attempt to come to the aid of the German-speaking residents in this area. To the southeast of Vienna, Hungarian forces occupied the region known as the Burgenland after defeating its Austrian defenders and refused to withdraw from part of it until 1921, while retaining control of its main city of Ödenburg. —Ed.]

II

Public opinion has been marked by an unfounded optimism, which even today fosters the belief that by some miracle unexpected help will come from somewhere to our rescue. People intentionally deceive themselves about the gravity of the situation and expect salvation from all sorts of possible events that in reality are incapable of significantly affecting the situation.

The Entente undoubtedly has a certain interest in maintaining our present political system and is therefore ready up to a point to make some sacrifices to support the economic system that is closely linked to this political system. The Entente states are not very well informed about our situation and are therefore inclined to give credence to our assurances that we are really incapable of feeding ourselves. They are quite ready, out of philanthropic motives, to grant us help (soup kitchens, food for children, etc.) and give us a hand by means of loans. But this aid will become increasingly scant and increasingly less capable of helping us. The day will come when the Entente will tell us that it sees no reason for supporting an untenable economic system at its expense. There is no prospect of our receiving sufficient help from the Entente to satisfy the insatiable desires of our syndicalists and to prevent inflation from progressing. As long as we are not able to accomplish that, the progressive decline of our currency will run its catastrophic course to the end.

The levy on capital is expected to have miraculous effects on the value of the currency. In truth, this levy will have no impact over and above what has already been achieved by the confiscation of foreign assets and measures of a similar kind. The state will proceed to expropriate the remnant of whatever transportable capital has not yet been expropriated and will convert into food the money received by its sale outside the country. This might stave off further inflation for a while, unless the loss of capital weakens industry to the point where current state revenues are correspondingly diminished and the expenses for the unemployed and for food distribution are commensurately increased.[13]

13 [The idea of a capital levy had been proposed as a financial means to reduce or eliminate the national war debt. Some of its proponents had advocated an actual "taxing" of physical plant and equipment. Joseph A. Schumpeter, who was Austrian minister of finance from March to October 1919, developed the actual proposal. He wished it to be used for retirement of the national war debt and not for current expenditures. It would start with a tax rate of 10 percent on assets of 15,000 crowns and rise up to 55.83 percent (though the base was not clarified in the document). Assets were defined as "the sum of money

Even if inflation continues, the collapse of the currency may be post-poned a little by the reintroduction of forward markets in foreign exchange on a regular basis. It would facilitate importers' purchase of foreign goods with domestic credit against crowns. Such transactions would undoubt-edly involve dangerous risks that businessmen are generally no longer will-ing to assume. In the absence of coverage on the forward market, businessmen must refuse payment in crowns even on the domestic mar-ket and must insist on payment in foreign currency. We already see many advertisements stating that only foreign currency will be accepted as pay-ment. The practice of insisting on foreign currency is becoming increas-ingly common even in retail sales. But no matter how urgently needed the reintroduction of forward markets in foreign exchange may be, it is highly unlikely that the Ministry of Finance will overcome its dislike of free foreign-exchange transactions. Public opinion, which is haunted by the bugbear of stock-market speculation, will also strongly resist the rein-troduction of forward markets in foreign currencies.

III

Our task is to prepare for the day on which traders, in a state of panic, refuse payment in crowns and demand payment exclusively in foreign

---

expressed in objects and rights of the tax subject regardless of whether they have a yield or not, after deducting debts and charges," including insurance claims of all kinds. The goal was to raise at least 15 billion crowns. The total war debt was calculated at 25 billion crowns. The outcome of the capital-levy proposal in relation to the fiscal situation in Aus-tria at this time has been summarized by Carlile A. Macartney, *The Social Revolution in Austria* (Cambridge: Cambridge University Press, 1926), pp. 108–109:

> The Socialists, while still in power, worked out the plans for a great capital levy, which they asserted would balance the budget. Their partners in government watered it down, the capitalists evaded it, and it produced in the end an amount grossly inferior to the expectations and the needs.... Yet, no taxes which Austria could raise would have met the deficit caused by the system of doles and subsi-dies, inaugurated and perpetuated by the socialists themselves; nor the other great drain of the salaries of the public servants, of which everyone agreed there were far too many; but none were dismissed, because at the first threat the political party to which they belonged threatened such fire and thunder that the Gov-ernment always ended in giving way.

For a detailed account of the theory behind and the experience with the capital levy in Austria at this time, see John V. van Sickle, *Direct Taxation in Austria* (Cambridge, Mass.: Harvard University Press, 1931), pp. 136–71.—Ed.]

currency. Should this process unfold slowly and without a panicky acceleration, no intervention on the whole would be required. Gradually, payment in foreign currency would extend more and more beyond individual branches of wholesale and even retail trade, where it has already become common. As the use of foreign currency expanded and individuals became accustomed to keeping fewer and fewer crowns and more and more foreign money, more foreign currency would become domestically available. There is no need for intervention in the free market, which is a self-regulating mechanism. We would receive foreign currency for shares and commodities that leave the country. Merchants and industrialists would adopt a system whereby wages would be increasingly paid in foreign currency. In the end, the state would have no choice but to do likewise in tax transactions and in salary payments to public servants.

This supposition rests not only on irrefutable theoretical considerations but also on historical experiences with currencies that have experienced a collapse. There are three instances of a complete devaluation of money: the American Continental money in 1781, the French *assignats* and land-warrants in 1796, and the paper dollars of the Confederacy in 1865.

The "Continental money" of the rebellious American colonies reached its nadir in 1781. As Horace White states, "Still, counterfeiting only hastened the impending crisis, and in that respect, it was a public advantage for, as soon as paper money was dead, hard money sprang to life, and was abundant for all purposes. Much had been hoarded and much more had been brought in by the French and English armies and navies. It was so plentiful that foreign exchange fell to a discount."[14]

The French land-warrants sank to zero in 1796. Thiers reports the following in his *History of the French Revolution*:

> Nobody any longer traded in anything but silver. This money, which had apparently been hidden away or exported abroad, took over the circulation. Whatever was hidden came into the open, whatever had left France returned there. The southern provinces were overflowing with piasters, which had come in from Spain because they were in demand. Gold and silver, like all commodities, move to where demand attracts them, their price becomes higher and stays at that level until the supply is adequate and the demand is satisfied. There were still some instances of knavery,

---

14 [Horace White, *Money and Banking* (Boston: Ginn & Co., 1935), p. 58. —Ed.]

when repayments were made in land-warrants, which remained legal tender and continued to be legally valid for settling written promises, but people rarely dared make use of this provision. As to agreements, these were all in metal coins. Only silver and gold were to be seen on all the markets and people's wages were paid in the same manner. One might have said that no paper money existed in France. Warrants were to be found only in the hands of speculators, who received them from the government and resold them to buyers of national assets. Thus the financial crisis continued to exist for the state but almost ceased to exist for individuals.[15]

We must of course not be misled by the previously mentioned three precedents in weighing the potential consequences of the catastrophe toward which our monetary system is heading. In 1781, the United States was a predominantly agrarian country, as were the southern states of the Union even in 1865. Similarly, even in 1796, France was lagging far behind in the development of the division of labor and the use of money, and in cash and credit transactions, compared to our present condition in Austria. The consequences of a currency collapse will be quite different in an industrial country like Austria, where half the population is urban, than it was in a country whose population was still deeply anchored in an agrarian economy.

It is almost too late to ask how these consequences—above all, the destruction of capital in the form of claims against debtors—can be best alleviated. For at the moment of the collapse, the more urgent problem will be the transition to the new currency situation. Here we must recognize another vital difference between the three examples of a monetary collapse already mentioned and the situation in Austria. In our country there is lacking a substantial hoard of metallic money and only a limited quantity of foreign currency is available. Shortly after the currency collapse, foreign money from the sale of goods outside the country will undoubtedly be injected into the domestic circulation. The issue remains how to bridge the vacuum created during the brief but highly critical transition period and how to prevent the difficulties that are bound to arise from the triggering of the political catastrophes that we have outlined. We must be prepared for the day when the collapse of the currency causes a panic.

15 [M. A. Thiers, *History of the French Revolution*, 4 Vols. (Philadelphia: Carey & Hart, 1842).—Ed.]

We must take steps for that day, even while hoping that it will never come to pass. Even if we believe that the complete collapse of our currency can be averted or that it will assume the less virulent form of a gradual transition, we must not let matters take their course. The danger arising from such a panic-like collapse is so immense that, however slight the chance of its occurrence, it is our most pressing duty to anticipate it. The leading economic policymakers and businessmen of the day would rightly be accused of the most unpardonable negligence if they failed to take such steps. They would well deserve whatever fate awaited them in the event of a Bolshevik uprising.

On this crucial day, means must be at hand in Vienna to pay out in foreign currency salaries and wages that are due, unemployment support and subsidies, as well as assistance to persons dependent on interest income and property income. For this purpose the amount of approximately 30 million Swiss francs in smallest currency units must be raised.

This amount was calculated as follows:

In Austria there are about 1.5 million employees (excluding the self-employed) working outside the agricultural and timber sectors of the economy. If we assume an average monthly income of 1,500 crowns, which is not too low a figure, since it includes youths and employed persons living in the country, the total monthly amount comes to 2,250 million crowns. If we convert crowns at the exchange rate of 1 crown = 1 centime—an exchange rate that will probably be reached in a few weeks and will constitute the last significant exchange rate for the crown—this amount equals 22.5 million Swiss francs. At the moment of the currency collapse, about 22.5 million francs would therefore be needed to pay the monthly income of Austrian employees outside the agricultural and forestry sectors. On the critical day when a currency panic breaks out, the banks should make this sum available to the government and to employers in commerce, trade, and industry in the form of foreign currency. A revolt can be averted only if workers and employees are assured that they will immediately receive a small amount in foreign currency equivalent approximately to their usual income, an amount that will tide them over during the first few difficult days. Let us assume, to be on the safe side, that monthly subsistence and unemployment distributions will absorb 100 million crowns and that another 50 million crowns will be needed for subsidies to persons on fixed incomes, etc., so that another 150 million crowns, that is, 1.5 million Swiss francs, must be added. Altogether 24 million francs would thus be needed. This amount is obviously based on vague estimates and should be increased by at least 25 percent in order to be prepared for all immediate contingencies. We should therefore set our sights on approximately 30 million Swiss francs altogether.

A different calculation produces the same amount. The circulation of notes in German-Austria will be at least 12 billion crowns at that critical juncture.[16] At most one-quarter is likely to be used in routine small-scale transactions, while the rest will come into the hands of farmers and the better-off, or will be used in wholesale trade. This supposition is confirmed by the notorious fact that large-scale merchants accumulate large sums of bank notes, which then find their way into everyday transactions. Hence about 3 billion crowns would be left over for the transactions of wage earners, for which, given the above ratio, 30 million Swiss francs should be adequate.

Advance plans need to be made only for the initial period and for small-scale transactions. Wholesale transactions will quickly adjust to the use of foreign money, which even today plays a rather large role. The sale of commodities and shares of stock to other countries will serve as an intermediate step through which wholesale transactions will inject whatever further sums are needed in retail transactions.

Hence our first objective is to procure 30 million Swiss francs from other countries and to have them readily available for domestic use. There are several possible ways of accomplishing this goal. Should the state succeed in getting the currency or food-supply credit or the much-discussed tobacco credit that it is currently seeking, it might proceed to set aside the 30 million francs or its equivalent in another foreign currency and write it off against this credit. At the critical juncture it could then use some of this reserve to pay its own salaries, etc. and make the rest available to the economy through the banks. In that case prior agreement with foreign credit suppliers would not have to be reached, nor would their approval be needed for this step. It would suffice to leave part of the credit untouched and to have it available at the critical juncture.

16 [In the first half of 1919, during the period when Mises wrote this essay, the Austrian money supply had increased from 4.7 billion crowns in March to 8.3 billion in July. The note issue reached 12 billion crowns in December 1919. The Austrian inflation would continue for another two years: By August 1920, the notes in circulation numbered 20 billion crowns, increasing to 58.5 billion crowns in August 1921 and 1.3 trillion crowns in August 1922. In August 1922, the League of Nations intervened at the request of the Austrian government and reached an agreement to extend a loan to enable the government to restructure the country's fiscal and monetary order under League supervision. — Ed.]

The state could also secure these means of payment by pawning or selling off its 50,000 shares in the *Alpine-Montangesellschaft* [Alpine-Mining Corporation], as well as its shares in the *Süddeutsche Dampfschiffahrtsgesellschaft* [South-German Steamship Line], and other enterprises that it currently owns.

In all likelihood, however, the government will be unwilling to have any part in this scheme. In that case, it will be up to the banks to raise the amount either by offering securities or by some other means. We will describe further on how the banks can avoid having this not inconsiderable sum in their coffers without it earning interest. What matters is that the sum be available in the smallest possible denominations. For purely technical reasons, the larger the denominations on hand, the greater will be the price rise triggered by the collapse of the currency. To keep prices that today amount to one or two crowns at their present level, we will need one- and two-centime pieces rather than ten- and twenty-centime pieces in foreign currency. It cannot be taken for granted that such a large number of coins can simply be withdrawn from the circulation of a foreign country. Switzerland will presumably object to the export of such a considerable portion of its supply of small coins. In fact, the quantities of one-, two-, and five-centime pieces we need are not even available. We must give some forethought to this matter. It would not be a workable expedient for the Austrian state to issue the small coinage of foreign currency covered by foreign money in larger denomination. The collapse of the currency will almost certainly have so thoroughly undermined general confidence in the state's monetary system that it will take some length of time before the public will again be willing to use any form of money issued by the state. For technical as well as constitutional and other reasons it is unlikely that foreign states, Switzerland, for instance, will be able to supply the requisite small denominations. The only solution is that domestic private banks (*not* the Austro-Hungarian Bank) take charge of issuing these small notes. Just as banks in America joined to form a clearing-house and issued clearing-house certificates at critical junctures, Viennese banks must form a consortium to issue these smallest-denomination units of Swiss currency up to the full amount of credits secured for this purpose in other countries.

Under these circumstances, it would be quite feasible to use the credit established outside the country by the consortium of banks in such a way that the money remains in productive use outside the country, without loss or minimal loss of interest, both prior to and after the moment when the money is issued.

In this entire matter, we have been quite cavalier about legal considerations. It is self-evident that, when the currency collapses, prohibitions that are in force against the issue of notes that are designed to protect the note-issuing privilege of the Austro-Hungarian Bank must not interfere with a rescue mission that is essential to safeguard the general interest. Technical considerations, however, are more critical. We must proceed at once to tackle the technical aspect of the printing of notes.

Another question deserves serious consideration. Might it not be more advantageous to seek a merger with the German rather than the Swiss currency? It is beyond doubt that some day we will carry through a political union with Germany. It is perfectly clear that at such a time the fusion of the Austrian and the German currency systems will take place. But that does not mean that such a fusion is appropriate at the moment that we have in mind. We must remember that the timing of such a currency merger is especially critical and that we would at that juncture be highly vulnerable to any negative reaction on the part of the Entente. The latter will not look upon any currency merger with favor, since it will view this step as a harbinger of a political union. It is quite conceivable for this reason that the Entente will make things difficult for the German Reich, should it envisage opening a credit for us as proposed. The German Reich would have to provide about 300 million marks for that purpose, and the Entente could put obstacles in the way of Germany's granting this credit. Moreover, the German currency itself seems to be heading toward an irredeemable, total collapse. In Germany, too, more and more notes are being printed, and the inflationist party (Knapp,[17] Bendixen,[18] Silvio Gesell,[19] and many others) still seems to hold the upper hand. In Germany,

17 [Georg Friedrich Knapp (1842–1926) made his reputation as a statistician specializing in mortality problems. He also wrote on the history of German agriculture in its eastern territories. He was considered a leading member of a group known as the "Socialists of the Chair," who advocated state socialism under imperial paternalism in Germany before the First World War. In 1905, Knapp published *The State Theory of Money*, in which he argued that the selection, use, and value of money were matters of government legislation, independent of the market.—Ed.]

18 [Friedrich Bendixen was a leading follower of Knapp's state theory of money. He served as director of the Hypothekenbank in Hamburg until his death in 1920. In 1919, Bendixen published the work to which Mises refers, *War Loans and Financial Distress*, in which he said that Germany's only salvation from the burden of its war debt was to print money to pay for it: "Only the transformation of the war loans into money can bring salvation."—Ed.]

19 [Silvio Gesell (1862–1930) was a German "monetary crank" who proposed imposing a 5.4 percent annual tax on the holding of cash. The idea was to stimulate the use of money in transactions, rather than its being held as idle "hoards." Gesell argued that money taken

a plan to "repay" the war loan by the issue of an additional 100 billion (!) Reichsbank notes goes unchallenged under the slogan "inflation as salvation." Were we to join the German currency, whose value is declining day by day, we may well end up undergoing two successive currency collapses, which is hardly an inviting prospect.

We want to merge with Germany eventually and establish a Greater-German currency union. There is no reason, however, to carry out this currency merger at the least favorable time imaginable. We are not abandoning the idea of a Greater Germany [grossdeutschen] when we envision a currency merger as a means to a joint ascension rather than as a means to a joint decline. On the contrary, we are rendering a service to the German people today by managing to avoid a major catastrophe in dealing with the currency collapse that is inevitable in our hopeless circumstances. We are offering them an example for the proper conduct in critical times like these.

The merger with a Swiss-franc currency has its own drawback. We cannot reject the possibility that domestic prices and wages will quickly reach parity with the world market. Our industry can become competitive with its exports, regaining its lost markets and winning new ones, only if our wage level is below the world level. Should this advantage be lost, the crises in our domestic production will be perpetuated. From that point of view, a merger with the mark currency would be preferable.

A merger with the dollar currency instead of the Swiss currency might of course also be feasible. But how this question is decided is of secondary importance. The circumstance that speaks in favor of the Swiss currency at the moment is that it could provide currency in smaller denominations, the advantages of which we have just discussed.

IV

By issuing 30 million Swiss francs or 300 million marks in smallest-note denominations, the banks would assume financial obligations the magnitude of which deserves consideration. On the one hand the banks acquire claims in foreign currency against the state (that is, against the individual provinces and large urban municipalities) and against industrial and com-

out of hoards and used for investment purposes would so increase the supply of capital that the rate of interest could be pushed down to zero. —Ed.]

mercial enterprises. There is no question about the viability of these claims; on the one hand, the amounts involved are not large, and on the other hand, all enterprises will certainly be almost debt-free at the time these claims are created. After all, the whole undertaking will only be set in motion when the crown has become completely worthless, a time when all debts in crowns will be completely wiped out. But security of a claim does not necessarily coincide with liquidity. On the one hand, banks acquire secure claims that are not liquid, while on the other hand, as issuers of the small-denomination notes they are obligated to trade these in against foreign currency at their owners' request. The banks could find themselves in a very difficult situation if large quantities of notes issued in this manner were simultaneously presented for exchange. This is a nonexistent danger, however. It may be assumed that transactions will absorb these small-denomination notes and that they will therefore not flow back to the banks. A more legitimate concern is that these notes will be hoarded.

In any case it may perhaps seem more prudent, from the banks' point of view, to limit the risk that they will run in this situation. They could do so by creating a special institute, of which all the banks were shareholders, that would become the issuer of the notes, rather than the banks themselves. An emergency note-issuing bank would thus be called into existence to carry through the whole scheme.

It is perfectly obvious that the whole concept of this note-issuing entity is incompatible with the principles of a sound policy for a note-issuing bank. Under the given circumstances, this consideration should not hinder the realization of such a project or one along the same lines. The issue here is to make provisions for the emergency stage of a critical transitional period.

Preparations down to the last detail must be made right now for this critical moment. Both the legal and the technical details of the operation must already be so fully planned that in a matter of days, and even, if need be, in a matter of hours, the operation can be put into effect.

It must be expressly stated once more that all these proposals are intended to be expedients for the moment of the collapse. But that is the only moment for which preliminary arrangements are needed. As soon as government interference in the monetary system is eliminated by the collapse of the currency, free-market forces will automatically come into play that will supply the economy with the exact amount of money it needs. Sales to other countries, which will build up at that moment, will attract the requisite money into the country. It is true that the economy will in fact suffer a blow from selling goods too cheaply, but that is the inescapable consequence of the disastrous currency policy that will have been pursued earlier.

Once the domestic transition to a currency in francs has been completed, legislation can spell out the legal consequences and regulate the manner in which old debts are to be liquidated. At that point the question might be examined whether it makes sense to establish a special Austrian note-issuing central bank at all and whether special Austrian notes should even be issued at all. But these are secondary questions. The currency change will be *de facto* completed as soon as the new currency is accepted in transactions.

CHAPTER 6

The Reentry of German-Austria into the German Reich and the Currency Question[1]

The Monetary System of the Comprehensive Austrian State

On January 24, 1857, the German-Austrian Coinage Union (*Deutsch-Österreichischer Münzverein*) was founded in Vienna, which facilitated German monetary homogenization on the basis of silver bullion. This treaty did not create a common German currency. In the north of Germany, it replaced the standard of 14 taler (with reference to the Cologne mark) by that of 30 taler (with reference to the pound of 500 grams). In Southern Germany, it replaced the standard of 24½ florins by one of 52½ florins, and in Austria the standard of 20 florins (the so-called "Convention" standard) by one of 45 florins. The proportion of the three new currency units was thus: 1 taler = 1¾ South-German florins = 1½ Austrian florins. However, with the Union taler, a new currency was introduced which was to be legal tender throughout the area of the Union regardless of which state had coined it.

Coinage unification could easily be achieved in the other contracting states, its implementation being only a technical problem. It was different in Austria. At the time of the Coinage Treaty, Austria did not really have a silver currency but a paper currency with a considerable silver agio.[2] As

1 [This article was written in German and completed at the beginning of July 1919. It originally appeared in Michael Hainisch, ed., *Wirtschaftliche Verhältnisse in Deutsch-Österreich* [Economic Relations in German-Austria], part of *Schriften des Vereins für Sozialpolitik* [Publications of the Association for Social Policy] (1919).—Ed.]

2 [Agio, or premium, is the amount by which an asset sells above par. The term is also used to describe the difference in value between currencies, or the percentage charged on changing paper money into a commodity money.—Ed.]

long as this situation prevailed, coinage unification existed, as far as Austria was concerned, only on paper. Section 22 of the Coinage Treaty provided that none of the contracting parties was entitled to issue paper currency at the specified value unless redemption on demand in silver coins by the holders of that currency was adequately guaranteed at all times. Any exceptions obtaining at the time of concluding the treaty were to be eliminated, at the latest, by January 1, 1859. Austrian public policy seriously endeavored to eliminate the exceptions to the specified conversion rate. On September 6, 1858, and thus before the contractually required date of eliminating them, the Austrian National Bank started making payments in silver. Only then was German coinage unification fully implemented.

It was to be of short duration. Austria became entangled in new wars, and her finances were again ruined. The war with France and Piedmont caused the note press to be used again.[3] On April 29, 1859, the Austrian National Bank ceased payments in silver. After the infelicitous end of the war, there were renewed endeavors to restore the currency and, by reducing the quantity of notes in circulation, to reduce the agio until parity was reestablished. These operations met with success. The metal agio that averaged 41.25 percent in 1861 sank to an average of 8.32 percent in 1865 and had all but disappeared by the beginning of 1866. The currency policy would therefore undoubtedly have achieved its objective if the new war on two fronts[4] had not led to a breach of Plener's Bank Act of December 27, 1862, which was modeled after Peel's Bank Act, and thus to a new wave of inflation.

The Peace of Prague, which obliterated German unity and expelled German-Austria from the political community of the German nation, provided also for the abolition of the Vienna Coinage Treaty. Section 13 made its annulment dependent upon special negotiations, which were concluded in Berlin by the treaty of June 13, 1867. This treaty invalidated the Vienna Coinage Treaty at the end of 1867 without, however, also obliterating all effects of the German-Austrian Coinage Union in the area of currency policy. The question of the Union taler continued to occupy legislation for several decades and was the topic of intergovernmental agreements.

Already during the negotiations that led to the German-Austrian

3 [See Chapter 2, "On the Currency Question," footnote 4.—Ed.]
4 [See Chapter 2, footnote 3.—Ed.]

Coinage Union, Austria had intended to adopt a gold standard. Vehement Prussian opposition, however, foiled these intentions. Upon dissolution of the Union, consideration was not given to returning to the silver currency but, instead, adopting a gold standard. A first step in this direction was the Austro-French Coinage Treaty concluded in Paris on July 31, 1867. The treaty between Austria and Hungary of December 24, 1867 on matters of tariffs and trade provided for the speedy introduction of a gold currency according to the principles laid down by the Paris Coinage Conference. The Austrian Act of March 9, 1870 (as well as the Hungarian Act No. 12 of 1869) prescribed the issuance of gold coins of 8 florins (equivalent to 20 francs) and 4 florins (equivalent to 10 francs). These coins were at first to circulate only for commercial purposes but were to serve in preparation for a future Austro-Hungarian gold currency. In 1871, the Austro-Hungarian Bank began to sell its silver bullion in order to purchase gold. The Act of March 18, 1872, permitted a greater role for gold, with the bank entitled to use its purchases to provide coverage for the currency.

In spite of all these moves, the restoration of a metal-based currency was not crowned with success. It was the prevalent idea of the time that reintroducing a sound currency system had to be preceded by operations to make the agio disappear. However, stringent economic arguments against such a currency policy were advanced. In the early 1860s, the economic consequences known to be connected with a rapid decrease of the agio on coins had already led to movements against continuing the restoration of the old parity value. Antirestrictionist tendencies now began to assert themselves. In 1872, the price of 100 gold florins (250 francs) averaged 110.37 Austrian florins (in paper) and with short interruptions increased, on average, to 125.23 florins by 1887. As long as the value of the currency was in decline, plans for a managed exchange rate could not count on support from industrial or agrarian circles, since higher exchange rates on the Vienna stock exchange impeded (much like protective tariffs) the import of foreign products; it also supported the export of domestic products (similar to export subsidies) and favored debtors vis-à-vis creditors as well.

This situation was not to reverse until 1888, when the value of the Austrian currency began to rise again — the price of 100 gold florins averaging only 115.48 florins in terms of paper currency in 1890. Producers and exporters, who saw themselves on the losing side of this exchange-rate movement, suddenly turned into advocates of the hitherto maligned exchange-rate reform. The abolition of the free coinage of silver coins in 1879, which severed the Austrian monetary system from its links with the metal silver, facilitated the disregard of previous difficulties. Thus currency regulation came into force.

By introducing gold coins, the Austrian laws of August 2, 1892 (Hungarian laws XVII to XIX of 1892) blocked the further decline of the exchange rates at the Vienna stock exchange. Since August 11, 1892, when the new currency laws entered into force, the Austrian florin (equivalent to two new crowns) could not significantly exceed the value of 2.10 francs or 1.70 marks. At this point in time, when the Austro-Hungarian Bank resumed payments in gold, imposing a lower limit on the value of the Austrian florin was still avoided. Notwithstanding vigorous resistance on the grounds of its potential inflationary impact, this was the actual currency-policy objective of the Christian-Socialist Party, which was at this time still small and in the opposition. The law, sure enough, never mandated the resumption of gold payments. It had nevertheless been the policy of the Austro-Hungarian Bank beginning in 1896, and most definitely after around 1900, to maintain *de facto* gold payments even in the absence of it being legally mandated. This was done by offering gold currency on the market at rates not much different from the parity fixed for coinage by the currency reform of 1892 and similar to the degree to which exchange rates deviated from parity in other countries maintaining payments in gold. This highly acclaimed currency regime of the Austro-Hungarian Bank was largely upheld until the outbreak of the war.[5] It was confirmed by the new (fourth) privilege granted to the bank in 1911. This required the bank to safeguard, in any way possible, that the value of foreign paper currency expressed in the rate of foreign bonds continued to be maintained in accordance with the parity of the coinage standard of the crown.[6]

5 [For histories of the development of the Austrian monetary system in the nineteenth century, including the establishment and functioning of the gold standard under the Austro-Hungarian Bank, see Charles A. Conant, *A History of Modern Banks of Issue*, 3rd ed. (New York: G. P. Putnam's Sons, 1908), pp. 209–34; Robert Zuckerkandl, "The Austro-Hungarian Bank," in United States Senatorial National Monetary Commission, *Banking in Russia, Austro-Hungary, the Netherlands, Japan* (Washington, D.C.: Government Printing Office, 1911), pp. 55–118; and Friedrich von Wieser, "Resumption of Specie Payments in Austria-Hungary," *Journal of Political Economy* (June 1893), pp. 380–405. — Ed.]

6 Knapp has variously misrepresented the exchange-rate policy of the Austro-Hungarian Bank (*Staatliche Theorie des Geldes*, Leipzig 1905, pp. 247ff.). It may suffice to refer to Knapp's claim that the exchange-rate regime had imposed a burden on the bank for which the state had then made additional compensation. On the contrary, the bank made ample profits from foreign-currency operations, large parts of which were paid out to the state as its owner. This very point is the essence of Knapp's explanation of "exodromic" policy. See on this my article, "Das Problem gesetzlicher Aufnahme der Barzahlungen in Österreich-

The Monetary System of German-Austria

Austria and Hungary also largely financed the World War by using the printing press.[7] At the very beginning of the war, the legislation was set aside that had imposed limitations on the expansion of bank notes by the Austro-Hungarian Bank, and on the use of credit by both states of the monarchy through their central bank. This cleared the way for inflation. The indebtedness of both states to the bank grew from month to month, the circulation of bank notes increased precipitously, and, in line with the proliferation of paper currency, the prices of goods and services and the rates of foreign bills of exchange increased.

When, in October 1918, the dual monarchy of the Habsburgs disintegrated into a number of separate national territories, some of them constituted as independent states while others incorporated into neighboring states, the Austro-Hungarian Bank finished its role as the joint institution enjoying the sole privilege of issuing currency for the entire monarchy. In the legal sense, its privilege of issuing notes continued until the end of 1919. However, in actual fact this privilege was only respected by German-Austria.

After the dissolution it was obvious that the Austro-Hungarian Bank would no longer be able to extend credit to the various successor states as it had extended to the Austrian and Hungarian states during the war. Only the implementation of previously arranged loans could be expected. Since lending activity to private parties had almost completely stopped during the war, a further expansion of currency circulation after the implementation of the pending credit operations could only have come about

---

Ungarn" [The Problem of the Legal Resumption of Gold Payments in Austria-Hungary], *Jahrbuch für Gesetzgebung, Verwaltung und Volkswirtschaft* 33 (1909), pp. 1027ff. It is remarkable that Knapp maintains his claim of losses incurred by the bank as a result of the exchange-rate policy even in the new edition of *Staatliche Theorie des Geldes* of 1918 though a glance at the bank's business reports should have made him abandon this erroneous opinion. [The English abridged translation of Georg Friedrich Knapp, *The State Theory of Money* (London: Macmillan, 1924), does not include the chapter containing the passages referred to by Mises in this footnote.—Ed.]

7 [On July 31, 1914, the number of notes issued by the Austro-Hungarian Bank in circulation numbered 3.4 billion crowns; by October 31, 1918, it had increased to 34.8 billion crowns. For a detailed account of funding of the war expenses of the government by the Austro-Hungarian Bank, see George A. Schreiner, "Austria-Hungary's Financial Debacle," *Current History* (July 1925), pp. 594–600.—Ed.]

through Lombard operations.[8] In contrast to the German Reichsbank, the bylaw of the Austro-Hungarian Bank authorizes the institution to incorporate loans granted against assets pledged to the bank into the coverage used to back currency in circulation. In the course of the war, the governments of Austria and Hungary have, in prospectuses upon issuing war bonds, guaranteed more favorable conditions for Lombard credit by the central bank. Pledged assets were to be accepted under a favorable interest rate and, as of the fourth war bond, under a limit of 75 percent of the nominal value. The issuance of every additional bond incurred a guarantee that these preferential conditions would be maintained for a certain period that was successively extended.

Upon dissolution of the Austrian state, statesmen and politicians of the new states, particularly those of Czechoslovakia, declined to honor the war bonds. The holders of war bonds were now understandably intent on reducing their impending losses by gaining Lombard credit against these bonds. For even though the successor states could repudiate payments of interest and principal on war bonds without harming their citizens, since nearly all war bonds were held by German-Austrians, it seemed impossible to apply the same policy to bank notes. During the war, particularly large quantities of notes issued by the Austro-Hungarian Bank had accumulated in the non-German parts of the monarchy. High agricultural price levels had led to a strong inflow of currency to the rural areas. But throughout the monarchy the share of non-Germans in the agrarian population was much higher than that of German speakers. Since agricultural producers were only partially subject to taxation, had largely abstained from buying war bonds, and instead had—for reasons of ignorance of banking, mistrust, or politics—kept their savings to themselves, they had accumulated tremendous amounts of Austro-Hungarian bank notes. In the fertile regions of Moravia and of southern Hungary (which was now occupied by Serbs and Romanians) individual farmers had stashed away hundreds of thousands or, in some cases, even millions of crowns.

German-Austrian holders of war bonds therefore were highly interested in receiving bank notes for bonds they wanted to pledge at the Austro-Hungarian Bank. The successor states, on the other hand, were interested in keeping such Lombard credit at bay, since they, as holders of war bonds, were afraid that the value of the crown would inevitably drop as a conse-

8 [Lombard business is credit usually extended by a central bank to commercial banks against securities, precious metals, or other mobile assets used as collateral.—Ed.]

quence of an increase in the circulation of the currency. From the very beginning, they therefore objected to the continuation of Lombard operations by the Austro-Hungarian Bank. At the same time, they envisaged the severance of their currencies from the common Austro-Hungarian currency.

At the beginning of 1919, the first step in this direction was taken by the Southern Slav government.[9] Czechoslovakia was to follow. The notes of the Austro-Hungarian Bank circulating within their territories were stamped, and all other notes were no longer legal tender. Henceforth, only stamped notes could be used to fulfill all contracts denominated in crowns. This completed the creation of Southern Slav and Czechoslovak crowns, though the technical implementation of these reforms may have been deficient from a monetary point of view.

Now German-Austria, also, had to act. It could no longer wait until all other states had made the transition from the Austro-Hungarian crown to separate national crowns. It had to give up the Austro-Hungarian crown in order to avoid there being notes that, for whatever reason, had not been stamped in the other states that would now flow back into German-Austria and increase the inflation within German-Austria. It had to prevent the Czechoslovak Ministry of Finance from using the half of its citizens' holdings of notes that had been retained upon the marking of currency for the purchasing of securities in German-Austria. Bank notes circulating in the Ukraine and in neutral foreign countries that totaled several billion crowns were not to be regarded simply as German-Austrian currency. This is why German-Austria, as well, applied a special mark to bank notes denominated in crowns and circulating within her territory. The decree of March 25, 1919, which had the force of law, withdrew legal-tender status from all obligations not so denominated. This created a separate German-Austrian currency. All further issues are then of a technical nature and pertain to the independent German-Austrian currency. Important though that may be, it takes second place behind the fact of the independence of the currency. Among the issues open for discussion is the question of whether or not to set up an independent German-Austrian central bank, and the further question of whether to keep the stamped notes in circulation or to replace them by newly designed notes because of the easy possibility of falsifying stamp imprints.

9 [The "Southern Slav government" refers to what later became known as Yugoslavia.— Ed.]

What is much more important than such technical issues is the question of whether German-Austria shall maintain the independence of her currency or a currency union with Germany should be envisaged.

This question admits no ambivalent answer. Political integration into Germany will necessitate adoption of the German currency. The theoretical possibility of maintaining a separate German-Austrian currency in spite of integration, or of a currency union with the other successor states of the monarchy, has not the smallest chance of realization. Not even partial and less so full unification in matters of politics, trade, and finance could be maintained if the currency systems remained separate. German-Austria must adopt the German currency if it wants to enter the German state.

Fiscal Aspects of Unifying Monetary Regimes

Instituting a currency union between the German Reich and German-Austria would be a rather simple and quick task if a solid monetary regime based on precious metal existed in both territories. If both countries had a gold currency, the transition to a common currency would be but a technical matter of coinage, monetary, and financial policy. Even if one territory used a gold currency and the other a silver currency, this transition would be an easy matter. The difficulties encountered in integrating German-Austria into the monetary system of the German Reich arise from the fact that both countries now use a paper currency.

These difficulties are first of all of a fiscal nature. At the present time, the public finances of both the German Reich and German-Austria are in a very precarious state. In both countries public expenditures far exceed revenues, and efforts directed at curtailing expenditure and boosting revenue so as to achieve a balanced budget, again, have met with insurmountable political impediments. Under such circumstances, there is hardly any other alternative but that of placing the printing press directly or indirectly into the service of the public finances and to obtain money by means of issuing notes. Inflation of bank notes is, however, not a commendable financial policy. It is an inappropriate means for managing public finances, since it distributes the fiscal burden in an economy in ways that run counter to the principles of sound finance. From the economic point of view, its disadvantages lie in the adverse social dislocations that are its unwelcome effects.

And, lastly, inflation is only a temporary alternative, since the issuers of bank notes must sooner or later show self-control and rein in the inflation if a catastrophic breakdown of the financial system is to be avoided. Inflation will, however, be continued for some time, and it will take time until the German people again realize that the first precondition of a reasonable economic policy is abstention from any inflationist experiment. At the moment the views on this subject are not very restrained, either in Germany or in German-Austria. But the fact cannot be ignored that inflation is an inappropriate tool for balancing the public budget, that it has detrimental economic effects, and that it must ultimately lead to a breakdown if it is not reined in within a brief period of time. But it is still considered by many to be a lesser evil than other possibilities. Today most people are very far from the principled views that distinguished, for example, the founding fathers of the German gold currency, who are very much misunderstood nowadays.

There is a historical example for the currency union of two countries on the basis of a paper currency. Austria and Hungary, two completely independent states since 1867, continued for decades the currency union based on the paper money that they had inherited from their predecessor, the unitary Austrian empire. But this sharing in a common currency was possible only by strictly adhering, over its entire duration, to the principle of not expanding the sum total of notes in circulation. The last expansion of notes in circulation came about by the law of August 25, 1866, at a time when Austria and Hungary were still a single state. After this date, the amount of paper money was never increased until, in the course of the currency reform, the notes were totally withdrawn from circulation.

The currency union of two states on the basis of a paper currency is hardly feasible unless there is, from the very beginning, an intention to abstain from any further inflation. Furthermore, this policy must be strictly implemented. As soon as inflationary measures are taken in order to generate funds for the treasury, differences of opinion are inevitable concerning the allocation of the money to be placed in circulation. Such differences can only be avoided if the public finances of both states are unified into one whole; failing this, a currency union must lead to severe disagreements.

It is therefore abundantly clear that the adoption by German-Austria of the German currency can only occur at a time when an irrevocable decision of political unification has been taken, since the implementation of currency unification must be preceded by an agreement on its implications for the public finances. This agreement can hardly be conceived as determining anything but a settlement under which Germany assumes over German-Austria all those powers of expenditure and revenue that she has in all the other federal states. Furthermore, that part of German-Austria's public debt that had been incurred for expenditures that in Germany are regarded as state expenditures will have to be converted into debt of the German state. Clearly, Germany will also have to take into account that the economy of German-Austria, one of the German lands least endowed by nature, has been particularly hampered by the war and its outcome. And it will have to be taken into account that the German-Austrians have, in relation to their smaller capacity, contributed a proportionately larger share to the war burden than the other Germans. It will thus be necessary for Germany to grant German-Austria a special subsidy so as to facilitate, for the first years, the transition into the new circumstances.

Another reason needs to be mentioned as to why monetary unification between German-Austria and the German Reich seems infeasible before a complete settlement of financial relations. The economy of German-Austria has made more use of war bonds than has Germany. Austrian entrepreneurs have invested greater proportions of their assets in war bonds than did German entrepreneurs. For them, a facility that would permit them to activate these bonds by pledging them under advantageous conditions is a matter of survival. Even if only imperfectly, this was provided for by the Austro-Hungarian Bank in the past. After implementation of the currency union it will, however, no longer be able to provide this facility. Lombard loans against war bonds will therefore have to be offered by lending institutions. It is obvious that the creation of new rules for loans against Austrian war bonds will be easier if their future has been decided upon. This decision, in turn, depends upon a binding and final determination of their acceptance by the German Reich.

The Ratio of Conversion

The other difficulty for currency unification on the basis of paper money in both countries concerns the determination of the ratio of conversion. If Germany and German-Austria both had a currency based on the same metal, such determination would be superfluous. In this case, we would not even have to deal with an exchange of currency but only with a change in the specification and names of monetary units. If both countries had currencies based on different metals, conversion would be effected on the basis of the ratio of the values of the two metals at a given point in time.

Many believe, as well, that the only correct basis for the conversion of paper currencies would be the ratio of the values of the two currencies at a given point in time. They therefore propose to make the transition on the basis of the prevailing exchange rate between mark and crown. Even those who propose to use statistical calculations of the purchasing powers of the two currencies for determining the exchange rate are guided by the same idea. Such proposals are based on the assumption that the depreciation of money in relation to commodities lags behind the devaluation in relation to foreign currencies, and that the "internal" or "true" value of money is better determined by resorting to the ratio of commodity prices instead of the ratio of currencies. However, this approach overlooks that this lag of commodity prices behind the increase of the exchange rate of currencies is only a temporary phenomenon. Exchange rates are in reality determined by nothing but the purchasing power of two currencies, this rate adjusting to that level that leaves the purchasing power the same regardless of whether a currency unit is used for the direct purchase of commodities or for first obtaining a unit of another currency in order to make such purchase. In the long run the exchange rate cannot deviate from the level warranted by the proportion of purchasing powers, which may be called the natural or static rate. As long as there is a discrepancy between the prevailing and the natural exchange rate, it is profitable to use a currency that appears to be undervalued in relation to its purchasing power to buy commodities and to sell these for currency that appears to be overvalued in relation to its purchasing power. This, however, triggers a demand for the currency that trades at undervalued rates and drives these rates up until they have reached the static level.

The purchasing power of a currency within an economy does not change at once and not at the same time in terms of all commodities. Price increases triggered by an expansion of the money supply do not come about overnight but take a certain period of time. The added money supply enters the economy at some point, and from there it slowly disseminates throughout the rest of the economy. At first it reaches particular sectors, only augmenting the demand for particular commodities and services but not for all of them. Subsequently, the prices of other commodities and services will rise. Exchange rates are, however, speculative rates, arising from the commerce conducted by businessmen who, in their decision making, do not only consider the immediate present but future developments as well. This is why exchange rates quoted on the stock exchanges already reflect inflation at a relatively early stage of its development, much earlier than the inflation has affected the prices of commodities and services in general.

The value of the crown has decreased to a greater degree and more rapidly than that of the mark. This may well explain why exchange rates for the crown have preceded the drop in its purchasing power more rapidly than exchange rates for the mark precede the drop in its purchasing power. A conversion rate determined on the basis of purchasing power would consequently be somewhat more advantageous for the crown than if it were determined on the basis of current exchange rates. However, as mentioned earlier, the difference may not be very significant.

Statistical determination of the purchasing power of currencies by comparison of commodity prices and wages faces so many theoretical and fundamental challenges—not even to mention the practical ones that are particularly intractable at the present moment—that this approach appears to be, as is commonly admitted, altogether unfeasible. If one were to start with the current ratio of the rates of the crown and mark, it would be best to take as a basis the ratio of price quotations on a neutral stock exchange.

There are various dissenting voices in Austria against the view that determination of the conversion rate may be based only on the current exchange rate between crown and mark or on a rate very close to it. It is pointed out that, since the beginning of the war, both the German Reich and Austria have had to debase their currencies by issuing bank notes. In doing so, Austria had to go farther than the German Reich, which led to the situation that her currency today has devalued not only in relation to both gold and foreign currencies but also in terms of the German mark, which has also internationally dropped in value. This is explained by the incontrovertible fact that Austria, particularly German-Austria, had to shoulder a comparatively greater burden of the war than the rest of the German population. Consequently, it is argued, as a matter of equity this imbalance should be abolished by conducting monetary and fiscal unification in such a way that it would be as if the unification had already occurred at the beginning of the war. It would be highly inequitable to make German-Austrians permanently suffer for the implications of the unfortunate separation of 1866, for which they are not guilty and which imposes on them a significantly higher share of the financial burden caused by the war.

This argument is incontrovertible as far as it concerns public finance issues surrounding monetary unification. It is clear that the basic principle guiding the fiscal dimension of unification must be to spread the war burden evenly to all of the German people according to their ability to pay—and that German-Austrians must not be singled out to defray financial charges arising from expenditures undertaken on behalf of the entire German people.

But in terms of the conversion rate, things are not so simple. Using the ratio of 100 marks = 117.56 crowns as a basis for currency unification would not only have implications for the finances of the state. It would not only make holders of Austrian war bonds better off but it would also increase the value of all other claims denominated in crowns. This ratio would make all creditors in crowns better off, it would impose a burden on all borrowers in crowns, and it would thus have dire social consequences much beyond public finances. The population of German-Austria cannot joyfully anticipate it without any further ado, since there are many who would be burdened by it.

Consequently, it hardly seems feasible to select a ratio that is very far from the one existing on the market at the time of conversion. There is no need to use the exact exchange rate on any particular day, which may be determined by chance and by momentary technical operations on the stock exchange. But it is impossible to ignore economic facts and manipulate a precipitous upward movement of the rate of the crown without causing economic dislocations the consequences of which would have to be determined and all of the effects of which may not be fully known for some period of time.

The severe sacrifices such a scheme would impose on the entire economy of German-Austria and the obvious advantages Germany would gain from it require adequate compensation as far as the public finances are concerned. Compensation would, at first, have to consist of Germany assuming that part of German-Austria's public debt which derives from expenditures that in the German Reich are regarded as state expenditure, at a different conversion rate from the one at which the currency is to be converted. Here the old prewar ratio of exchange may well apply. Then, however, Germany would have to make a special contribution to cover the expenditures of the Federal Republic of German-Austria for an initial period of several years. It would have to be a period of time long enough to facilitate the transition of German-Austrian public finances into the new order of things.

The question of the exchange ratio for unification is also connected with the issue of what direction the German Reich will follow in terms of its future currency policy. There is a large number of people in Germany who are presumably convinced, even today, that a reinstitution of sound currency conditions requires bringing the devalued currency back to the level of the coinage parity defined by the monetary reform of 1873. They take it for granted that the only goal of currency policy can be the lowering of the agio of the gold mark. They thus ignore another option, namely stabilization at the current value of money. Whether one or the other path should be taken must be a matter of extremely careful economic policy decision-making. Reducing the gold value of the mark to that of 1914 would put at a disadvantage all debtors, primarily in the Reich, the federal states, and the municipalities; it would favor all creditors. The repercussions of such a policy on foreign trade would be even more severe. As long as the value of the currency is increasing, the importing of foreign goods is facilitated and the exporting of domestic goods is impeded. However, over the next years German trade will undoubtedly run up against so many difficulties that lifting export barriers will be one of the principal tasks of German economic policy. With all probability, therefore, German policy will not follow the direction that would reduce the German currency to its old gold parity. Instead, currency reform is likely to be confined to stabilizing the currency at the current value or a rate not significantly higher than that.

In any case, since it is among the most important economic questions of the immediate future, it would be desirable that Germany clarified this issue before a decision is made about the conversion ratio for the monetary integration of German-Austria into the German Reich.

Preparing the Way for Currency Union

Without a doubt the ultimate goal of German-Austria's integration into the German monetary system must be the implementation of a full union in terms of every aspect of the monetary and banking regime. It is another question whether this goal should be approached immediately or through a transition of several stages.

The Mark as a Core Currency

It would seem possible to unify the monetary systems by German-Austria, in the first stage, adopting the mark as a core currency. Implementation of this would hardly be difficult. The German-Austrian state would institute a special central bank by either setting up a new bank or by transforming the branch offices of the Austro-Hungarian Bank situated on its territory.

This German-Austrian central bank would exchange its own notes for every stamped note of the Austro-Hungarian Bank circulating in its territory. The bank notes thus received are given to the German-Austrian state as an interest-free loan and are used by the state to repay the share of the old Austrian state's debt to the Austro-Hungarian Bank.

In addition to bank notes to be issued in exchange for stamped notes of the Austro-Hungarian Bank, the German-Austrian central bank would be permitted to issue notes only for commercial and industrial business. An endorsement by state institutions (such as the War Crops Office) should not be regarded as a sufficient basis for issuing such notes, because otherwise the printing press again would be indirectly placed at the service of the financial administration of the state. Inevitably, it will be also permissible to issue notes, also Lombard credits. It is true that the use of lending operations for covering notes was peculiar to the Austro-Hungarian Bank. But one must not forget that in the German Reich, as well, Lombard credit is nowadays used for creating circulating credit through lending institutions.

A maximum amount for admissible currency in circulation should in some form be imposed on the German-Austrian central bank. This may have no material importance if, as is indispensable, the bank is strictly committed to paying its notes in marks. But when regulating central banks, the sentiments and biases of the public must also be taken into account.

The foremost and only decisive task is to impose on the German-Austrian central bank the duty of exchanging its notes at any time into marks at a fixed rate and, vice versa, to exchange marks for crowns at the same rate. On the assumption that this rate is 2 crowns = 1 mark, the German-Austrian central bank would be obligated to exchange on demand and at any time one mark for two crowns and vice versa. As soon as this is strictly implemented, the German-Austrian crown will have lost its independent value and be nothing but a proportional fraction of the mark. It will proportionately follow all movements in the value of the mark, both in relation to commodities and to foreign currencies. The integration of German-Austria into the German currency regime will then be completed, and the crown will be no more than the designation for a part of the mark.

Determining the ratio of exchange between crowns and marks attains a great importance in this context. If this ratio does not correspond to the exchange relations on the market, serious difficulties will arise that might imperil the entire project. If the crown is overvalued in relation to the free-market rate when the conversion ratio is fixed, vast quantities of crowns will be presented for exchange, while in the opposite case vast quantities of marks will reach the banking system to be exchanged for crowns. If, on the other hand, the conversion rate corresponds to the conditions prevailing on the market, exchange will be limited to those small amounts that are needed for travel and for payments of low-priced items. In this case, the German-Austrian central bank will need but a relatively small amount for complying with requests for currency exchange.

To comply with popular expectations concerning cover for the notes, the German-Austrian central bank would have to borrow the marks required for this purpose plus a further large amount of marks by way of a loan from the German Reichsbank in the amount of 500 to 1,000 million marks. Granting such a loan by issuing further bank notes would be unobjectionable since the Reichsbank would place these notes in circulation only upon withdrawal of a corresponding amount of crown notes. Greater Germany [*Grossdeutschland*] should thus not experience an increase in inflation.

Some will regard this model of the mark as a core currency as infeasible because German-Austria has a passive balance of payments with Germany. All objections from this standpoint are misplaced. The mutual exchange relation of two currencies does not depend on the balance of payments but on the purchasing power each currency has with regard to commodities.[10] Just as all the money in Bavaria cannot be drained off and go to Prussia because of Bavaria having an unfavorable balance of payments with Prussia, so the analogous case will not happen between Austria and Germany.

For the unhampered functioning of the system that has been described above, it will be crucial as to whether or not the German-Austrian bank abstains from any expansion in the circulation of notes. Any such inflationist measures should best not be done. If it is found to be impossible to completely avoid this in the initial stage, then any expansion must at least be uniform throughout the entire currency area. The German-Austrian state would thus have to forego undertaking any future loans from its bank

10 See my paper "Zahlungsbilanz und Devisenkurse," *Mitteilungen des Verbandes österreichischer Banken und Bankiers*, 1919, p. 39ff. [An abridged translation of this article under the title, "Balance of Payments and Foreign Exchange Rates," may be found in Percy L. Greaves, ed., *Von Mises, On the Manipulation of Money and Credit* (Dobbs Ferry, N.Y.: Free Market Books, 1978), pp. 50–55. —Ed]

of issue for which this bank would have to issue new notes. If the state requires funds, it should raise the funds only by borrowing from the German Reichsbank. Such loans could, as has been mentioned, be given to the German-Austrian state in the context of the special support it needs from Germany, especially because of the disproportionately large financial burden Austria shouldered during the war in the interest of the entire German people.

The special advantages accruing from a currency unification that initially establishes the mark as a core currency in German-Austria will be seen in the areas of international law and of constitutional law. Adopting the mark as a core currency does not require any action by the German government, and the obligations the German Reich has accepted in the peace treaty with regard to the independence of German-Austria will remain unaffected. A loan extended by the German Reichsbank in the form of foreign currency can formally be brought into conformity with these obligations under the treaty if a consortium of German private banks is introduced as an intermediary. Adoption of the mark as a core currency is a unilateral action by the German-Austrian state, and the German-Austrian state can no more be prevented from accepting the mark as a core currency than it can be prevented from adopting the dollar or the pound sterling as a core currency.[11]

An expansion of the sphere of activity of the German Reichsbank to the territory of German-Austria, as would be required by the immediate full integration of German-Austria into the German monetary system, could cause complications as long as political unification [*Anschluss*] had not been achieved. This would result from the fact that the agents of the Reichsbank would be seen as German civil servants so that, in the legal sense, their activities outside German territory would engender difficulties under constitutional and international law. But these difficulties will not impede the adoption of the mark as a core currency.

If German-Austria were to introduce the mark autonomously, the state would have to be able to keep its budget balanced without further inflation. In this sense the adoption of this currency is still fraught with consider-

11 [Both the Treaty of Versailles, which ended the war between the Entente and Germany, and the Treaty of Saint-Germain, which ended the war between the Entente and Austria, prohibited the unification (*Anschluss*) of Austria as a part of the political territory of Germany. —Ed]

able problems. But these will be overcome as soon as the recognition of the detrimental effects of an inflationary policy will have led to the renunciation of any further inflationist experiments.

Full Banking and Currency Unification

The second way in which currency unification might be implemented is through the immediate and complete integration of German-Austria into the German monetary and central banking system. In terms of currency policy, German-Austria would then have no other status than the other German federal states.

Having defined the conversion rate between the crown and the mark, the stamped crown notes that are circulating in German-Austria would then be replaced by notes of the German Reichsbank. The Reichsbank would extend its activity into German-Austria and replace every office of the Austro-Hungarian Bank by one within its own network. It would raise the funds for expanding the circulation of its notes by issuing new bank notes and treasury bills. This procedure seems unobjectionable and will not trigger any detrimental inflationary effects since the area of circulation of the notes will be expanded and the demand for German paper money will thus be increased.

The stamped notes of the Austro-Hungarian Bank that will be taken out of circulation by the German Reichsbank through such exchange operations will be paid over to the German Treasury. The German Treasury will in turn use these notes to redeem a part of the Austro-Hungarian Bank's claims that are outstanding against the old Austrian state at the time of liquidation; upon integration, these will become claims on the German state.

At the end of June 1919, 7.6 billion stamped crown notes were in circulation in German-Austria. At the same time, the German Reichsbank's note circulation amounted to 30 billion marks, along with 12 billion marks of treasury bills in circulation, for a total sum of 42 billion marks. If, on the basis of the exchange rate on the Zurich stock exchange, the ratio in exchange between the crown and the mark is assumed to be 1:2.25, an amount of about 3.4 billion marks would suffice for the conversion of the crown notes circulating in German-Austria into Reichsmark notes. If Germany, upon currency unification, wanted to expand its circulation of notes and treasury bills in proportion to the increase in population, it could issue new notes in the amount of 4.2 billion marks, since Germany's population is about ten times that of German-Austria. A fraction of this amount —800 million marks—could be spared, which the German Reichsbank could grant as a loan to the German-Austrian state for rebalancing the public budget, under the same conditions under which the German state had received loans from the Reichsbank.

At the time of the actual implementation of currency unification, this calculation may well be different. The currency in circulation in German-Austria is likely to increase as a result of withdrawals from demand deposits held at the central bank and from the cashing in of treasury bills. It cannot be excluded, therefore, that the amount necessary for converting the number of crowns in circulation into marks may exceed the amount which the German Reichsbank may be able to issue upon integration in accordance with the now larger population. This will create the necessity for placing additional mark notes in circulation by this amount.

It should be remembered that, upon creation of the German Reich, special measures also were taken in order to eliminate the paper currencies of the individual states that were in use at the time.[12] The sum total of paper money amounted to 61.3 million taler, equivalent to 184 million marks. The law on treasury bills of April 30, 1874, limited the amount of treasury bills to be issued to 120 million marks. The debt was distributed among the individual states in proportion to their population (at 3 marks per inhabitant), so that even those that had hitherto not issued paper money would have their share. In order to facilitate the retirement of this debt in states that had more paper money than this in circulation, the state advanced them two-thirds of the surplus of their individual paper money over their share in the national amount of paper money. This advance, which amounted to 54.7 million marks, was paid off in fifteen annual installments beginning on January 1, 1876, until, in 1891, the amount of treasury bills in circulation had reached the level of 120 million marks as prescribed by law.

The disparities deriving from the different per-capita quotas in Germany and German-Austria would have to be remedied in a similar fashion. If the per-capita quota of notes should turn out to be larger in Austria than in Germany, the excess amount would have to be repaid, within a certain

12 [Mises is referring to the formation of the German Reich, when several German states were unified under Prussian leadership in 1871. While these states retained a degree of autonomy, they lost the authority to issue their own currencies. —Ed.]

period, as an interest-free loan to be extended to the German-Austrian state by the Reichsbank.

There can be no doubt that the full implementation of the currency union between German-Austria and the German Reich must be the ultimate goal of any integration policy in the field of currency relations. It is quite another question whether this path should be taken immediately. In German-Austria, concerns are sometimes raised about the immediate implementation of full integration into the German monetary and central banking system. One of the arguments is that the economy of German-Austria has certain characteristics that would require special treatment of its financial sector over the next several years. The apprehension is based on the idea that the agencies of the German Reichsbank may not always have the requisite understanding for the difficult position of the German-Austrian economy. Years may have to pass before they will have given up the Northern German habit of regarding everything that is Southern German, and particularly everything Austrian, as inferior and foreign.

The Cartel Banks

These considerations were at the root of the idea of first bringing about currency unification over a transition period by participating in a cartel relationship between the German Reichsbank and the future German-Austrian central bank. Both banks would formally retain their independence, though they would have to conduct their business according to the same principles. The legal foundations for their banking policies would thus have to be identical, and an agreement between the governors would have to guarantee uniform procedures in all matters of banking policy.

History knows no example of such an arrangement between independent central banks. When Hungary regarded the continuation of a common central bank as incompatible with its legal claims and economic interests, consideration was repeatedly given to the idea of instituting two cartel banks in Austria and Hungary. These proposals were never implemented, probably because of the great hurdles that would have had to have been overcome from a practical point of view. The relationship between German-Austria and Germany would, however, be a different case. German economic preeminence is such that the relationship between the two cartel banks could hardly be seen as that of equal partners over any extended period of time. This would drive the German-Austrian central bank into dependence on the Reichsbank. Already during the war, the Vienna Stock Exchange and the Austrian currency had become heavily dependent on the Berlin Stock Exchange and the German currency, although all the economic forces of the entire Austro-Hungarian economic area were at the time still concentrated in Vienna. The position of the German-Austrian bank vis-à-vis the Reichsbank would then hardly be stronger than that of private banks of issue.

The advantages the several federal states today draw from the existence of their central banks are so small that they are not worth the effort of setting up a special German-Austrian central bank modeled after them, or to subsidize them into a position of insignificance. The particular privileges that are claimed by German-Austria for her financial sector, before the creation of a German-Austrian central bank, are likely to be attainable by setting up a state bank without the privilege of issuing bank notes. Such a German-Austrian state bank is already in existence today. It is the German-Austrian Post Office Savings Bank, which, upon German-Austria joining the German Reich, is likely to lose its deposit business to the German Reichsbank and may then fully concentrate on loans.

Coinage Issues of Currency Unification

Given the conditions under which the transition to the mark as a single currency would have to take place, particular dispositions as to the gold and silver coins in circulation are unnecessary. This applies also to the silver florin. It is sufficient if the German-Austrian state calls these coins up for exchange into notes and, after a certain period, terminates their legal-tender status. The public will let this period pass unused, since the metal value not only of gold coins but also of silver coins by far exceeds the value of the Austrian currency. These are the relations (assuming a price of 700 crowns for one kilogram of silver):

	STANDARD WEIGHT (GRAMS)	VALUE (IN PAPER CROWNS)
One-crown piece	4.175 g	2.92
Two-crown piece	8.350 g	5.85
Five-crown piece	21.600 g	15.12
Silver florin	11.110 g	7.77

Special rules have to be established for coins made of nickel, bronze, and iron. But this is a question of lesser importance that can be easily solved.

The German-Austrian state needs to give no more regard to the coinage and currency treaty between Austria and Hungary than it does to the successor states that have been proclaimed on the territory of the old Austrian monarchy. Hungary has for her own part voided the coinage and currency treaty by violating, in total disregard of the privileges of the Austro-Hungarian Bank, the status of the Bank's subsidiaries located on Hungarian territory, and by renouncing the legal-tender status of notes issued by the Bank. Hungary, therefore, could not raise any claims against German-Austria based on this treaty. To an even lesser degree could the several successor states raise such claims, since they have done the same as Hungary, only at an even earlier date.

A Policy of Sound Money

The importance of currency unification must not be overestimated. Little would be gained if Germany and German-Austria were to become a common-currency area in the future while this area then suffered the consequences of a constantly inflationary paper currency. The positive effects of having overcome the pernicious effects of monetary "particularism," and of having revived the policy which was so calamitously interrupted by the war of 1866, will not be enjoyed by the entire German people unless in matters of currency policy they will have taken a stance in favor of renouncing any inflationary measures.

CHAPTER 7

Foreign-Exchange Control Must Be Abolished[1]

In the course of the current discussions, questions concerning foreign-exchange policy have been repeatedly asked.[2] As a matter of fact, it is quite impossible to talk about a controlled economy and foreign trade without at the same time discussing foreign-exchange policy. Thus, I shall be brief, especially in view of the declaration made yesterday by the government representative before a subcommittee of the constituent National Assembly, that the government also has realized that the system of the foreign-exchange control is untenable. The government is to change direction in order to fight the unfavorable situation created as a result of the existing rates of exchange.

From the information provided by the representatives of the government, as well as from the remarks made by the spokesmen for the various political parties following the debate, it is now the intention to limit future activities of the Foreign Exchange Office to a single purpose, namely to serve as an agency for obtaining the foreign exchange needed by the state. If this plan is actually put into practice, then the present system of

1 [This article was originally delivered in German as a lecture at the Vienna Chamber of Commerce in the autumn of 1919. It has not been previously published.—Ed.]

2 [In the face of large outflows of gold and foreign exchange from the Austrian central bank during the First World War, the Austrian government established a Foreign Exchange Agency on February 22, 1916, and a similar institution was put into place in the Hungarian part of the Austro-Hungarian empire on February 24, 1916. All foreign exchange received by exporters was to be sold to the central bank at the official rate of exchange. All importers requiring foreign exchange for purchase of goods from abroad were to receive permission and an allotment of foreign currencies from the Foreign Exchange Agency at the fixed rate of exchange. The foreign-exchange control remained in place following the end of the war in November 1918, and was not lifted officially until November 1920.—Ed.]

foreign-exchange control will be eliminated. The task assigned to the Exchange Office could just as easily be carried out by any bank, e.g., the Postal Savings Bank, or by the Central Bank. To perform this task does not require any special authority or any official interference by government representatives in matters concerning foreign trade. The Foreign Exchange Office will then simply be an institution that acquires foreign exchange in the free market at market prices or, to be more precise, from those who are willing to sell foreign currency.

What now constitutes the core function of the central Foreign Exchange Office, namely the compulsory surrender of foreign exchange from commercial and industrial businesses, will be abolished. In order to maintain stable commercial-trading relations with foreign countries it is not enough that decrees of such great importance as this one should technically remain part of the law, with circumstances dictating whether they are to be enforced or not. At present, every businessman must obtain the approval of the Foreign Exchange Office prior to concluding any foreign business transaction. When making purchases from abroad, he has to ask if the Exchange Office is willing to let him have the required foreign exchange, and whenever sales made abroad are concerned, he has to inquire if the Exchange Office demands that he surrender the foreign exchange he has earned or whether they will waive its claim against him.

The very obligation of having to approach the central Exchange Office prior to any business transaction means that, under present conditions, it is not only more difficult to do business, it is practically impossible. As things are now in the market place, offers must often be instantly made, accepted, or rejected. No foreign seller or buyer is willing to wait until a decision is made by the Exchange Office, when as a government agency it works at a considerably slower pace than is required in the world of business. The losses suffered in our economy due to this situation—namely, that many advantageous transactions could not be concluded because it was impossible to obtain in time the necessary authorizations from the various government offices—are much more significant than one is inclined to assume.

Modern-day commerce cannot be made to function on the basis of every business transaction being dependent on the arbitrarily applicable rules of government agencies. The businessman has to know what he may or may not do. Therefore, it is not enough to formally retain the foreign exchange regulations on the books, but then merely try to eliminate the obstacles they place in the way of doing business by acting in the manner that is so popular with us, i.e., to apply them more mildly. Commerce requires a more solid and reliable legal basis; it does not want to depend on the arbitrariness of officialdom. (*Applause*)

I shall only briefly touch on what happened yesterday in the subcommittee of the National Assembly, since I assume from the vigorous applause that followed my last remark that all of you gentlemen completely reject the policy of foreign-exchange regulations. However, I do want to point out certain interrelated facts regarding our currency-policy problems as well as others needing to be addressed right now. During today's debate, it was pointed out time and time again that for currency-policy reasons it seems advisable to continue with the controlled economy, or at least to keep in effect certain specific restrictions on the freedom of trade. It is argued that the controlled economy must be continued because, considering the unfavorable prices for foreign currency, it would be impossible to buy goods from abroad. This is a misconception. Not even a controlled economy can reduce the amounts of Austrian crowns we have to expend when buying foreign goods. Equally incorrect is the idea that restrictions on imported foreign goods will bring down the demand for foreign currency. Even without government intervention, the increase in the price for foreign currency will reduce the demand for imported goods. The rise in the price for foreign exchange limits imports and stimulates exports.

Furthermore, an allusion was made to the fact that foreign-exchange transactions are not always in the hands of honest businessmen and that, consequently, there would be undesirable effects from completely eliminating the foreign-exchange decrees. It is true that there are elements active in the currency market nowadays that should not be in it. But that the business in foreign exchange actually has been taken over by these elements can be blamed on the foreign-exchange decree. Doing business in foreign exchange was taken away from the banks and bankers and channeled into the hands of people for whom prohibitions and fines only mean they have to find a way around these inconveniences. The business in foreign exchange only can be rescued from such people by repealing the prohibitions. The banks once more would be able to freely dedicate themselves to the business of foreign exchange. (*Applause*)

It is in the public interest that the business in foreign exchange be returned to the respectable hands of bankers and banking.

Defenders of the foreign-exchange regulations constantly point out that it is necessary to keep certain goods off the domestic market. It needs to be pointed out, as well, that the unfavorable situation with regard to foreign-exchange rates is not caused by an unfavorable balance of payments. It is caused by inflation. But even if one believes that certain types of goods should be prevented from being imported, this can be done just as easily by listing certain goods as being subject to import duties or simply prohibiting their importation.

The present state of affairs is almost intolerable. We practically have a general ban on imports. If one wants to purchase goods from abroad, a special permit has to be obtained from various government offices. For all practical purposes, this makes any domestic commercial or industrial enterprise impossible. The industrialist who wants to purchase semifinished products or machine parts for a few hundred marks has to demonstrate the necessity for this purchase at the government offices. An importer has to carry out a sizable number of manipulations—taking days, weeks, or even longer—in order finally to obtain the needed goods after having overcome indescribable difficulties. This state of affairs is unacceptable in a country whose industry has maintained very close ties with old and new foreign countries.

I believe, dear sirs, I can recommend that you accept the arguments conveyed in this paper. (*Lively applause*)

CHAPTER 8

Direct Taxation in City and Country[1]

I

Before the war, the urban and commercial segments of the population shouldered the main burden of taxation. The owners of landed estates contributed comparatively little to the fiscal revenue. It is telling that, while revenue from all other direct and indirect taxes has increased steeply for decades, only revenue from the tax on rural buildings, the so-called building category tax, has remained more or less stable and the revenue from the land tax has actually declined. Only 7.25 percent of the aggregate gross income declared for income taxation in 1913 was from land ownership, a share much smaller than the proportion of agrarian to nonagrarian income. True, taxation on the basis of land ownership was slightly increased during the war. But one must remember that inflation has reduced the amount of agrarian income taxes to a small fraction of their original amount, unlike the primarily urban taxes that are based on fixed rates. Given present exchange rates and prices, the tax rates on land would have to be more than twenty times higher in order to yield the same revenue as in 1913. The war surcharges have, in fact, not even doubled the land tax. On average, those in the agricultural sector are not any worse off than they were before the war. If they were in debt, inflation has even made them better off. But their tax payments today, when inflation is taken into account, are significantly lower than in 1914. For even the war tax affected them only in exceptional cases, and rural income-tax liabilities have fallen far behind the nominal increase in land rents.

1 [This article originally appeared in German in two parts in the *Neues Wiener Tagblatt*, Nos. 324 & 326 (November 27 & 29, 1919). Some modified passages in part two of this article were incorporated by Mises into "Vienna's Political Relationship with the Provinces in Light of Economics," Chapter 9 of the present volume. — Ed]

Changes in the taxes from rent on land have moved in only one direction. Technically, from the financial perspective, forests belonging to the large estates have been hit with a special tax. The Office for Forestry Management deprives the owners of wooded estates from keeping the total price for timber that can be obtained under the given world-market conditions. A substantial part of this accrues to the public entities. By permitting an arbitrary administration by the civil servants, this type of taxation, apart from it having a questionable constitutional foundation, militates against the first and foremost principle of public finance: the determinacy of any tax. Furthermore, it is exposed to the severe criticism that collecting this tax involves disproportionately high costs. And that its sizable revenues for the most part benefit neither the state nor even the federal provinces but entities under no control whatsoever, which in turn use them for various welfare purposes. The first objective of a somewhat more reasonable financial policy would have to be the termination of such untenable practices. The taxation of forests would have to be fully incorporated into the structure of the tax system in order for it to serve a useful fiscal purpose. So far, however, all endeavors in this direction have been rebuffed by the provinces and by the agricultural dictators.

It should at long last dawn on us that any stabilization of our public finances depends on including the large estates in the system of taxation. Landed property in agriculture and forestry is the only natural resource in our country, if we may disregard deposits of ore, magnesia, and some minor minerals, in addition to the as-yet-untapped hydroelectric power. It is an anomaly that, during the war, those in the agriculture sector could even greatly expand their inherited privilege of paying much less in taxes.

Farmers complain that regulations governing sales force them to sell a part of their produce to the economic authority set up by the government at prices far below market prices and usually not even enough to cover their costs of production. These complaints are not unjustified.

II

The first part of this article claimed that the complaints made by the agricultural sector about irrational sales regulations are not unjustified. This agrarian policy was as unsuccessful as all the other economic-policy measures that were implemented during the war. Instead of expanding agricultural taxes in line with the rise in the prices of agricultural products, landowners were compelled to make contributions in kind. The officers of the general staff and other dilettantes who were responsible for this policy were, of course, ignorant of all the reasons why the fiscal authority already centuries ago abandoned payments in kind and instead adopted payment of taxes in the form of money. They did not take into account that the in-kind payment is calculated on the basis of the gross revenue from the land and not its net profits. Neither does it tax the individual landowners uniformly, and the variability in this burden is also bound to generate a great deal of resistance.[2] Collecting in-kind contributions is, furthermore, extremely difficult and difficult to control, while over time the fiscal authority has developed efficient and tested ways of forcibly collecting tax payments in the form of money.

The outcome from this levy is very different depending on the regions concerned. In some areas its yield is low, while in others it is made more abundant due to the local balance of power. But it is precisely from these latter regions that there flow the least amounts to the urban and commer-

2 [In 1919 the local and provincial authorities used their powers to restrict and often prevent the "export" of foods and other goods from their rural areas to the cities, including Vienna. The imposing of fixed and artificially lower prices for agricultural output and the imposition of forced requisition of agricultural goods resulted in a fierce resistance by the farm communities. See David F. Strong, *Austria (October 1918–March 1919: Transition from Empire to Republic* (New York: Octagon Books, [1939] 1974), pp. 193–94:

> As the system of wartime emergency was continued, the vice of the wartime measures also carried over. The initiative in the organization of the Food Administration in the early months of the Republic seems to have been taken by the self-appointed and rather independent Provincial Administrations. Here there was obviously developing a movement intended to retain what food they had rather than permit it to be sent out of the Province for the relief of distant communities. In general, this method worked to the satisfaction of the dweller in the less densely populated rural regions, but the problem of supply, and with it the issue of administrative authority, became acute in the larger urban areas. . . . In part as the result of attempts made to force the rural districts to give up supplies for the provisioning of Vienna, there grew up a feeling of rebellion, during this early period, within the ranks of the agriculturalists. . . . The unpopular wartime policy of rationing the population on the basis of the estimated food and fuel supply [was] continued, and also the unpopular system of reduced prices at the source combined with the inevitable requisitioning of supplies. This method proved unsatisfactory, for the producers merely continued the devious methods employed in the war years to prevent the supplies from reaching the official channels for distribution. The opposition of the peasant producers to this system of distribution stiffened more and more.

—Ed.]

cial population centers. The fact that food is scarce in the cities only weeks after the harvest sheds a telling light on this system.[3]

Under the circumstances, the compulsory contribution of agricultural produce will sooner or later have to be repealed. It should be the task of a targeted financial policy to combine this with a fundamental tax reform for agricultural revenue.

While the fiscal burden of farmers has been lowered to a fraction of the already low prewar level, fiscal policy during the war has downright exploited the urban population.

The circulating capital in the hands of commercial and industrial en-

---

3 [Mises is referring to the vast black-market network that was a major source of food supplies from the countryside to the cities, and especially to Vienna. See David F. Strong, *Austria (October 1918–March 1919: Transition from Empire to Republic*, pp. 196–97:

> Food control was further complicated by extra-legal methods of distribution. Schooled in his business during the later years of the War, the smuggler was practically unhampered in the early days of the Republic. In fact his position in the economic life of the urban centers was recognized publicly, though by no means officially condoned. . . . Smuggling was practiced widely and by four different types of people. There were what might be called the purveyors, regular and irregular; then the producers; and finally, the ultimate consumer. There was first of all the professional smugglers who had well-established businesses with headquarters usually in hotels—rendezvous known to the authorities and gleefully raided at intervals by the *Volkswehr* [the People's Defense Force]. These professionals had their business contacts and regular clientele. They could offer provisions, otherwise unobtainable, to the housewife able to pay the premium, which was, needless to say, far above the official price at the government dispensaries. "My smuggler" was a familiar household expression. Although currency may have been accepted at first, by the end of the year the smuggler demanded "real value" in preference to an inflated currency. A gold watch brought four sacks of potatoes. Fifty cigars, of a superior quality because purchased before tobacco was rationed, brought four pounds of pork and ten pounds of lard—a considerable amount in view of the fact that it was unobtainable through the authorized channels. . . . In fact, the administration played directly into the hands of the smuggler, for during official "meatless weeks" the well-to-do housewife naturally patronized the smuggler. In these frequent periods, he did a thriving business. . . . In the face of a serious food shortage, aggravated by the sudden disruption in communications and transportation, the Department of Food Supply strove to distribute available supplies equitably to all sections of the population. The producer, however, found that he could obtain a better price from smugglers or from the consumer directly, and consequently withheld his goods. The prestige of the new administration suffered accordingly, since it was neither willing to raise the retail price at the dispensaries to a level that could compete with illicit transactions, nor was it possessed of sufficient police power effectively to check either smuggling or hoarding.

—Ed.]

terprises is continuously being transformed back into money, and as such is continuously channeled through ledger books in the form of money. As the monetary inflation increases, the greater becomes that same amount of capital when expressed in money terms. Since all accounting rests on the tacit assumption that the value of money is unchanging, the increase in that monetary sum appears as a profit on the balance sheet. As long as the inflation continues, merchants who turn over their inventory several times during the year make, in addition to the profit they would normally earn, an additional nominal profit resulting from the increase in the monetary value of their inventory. This is the foremost source of the so-called war profits. They were not any real profits but to a great extent only changes in their monetary expressions because of the inflation. Since the war created advantages for certain individuals and for some entire industries, real profits were also certainly made. In Austria, however, even these real war profits, which taxation reduced to a minimum anyway, were actually fictitious; at the end of the war, the most important of the suppliers to the armed forces were owed far more by the army than they had ever earned during the war. Since these outstanding claims must pretty much be written off as bad debt, an easy calculation reveals that real war profits in this country were made only by a few members of the urban population.

A merchant who ran his business before the war with a capital of one million crowns would today require 20 million crowns for the same volume of business, taking no account of commodity price increases. If this merchant today had a capital of 20 million, he would not be any richer than he was before the war. The government's tax policy, which in relation to the urban population has always taken the position that a crown is equal to a crown, has tried and succeeded to a large extent in taxing away any amount exceeding one million crowns. Tax policy did not treat the business sector's fixed capital very differently. Machines and other factory equipment need to be replaced after a certain period of time. But at the present time, such replacement requires far more financial capital than before the war. Businesses are hardly able to make these replacement investments because the necessary funds have been taken away through the taxation of wartime profits. If the government had treated the agricultural sector in the same manner that the industrial and merchant sectors are being treated, then the state would have to take away 15 to 18 hectares of the farmer's land from the 20 hectares he owned in 1914.

Serious flaws have been made in our fiscal policy because of the misunderstanding of the true nature of these much-discussed war profits of industry and commerce. It has acquired political importance because of the way in which these apparent profits have been used in political agitation. Mistakes are constantly made in the assessment of our economic situation because of the flawed view on this issue. The fact is ignored that our industrial and commercial sectors will have to overcome difficulties of the highest magnitude in order to survive. One must realize that, in the years to come, taxation of industrial and commercial businesses will hardly yield any significant fiscal revenue. During the war and in the first postwar year, the government has lived by confiscating through taxation the lion's share of industrial and commercial capital and using these funds for consumption. It is clear that this cannot continue.

Our urban population can only prosper through commerce and industrial activity directed toward export. Today, both commerce and industry rely on the availability of ample foreign financial means, since the capital of our own entrepreneurs has been reduced to a fraction of its prewar value. But foreign capital will only come here if it can be put to a more profitable use than abroad. This requires that our tax policy be entirely placed on a totally different foundation.

CHAPTER 9

Vienna's Political Relationship with the Provinces in Light of Economics[1]

The German-Austrian State, or Austria as we are now asked to call it, leads only an illusory existence. The power of the state's institutions, headquartered in Vienna, barely extends to the borders of Lower Austria.[2] In the rest of the provinces the laws are observed only when and as far as they coincide with the wishes of the provinces. In Vorarlberg, Tyrol, and Salzburg, people talk quite openly about joining Switzerland or Bavaria, and if at present these provinces still remain within the federation of our state this circumstance is attributable solely to the fact that the Entente wishes that our state be kept to its present size.[3] It was only a short while ago that Upper Austria declared its sovereignty. The state authorities have not implicitly recognized the sovereignty of the province of Upper Austria; only when Upper Austria was faced with a conflict due to the decisiveness of the state authorities did it accept a compromise and abandon the road it had initially chosen.[4] Each of the provinces is trying to independently open talks with foreign countries. Their policies constantly thwart the goals of the government in Vienna. In light of this state of affairs, it requires all of the indestructible Austrian optimism still to speak of a State of Austria. Let us not fool ourselves. Except for Lower Austria, very few of the provinces have

1 [This article was delivered in German as a lecture at the 258th Plenary Assembly of the Association of Austrian Economists on December 2, 1919. It was published in the *Jahrbuch der Gesellschaft Österreichischer Volkswirte* (1920).—Ed.]

2 ["Lower Austria" refers to the eastern province of Austria surrounding Vienna.—Ed.]

3 [See Chapter 4, "The Austrian Currency Problem Prior to the Peace Conference," footnote 3.—Ed.]

4 ["Upper Austria" refers to the province west of Lower Austria that borders on Bavaria, with the city of Linz as its capital.—Ed.]

any desire to be a part of this state.[5] But the final result from inhabitants rejecting the states in which they reside is something we have already experienced quite recently with the disintegration of the old monarchy.

Being faced with this problem, our statesmen do not know what to do. They try to get rid of the difficulties of the political situation through constitutional procedures. But writing or copying a beautiful national constitution does not resolve the political problem;[6] this also is a lesson that we can learn from the history of the old Austria.[7]

When viewed solely from the perspective of the relationship between the state and the provinces, matters can be looked at in the following way. Legally, the old Austria was a political association consisting of a number of Crownlands. A firm cohesiveness for this association was provided solely by the governmental administration and was ruled by the Crownlands' bu-

---

5 [See Malcolm Bullock, *Austria, 1918–1938: A Study in Failure* (London: Macmillan Co., 1939), p. 21: "The hostility between town and country had sharpened during the war, and there was a great provincial feeling against Vienna. The provinces formed their own Governments as soon as the Republic was proclaimed, and Vienna was surrounded by a circle of unfriendly provinces as well as by the Allied blockade. An Austrian citizen now needed a passport in order to go from one province to another. Lower Austria and Vienna remained an administrative unit till 1920 and it was not until 1921 that Austria assumed the appearance of a single State."—Ed.]

6 [In October 1919, the coalition Austrian government commissioned the respected constitutional lawyer, Hans Kelsen (who had been Mises's fellow student and friend in the *Akademisches Gymnasium* in Vienna when they were teenagers in the 1890s), to prepare a new constitution for the Republic of Austria. This new constitution was promulgated a year later on October 5, 1920. It established a democratic form of government and a federal structure with a variety of powers divided between the central government, the provinces, and the city of Vienna. For a detailed, critical exposition of the Austrian constitutional order in the period between the two world wars, see Mary MacDonald, *The Republic of Austria, 1918–1934: A Study in the Failure of Democratic Government* (Oxford: Oxford University Press, 1946).—Ed.]

7 [The *Ausgleich* (or Compromise) of 1867 reorganized the Austrian empire into the dual monarchy of Austria-Hungary. Under the new constitutional arrangement, Austria and Hungary were independent administrative units for all domestic affairs, with foreign affairs, defense, a customs union, and a joint administrative budget coming under a unified political structure for the empire as a whole. The emperor ruled over the combined monarchy, with the term "Imperial and Royal" (*Kaiserlich und Königlich*) applied to the branches of the bureaucracy that were responsible to the administration of the joint ministries. The Austrian portion of the empire was divided into "Crownlands," with each possessing a high degree of territorial autonomy but with a layer of administrative bureaucracy just above the local authorities that was appointed by and responsible to the emperor.—Ed.]

reaucratic apparatus. During the very first hours of the revolution the state's institutional structure was broken up when the governing bodies of the provincial offices, together with its entire subordinate executive organizations, were surrendered to the local, autonomous administrations. This step now must be somehow undone. But this cannot be accomplished openly. The provinces' aversion for any such action is too great. They still associate Vienna with the image of the centralized bureaucracy of the old political authority; consequently, it must be done covertly.[8] This is precisely the role of constitutional and administrative reform.

The only thing that can be said here with any certainty is that the revolution broke up the old state structure and replaced it with anarchy. Or described more correctly, it replaced the coexistence of various governing

---

8 [See Carlile A. Macartney, *The Social Revolution in Austria* (Cambridge: Cambridge University Press, 1926), pp. 94–95:

> When the unifying power of the Habsburgs was gone, every man felt himself a citizen of his province: a Styrian, a Carinthian, or a Viennese. Pending the passing of a new Constitution, the provinces were indeed practically and to a large extent legally independent of one another. A hurried provisional law transferred the powers of the old Imperial governors to provincial Diets, with democratic councils as executive organs and elected Presidents and Vice-Presidents at their heads. Even before this law was passed, several provinces had already formed for themselves provincial Governments which had indeed often to act with sovereign and summary powers: to preserve the food supply of their constituents, to save their homes from the plunderings of the returning army, in some cases even to defend their frontiers against foreign aggression.... Economically, the Alpine provinces were far more independent of Vienna than were Bohemia or Moravia; and even from the national point of view, there was little community between the essentially parochial Germans of the Alpine valleys and the no less essentially "Weltburger" of the capital. On the other side, there was the antagonism between the agricultural and industrial classes, which the privations of wartime had fanned into a lively hate; between the socialism of the factory hand and the obstinate individualism of the peasant proprietor; between the freethinking of the city and the clericalism of the province.... It was not surprising that the provinces, which the new laws had delivered over to the control of the peasants and their traditional rulers, showed an energy and ingenuity in turning their backs on Vienna.... Vorarlberg held a plebiscite and voted for union with Switzerland; the Tirol with Germany. Both Tirol and Styria were known to have worked out plans in every detail for cutting loose altogether from Austria if occasion arose.... Every province, even every parish, enclosed itself in a watertight compartment of restrictions, designed to jealously guard the all-important food supply. An Austrian needed a passport and a visa to travel from one province to another of his own country. On the journey his pockets were searched exhaustively, not for cocaine or diamonds, but for flour and potatoes.

—Ed.]

bodies. But that is the nature of all revolutions. It is what differentiates a revolution from a putsch and a palace revolution, both of which leave the old governing apparatus intact and only transfer the leadership to other individuals. It was unavoidable that our revolution would abolish the existing administrative dichotomy. The elimination of that unsustainable system of a dual administration only could be initiated by first placing the government and local autonomous bodies under one authority. It is obvious, of course, that in a democratic state this could not have meant for the local autonomous administration to be surrendered to the bureaucracy. The peculiarity of our circumstance is not that the revolution initially resulted in disorder, but rather that it was not undertaken to build a new governmental order upon the ruins of the old one.

If one asks for the reason behind this striking phenomenon, the answer is that the provinces just did not want to have anything to do with Vienna. Farmers and lower middle class villagers and the people in rural towns did not subscribe to the socialism supported by the working population in the cities. That is undoubtedly true. But in fact the interconnection between these matters is not as simple as is usually assumed. Even if there is no love lost between the Social Democrats in the cities and the farmers, in principle the farmers are not at all opposed to the socialization of big industry. Furthermore, the farmers and lower middle class people are not the only ones who have no use for Vienna. This also applies to the civil servants, the employees in the private sector, and the workers in the provincial capitals, all of whom constitute a segment of the population whose social radicalism is hard to surpass. It is necessary for a more in-depth investigation into the relationship between Vienna and the provinces to discover the root of the feud that threatens to wreck this state.

The German Alpine provinces are not well endowed by nature. They do not offer any especially favorable conditions for agriculture. Their only riches are their hydroelectric water resources, whose development was impeded over the decades by the étatism[9] of the state and the provinces. Consequently, they played a rather minor role in the economic system of old Austria. They contributed little, but received much. And all the gifts they received under the old regime fell into their laps without their having to make much of an effort. They did not have to undertake any particular fight in order to obtain high protective customs duties for their agricul-

9 [See Chapter 5, "On the Actions to Be Taken in the Face of Progressive Currency Depreciation," footnote 10.—Ed.]

tural products as well as an import ban on cattle and meat—both of which were very lucrative for them. That battle was already being fought for them by the Hungarian landowners, and—insofar as Austrian support was still needed—by the landowners in the Sudetenland[10] and Poland.[11]

On the other hand, the Alpine provinces were incredibly favored when it came to taxes. Due to the pressures being exerted by the Czech and Polish landowners, the state tried to shift the major portion of the tax burden on to Vienna's German industry, the area around Neustadt,[12] and the Sudetenlanders. The rural property taxes—the residential and land taxes —were low. The tax levied on income (earned on capital) impacted the Alpine provinces only to a relatively low degree; the income tax assessment also was not implemented as strictly as in Vienna and, correspondingly, inheritance tax assessments were more moderate as well. Under the circumstances, the tax on income from rental housing and the tax on capital earnings hardly applied at all to the Alpine provinces. The farmers' distilleries enjoyed great benefits from indirect taxation, and the law also provided relief for smaller Alpine breweries. All this benefited the Alpine provinces without any particular effort on their part. However, during the last years of this struggle, they did provide the leader, the parliamentary deputy, Steinwender. But the people who secured the victory were the Czechs, Poles, Ukrainians, and Slovenians, who were ever ready to shift all state expenses onto the shoulders of the German cities.

This system was developed to its maximum under the fiscal policy that followed during the war. Taxation on farming was increased very little. While the prices for farm products increased twenty, thirty, forty times, and sometimes even up to one hundred times what they were during peacetime, the tax on land was not even doubled. The taxation during the

10 [The Sudetenland was the western part of Bohemia bordering on Germany and Lower Austria in the old Austro-Hungarian Empire. It was incorporated into the new state of Czechoslovakia at the end of the First World War, in spite of its large German-speaking population that had wanted to be part of the new Austrian Republic.—Ed.]

11 ["Poland" refers to that portion of the Austrian Crownlands known as Galicia, the easternmost area of the Imperial Austrian domains under the old Austro-Hungarian Empire. It included the city of Lemberg (now Lvov), the birthplace of Ludwig von Mises. Galicia was incorporated into the reborn nation of Poland after the First World War. The eastern half, including Lemberg, was annexed by the Soviet Union during the Second World War, and it is now part of independent Ukraine.—Ed.]

12 ["Neustadt" refers to the region around the city of Wiener Neustadt, approximately sixty miles south of Vienna.—Ed.]

war hardly affected the farmer and, for a long time, the income tax paid by the landowners did not keep up with the increase in the rental price on land. In general, today's farmer is not much poorer than he was in 1914; if he had been in debt before the war, then he even made a profit during the war. Taking into account today's monetary inflation, he presently pays much less in taxes than he did before the war. If, then, the tax burden on the farmers had been lowered to a fraction of their already low prewar tax level, the city population was practically squeezed dry by the wartime fiscal policy.

The circulating capital in the hands of commercial and industrial enterprises is continuously being transformed back into money, and as such is continuously channeled through the ledger books in the form of money. As the monetary inflation increases, the greater becomes that same amount of capital when expressed in money terms. Since all accounting rests on the tacit assumption that the value of money is unchanging, the increase in that monetary sum appears as profit on the balance sheet. As long as the monetary inflation continues, the merchants who turn over their inventory several times during the year make, in addition to the profit they would normally earn, an additional nominal profit resulting from the increase in the monetary value of their inventory. If prior to the war [a merchant] operated his business with a capital of one million crowns, then at present (leaving completely aside the increase in commodity prices) he will require at least 25 million crowns in order to operate his business at the same volume as before. If today he has 25 million crowns, he would not be any richer than he was before the war. The government's fiscal policy, which in relation to the urban population has taken the position that a crown will always be equal to a crown, has now tried and succeeded to a large extent in taxing away any amount exceeding one million crowns.[13]

13 [The phrase "a crown is a crown" had its origin in an executive order (*Verordnung*) signed on March 25, 1919, by Joseph A. Schumpeter, then the Austrian Minister of Finance, and issued the following day as "1919 No. 61." It stated that the only legal tender was bank notes originally issued by the Austro-Hungarian Bank that had been "officially stamped with a 'guillodierte' frame containing in red color the word Deutschösterreich (German-Austria)....The notes marked for circulation in Deutschösterreich...are sole legal tender which must be accepted for all payments denominated in crowns....They must be accepted to their full nominal value by everybody, as well as by all public authorities." This meant that the settlement of all debts were payable in the nominal amounts at which they were originally contracted, in spite of the dramatic depreciation of the crown due to the wartime and postwar inflation in Austria. Thus creditors would receive payment in basically valueless paper money. In 1924, this became the basis of a court case in which the judgement came down that the executive order of 1919 was valid and to be upheld. See

Tax policy did not treat the business sector's fixed capital very differently. Machinery and other factory equipment need to be replaced after a certain period of time. But at the present time, such replacement requires far more financial capital than before the war. Businesses are hardly able to make these replacement investments because the necessary funds have been taken away through the taxation of wartime profits. If the government had treated the agricultural sector in the same manner that the industrial and business sectors are being treated, then the state would have to take away 15 to 20 hectares of the farmer's land from the 25 he owned before the war.

Thus, the result from the fiscal policy followed during the war is that primarily the agrarian provinces received tax relief, while on the other hand the greater part of all liquid capital was seized by the state, transformed into consumer goods, and used for nonproductive purposes during the war. If we look at the fiscal policy of the past twenty years, and particularly since 1914, we have to conclude that it is the city population, and not the provinces, that has reasons to complain. But here we encounter a phenomenon that is extremely important for shedding light on the relationship of the city to the agrarian population, i.e., of the city of Vienna and Lower Austria to the provinces. The city population has become so biased in favor of the "natural economy," mercantilist and petty bourgeois ideas that it does not even realize when it is being discriminated against in favor of the agrarian population. Not only does it fail to complain that it is being discriminated against, it even thinks that this fiscal policy is not sweeping enough. This very city population rashly demands the total taxing away of war profits. In light of the depreciation of our national currency, taxing away war profits signifies that owners of liquid capital, i.e., capital that is recorded in the books of businesses or represented in the form of securities, will be divested through taxation of their financial means for invest-

Wolfgang F. Stolper, *Joseph Alois Schumpeter: The Public Life of a Private Man* (Princeton, N.J.: Princeton University Press, 1994), pp. 224–27. Friedrich A. Hayek has commented in "The Denationalization of Money: An Analysis of the Theory and Practice of Concurrent Currencies," [1978] in Stephen Kresge, ed., *The Collected Works of F. A. Hayek, Vol. 6: Good Money, Part II, The Standard* (Chicago: University of Chicago Press, 1999), p. 148 n. 34: "In Austria in 1922 the name 'Schumpeter' had become almost a curse word among ordinary people, referring to the principle that 'Krone is Krone', because the economist J. A. Schumpeter, during his short tenure as Minister of Finance, had put his name to an order of council, merely spelling out what was undoubtedly valid law, namely that debts incurred in crowns when they had a higher value could be repaid in depreciated crowns, ultimately worth only a 15,000th part of their original value." — Ed.]

ment, considering that they are no richer now than they were in 1914 in terms of an imaginary crown of stable value.

But it does not occur to anybody to apply the same principle to agrarian property. The city dweller finds it completely reasonable that a different yardstick is used, one that favors agrarian property when determining the amount of property taxes. The city's working population is so much under the spell of the ideas of the class struggle and irreconcilable differences of interest between the entrepreneur and the worker, that they do not realize that due to this fiscal policy the basis of their very existence is being reduced through the erosion of liquid capital. The difficulties with which our industry has to struggle nowadays are primarily due to the fact that because of the lack of capital they cannot successfully compete against foreign industry. The level of real wages in our country will have to be kept below that of the foreign worker until, as a result of many years of hard work and economizing, we will again be financially sound and thus more competitive.

That the urban population does not realize that they are being discriminated against in favor of the agrarian population is of great psychological importance. If the negative effect of this fiscal policy on municipal interests were commonly understood, the conclusion drawn would be that it is Vienna that has a motive for insisting on being separated from the provinces. At least the burden caused by Vienna's fiscal policy should be used as a bargaining chip for obtaining possible concessions that the provinces would not otherwise have to make to the city of Vienna. But as it stands now, the most important advantage that the municipalities of the state can give to the provinces is given away without anything being received in return.

There was no reason whatsoever for the farmers to be discontented with the wartime fiscal policy. Therefore, their complaints are not directed against the fiscal policy followed during the war, but against the wartime commercial and agrarian policy that obligated them to render extensive services to the state under the taxation and requisitioning system. This agrarian policy was as unsuccessful as all the other economic policy measures that were implemented during the war. Instead of expanding agricultural taxes in line with the rise in the prices for agricultural products, it was preferred to have the landowners make payments in agricultural produce for which a relatively low compensation was paid. This represented the easiest way out for the mercantilist reasoning of the officers of the general staff and other dilettantes who were responsible for this policy. They were oblivious to the reasons that for hundreds of years has made the fiscal authority prefer payments in money rather than payments in kind. They did not take into account that the in-kind payment is calculated on the basis of the gross revenue from the land and not its net profit. Neither does it tax the individual landowners uniformly, and the variability in this burden is bound to generate a great deal of resistance. They brought the indignation of the rural population to a boiling point when they used military requisition detachments for collecting the in-kind payments that were owed, instead of having civil servants from the administrative body or the courts do the job. The farmers of the Alpine provinces sent their sons willingly into that hopeless war from which many were never to return. But their loyalty to the emperor quickly made an about-face the moment the military commercial inspectors for the district began the forced collection of the imposed quotas. In the struggle between the brute force of the military and the cunning of the peasantry, the latter won. The collection results worsened from day to day.

The Republic intensified even further the Imperial economic policy. It expanded the state-socialist and mercantilist tendencies that are found in militarism. In this respect the system does not appear to be at cross-purposes with the imperialist policy, but is its completion and culmination. More than ever, the imperialist and mercantilist theory of an economic territory and self-sufficiency seemed to permeate all economic thinking after its most prominent and literary leader became the head of state.[14]

City residents have to live on what they make through commerce and trade. This is already reflected in the very concept and nature of the city. The manufacturer who does not produce any raw materials and foodstuffs can obtain the raw materials he processes and the foodstuffs he consumes only by purchasing them from other producers. But if that is the case, then it does not matter if he purchases them domestically or from abroad. It is certainly a disadvantage if an industry is located far from the areas in which raw materials are produced, especially if these materials are bulky or of little value, but it does not really matter if they are on the other side of a

---

14 [This refers to Karl Renner (1870–1950), a leading Austrian socialist who headed two coalition governments of the new Austrian Republic between November 1918 and the summer of 1920. In April 1945, he formed a provisional government that proclaimed the reestablishment of Austria as a democratic republic; in November of that year, he was elected president of Austria, a position he held until his death.—Ed.]

political border. Only the intervention of foreign-trade policies makes this fact important. Tariff wars and other commercial chicanery only ensue when such an interventionist trade policy is introduced.

If we, the Viennese, want to eat, then we must do business and produce and sell commercial products, so that we can use the profits to procure what we are not able to produce ourselves, namely raw materials and foodstuffs. The notion that one ought to produce foodstuffs and raw materials domestically, and that one ought to have control over the areas in which they are produced, is an imperialist notion that is not at all in accordance with the conditions of differentiated production in the world economy. A Viennese does not have the right to call the ore mines "his own" or to lay title to the African gold mines; he must buy the Austrian farmer's grain just the same as he has to buy the coffee harvested by a Brazilian. A state is not rendered unfit to live because its territory lacks some raw materials.

Our public's opinion and our ideas about economic policy regarding raw-material supplies are completely untenable. We demand from our farmer that he supply us with foodstuffs at a price that is far below the price quoted on the world market, and we demand from foreign countries that they make us a present of their foodstuffs and raw materials. All our endeavors are directed towards bringing down even farther the already unnaturally low domestic prices, instead of finding ways our low incomes can be increased by providing work. Our municipal-supply policy tries to contribute something to alleviate the lack of foodstuffs by fostering garden allotments for planting vegetables and by issuing permits for cultivation in public parks and gardens. But a city can never live on the potatoes and vegetables that are planted in such places at a high cost. The granaries of the city of Vienna are not the construction sites that are planted with cabbage; they are the workshops of the Viennese industry making finished goods, with whose products we would be able to buy foodstuffs on the world market. To keep ourselves supplied we need to look after how well the city's commerce and industry are doing; what is raised on the farms is not decisive in this regard.

We subscribe to the delusion that we can keep the domestic price level below the price level of the world market through public rationing of supply. It is the state that pays the difference between the world-market price and the domestic price, and it obtains the means for doing so by going into debt and by printing money. That is the essence of our much vaunted supply policy.

Our ideas about supplying our cities do not correspond to the reality of a city whose working population is made up of entrepreneurs and workers, but reflects the notion of an idle city proletariat that wants to live off the fruits of the farmer's diligence. Some politicians think that the supply situation is similar to what those in power in ancient Rome tried to give to the populace: bread and circuses. But to set up a National Food and Agricultural Ministry and a National Film Department does not solve the problem. The essential element is missing that made the policy of the Romans possible: the legions that dominated the world. An imperialist policy is understandable if it is backed by impressive military might. A militarist policy without a powerful army looks ridiculous.

As long as we intend to somehow obtain the foodstuffs we need without paying for them in full, it follows that we can call only upon areas in which we can apply political power. But as soon as we decide that we intend to work to pay for the things we need, that we want to purchase and not seize or requisition, then it does not matter if we have to obtain the goods domestically or from abroad. What we need in the way of foodstuffs we have to pay for with the goods we have produced. And when we buy less domestically and more from abroad, it follows that we will be exporting more and selling less to the farmers at home.

In the present situation we take in very little. Very little is obtained domestically because we do not have the power to force the farmers to deliver, and little comes in from abroad because we lack the means to pay for what we want.

The general opinion tends to be that only the farming sector in the provinces is opposed to Vienna and the unified Austrian state, and that the civil servants, employees, and workers favor centralism. But when one takes a good look, it turns out that this opinion does not correspond at all to the facts. It is true that employees in the public and private sector—in short, those broad sections of the population that now simply call themselves consumers—do want a continuation of a *Zwangswirtschaft* (controlled economy).[15] But this is not at all in the sense of a desire for centralism.

15 [Mises in his later writings referred to *Zwangswirtschaft* as the German pattern of economic planning, in *Planned Chaos* (Irvington-on-Hudson, N.Y.: Foundation for Economic Education, 1947), pp. 19–20; reprinted in *Socialism* (Indianapolis: Liberty Fund, [1951] 1981), p. 485: "The German or *Zwangswirtschaft* system ... seemingly and nominally, maintains private ownership of the means of production, entrepreneurship, and market exchange. So-called entrepreneurs do the buying and selling, pay the workers, contract debts and pay interest and amortization. But they are no longer entrepreneurs. ... The gov-

They are in favor of keeping the ties that link the provinces to Vienna and Lower Austria, because—due to their few numbers—they are too weak to ensure the continuation of the controlled economy without the help of Vienna and Lower Austria. Especially the workers in the provinces who are Social Democrats know that without the assistance of the party members in Lower Austria they would hardly be in a position to maintain their present political clout.

However, they are very much opposed to any benefit that the city of Vienna might obtain from the controlled economy in the provinces. They oppose grain from the provinces being sent to Vienna. After all, they were the ones—contrary to the wishes of the farmers who would have liked very much to send their products to the Viennese market—who put the conditions on the export of foodstuffs from the provinces to Vienna, conditions that practically amount to an export ban. When the Viennese make common cause with these non-farm sectors in the provinces concerning the question of continuing the controlled economy, they are supporting keeping in place artificially lower foodstuff prices in the provinces. This means that the food supply flowing from the provinces to Vienna will continue to be artificially hampered. In short, they support a policy that results in their own starvation. They even support the internal hunger blockade, i.e., the economic war that the provinces wage against them.

The interests of Vienna's population and the population of the industrial cities of Lower Austria are severely damaged by the policy that is being pursued by the towns of Graz, Linz, Salzburg, etc. But the population of our city is so much under the sway of autarkic ideas that it does not perceive the conflict that exists between their interests and those of the provinces. But even where they clearly do discern it, because even the simplest person is able to see the conflict, the population turns to mistaken countermeasures due to their mercantilist way of thinking. It may be debatable whether the summer resorts and spas are acting wisely when they curtail the length of time the Viennese may stay there. But it is definitely a mistake when the city of Vienna retaliates by restricting entry into Vienna. A city whose livelihood depends on commerce and selling industrial products has to rely on visits by people from elsewhere; it must

---

ernment tells these seeming entrepreneurs what and how to produce, at what prices and from whom to buy, at what prices and to whom to sell. The government decrees at what wages laborers should work and to whom and under what terms the capitalists should entrust their funds. Market exchange is a sham."—Ed.]

desire and foster such visiting and not restrict it under any circumstances. The notion that visitors from Graz, Budapest, and Laibach eat up some of our food supplies is completely without foundation. On the contrary, the food that is available for our consumption is brought in solely because we are visited by people who do business with us here in the city. It is village politics of the worst kind that we are pursuing and not by any means the policy of a great city.

It is also a well-known fact that the attempts at nationalization also have created a conflict of interests between the state and the provinces that threatens to endanger the former. But there are misconceived opinions circulating regarding the root and the essential nature of this conflict of interests. It is said that the provinces are influenced by the interests of the farm-owning peasants and, therefore, view nationalization differently than does the proletariat in the city. But in reality it has to be admitted that, in principle, there is no difference between these two groups concerning their views about the question of nationalization. The farmers know very well that at present it is out of the question that farm property will be nationalized, and they are not fearful that nationalization might include their own land. On the contrary, they hope that nationalization may result in the breaking up of the large landed estates or, at the very least, that it would expand their own woodlands.

But precisely the fact that the majority of the population is in favor of nationalization is a threat to the unity of the state. The idea behind those who favor nationalization is, of course, that they want to increase their own income through the distribution of the profits of the enterprises that are to be nationalized. But the greater the number of people participating in this distribution, the lower will be the per-capita dividend. Thus, it is quite understandable that when there is talk about the nationalization of the Alpine Mountain Company or the Veit Magnesite Plant, the Styrians[16] advocate that the nationalization be effected by the province, so that strangers would be excluded from sharing the dividends. The provinces present a common front as long as it is about taking nationalization out of the state's hands and turning it over to the provinces. But as soon as this fight ends in favor of the provinces, the inhabitants of the various political districts where the enterprises to be nationalized are located will enter the picture and demand that the nationalization be decided in favor of the district; then the

16 [Styria was the province southwest of Vienna and Lower Austria containing the city of Graz.—Ed.]

municipalities will come in and will want to undertake the nationalization themselves. And even before matters have gone this far, the workers of these enterprises will also appear on the scene, and they cannot imagine nationalization other than with themselves as the masters and sole beneficiaries of the enterprises. It shows that the notion of nationalization, when looked at in conjunction with the idea of an economic territory, will rapidly lead to syndicalism and the dissolution of all higher political associations.

There is another conflict between industry and the rural population. The nationalization problem in an exporting nation is exclusively an export-industry problem, especially when the national territory is so small and the inhabitants are so few that no industry can financially make do with only the domestic market. German-Austria is too small a market for any medium-sized factory to be able to generate sufficient revenues within its area, particularly in view of the specialization that is needed nowadays. This has been thoroughly misunderstood with regard to the nationalization projects that have been formulated up to now. In fact, nationalization in this country has not foundered because its opponents fought it, but because its most fervent supporters were not able to formulate the idea of an export business on a socialist basis. The socialists are at a loss when faced with the real problem of Austrian industry, i.e., to produce industrial goods that are to be sold in foreign markets. All they know is to nationalize production for the domestic market. This, however, signifies a constraint for the purchasers. If the shoe industry is placed on a socialist basis, this means that the rural consumer has to buy shoes from this particular enterprise, and this will produce a stormy opposition in the farm sector. Just as the farmer subscribes to the idea of free enterprise when selling his own products, he will also apply it when he is the buyer.

We all know that the theory of an economic territory teaches that the economic policy of the state binds together its various parts, so that possible centrifugal tendencies cannot take place. But the contrary point needs to be made, that economic interventions create conflicts of interest that threaten to break up the unity of the nation. Looked at from the purely economic point of view, the only valid aspect of the theory of an economic territory is the advantage if production and commerce are hampered as little as possible. The demand will be for free trade, and not at all a demand for a large protectionist customs area. If the theory of an economic territory paints a pretty picture of the benefits from large economic territories, it forgets to mention that what constitutes the largest economic territory is the entire populated part of the earth.

The defenders of the existing politico-economic system usually cite the Entente's prohibition on our *Anschluss* with Germany as the cause for the failure of their policy. They say that a nation without coal and food is preposterous; that a metropolis that contains one-third of the country's total population is not viable; and that after the fall of the Austro-Hungarian monarchy, there was left only one way to rescue Vienna, namely unification with Germany.

Furthermore, they say that the entry of German-Austria into the German Reich is a political matter of the utmost importance for the entire German nation. Only the union with Germany would really demonstrate that the period of Prussian autocracy in German history had finally come to an end. This would be the crowning piece in rebuilding the national German state and, therefore, the starting point for a calm and peaceable development of the situation in Germany.

The demand for a unified German state is a political and moral necessity, but not even the supporters of the theory of an economic territory can say that it is an economic necessity. Even in the context of the theory of an economic territory it cannot be argued that the German and Austrian economies would be mutually complementary. If we are short of food, the Germans in the Reich are not exactly well supplied with it either, nor can they supply us with the raw materials for which we are so urgently in need. Even today, nothing prevents us from supplying to the Germans in the Reich everything that we have and that they need, and to purchase everything from them that they can supply. As a matter of fact, the greater part of our coal and industrial-goods imports is of German origin. The fact that the Czechs can stop the coal trains that come from Silesia[17] would not be changed by any unification. Today we are also at liberty to buy coal from Germany, shipped via Passau,[18] and, as we found out again only a few days ago, the Germans of the Reich are willing to help us out with foodstuffs, in spite of the fact that unification has fallen through.

From the economic perspective, the idea of unification is actually

17 [Silesia was an area of Germany southeast of Berlin bordering on the Czech regions of Bohemia and Moravia. It was incorporated into Poland after the Second World War.—Ed.]

18 [Passau is an Austrian town on the German border northwest of the city of Linz.—Ed.]

being hindered rather than fostered by the way for which it has been argued. That for some time the idea was given a somewhat cooler reception in the German Reich can be attributed to the fact that, to a certain extent, we tried to construe it as meaning we had a justifiable claim to aid. In the present situation, the German Reich is not in a position to afford the luxury of being a member of a state that would have to support the other members. Even if we were to be part of a union with the German Reich, this would not solve our problem of resuming production. When it is pointed out that a part of German industry has already obtained raw materials and is working again, it also should be observed that we too could do exactly the same. That "opening in the West" that was forced on the Reich could easily be created by ourselves as well, if we would open our frontiers to imports. Nothing stops us from doing so except our own prejudices.

During the old Austro-Hungarian monarchy, the city of Vienna did not live on either aid or provincial tributes, but on the proceeds from its industrial and commercial activities. It is true that a certain amount of the income that Vienna formerly derived from today's new successor states will not be available in the future.[19] The city of Vienna will have to cover this deficit. On the other hand, however, let us not forget that right now — or at least during the critical transition period before the economy has adapted to the new circumstances — the city of Vienna is in an extremely favorable economic position, in fact it is in a boom. Vienna was never a major commercial center, but it has developed into one during the past year. Many large cities that formerly were Vienna's competitors are now out of the running. Moscow and Saint Petersburg are in ruins, and it will be a long time until Budapest recovers; Trieste and Fiume have suffered immensely due to the Italian annexation.[20] The tense political situation that exists between the various successor states does not allow direct trad-

19 [The "successor states" were the new or enlarged countries carved and created out of the old Austro-Hungarian empire following the First World War. They were a new Czechoslovakia and Yugoslavia, an independent Hungary, a reconstituted Poland, an enlarged Romania, and the new, smaller Austrian Republic. — Ed.]

20 [Trieste and Fiume are port cities on the Adriatic Sea that had been part of the Austro-Hungarian empire. At the end of the First World War, Italy annexed them. After the Second World War, the city of Fiume and its surrounding area were incorporated into Yugoslavia; it is now a part of Croatia under the name of Rijeka. — Ed.]

ing between them. More than ever, the industry of the Sudetenland and the consumers in the east, southeast, and northeast depend on Vienna as their transfer and intermediate trading place. More than ever, today's Vienna is the place where East and West meet. All that is needed is the ability to offer Vienna ample substitution for the losses it sustained when a number of owners of large estates and enterprises departed for the successor states. The daily occurrences that hamper and impede this development must be stopped.

Nothing could be farther from the truth than trying to explain our country's present economic conditions by referring to the war and its consequences. The war has brought terrible misery and those who instigated it should be made responsible for it. The war has impoverished us terribly, and perhaps it may take centuries to overcome its effects. But none of this is an excuse for the policy we pursue today. He who today holds the war responsible for all the damage done to our economic activities, who excuses everything as being a consequence of the war that just has to be accepted, is a person who shows that he has no understanding of what is required at the present time. The motto "there is nothing to be done" is probably the worst maxim in politics. It is the last fallback position, nowadays, of a system that only leads to decline. All around us we see the new possibilities for a recovery of our industry and commerce. One should encourage the population to adapt to these new circumstances, instead of telling them time and again: "You are unable to cope with life anyhow, you will die."

Vienna and the German-Austrian Alpine provinces suffered the same political fate during many centuries. Since for some time to come, hopefully only a short one, they will not be allowed to join the German Reich, they could still create a state in which a strong consciousness of statehood might soon develop. That such a state consciousness is absent, and that the state has hardly been created when it is already plagued by severe crises, can be attributed to the attempt to treat it as a separate economic territory. In principle, such experiments are not entirely hopeless; they always succeed where they are supported by a strong political and military power. This is believed by all who today continue to call for a strong hand, and who do not care if this strong hand belongs to a Hungarian or Italian, to an American or a Frenchman, just as long as it is a hand that is strong and generous. The advocates of the system of a controlled economy and socialism really just want an authority that comes from the outside. The state authority is unable to achieve this on its own. But a foreign state authority that is supported only by foreign sources of power is incompatible with the character of a democratic state. In fact, a controlled economy and socialism are incompatible with democracy. That we did not realize this can only be attributed to the fact that the peculiar political configuration in Germany, France, Austria-Hungary, and Russia enabled for some time the development of a party that was allowed to call itself both socialist and democratic at the same time. From the moment that this party came to power, it had to become apparent that democracy and socialism are incompatible and that the term Social Democrat contains an inner contradiction. Of necessity, democracy requires free trade.

All those conflicts of interest that exist today between Vienna and the provinces would disappear with free trade. There would be no conflict, no conflict over the seizure of grain, the supply of foodstuffs, entry visas, nationalization questions, compensations, and similar matters. As soon as we get rid of the idea that a city can obtain its foodstuffs by means other than commerce and industry, as soon as we understand once again that we have to produce and sell, then foreign countries will perceive us in a completely different light. The weakness of our political position, domestically as well as abroad, lies in the fact that we appear on the market as petitioners and not as purchasers and sellers. People say that nowadays we do not have any foreign currency. The reason for this is because we neither produce nor export anything. If we do not have enough capital to operate our industries without having to recur to means other than our own, then we have to borrow abroad. But, surely, that has to be considered an entrepreneur's production loan, not a consumption credit for the state. But the so-called foreign credits for food from abroad that we have been using are plain consumption credits. And sooner or later they will dry up. At some point the foreigners will get tired of lending to support our economic system.

It is common practice to defend the existing system against all politico-economic objections by saying that free trade is impossible under the present extraordinary circumstances. It is pointed out that even the successor states cut us off, and the considered opinion is that they should start to lift the regulations that impede commerce. People who voice this opinion overlook that the successor states are intent on trying to damage our commerce out of blind chauvinism, even in situations where they hurt their own commercial interests. Not in order to do them a favor but for our own good, we have to try to reinstall free trade as much as possible. It remains to be seen if our example will induce them to lift their restrictions as well. I would like to add that the Czechs are dependent to a much larger extent on Germany and Austria for transshipments of their goods than we need any transshipping through Czech territory. Should the successor states persist in their system of hampering trade, this would only strengthen Vienna's position as a free commercial city and transshipment center. We can't expect anything from the good will of the Czechs, South-Slovenians, and Hungarians, but only from their own self-interest. They will open up trade with us as soon as they can buy and sell here.

What we lack are not foodstuffs and raw materials, but the spirit that has to pervade a nonagrarian population if it wants to survive, and that is the modern, capitalist spirit of profit-making commerce. The people who live in our cities today are citizens of a modern city only in name. Because of their way of thinking and feeling they are much closer to the inhabitants of a medieval castle hamlet or a prince's residence in the seventeenth century than to modern man. An industrial state can survive without coal, but not without the spirit of a modern economy.

For us, the city inhabitants of this state, there is no other way out than to try to succeed through commerce and industrial operations. At present, we survive by selling the last remnants of our former affluence. We sell our capital instead of working with it. We live on borrowed food and forget that some day we will have to pay for it. The system that is prevalent among us today does not live on the fruits of its own work; it lives off the riches that were accumulated during the times of a freer economy. Every day brings this system nearer to its downfall, and it is only a question of time about when the catastrophe will occur. It is a given that it has to occur, if the system is not changed in time.

All these processes lose their transparency because of the effects of inflation. The depreciation of our currency gives us the false image of a somewhat bearable situation while in fact we are going under. While the shares of our enterprises, paid for in sound money, fall day after day, their prices expressed in crowns go up, so that the apparent picture of the stock market still fakes a bullish movement whereas in reality all prices are falling. A year ago, the shares of the Alpine Mountain Company stood at 900 crowns, and today they are at 3,000 crowns. But a year ago, 900 crowns were still worth about 360 Swiss francs, whereas today 3000 crowns are barely worth 120 Swiss francs. This is what the fabulous, bullish stock market really looks like. The person who owns shares believes that he becomes richer by the day. The person who sells old furniture and receives a price many times over what he paid for it at the time believes that he has made a profit that he can spend without qualms. In reality all this glitter is a result of the monetary printing press being cranked up. But even the monetary printing press will have to fail some day. It is impossible to picture the disaster that will befall us when the crown's day of reckoning arrives.

Since we cannot successfully fall back on anything else, we appeal to the good hearts of our fellow citizens in the provinces. They may take pity on us in our misery and desperate straits and send us food so that we do not starve to death. But we are just as unsuccessful in appealing to their kindness as we were with decrees demanding forced delivery. People simply do not believe that we are in dire straits since all they continuously hear is talk about war profits. It should not surprise us that they do not understand how things are interconnected, that they are unable to see how the inflation is covering up the real economic situation, since we who are much more affected by it accept the most flagrant deceptions. Out in the provinces they really believe everything that the daily papers say about war profits and war profiteers, about the stock market boom and increasing wealth.

In the long run, a state cannot be built on the charitable spirit of the public. The national community may be based on the forced subjugation of one group by the other, or on a free union because parties recognize their mutually beneficial common interests. If we approach the provinces as petitioners then we should not be surprised when we are treated as one treats bothersome beggars.

It is obvious that the malady that we are suffering from is of a type that makes it seem hopeless to try to cure it with constitutional and similar reforms. It does not matter if one introduces centralism more energetically on paper as an austere transition or if one gives greater rein to provincial autonomy, or if one integrates workers' councils in the constitution or lets them carry on –without any legal basis—as a "permanent revolution." All these are unimportant matters compared to that great fundamental problem of our economic policy. Measured against this huge problem, it even seems quite unimportant if the unification with Germany will become a reality, or if we set up a Danube federation, or if we stay independent, or if we prefer the monarchical or republican form of government, and it is completely uninteresting if the left-wing or right-wing Social Democrats or the Christian Socialists or the German Nationalists are in power. Because there are much greater things at risk than political problems: naked existence is in doubt.[21]

The problem of Vienna's and Lower Austria's political and constitutional relations with the provinces represents only a small part of the problems confronting us, and all these problems lead up to one big question: Will we be able at all to create an economic foundation for ourselves? If

21 [Throughout 1919 and into 1920, Vienna was facing near-starvation for a sizable portion of its population. During this period it was heavily dependent upon private charity and aid from the governments of the Allied powers. See Friedrich von Wieser, "The Fight Against the Famine in Austria," in Lord Parmoor, et al., *The Famine in Europe: The Facts and Suggested Remedies* (London: The Swarthmore Press, 1920), pp. 49–50 & 52–53:

> Milk can only be supplied to babies and invalids. In peace time the daily consumption in Vienna amounted to between 800,000 and 900,000 liters. Now, barely 70,000 liters are available, because Hungary and Czechoslovakia have completely stopped their milk supply to Vienna, and milk production in the Austrian provinces are much reduced. In Vienna today no milk can be given to children over two years of age. Children up to one year receive one liter a day, and those between one and two years receive three-quarters of a liter. We need not dwell on the horrible effects on child mortality.... The nourishment of the population is extremely inadequate, the state of public health very low, and death claims many victims. The number of crimes committed in this extremity, and the number of suicides is extraordinarily high.... The coal shortage and the transport difficulty connected therewith are so severe that we fear we may not be able to forward in time, to the consumer, even the foodstuffs which can be procured. The railroads have no stocks of coal, and when the lines will be blocked by the winter snow, traffic will have to cease everywhere.... Shortage of coal and the transport crisis hamper our industrial production. Even the farmer has to wait for the coal which he needs to thresh his harvest. In the towns, especially Vienna, the supply of gas and electric light is reduced to a minimum, and we fear from day to day that it may have to be stopped altogether. For the two million inhabitants of Vienna, there is at present [autumn of 1919] only enough coal to cover the most urgent kitchen requirements. Till now no supplies are available for the heating of rooms.... Deprived of millions of her own race, who have been assigned as subjects to alien national States; cut off from her industrial undertakings, which she had established and guided throughout the former empire; without food for more than half her inhabitants, almost without coal, without raw materials from abroad—with her railways and workshops worn out, bowed down under the burdens of the War and under those of the Peace Treaty—we [Austrians] must indeed doubt whether she [Austria] will be capable of surviving when once the time has come when she may use her powers in peaceful and free competition.

In the same volume, see especially the contributions by Friedrich Hertz, "What the Famine Means in Austria," pp. 17–26; and by Dr. Ellenbogen, "The Plight of German Austria," pp. 39–48. See also David F. Strong, *Austria (October 1918–March 1919: Transition from Empire to Republic* (New York: Octagon Books, [1939] 1974), pp. 241–73.—Ed.]

this can be accomplished, if we start working again, then we will have a future. Maybe we will not have riches, but at least some degree of prosperity and the possibility to earn enough to satisfy our needs. Then also, it will be easy to solve satisfactorily the issue of our relations with foreigners and our relationship with the Germans in the Reich and with the provinces. But if this cannot be accomplished, then our cities will decline. We will become a country of peasants, the same as Russia and Hungary perhaps will become after their great social struggles. Our cities will go under, the population of our cities will sink deeper and deeper into poverty, and Vienna will become deserted. It is entirely up to us which of the two roads we choose. But should we go under, we will not have perished due to a lack of coal and food, but because we lacked the spirit that builds cities and makes them flourish: the bourgeois spirit.

CHAPTER 10

Viennese Industry and the Tax on Luxury Goods[1]

The basic idea underlying the luxury sales-tax laws that have been introduced in various countries during the last few years is that this tax is passed on to consumers, so that the ones who consume luxury goods are the ones who are taxed. We shall not discuss the extent to which this condition is actually met. In Austria and especially in Vienna, at least, things are completely different.

Among the industrial sectors in Austria, the production of finished items classified as "luxury goods" occupies a prominent place.[2] It may be

---

1 [This article originally appeared in German in the *Neues 8 Uhr Blatt*, No. 1987 (May 13, 1921).—Ed.]

2 [In 1920 and 1921, following the establishment of the city of Vienna as having the constitutional status of a separate "province," the Social Democrats who controlled a large majority in the city council proceeded to undertake a vast program of social-welfare legislation. To cover the costs of this program the socialist city government introduced a series of taxes meant to "soak the rich." Among them were eighteen categories of "luxury" taxes, including entertainment levies that placed a 10 percent tax on operas, theaters, and concerts and a 40 percent tax on movie-theater tickets, which was meant to induce the "working class" to listen to classical music rather than watch Hollywood films. The tax for attending horse races or boxing matches was 50 percent, under the presumption that these were the spectator sports of the wealthy and the comfortable middle class. There was a 33 percent tax on any person giving a luncheon or dinner party, or if music was played at a funeral, again under the assumption that only the rich had such parties or could afford to have musicians play at a funeral service. There were heavy taxes on "luxury" apartments and automobiles, as well as on horses used for riding or for drawing a carriage. There was a tax on the employment of more than one servant in a household, with the rate set at 50 schillings a year for the second servant, if female, 300 schillings for the third, and an extra 250 schillings per year for each additional servant after that. There were steep taxes for food and drink served to patrons in bars, cabarets, variety clubs, concert cafes and concert restaurants, *"Heurigen und Buschenschenken"* (popular taverns and inns in the suburbs of Vienna), and liquor and breakfast houses; the tax rates on these establishments were set anywhere between

said without exaggeration that Vienna's industrial importance is predominantly based on the production of such goods. The Viennese retail sector largely markets them to the final consumer. Foreigners visiting Vienna only briefly for shopping purposes buy the lion's share of all luxury goods. Without the extraordinary services provided by the retail businesses in Vienna, the Viennese luxury industry would not be able to market its own products and would deteriorate.

Over the past years, complaints have been made that industrial production in Vienna is too concentrated on luxury goods. It has been claimed that, instead, our industry should produce inexpensive consumer goods for the masses. Those romantics who lack any economic understanding and who advance such arguments against Viennese industry fail to appreciate that our urban population can only be fed nowadays if we export final products. Among our finished products, however, it is predominantly luxury goods that are exportable. In spite of all the impediments created by economic policy, our entrepreneurs have succeeded in developing and keeping competitive a flourishing industrial sector. Let us hope that they will be equally successful in producing inexpensive products for mass consumption at quality levels that already characterize our other products, and which have established the excellent reputation of Viennese goods throughout the world. However, for as long as we have not yet succeeded in overcoming the extraordinary difficulties that stand in the way of developing mass production in Austria, it would be downright frivolous if we were wantonly to destroy our luxury industry for the sole purpose of pleasing some doctrinaire fanatics.

Any Austrian luxury tax primarily would put a burden on export goods and thus considerably impede our industrial marketing efforts. If the tax on luxury goods is seen as an indirect tax aimed at consumers, then one must try not to impose it also on foreigners. After all, foreigners can escape the tax by simply withdrawing their orders from Austrian producers. Luxury consumption is particularly sensitive to price. All laws introducing indirect taxes therefore exclude exports from the tax base. Article 2 of the Ger-

---

2 and 15 percent at the discretion of the tax officials, depending on how they classified the income categories of the clientele in each one. The tax on luxury goods imposed by the city of Vienna, which is the focus of Mises's article, was abandoned in April 1923, when the federal government of Austria put into effect a general "turnover tax" of one percent that was raised to 2 percent in 1924. Through most of the remainder of the 1920s, it provided approximately one-third of the total that was raised in joint taxes that were divided among the provinces, cities, and towns. — Ed.]

man Sales Tax Law of December 24, 1919, provides for the exclusion of export sales.

The bill on a Vienna luxury tax prepared by the Viennese city administration not only fails to contain such a provision, it even makes taxable shipments to communities outside Vienna. It is not sufficient if the tax on Austrian and especially on Viennese luxury goods only exempts those that are shipped and sold abroad. To avoid dealing a deadly blow to luxury sales by retailers selling directly to foreign tourists, the law would have to provide for the exemption of all sales to persons with legal residence outside of the Republic of Austria. It may be freely admitted that the technical implementation of such provision would be impossible. But then the whole idea of a tax on Viennese luxury goods is simply unfeasible. If one does not want to take the bread out of the mouths of the merchants, retail employees, and workers who make their living from the production and marketing of luxury goods, then such a luxury tax must not be imposed in Vienna.

One of the arguments advanced in favor of the tax on luxury goods is that similar taxes already have been introduced in the German Reich and in Czechoslovakia, as well as in other countries. But in Germany, where production of luxury goods holds a comparatively minor role in industry, direct sales to tourists play a secondary place in the economy. The previously mentioned passage in the German law is sufficient not to curb the German export trade. As explained already, the situation in Vienna is totally different. Its importance as a city of trade results from its location on the border and its having retained the status of the commercial center of a region that since 1918 has disintegrated into several independent states. And as concerns the luxury sales tax of Czechoslovakia, we must note that Czechoslovak industry by and large does not produce luxury products; its consumption of luxury items is centered on imported goods that are mainly of Austrian origin. The Czech luxury tax is a link in the chain of numerous economic measures the Czech government has taken against Austrian industry, and particularly against the position of Vienna as a city of industry and commerce.

There should be no confidence in the assumption that luxury consumption could easily accommodate a price hike of 15 percent. It is not required for Czechoslovaks, Hungarians, or Poles to order their clothes and furniture in Vienna or to buy their jewelry and furs in Viennese stores. They can shop around with the competition. The economic policy of the new successor states will be very intent on using this felicitous moment for supporting their own industrial production over that of the Viennese market.

CHAPTER 11

A Serious Decline in the Value of the Currency[1]

The constant decline for several months now in the value of the currencies of those European countries that took part in the war continued to an aggravated degree yesterday and today. In Zurich the Austrian crown is still quoted at only 1.60 Swiss francs, the German mark and the Czech crown at 5.50, the pound at 19.55, the French franc at 42.75, and the lire at 37. These are rates of exchange that only a year ago would have seemed incredible. For those who understand the deeper reasons for these declines, the new fall in the rates of exchange, of course, comes as no surprise. As long as an inflationary policy is followed, the rates of exchange will keep falling lower and lower until they finally reach that point beyond which there is no room left to go, the zero point. History offers many examples of such a complete collapse of a currency. The best-known are the collapse of the so-called "Continental Notes" of the North American states in 1781[2] and of the French *assignats* and *mandats territoriaux* in 1796.[3] If

1 [This article was originally published in German in *Neue Freie Presse*, No. 19907 (January 28, 1920).—Ed.]

2 [Continental notes were issued by the Continental Congress during the American Revolution to finance the expenses of the war against Great Britain. Their issuance resulted in a high inflation throughout the thirteen colonies. After the revolution, they were partially redeemed, but at far below face value. See J. Laurence Laughlin, *A New Exposition of Money, Credit and Prices*, Vol. II (Chicago: University of Chicago Press, 1931), pp. 147–67.—Ed.]

3 [*Assignats* were the paper money issued by the Revolutionary government of France between March 1790 and December 1795, during which time they generated an extremely destructive inflation, resulting in the imposition of price and wage controls. The *mandats territoriaux* were the new currency issued in place of the *assignats*, but they also were soon increased in such quantities that another inflationary process was set in motion. See Richard M. Ebeling, "Inflation and Controls in Revolutionary France: The Political Econ-

the European nations do not soon change their policy, they will experience a similar catastrophe. Certainly the effects of such a catastrophe would be far more severely felt today than they were in the United States of 1781 or in the France of 1796, when both countries were predominantly agrarian. The consequences from such collapse would necessarily produce completely different effects in an industrial nation than in a country whose population still widely operates on the basis of barter transactions.

The sharp decline in the exchange rate of the mark is especially worthy of attention. At the moment, the mark no longer stands higher than the Czech crown. The negative expectations in neutral countries concerning the value of the mark can be attributed as much to fears about future inflationary tendencies as to the degree to which inflation has already occurred. For a decade and a half, an inflationist theory has been successfully spread throughout Germany. The writings of Georg Knapp[4] and Friedrich Bendixen[5] have found enthusiastic supporters, and it is reasonable to say that their viewpoints on monetary theory are the dominant ones today, shared by all the leading political experts. Recently, Bendixen zealously proposed that Germany's entire war debt should be redeemed through issuing an additional 100 billion marks. His proposal aroused very little opposition in Germany, while it has been met with the greatest unease in other countries. The sharp decline in the mark's rate of exchange can be attributed primarily to the floating of this idea.

During the war, billions of German mark notes were speculatively purchased in the neutral countries. These marks were held on to, in spite of the unfavorable outcome for Germany in the war, because the speculators were confident that Germany would succeed in getting its monetary house back in order. But when they saw that the proposals of inflationists like Bendixen were not rejected by the German public, they became fearful that a further depreciation in the purchasing power of the mark would occur, and they tried to sell off their holdings of the currency as quickly as possible.

---

omy of the French Revolution," in Stephen J. Tonsor, ed., *Reflections on the French Revolution* (Washington, D. C.: Regnery Gateway, 1990), pp. 138–56.—Ed.]

4 [See Chapter 5, "On the Actions to Be Taken in the Face of Progressive Currency Depreciation," footnote 17.—Ed.]

5 [See Chapter 5, footnote 18; also Gerald D. Feldman, *The Great Disorder: Politics, Economics and Society in the German Inflation, 1914–1924* (Oxford: Oxford University Press, 1997), p. 152.—Ed.]

The report issued two weeks ago by the German Currency Commission, which is composed mostly of a number of prominent businessmen, clearly shows that leading circles in Germany do not clearly understand that the cause of the currency's depreciation is to be found in the inflation of the money supply. The commission proposed administrative measures, such as restrictions on foreign trade and a toughening of the foreign-exchange regulations, to counter the depreciation of the currency. For those who understand the real situation, this report had an unfavorable effect both in Germany and abroad.

In addition, there are the negative effects resulting from German fiscal policy. The tax on iron-ore mining is especially severe and extreme. If it were enforced to the letter of the law it would mean nothing less than the destruction of German industry and commercial activity. Germany lives off the export of industrial products. But industrial production will be completely paralyzed by the iron-ore mining tax; the importation of capital from abroad, which German industry urgently needs today, will be interrupted.

This fiscal policy demonstrates an unwillingness to accept the fact that Germany's unfavorable financial situation can only be turned around through a complete change in German economic policy. Reestablishing a balanced budget is impossible for as long as the German government is responsible for deficits in the billions of marks, so that a part of the work force may continue to be employed in unprofitable and inefficient public undertakings, including highway construction, military facilities, etc.[6]

The most urgent fiscal problem at the present time concerns the need to sell off German public enterprises. But denationalization and demunicipalization of enterprises are roundly unpopular today. In addition, there is the dangerous threat of a domestic revolution. On the one hand, the widely proclaimed Bolshevik military offensive threatens Germany from the east, an offensive that Poland seems hardly able to resist.[7] On the other hand, the future of Germany's economy is threatened by the count-

6 [For the fiscal year of 1920, during which Mises wrote this article, the German government's expenditures were 9.7 billion (gold) marks and tax revenues were 3.5 billion (gold) marks, with a resulting budget deficit of 6.2 billion (gold) marks, representing a deficit that was equal to 64 percent of government expenditures.—Ed.]

7 [From 1919 to 1921, a war was fought between the new Poland and the Bolshevik government in Russia. At first, the Poles advanced far into the Ukraine, capturing the capital of Kiev. The Red Army counterattacked, forcing the Poles back to the gates of Warsaw. The Poles mounted a new offense, and had driven the Red Army far back into Ukrainian and Belorussian territory by the time a peace treaty was signed.—Ed.]

less demands that the Entente[8] is making, especially France in her blind desire for revenge.

If the German people see no prospect for themselves other than to be working for decades as the slaves of France, then it is not surprising that a mood has spread among a growing number of people that strongly encourages the advancement of Bolshevism. A Bolshevik Germany would, however, mean not only the destruction of Germany itself; it would also harbor the greatest dangers for the rest of Europe. It is very doubtful whether France and Belgium would be able to keep Bolshevism from crossing their borders, once it will have taken hold in Germany. And it is certain that Italy and Czechoslovakia would succumb to a German Bolshevism.

England and France are going to have to realize that Europe's problems cannot be solved in as easy a manner as their representatives imagined when they negotiated the Treaties of Versailles[9] and Saint-Germain.[10] Germany cannot be brought to destruction without dragging all of Europe into ruin along with it. A revision of the Treaties of Versailles and Saint-Germain seems imperative, not only in the interest of Germany but equally in the interest of the rest of Europe, indeed, in the interest of Western civilization in general.

The events on the foreign-exchange market represent a serious warn-

8 [The Entente was the term for the Allied powers in the First World War. Originally, Great Britain, France, and imperial Russia were the major Allies. In 1915, Italy entered the war on the Allied side. In April 1917, the United States declared war on imperial Germany and joined the Allies. In March 1918, the new Bolshevik government in Russia signed a separate peace with Germany and formally withdrew Russia from the Allied side. — Ed.]

9 [The Treaty of Versailles was signed in May of 1919, ending the First World War. It imposed heavy reparations payments on Germany, to be paid to the Allied powers; limited the size of the German armed forces; restored Alsace-Lorraine to France; transferred Prussian Poland, most of West Prussia, and part of Silesia to the new state of Poland; made Danzig a free city; transferred Germany's African and Asian colonies into mandates of the League of Nations; placed the Saarland under French administration; called for plebiscites in various territories formerly controlled by Germany and Austria-Hungary; and required the demilitarization of the German Rhineland. In 1935, Hitler unilaterally abrogated most of the terms of the Treaty of Versailles. — Ed.]

10 [The Treaty of Saint-Germain was signed by Austria and the Allied powers in 1919. It ended the state of war between them and formally dissolved the territory of the former Austro-Hungarian empire into a new, small Republic of Austria, the independent states of Hungary and Czechoslovakia, an enlarged Romania, a re-created Poland, and a Serb-dominated Yugoslavia. — Ed.]

ing for Austrian economic policy. It is true that we are not the only country whose money is constantly declining in value, and that the currency problem that afflicts us today is a European-wide problem and not one that is specifically Austrian. But at the present we are the ones who stand nearest to the abyss, and therefore we cannot wait until the general problems of Europe are solved. Otherwise, it might very well happen that help reaches us when it is already too late. The first step toward alleviating the present conditions is recognizing that the evil has its origin only and exclusively in inflation. Stopping inflation, however, demands a complete turnaround in our economic policy. An economic system cannot maintain itself for long when it does nothing but consume the capital that the free economy has accumulated over several decades.

CHAPTER 12

The Abolition of
Money in Russia[1]

According to a report from Copenhagen, the Soviet government has abolished money. In the future, payments are no longer to be made in rubles but in requisition vouchers that the state distribution facilities must honor. If the requisition vouchers are not used within two months, they expire; this is to prevent them from being kept in circulation as a kind of money. It is not clear whether these requisition vouchers are to be denominated in money or in specified quantity of goods. In the former case it would be nothing more than the issuance of a new kind of paper money. All governments that have fought against the depreciation of their own money have tried to prevent a complete loss in its value by issuing a new kind of money, which they try in some way to keep in circulation. When the *assignats* were not accepted for very long during the French Revolution they were replaced with the *mandats territoriaux*.[2] Similarly, the United States undertook the issuance of a new money of "new tenor" in 1780 when the "Continental notes" had completely failed.[3] Only if the new Russian requisition vouchers are redeemable in goods instead of money would it represent a new experiment.

From the sparse reports it cannot be judged what really was decreed in Russia. The official Russian version that is offered is as rose-colored as the publications of the old czarist regime used to be; and the few foreigners who are permitted entrance into Russia are only shown Potemkin vil-

1 [This article originally was published in German in the *Neue Freie Presse*, No. 20195, on November 17, 1920, in a column called "The Economist." — Ed.]

2 [See Chapter 11, "A Serious Decline in the Value of the Currency," footnote 3. — Ed.]

3 [See Chapter 11, footnote 2. — Ed.]

lages and Potemkin factories.[4] On the other hand, the descriptions given by the opponents of the Bolsheviks are not based on a clear picture of the situation, either. For any impartial observer, there can be no doubt that Bolshevism can only lead to the complete destruction of the Russian economy, that it can only bring distress and misery, and that it has already done so. But there can be a lot of deception during the time that it takes for all of these effects fully to come to light. The Bolsheviks are following the same policy that the Jacobins once pursued.[5] The Jacobin system lasted longer than many people had predicted. The economic reserves that a rich and powerful nation has accumulated over the years can be so great that even the worst policy requires a certain amount of time before the country's wealth can be wholly and completely squandered away.

In the socialist commonwealth, in which the ownership of all the means of production belongs exclusively to the state, there can be only a very restricted area in which money circulates. In such a community the means of production stand outside the arena of exchange. They are, as the jurists say, *res extra commercium*. Since the means of production can be neither bought nor sold for money, prices for them cannot be formed on the market. Consumer goods are allotted to the individual comrades of the socialist commonwealth by the state. With these allotments money cannot come into use. Only insofar as the exchange of luxury goods between comrades is permitted and actually occurs can a generally accepted medium of exchange—money—come into use. After all, it is possible to imagine that in a socialist commonwealth even the bartering of luxury goods is completely forbidden. In this case there would be no money at all.

Up until now the Soviet regime has, in fact, not battled against the institution of money on such a broad basis. It has only attempted to partially bring its socialist program into existence. The efforts to socialize agriculture, the primary branch of production in Russia, broke down in the first

---

4 [The expression "Potemkin villages" dates from the time of the Russian empress, Catherine II (1729–96), and is named after Catherine's advisor and lover who would arrange for artificial structures to be constructed along routes that Catherine would take around Russia to give the false impression of prosperity and progress. — Ed.]

5 [The Jacobins were a radical political group during the French Revolution. Known for their extreme egalitarianism, they actively participated in the Reign of Terror after the establishment of the revolutionary dictatorship in 1793. They were called the Jacobins because they frequently met in a former Dominican convent in Paris, where the Dominicans were known as Jacobins. — Ed.]

weeks of the Soviet regime. Land was not socialized but distributed to the proletarian sectors of the rural population. Industrial enterprises were nationalized, that is to say, socialized. But the socialization of industrial enterprises also seems not to have been carried out completely. In many cases they were not actually transferred to the ownership of the state but, instead, to the ownership of the workers of the company. Out of socialization there has developed an unexpected syndicalism. Commerce and trade also could not be completely suppressed. In Russia buying and selling still takes place, and even the government participates as a buyer and seller.[6] In order to make its purchases, the government has printed money without restraint, bringing the foreign-exchange rate for the Soviet ruble to a low that is not very far from the last exchange rates that were recorded for the *assignats* during the French Revolution.[7]

Since the farmers refuse to willingly deliver anything for these rubles, agricultural goods and raw materials are requisitioned in the countryside. The Russian rulers may justify their policy of an unrestrained expansion of the supply of rubles as a means gradually to undermine the institution of money; but this is an *ex post* and contrived rationale for a policy they have been driven to by the force of circumstances. Inflation is in truth the *ultima ratio* of all authoritarian governments that wish to suppress economic freedom.

If the Soviet regime is now undertaking to abolish money, it is probably due to some such force of circumstance. The Soviets, no doubt, are issuing a new kind of requisition certificate as a means to resist the dramatically higher prices that are being demanded by producers in Russia. They, perhaps, hope that the requisition of goods will proceed more smoothly if it is done through the new requisition voucher, instead of the rubles that are rejected by the farmers. It remains to be seen whether this attempt to stimulate the farmers to increase their production and the delivery of their output will have better success than the previous attempts

6 [On Soviet economic policy and practice during this period, known as War Communism, see Silvana Malle, *The Economic Organization of War Communism, 1918–1921* (Cambridge: Cambridge University Press, 1985).—Ed.]

7 [Between the beginning of 1918 and the middle of 1920, shortly before Mises wrote this article, the foreign-exchange rate of the ruble had fallen in terms of the British pound from 45 rubles to 10,000 rubles. On Soviet inflationary policies during this period, see S. S. Katzenellenbaum, *Russian Currency and Banking, 1914–1924* (London: P. S. King, 1925). —Ed.]

that have all failed. The fate of the new vouchers will depend on whether the government is able to honor them promptly. They will rise or fall with the greater or lesser chance of their being honored.

Of course, even a temporary success cannot prevent the final collapse of the Bolshevik system. If this attempt at first succeeds, it will be a success based on the use of the soldiers and executioners of the Soviet Republic. Such successes always only last for a short time. The problem that the Soviet regime faces in carrying out a full socialization of the Russian economy is much deeper and far more difficult to solve than the majority of its followers and friends realize, among whom there are not only criminals but also many noble and sincere idealists.[8] The question is whether it is at all possible to carry on economic calculation in a purely socialist commonwealth. Economic calculation requires the ability to reduce the value of goods and resources to a common denominator. This is only possible if not only consumer goods but also the means of production are bought and sold, and exchange is facilitated through the use of money. Economic calculation is not possible if money prices for the means of production cannot be generated on the market. And without economic calculation there is no economic rationality. Statistics cannot help to overcome these difficulties because, like trying to calculate in kind, they do not provide the possibility for expressing revenues and expenditures in terms of a common denominator. Trying to calculate in terms of hours of work performed also does not solve this problem because it ignores the use of natural resources that enter production and offers no method for reducing the different qualities of work performed to any "simple labor" standard.

All of these problems were acknowledged by Vladimir Lenin, the leader of the Soviet republic, when soon after he came to power he declared that the first task of Soviet power was to carry out an inventory of the accounts of enterprises and to assume control over socialized companies by enlisting the use of the "bourgeois experts." But "bourgeois bookkeeping" either calculates in terms of money, or it does not calculate at all.

This is the primary and fundamental problem confronting the social-

8 [On the pronouncements by the Bolsheviks on abolishing money and the effects of this abolition in the first years after their coming to power in Russia, see L. N. Yurovsky, *Currency Problems & Policy of the Soviet Union* (London: Leonard Parsons, 1925), pp. 20–37; and Arthur Z. Arnold, *Bank, Credit, and Money in Soviet Russia* (New York: Columbia University Press, 1937), pp. 72–110.—Ed.]

ist commonwealth. Several generations of socialist writers have not succeeded in theoretically solving it. Quite to the contrary. It can be said that scientific economics has provided the proof that there simply cannot be a socialist solution to this problem.[9] The Soviet experiment will also fail to solve this problem in any manner that will be favorable to socialism. Violence and compulsion can achieve nothing.

9 [The present article appeared the same year as the publication of Mises's famous essay, "Economic Calculation in the Socialist Commonwealth" [1920] in F. A. Hayek, ed., *Collectivist Economic Planning: Critical Studies on the Possibilities of Socialism* (London: Routledge & Sons, 1935), pp. 87–130; and in Israel M. Kirzner, ed., *Classics in Austrian Economics: A Sampling in the History of a Tradition*, Vol. III (London: William Pickering, 1994), pp. 3–30. Mises expanded his critical evaluation of the possibilities for socialism two years later in his 1922 treatise, *Socialism* (Indianapolis: Liberty Fund, [1951] 1981). He restated and refined his criticisms of the viability of a socialist-planned economy in *Human Action: A Treatise on Economics* (Irvington-on-Hudson, N.Y.: Foundation for Economic Education, 4th rev. ed., 1996), pp. 689–715. —Ed.]

CHAPTER 13

Inflation and the Shortage of Money: Stop the Printing Presses[1]

When businessmen talk of a shortage of money they mean a shortage of short-term capital on the loan market, when an increasing demand for loans is not met with an increase in the supply of loanable funds. A shortage of money results in an increase in the interest rate for short-term capital.

The belief that a shortage of money can be alleviated by an increase in the quantity of money in circulation is an ancient fallacy disposed of long ago by David Hume and Adam Smith. Since businessmen calculate the amount of their capital in terms of money, and since all demand for capital appears to be a demand for loanable funds on the market, it is not surprising that the reason for an increase in the interest rate appears to be a shortage of money. However, if the quantity of money is increased, it affects only the prices of goods and services; prices and wages go up. The interest rate is not reduced at all as a result. Quite the contrary!

If inflation is expected to continue, anyone who lends money recognizes that the amount of money that the debtor returns at the conclusion of the credit transaction will represent less purchasing power than the sum he originally lent. For instance, if someone should lend 100,000 Austrian crowns at a time when the U. S. dollar exchanges for 500 crowns, and is repaid when the dollar costs 5,000 crowns, he lends $200 and receives back only $20.[2] If he does not lend that sum, but uses it to buy stocks, com-

1 [This article originally appeared in German in the *Neue Freie Presse*, No. 20666 (March 11, 1922).—Ed.]

2 [Between January 1919 and March 1922, when Mises wrote this article, the exchange rate between the U.S. dollar and the Austrian crown went from one dollar trading for 17.09 crowns to one dollar trading for 7,487.5 crowns. The crown fell to its lowest level in August of 1922, when one dollar traded for 77,300 crowns.—Ed.]

modities, or even foreign exchange instead, he would do far better; he would lose less, or perhaps not lose anything at all. On the other hand, the debtor makes out very well. If he buys goods with the borrowed money and then sells them after a time, a surplus in crowns will be left over after the borrowed money is returned. In this way, the illusory profit that the inflation creates becomes for him a *real* profit. Thus it is easy to understand that so long as monetary depreciation is expected to continue, the money lender will demand higher interest and the borrower will be willing to pay that higher interest. The fact that in Austria in recent years previously unheard-of interest rates have been asked for and agreed to in the money-lending business is due primarily to the inflation. Should Austria succeed in creating a more dependable currency, the interest rate will significantly decline.

It is not surprising that we suffer from a shortage of money following every increase in the notes in circulation. A shortage of money prevails, not in spite of the inflation, but precisely because of the inflation.

One should not speak of a shortage of money or of an abundance of money in any other meaning than the one mentioned here. These expressions refer to the ratio between the supply of and demand for money, and not the supply and demand of funds available for loans. Changes in the ratio of the supply of money relative to the demand for money, for all economic purposes, bring about changes in its purchasing power. The utility of money rests entirely on its purchasing power. And since its purchasing power is always high enough to bring supply and demand into balance, the economy and its participants are always in a position to gain the greatest satisfaction possible from the use of money. Increasing the quantity of money will not make either the world or an isolated national economy any richer.

It is frequently observed that presently the notes in circulation in Austria are not increasing as rapidly as their value is depreciating. Attempts have been made to show that in terms of gold the value of the quantity of money that circulated in this country's geographical area in 1914 was greater than the value in gold of the money in circulation today. Objections can be raised to the method by which these calculations are made. For one thing, one should not only consider the supply of specie and notes and ignore the checking deposits at the banks that also serve as money. Nor is it proper to calculate the gold value of the quantity of money currently in circulation without noting that formerly the crown's purchasing power within the country was higher than its value in foreign exchange or bills of exchange. Moreover, it is wrong to assume *ceteris paribus* that we, who are much poorer than we were in 1914, still need the same quantity of money as we used before the war. At the very least it should be mentioned that foreign money is now satisfying a part of the demand for money within the country. The people, especially those living near the border areas, no longer hold Austrian notes, or at least they do not exclusively hold them; they also hold foreign money. And a certain portion of our business transactions also is now being conducted in foreign money.

Still, irrespective of the method by which these calculations are made, it is certainly true that monetary depreciation is now proceeding faster than new money is being created. Didn't business suffer from a shortage of notes for completing transactions during the critical final weeks of last year? How can that be explained? Shouldn't this shortage of money have brought about a tendency toward a rise in the value of our money, with an increase in the purchasing power of the monetary unit making this shortage disappear?

A speculative element is always present in the evaluation of money relative to goods and foreign money. That is, the anticipated future ratio is always taken into consideration. If it is assumed that the monetary depreciation will continue, because the government is unwilling to observe moderation in the demands it makes on the printing press, then the value of the monetary unit will be lower than if no further inflation were expected. Because monetary depreciation is expected to continue, the people try, by the purchase of commodities, bills of exchange, or foreign money to rid themselves as quickly as possible of their domestic money that is daily losing its purchasing power. The panic buying in the shops, where the buyers go in droves in the attempt to acquire anything tangible, anything at all, and the panic buying on the exchange, where the prices of securities and foreign exchange go up by leaps and bounds, race ahead of the actual situation. The future is anticipated and discounted in these prices. These prices indicate a greater depreciation of the Austrian crown than is actually warranted by the notes in circulation at the moment.

We must admit that at present there is a shortage of notes for day-to-day commerce. This shortage of notes, like the panic buying, is a phenomenon of the advanced state of inflation.

There is only one way to combat all these evils: stop the printing presses. If the issuing of notes is increased to alleviate the shortage of money available for daily cash transactions, this would only make conditions worse. This would not correct the ratio between the monetary depreciation and the quantity of money in circulation, as some believe. Rather, it would exaggerate it. The panic would continue and bring on the collapse of the monetary system.

No matter how one reasons back and forth over the arguments, there is no possible way to justify the further increase of the notes in circulation.

CHAPTER 14

The Return to the Gold Standard[1]

It is not insignificant that among the evils left behind by the events of the last decade has been the interruption of the exchange of ideas between nations. Just as traveling is much more difficult today than it was before the war, so it is also more difficult nowadays for ideas to pass from country to country. Believing that they have enough to do just taking care of their own day-to-day problems, at the present time people devote far less attention to what is happening beyond the borders of their own country. The intellectual unity that was shared between Europe and America before the war has been destroyed, and many years will be required to build it up again.

This intellectual isolation between peoples has also happened in the realm of economic ideas. It is understandable that people first turn their attention to the difficult economic problems that are posed by the day-to-day politics of their own country. But it is precisely in the arena of economic policy that such a narrowing of the intellectual horizon is especially harmful, and its damage must very soon come to light. No country can withdraw from involvement in world affairs; changes that take place in one country must sooner or later also have an effect in other nations. We in Europe cannot be indifferent to what happens in America, to what happens in the Far East or in Australia; and it is necessary for us, once again, to take more of an interest in the remoter parts of the world than we have

---

1 This article was first published in German in *Mitteilungen des Verbandes österreichischer Banken und Bankiers*, Vol. 1, No. 2 (1924). A greatly abridged and slightly reworded version of this article appeared under the title, "The Gold Standard," in *Neues Wiener Tagblatt*, No. 101 (April 12, 1925). — Ed.]

in recent years. If this is true for all economic questions in general, it is true to an even greater extent in reference to problems of monetary policy. There is no doubt that it is least possible to follow a policy of autarky and regional autonomy when it concerns matters surrounding monetary policy.

In the United States and Great Britain, problems in the field of monetary policy are being discussed that have so far aroused on the continent either no attention at all or certainly not the attention that reflects their importance. They involve questions that are of the greatest significance for all the countries of Europe, whether they like it or not. It is nothing less than the question of whether the gold standard, which was the foundation of the monetary system of the world before the war, should be retained or whether it should be replaced by a completely new monetary system that up to now has neither been put into practice in any country nor as of yet proven its practical usefulness.

In all the nations of Europe that took part in the war or that, without being directly involved in the war, participated in the financial problems related to the war, the monetary policy of the last few years has been a policy of inflation. Among the system of ideas that resulted in the nations of Europe being drawn into a war ten years ago was the notion that there was no particular danger from the state putting the printing presses in motion to provide the required financial resources for the pursuit of its goals. Among the proponents of a policy of inflation, there was a spectrum of views concerning its likely consequences. In their writings and speeches, some of them seriously argued that the monetary depreciation that necessarily results from a policy of inflation was beneficial to the whole country.

Others were more cautious and only recommended an inflationary policy as a necessary evil, rather than as something positive in itself. They said that if the state had a choice between acquiring the resources it needed through either taxation, borrowing the funds, or issuing new bank notes, the latter was the least oppressive. The losses that one part of the population suffered through the rise in prices could be considered as a sort of tax, and it was not inappropriate to prefer inflation to the other ways of providing the money needed by government.[2]

---

2 [For Mises's analysis of the effects resulting from these different methods for financing a government's war expenditures, see Ludwig von Mises, *Nation, State and Economy* (New York: New York University Press, [1919] 1983), pp. 151–71.—Ed.]

It is unnecessary today to waste many words on these inflationist theories. The results of inflation have shown them to be absurd. The most powerful objection that the calm reflection of the theoretician could raise against such an inflationary policy was precisely that it would inevitably lead in the end to a collapse of the monetary system. It really was not necessary for some of the nations in Europe to take inflation to the extreme to furnish proof once more that such a policy must finally end in a collapse.[3]

Long ago, economic theory had already clearly proven all of this, and history has provided a whole series of outstanding examples confirming the validity of these theoretical deductions. The old saying that the only thing that is learned from history is that people learn nothing from history has been confirmed once again; and it must be sadly added to this that it seems that people also learn nothing from theory.

After various nations had suffered from and learned of the harmful effects that result from a continuous increase in the quantity of money from their own bad experiences, when they realized that the boom in business that accompanies inflation is only an illusion of prosperity that is followed by a process of decay, they then fell into the opposite error of believing that an increase in the value of the monetary unit could be beneficial. To the layman it must have seemed absolutely obvious that, if a fall in the value of money was harmful, then increasing the value of money would bring positive consequences. It is not necessary, today, to waste much time on this idea, particularly in this country.[4] But once again the reproach must be made that people learn nothing from either theory or history. If they had turned to theory and history with the question of what the effects are of increasing the value of money, an answer would have been given

3 [For Mises's analysis of the factors behind the collapse of the mark during the Great German Inflation, see Ludwig von Mises, "Stabilization of the Monetary Unit—From the Viewpoint of Theory," [1923] in Percy L. Greaves, ed., *On the Manipulation of Money and Credit* (Dobbs Ferry, N.Y.: Free Market Books, 1978), pp. 5–16.—Ed.]

4 [This article was first delivered as a lecture at the annual assembly of the General Federation of Industry in Teplitz/Schönau, Czechoslovakia, on March 15, 1924. In 1919, the Czech crowns in circulation numbered 7 billion. By 1921, the number of Czech crowns in circulation had increased to 12 billion. Between 1922 and 1924, the Czech central bank followed a policy of monetary deflation, until by mid-1924, the Czech crowns in circulation had declined to 8 billion, a one-third decrease from its high in 1921. Between January and December 1922, when the monetary deflation was being most vigorously followed, prices in general in Czechoslovakia fell by about 40 percent.—Ed.]

without them having to relearn it all again through their own bitter experience.[5]

But even if someone had not wanted first to find out what theory and history might have told them, he should have been able to imagine from his own business experience what effects would follow from a fall in prices. And then, even before the attempts that were undertaken in Europe and in America to lower prices, he would have realized what today is taken for granted, that increasing the value of the monetary unit also unleashes consequences that are clearly undesirable.[6] In saying this, it is far from my intention to direct any special criticism against the monetary policy that the Czechoslovak Republic pursued for a time, a criticism that as a foreigner I can claim no right to make. The Czechoslovak Republic certainly does not stand alone in its endeavors to alleviate the effects resulting from a policy of inflation by introducing a policy of deflation.[7] England, the United States, and France, not to mention other countries, also tried a policy of deflation for a time, and there, too, the results were no different from those that must inevitably arise from every implementation of a deflationary policy.

After the failure of both inflationary and deflationary policies, the nations of Europe and America finally returned to the monetary system that

5 [For Mises's analysis of the effects resulting from a deflationary process, see Ludwig von Mises, *The Theory of Money and Credit* (Indianapolis: Liberty Fund, 3rd rev. ed., [1924; 1953] 1980), pp. 262–68.—Ed.]

6 [See Ludwig von Mises, "The Non-Neutrality of Money," [1938] in Richard M. Ebeling, ed., *Money, Method and the Market Process: Essays by Ludwig von Mises* (Norwell, Mass.: Kluwer Academic Press, 1990), p. 76: "[A]ll proposals for stabilization, apart from other deficiencies, are based on the idea of money's neutrality. They all suggest methods to undo changes in purchasing power already effected; if there has been an inflation, they wish to deflate to the same extent and vice versa. They do not realize that by this procedure they do not undo the social consequences of the first change, but simply add to it the social consequences of a new change. If a man has been hurt by being run over by an automobile, it is no remedy to let the car go back over him in the opposite direction." —Ed.]

7 [For a brief history of Czechoslovakian monetary policy and reform in the years immediately after the First World War, see Leland B. Yeager, *Experiences with Stopping Inflation* (Washington, D. C.: American Enterprise Institute, 1981), pp. 80–85; and Thomas J. Sargent, *Rational Expectations and Inflation* (New York: Harper & Row, 1986), pp. 95–100. —Ed.]

was their ideal and goal during the greater part of the nineteenth century: the gold standard.[8]

The employment of gold for monetary purposes is sometimes described as an outmoded use for the metal and an irrational carryover from the past, an atavism.[9] The argument is made that it is completely understandable that, in ages past, gold possessed an especially high value in the market and was widely accepted as a general medium of exchange, due to its brilliance, its particular suitability for ornamentation and decoration, and its relative scarcity. But it is completely incomprehensible that even today this old custom is still retained. It is intolerable, these critics say, to think that increases and decreases in the value of the monetary unit, along with the social consequences that accompany changes in the value of money, should be dependent on the accidents of gold production.

It would be far more reasonable if countries were willing to establish independent national currencies, and create a monetary system free of the uncertainties surrounding the profitability of gold mining. Such a currency would have its value determined by the conscious will of the nation as reflected in the decisions of its government. A special advantage of such an independent monetary system, it is said, would be that its implementation would involve relatively minor costs in comparison to the capital and labor presently tied up in gold production that then would be freed for producing far more useful things.

These arguments sound as enticing as they are mistaken. They ignore the insuperable obstacles that stand in the way of a monetary system in which changes in the value of money would be regulated by measures im-

8 [For an exposition of Mises's views on money, gold, and the limits to monetary policy attempting to manage or manipulate the price level for purposes of economy-wide stabilization, see Richard M. Ebeling, "Ludwig von Mises and the Gold Standard," in Llewellyn H. Rockwell, Jr., ed., *The Gold Standard: An Austrian Perspective* (Lexington, Mass.: Lexington Books, 1985), pp. 35–59.—Ed.]

9 [See John Maynard Keynes, *A Tract on Monetary Reform* (New York: Harcourt, Brace, 1924), p. 187: "In truth, the gold standard is already a barbaric relic.... Advocates of the ancient standard do not observe how remote it now is from the spirit and the requirements of the age." Keynes (1883–1946) was one of the most influential British economists of the twentieth century, most famous for his 1936 book, *The General Theory of Employment, Interest and Money.* This work served as the basis and inspiration for the development of modern macroeconomics, especially in the form that became known as Keynesian economics. Keynes argued that a market economy, when left to itself, has a tendency to fall into a state of relatively high unemployment and idle resources, the solution for which required active monetary and fiscal policy by government.—Ed.]

plemented by the political authority. Gold did not possess its position as money in the nineteenth century because it shines and is appropriate for jewelry but because people wanted a monetary system under which variations in the value of money were independent of governmental influences.[10]

Precisely what the opponents of gold regard as an advantage of the system they recommend—that changes in money's value would be independent of the uncertainties of the profitability of gold production and would depend exclusively on the decisions of the political entities whose job it would be to regulate the monetary system—seems to the proponents of the gold standard as exactly the biggest drawback to this heralded ideal of a paper-money system. The advocates of liberal economic policy who recommended the gold standard, and who led it to victory and defended it, sought in the gold standard, above all else, protection against govern-

10 [See David Ricardo, "The High Price of Bullion," [1811] in Piero Sraffa, ed., *The Works and Correspondence of David Ricardo*, Vol. III (Cambridge: Cambridge University Press, 1951), pp. 98–99: "It is said…that the Bank of England is independent of Government. …But it may be questioned whether a bank lending many millions more to Government than its capital and savings, can be called independent of that Government.…This is a danger to which the Bank, from the nature of its institution, is at all times liable. No prudence on the part of the directors can perhaps have averted it.…It was then owing to the too intimate connection between the Bank and Government, that the restriction [the suspension of redemption of Bank of England notes for gold] became necessary.…The only legitimate security which the public can possess against the indiscretion of the Bank is to oblige them to pay their notes on demand for specie." See also John Stuart Mill, *Principles of Political Economy, with Some of Their Applications to Social Philosophy* (Fairfield, N.J.: Augustus M. Kelley, [1871] 1976), pp. 544 & 546:

> [N]o doctrine in political economy rests on more obvious grounds than the mischief of a paper currency not maintained at the same value with a metallic, either by convertibility, or by some principle of limitation equivalent to it.…All variations in the value of the circulating medium are mischievous: they disturb existing contracts and expectations, and the liability to such changes renders every pecuniary engagement of long date entirely precarious.…Great as this evil would be if it depended on accident [gold production], it is still greater when placed at the arbitrary disposal of an individual or a body of individuals; who may have any kind or degree of interest to be served by an artificial fluctuation in fortunes; and who have at any rate a strong interest in issuing as much [inconvertible paper money] as possible, each issue being itself a source of profit. Not to add, that the issuers have, and in the case of government paper, always have, a direct interest in lowering the value of the currency, because it is the medium in which their own debts are computed.…Such power, in whomsoever vested, is an intolerable evil.

—Ed.]

ment interventions that were meant to influence the value of money. Those of us who in recent years have seen what government intervention leads to when directed at the value of money will understand these arguments in favor of the gold standard far better than they were understood in the decades immediately preceding the World War.

Of course, advocates of an ideal paper money refuse any responsibility for the recent excesses from both inflationary and deflationary policies. Their goal, they say, is a monetary system in which increases and decreases in the supply of money would exactly match the demand for money. Since the demand for money cannot be directly determined, the procedure would be to control the supply of money in such a way as to try to keep the price level stable. An index of prices would be calculated and the money supply would be constantly manipulated so that the value of this index remained unchanged.

This proposal would be excellent if its foundation — a system of index numbers — was as firm and solid as its proponents assume. If a system of index numbers made it possible for us to measure changes in the value of money more or less in the same way that we are able to determine length or measure areas, then a monetary system based on a price index would be equivalent to the goal we stated above: The value of the monetary unit would be independent of the changing views and purposes of those in positions of political power, as well as of political parties and interests. The advocates of such an index-number system enormously overrate its capability for the measuring of changes in the value of money.

The oldest and most primitive methods of indexation were based on the procedure in which one took the wholesale prices of a number of goods in a year chosen as the starting point for an initial value; then, year by year, a comparison was made to determine whether the sum of the prices that had to be paid for the same quantity of goods had risen or fallen. The best known index that was constructed using this method is that of the London *Economist*. The *Economist* took the wholesale prices of twenty-two articles in the years from 1845 to 1850 as its starting point. The average price of each one of these twenty-two articles was made equal to one hundred. And the initial value for all twenty-two articles was 2,200, in relation to which, then, the computed price relationships for the following months and years were compared.

It is readily obvious that with this method everything depends on which goods are chosen for the calculation of the index number. Among the twenty-two articles that the *Economist* uses for its calculations there are no fewer than seven materials from the textile industry, to wit, cotton four times in different stages of processing, as well as raw silk, flax, hemp, and wool; in contrast, foodstuffs and luxury items are represented only six times. It is clear that every single change in the prices of textile materials must considerably influence the computed index number. Thus during the American Civil War, when there was an interruption in the supply of American cotton to Europe, the *Economist*'s index rose significantly. In January 1860 it stood at 2,692, in January 1864 at 3,787, and in January 1868 again at 2,682. This rise in the index number was not caused by an increase in the costs of goods resulting from a change in the value of money; it was caused by the rise in the cost of a particular group of goods affected by a special situation.[11]

It is also clear that the index-number system is essentially arbitrary as long as it does not include all goods. It is not sufficient to use the prices of goods in the wholesale trade. One should start with consumer goods rather than with raw materials, because it is changes in the prices for finished goods that induce changes in other prices. Furthermore, in using the prices of raw materials and semifinished products there is no way to avoid the problem that these goods have multiple uses. The practical solution to this problem would be to include the prices of all consumer goods; this is, however, completely and absolutely impossible. Also, the prices of consumer goods are not comparable over time. Last year's wheat price can be compared to that of today's, but the prices of consumer goods whose qualities change with fashion and technical progress cannot be compared in the same way.

In addition, it is clearly unreasonable to allow the price of each individual good to have the same importance in the determination of the index. If the changes in the price of wheat and the changes in the price of tobacco were to be given the same weight in the construction of the price index, as the *Economist* does, then a doubling of the price of wheat and a lowering of the price of tobacco by half would compensate each other in the establishment of the price index, which is obviously absurd. The price of the individual goods would have to be multiplied by the quantity (or weight) that they represent in the total consumption basket.

But besides the practical difficulties that stand in the way of the

11 [On the types and categories of commodities included in the *Economist* index, see William Stanley Jevons, *Investigations in Currency and Finance* (New York: Augustus M. Kelley, [1884] 1964), pp. 50–53.—Ed.]

establishment of a correct price index there are other fundamental difficulties that are unsolvable. Consumer demands constantly experience changes that, if longer periods are compared, are so considerable that the basis for comparison with the use of the price index largely disappears. Precisely if one wants to multiply the prices of the individual goods by the quantities of them that are consumed, in order to include them in the price index, insuperable difficulty results from the fact that at both points of comparison—the starting year and the later year—different multiplying factors must be used. And what about new goods that appear on the market whose prices would not be included? These difficulties cannot be overcome. They would only cease to exist in an economy that was completely dead, in which there are no changes, no progress, and no new innovation.

Another insuperable and fundamental difficulty is that the price index is different according to the way in which the average of the different prices is calculated. We reach a different result depending on whether we take the arithmetic, the geometric, or the harmonic mean or whether we take the densest value or the median value. And the use of all of these average values is equally legitimate.

From all of this, it is clear that a price index cannot provide what is expected from it. Changes in value of money cannot be precisely determined in the same way in which we measure changes in the size or weight of an object. It will always be possible to defend different views about whether this or that way of calculating the price index is more accurate. Under a monetary system based on a price index, the answer as to which method of measuring price changes should be used would have crucial importance for the distribution of income and wealth among individuals and entire groups in the society. These differences of opinion will not be merely settled in the quiet of the scholar's study, far from worldly conflicts of interest. They will move to center stage on the political battlefield. Debtors and creditors will have different interests and will try to make their respective interests triumph.[12]

---

12 For Mises's critical analysis of the construction and limits in the use of index numbers for price-level stabilization purposes, see Mises, *The Theory of Money and Credit*, pp. 215–23; "Monetary Stabilization and Cyclical Policy," [1928] in Israel M. Kirzner, ed., *Classics in Austrian Economics: A Sampling in the History of a Tradition* (London: William Pickering, 1994), pp. 48–52; "The Suitability of Methods of Ascertaining Changes in Purchasing Power for the Guidance of International Currency and Banking Policy," [1930] in Richard M. Ebeling, ed., *Money, Method and the Market Process: Essays by Ludwig von*

It is these shortcomings in the construction of index numbers that has, up to now, resulted in the rejection of every project for monetary reform built upon their use. For more than a hundred years proposals have been made over and over again to supplement or replace a precious-metal currency, at least for debtor-creditor relationships, by a compensating currency based on a price index. To avoid gains and losses from long-term debt contracts, it was proposed that such long-term contracts should no longer be serviced and repaid, as they have been up to now, by the payment of a certain fixed sum of money. Instead, interest should be paid and principle repaid with that nominal amount of money that corresponds to the purchasing power of the amount of the loan at the time the debt was assumed. Thus if a mortgage debt of 100,000 crowns was assumed at a time when the index stood at 100, then if it is repaid years later at a time when the index stands at 120, it should be repaid not with 100,000 crowns but 120,000 crowns.

These proposals were discussed in the most thorough and fundamental way, especially in England and America, but they were never carried out because it was fully recognized that no system of index numbers offered a sound and solid foundation for long-term loan contracts.[13] In the Anglo-Saxon countries, unlike on the Continent, people never closed their eyes to the fact that changes in the value of the precious metals very strongly influenced the importance of long-term contracts. How great is this influence is shown by the fact that, from 1896 to 1912, the purchasing power of gold fell by the ratio of 100:66; that means, then, that the saver who invested his savings in fixed-interest assets lost a third of his savings over this time. But the opinion was expressed that even this situation was still to be preferred to one in which the amount of principle and interest repaid on a loan would be dependent upon the changing opinions of legislators and judges. The gold standard was retained in spite of the fact that its defects were recognized, because it was considered that any other system had incomparably greater defects.

Mises, pp. 78–95; *Human Action: A Treatise on Economics* (Irvington-on-Hudson, N.Y.: Foundation for Economic Education, 4th rev. ed., 1996), pp. 219–23.—Ed.]

13 [See N. G. Pierson, "Further Considerations on Index-Numbers," *Economic Journal* (March 1896), pp. 127–131, who concluded after critically examining various methods for constructing index numbers—including those developed by Sauerbeck, Jevons, and Laspeyres—that "the only possible conclusion seems to be that attempts to calculate and represent average movements of prices, either by index-numbers or otherwise, ought to be abandoned."—Ed.]

But during the last decade a change has taken place in the monetary situation of the leading countries of the world that threatens the gold standard from a different direction. The classical English gold standard, as it was established after the currency chaos of the Napoleonic period and organized by the Peel Bank Act of 1844, was so constituted that considerable quantities of gold were in effective circulation.[14] Since the smallest notes represented five pounds and the largest silver coin, the crown, had the value of five shillings, the entire retail trade had to make use of the gold sovereign. The situation was the same in France, where there was a wide gap between the highest silver coin of five francs and the lowest note of fifty francs. And the German monetary system was set up in a very similar way after the unification of the Reich. We all know from personal experience that before the war gold coins actually circulated in considerable quantities in England, in Germany, in the countries of the Latin Monetary Union, and in a number of other states.

But in the last decades before the war, gold standards were created that for different reasons failed from the beginning to put gold-money in the hands of the public. For domestic transactions, bank notes and small coins were used exclusively, and gold remained in the vaults of the central banks as backing for the bank notes. This type of currency, which was introduced in India, the old Austro-Hungarian monarchy, and other countries, is called a gold-exchange standard or the "gold-core currency." It, too, was a gold standard since, either on the basis of special legal regulations or common practice, the currency could be redeemed for gold or in gold-backed foreign exchange.

But things did not stop there. Already some years ago a succession of note-issuing central banks, especially those of small and financially weaker states, had found that the holding of large gold reserves involved costs that could be saved. They set about exchanging a part of their gold reserve, which was lying in their vaults earning no interest, for short-term gold claims on foreign countries, gold claims that in contrast to non-interest-earning gold ingots and stocks of coins did earn interest. Decades ago the Austro-Hungarian Bank already had been given permission to include a part of its holdings of foreign exchange in the legally prescribed backing for its bank notes. The bank likewise invested the greater part of the reserves that it held beyond the legally prescribed minimum not in actual gold but in foreign exchange. This system, the financial advantages of which were obvious for the note-issuing banks sharing the proceeds resulting from this arrangement, was already extraordinarily widespread before the war; after the war it was elevated to the ideal of a cheap but sound monetary system.

When the countries of Europe whose monetary systems were wrecked by the war and its aftermath think about monetary reconstruction, they all have in mind, in the first place, the setting up of a gold-exchange standard in which all or at least the greater part of their gold reserves are to be invested in gold-backed foreign exchange. For the time being they are giving no thought to bringing gold back into use for domestic transactions. What they have in mind is simply and only to establish the stability of the rate of foreign exchange through the stipulation of an obligation to redeem the notes that are circulating within the country. In Austria we have virtually had such a currency since the end of 1922; the Austrian National Bank has not added a single gold coin to its vaults for purposes of currency redemption. All that the Austrian National Bank has procured for this purpose are foreign claims to gold.[15] Whoever follows the policies of the other note-issuing central banks of the world will easily recognize that this is the ideal that all these banks have in common. For considerations of prestige they might, in general, refuse to diminish the stock of gold that already resides in their vaults; but they want to avoid buying any gold that adds to their existing stock. They want to keep their reserves with the least possible sacrifice, and the best way to do it is to invest it in interest-bearing claims abroad.

It is obvious that every country in the world cannot follow this policy. Let us assume that all countries were to act according to this policy; the result would be that there would no longer be any room in the world for that part of the gold supply not being used for other, industrial purposes. This system, therefore, can only survive because there is, temporarily at least, still one country in the world that does not practice the principle of the gold-exchange standard and hold its reserves in the form of a foreign-

15 [See J. van Walre de Bordes, *The Austrian Crown: Its Depreciation and Stabilization* (London: P. S. King and Son, 1924), pp. 219–20: "Austria has therefore at present a *gold exchange standard*, and in the purest form — *with practically no gold.* . . . There is no gold in circulation, and the gold reserve of the Austrian National Bank is insignificant. At the end of 1923 the gold reserve amounted to 6.5 million gold crowns, and there was a foreign exchange reserve of 298.6 million. On several occasions during 1923 the Bank sold gold, probably because it preferred to have a reserve of interest-bearing foreign bills than of unproductive gold." (Italics in the original.) — Ed.]

currency claim to gold. The United States still has a real gold standard in the old sense. All newly mined gold not going into various industries that use gold as a raw material flows into the United States, where it ends up either in circulation as coins or, to a greater extent, in the coffers of the banks that are subordinate to the Federal Reserve System.

These circumstances have led an English writer on monetary policy, John Maynard Keynes, to express the opinion that the gold standard can no longer be considered independent of the influences of governments.[16] Instead, according to Keynes, the value of gold is today already dependent in a very blatant way upon the decisions of one government, namely, the government of the United States of America. If the United States were to decide to set a limit on any further inflow of gold by abolishing the right of free coinage of gold and through the suspension of gold purchases by the banks, then the value of the dollar would rise above its gold value while the value of uncoined gold or gold not coined into dollars would have to fall considerably. Keynes thinks that, within the foreseeable future, the United States will come to this decision because in the long run it will not find it expedient to deliver large quantities of goods—it is a matter of from 50 to 100 million pounds' worth of goods per year—in order to receive in exchange a metal with which it can do nothing except store it away in bank vaults. As long as the newly produced gold can flow into the United States, a continuous inflationary pressure is exerted on the value of the dollar and a tendency toward rising prices is created. It could happen, according to Keynes, that a movement advocating going off the gold standard could arise in the United States as a reaction against a continuing rise in prices.[17]

Keynes apparently sees nothing disturbing in this possibility because he is obviously of the opinion that a paper currency disconnected from gold can function satisfactorily, if it is anchored to a price index. He thinks it is an exaggerated anxiety to object that such a currency will no longer be independent of the decisions of governments. The gold standard is already no longer independent of governmental policy today, as it once had been, when the gold standard could be seen as a useful device to remove government interference from the monetary system.

In any case, one has to agree with Keynes that the present system of currency arrangements cannot continue. Although rarely explicitly expressed, the reform ideal of most monetary-policy advocates in the smaller

16 [Keynes, *A Tract on Monetary Reform*, pp. 177–82.—Ed.]

17 [Ibid., pp.182–83 & 213–21.—Ed.]

and poorer countries is the gold-exchange standard, with a redemption fund formed either entirely or at least chiefly out of claims to gold, not in gold itself. Even if this system should be accepted by the great economic powers of the world, by England, Germany, France, and the other great nations, this would mean that the entire costs of holding the gold reserves of the world would be placed on the shoulders of the United States. The United States would, of course, thereby have the honor of managing the gold reserves that constitute the foundation of all the world's currencies; but it would have to pay rather dearly for this honor. Keynes thinks that at the moment when the United States realizes this fact, which is still hidden from the mass of the American public, it will decide in favor of abandoning the gold standard.

There is, however, another course of action that is conceivable and possible. The United States and the few other countries in which the gold standard is still in effect today could make all the other countries of the world restructure their currency legislation in such a way that they would have to accept a considerable part of the new gold entering the market. This could be done by requiring these countries either to hold a correspondingly larger stock of real gold in their note-issuing central banks or to apportion their notes and coins in such a way that real gold coins would have to be used in transactions. It is certain that the United States, which today occupies the dominant position in the capital market, has the power to force the other nations of the world to conclude and keep such an agreement. By such a method, it would protect its own monetary system and that of the rest of the world from further disruptions.

Keynes is, however, completely mistaken if he thinks that there would be no harmful consequences for the United States if it broke away from the gold standard. The abandonment of the gold standard by the United States would weaken the purchasing power of gold and would cause a difference to arise between the value of the dollar and the value of gold. As a result, great disagreements would develop between America and its debtors. The debtors, whose obligations are payable in dollars, would make the claim that they were only obligated to pay as much gold as corresponded to the weight of the dollar at the time they assumed their loans. It will not always be easy for the United States to reply with counterarguments against those of the debtors, and it would be even more difficult for the United States actually to impose its own view on others.

If the United States, after freeing the dollar from the gold standard, has a currency that rises in value relative to the currencies of other countries, then all Americans who draw income from foreign countries will have an unpleasant experience, and American industry will have to struggle against increased imports at the new foreign-exchange rate.

Every step that detaches the United States and the other countries from the gold standard will produce a long transitional period of fluctuations in the exchange rates between their currencies, which otherwise could have been avoided. Such fluctuations are apt to gravely damage international trade, and the countries that would suffer the most are those that are most heavily involved in world trade; and those are, again, the United States and the other American regions that are bound to it by numerous economic ties. So it will not be as easy for the United States to abandon the gold standard as Keynes believes.

If Keynes thinks that it would be very easy for England to abandon the gold standard, he is wrong there as well.[18] It is true that the greater part of England's foreign assets is payable in English pounds sterling and not in gold. But if, through the abandonment of the gold standard by England and the United States, a situation should develop in which gold is below the value of the pound, then debtors certainly would not be so easily persuaded to share Keynes's legal opinion that they owe pounds sterling and not gold. They will defend the view that by pound sterling nothing more can ever be understood than the quantity of gold that corresponded to the debt at the time it was assumed. And here, too, it is questionable whether England will be in a position to prevail against this kind of argument. But most especially, England must consider the fact that by adopting a currency whose value rises against foreign currencies it will, for a period of transition, further increase the difficulties of its industrial sector. We have seen only recently that in England many politicians, in their efforts to find a way out of the difficulties of the industrial crisis, have even turned to the desperate idea of creating inflation for the purpose of facilitating exports.

For the present, Keynes's ideas have not met with any approval in England. In the United States, as well, public opinion is far from agreeing with the sort of plans that Keynes proposes. The practical spirit of the American resists risking an experiment whose outcome would hardly be favorable. On the other hand, in the United States today another, and no less dangerous, project is being considered that, although fundamentally retaining the use of gold, wishes to introduce price indexing into its monetary sys-

18 [Ibid., pp. 193–213. –Ed.]

tem. This is the proposal of the American economist, Irving Fisher.[19] The basic idea behind his plan for stabilizing the purchasing power of money is to replace the gold standard as it exists today with the compensated dollar standard. I have already pointed out that the proposal has been repeatedly made to supplement the precious-metal standard by a compensated currency standard. Obligations in money that become payable after the expiration of a certain time should, either by virtue of universally obligatory legal provisions or by virtue of special contractual agreements between the parties, be paid off not in the nominal sum of money in which they are written but by that amount of money whose purchasing power at the time of the payment of the obligation equals the purchasing power of the borrowed sum at the time the obligation was entered into. As for the rest, all of these proposals would leave gold in its place in the monetary system.

But Fisher wishes to go beyond this. According to his proposal, the compensated dollar standard would not merely complement the precious-metal standard, instead it would replace it completely. This would be achieved through a combination of the fundamental idea of the gold-exchange standard with the fundamental idea of the index standard. Under the gold-exchange standard the money substitutes in circulation are redeemable in gold—or also in gold-backed foreign exchange. Fisher also wishes to retain redeemability in gold, but in his construction the money substitutes in circulation would no longer be redeemable as a specific weight of gold but as that amount of gold corresponding to the purchasing power of the monetary unit at the time the plan was introduced. The dollar, according to the model elaborated by Fisher for the United States, ceases to be a fixed amount of gold with a variable purchasing power and instead becomes a variable amount of gold with an unchanging purchasing power. From month to month it is to be determined by surveys of price statistics, which are used for the calculation of a price index, by how much the purchasing power of the dollar has risen or fallen in comparison to the preceding month. Accordingly, then, the amount of gold that is to correspond to a dollar increases or decreases. The dollar is

19 [Irving Fisher, *Stabilizing the Dollar* (New York: Macmillan, 1920). Irving Fisher (1867–1947) was one of the most prominent American economists in the first half of the twentieth century. He formulated a widely used version of the quantity theory of money, utilizing the equation of exchange in *The Purchasing Power of Money* (1911). He advocated using a system of index numbers to vary the gold content of the dollar to maintain a stable purchasing power of the monetary unit. A professor of economics at Yale University, he also was an advocate of eugenics and unusual health-food diets.—Ed.]

redeemable at the redemption office for this amount of gold, and for this amount of gold it must hand over a dollar to anyone who demands it.

Fisher's proposals are also unacceptable. In the first place, the shortcomings of a price index, which we have already described at length, must speak against it. This defect and others, which cannot be reviewed here because of the brevity of the time at our disposal and which I have discussed thoroughly in another place,[20] mean that the implementation of Irving Fisher's project would fail to eliminate, in spite of what he claims, those social consequences that accompany changes in the value of money that are universally considered as an evil. The Fisher project has been thoroughly discussed in the United States, and the House of Representatives has set up a special committee to study it. I believe, however, that the United States does not intend to follow the path that Fisher has proposed.

All attempts to put something better in place of the gold standard must fail because the price-index system provides no clear solution and because conflicts between interested parties would inevitably break out about which of the many possible solutions to use that would never leave the economy in peace. It would be an intolerable situation if we had to carry on discussions forever and ever about whether at every instant measures for the raising or lowering of value of the currency were to be recommended or rejected. Continuity of economic development would be endangered, and the evil that we have been enjoying so fully in these last few years would be perpetuated.

The gold standard's future does not appear to be as unfavorable as Keynes sees it. Of course, in this sphere as well as in many others, it is no longer acceptable that each individual nation carries on its own economic policy without any consideration for neighboring countries. In the realm of monetary systems it will be necessary to make international agreements. The goal of these international agreements must be to reintroduce the gold standard in every single country of the world, which can be achieved without difficulty if the League of Nations imposes a punitive duty on the exports of those countries that refuse to stabilize their monetary system. If the nations of the world once again agree to accept the gold standard we will once more have a monetary system that is not dependent on the influences of one or several individual governments. This monetary system

---

20 In the new [1924] edition of my *Theory of Money and Credit*, pp. 438–45, which will appear in about three months.

would also guarantee the stability of foreign-exchange rates and thereby the stability of international capital and bank transactions.

But if we wish to undertake the creation of a monetary system that is divorced from gold, then in every single country we shall see conflicts arise between special-interest groups who want to change the value of money in one direction or another. If people within their own countries cannot even come to an agreement about the monetary-policy measures to be undertaken, then it will be even less possible to achieve unanimity in international arrangements. A currency system detached from gold, which would be regulated by the different points of view in each individual country, would be synonymous with the perpetuation of fluctuations among the foreign-exchange rates, and international-capital transactions would suffer severely from these fluctuations. The monetary chaos would be aggravated and become a lasting institution.

We have only the choice between the gold standard and a currency manipulated by governments. With the gold standard we are dependent upon the accidents of the profitability of gold production; with an independent currency we are dependent upon the changing political currents. With the maintenance of the gold standard we have at least a possibility of seeing foreign-exchange rates stabilized again; with currencies unconnected with gold this is hardly likely to be achieved. In such circumstances the choice can surely not be difficult. The gold standard is not an ideal monetary system, but in the given circumstances it is the best one possible.

In these conditions it would be absolutely mistaken to argue that the policy of those countries whose currencies were wrecked by the war are today going in the wrong direction. All of these countries are striving for a gold-exchange standard backed up by a reserve fund invested in foreign exchange. It is true that this conception of a currency system cannot be the ultimate goal of monetary reform and policy. But it is equally true that it represents the first step on the way to rehabilitating the ruined monetary situation.

CHAPTER 15

Restoring Europe's State Finances[1]

It is a mistake to view the Great War or the ensuing economic hardships as natural calamities, like earthquakes or floods, as the result of which humanity was the innocent victim. Later generations will recognize more clearly than is possible today that the groundwork for the collapse of European civilization was already carefully laid by literary and sociopolitical trends in the decades immediately preceding the Great War. Imperialist doctrines of power and force and theoretical justifications for protective tariffs have led straight to military catastrophe and economic warfare, while socialist doctrines and the destructive teachings of literary figures like Leo Tolstoy are directly responsible for Bolshevism. In the same way, current financial problems are the product of misguided fiscal theories that have been propounded and propagated for decades.[2]

There was a time when it was conventional wisdom that taxes were an evil to be avoided as far as possible and that a finance minister's only virtue was frugality. In those days the representatives of the people in parliament were at great pains to trim budget proposals in order to save the population from excessive tax burdens. Unfortunately, this principle was abandoned in the decades prior to the war. The pernicious doctrine arose that there was a fundamental difference between the public budget and

1 [The article was delivered in German as a lecture in Cobden-Szövetség, Hungary in October 1924. It has not been previously published.—Ed.]

2 [On Mises's diagnoses of the economic ills of Europe in the period between the two world wars and his economic policy prescriptions for reestablishing both freedom and prosperity, see Richard M. Ebeling, "Planning for Freedom: Ludwig von Mises as Political Economist and Policy Analyst," in Richard M. Ebeling, ed., *Competition or Compulsion? The Market Economy versus the New Social Engineering* (Hillsdale, Mich.: Hillsdale College Press, 2001), pp. 1–85.—Ed.]

household budgets. In household budgets, it was believed, expenditures were to be based on income, while in the public budget expenditures were to determine revenue. While no fiscal theorist ever dared to proclaim this principle openly and without reservations, nevertheless, for the last several decades it has by and large served as the basis for scholarly discussion.

The principle was reinforced by a singular interpretation of the impact of direct and indirect taxes. It was thought that only indirect taxes on items of mass consumption affected broad segments of the population, while direct taxes were believed to target only the wealthy and the owners of property, without otherwise burdening the economy. Ferdinand Lassalle did a lot to popularize this idea, which became the accepted gospel on taxation for all radical politicians, and in particular the Social Democrats.[3]

In the eyes of the older liberals, taxation of income and the interest on capital had the negative effect of slowing down the process of capital formation and hence retarded economic progress.[4] This objection was now cavalierly dismissed. Progressive income taxes were introduced and par-

3 [Ferdinand Lassalle (1825–64) was a leading advocate for the German socialist movement. An associate of Karl Marx, he was one of the founders of the German labor movement. He argued for nonrevolutionary change in the direction of socialism through welfare-state policies introduced by the imperial German government. He referred to the State as "God," and condemned free-market liberalism as "the Night-watchman State." In 1863, Lassalle published a pamphlet on "Indirect Taxation and the Position of the Working Class," in which he advocated a shift to a system of direct taxation targeted at the capitalist owners of the means of production. He was killed in a duel over the affections of a woman. — Ed.]

4 [See, for example, David Ricardo, "On the Principles of Political Economy and Taxation," [1821] in Piero Sraffa, ed., *The Works and Correspondence of David Ricardo*, Vol. I (Cambridge: Cambridge University Press, 1951), pp. 152–53:

All taxes must either fall on capital or revenue. If they encroach on capital, they must proportionally diminish that fund by whose extent the extent of the productive industry of the country must always be regulated; and if they fall on revenue, they must either lessen accumulation, or force the contributors to save the amount of the tax, by making a corresponding diminution of their former consumption of the necessaries and luxuries of life. Some taxes will produce these effects in a much greater degree than others; but the great evil of taxation is to be found, not so much in any selection of its objects, as in the general amount of its effects taken collectively.... It should be the policy of governments...never to lay such taxes as will inevitably fall on capital; since by so doing, they impair the funds for the maintenance of labour, and thereby diminish the future production of the country.

— Ed.]

ticularly high taxes were levied on joint-stock companies, which are the most important type of enterprises. While in the past parliament had resisted budgetary requests and tax proposals, the representatives of the people now demanded new expenditures and voted for such large tax increases that they had to be restrained by more farsighted finance ministers.

Whenever discussion turned to a new and popular expenditure, the representatives of the people were inclined to approve it, as long as it was not paid for through additional indirect taxes but only by new direct taxes. Some of the direct taxes, for instance inheritance and capital-gains taxes, targeted wealth in the form of capital as a source of tax revenue. In the case of taxes on income and profits, the idea was originally to tax only real income. In the wake of monetary depreciation and the resulting taxation of paper profits, even taxes on income and profits have now been converted into taxes on wealth. A portion of the existing capital has been taxed away, converted into consumption goods, and used up. By its very nature, this fiscal policy has reduced the economy's wealth. But so great were the social and political delusions that it was considered a desirable feature of direct taxation that it taxed away the country's patrimony. Feelings of envy such as this generated the belief that the impoverishment of entrepreneurs and the owners of capital was beneficial to the economy. The fact that the economy as a whole, not just the owners of capital, became poorer was completely disregarded.

It became an article of faith that the bounty of the state treasury knew no limits and the demands placed on the treasury knew no bounds. During the war and the postwar years, this belief culminated in the demand that large amounts of money be disbursed by the state to its citizens in the form of food subsidies. Future historians will study the motives that led to this system of government food distribution.

Easy credit also played a large share in the cavalier attitude that developed toward increasing public expenditures. In the past, even finance ministers of large and wealthy states were hard-pressed to raise even modest loans, and such attempts often were rebuffed. This situation changed completely in the last decades before the war. Europe's wealth had grown so rapidly that all public loans were fully subscribed. Banking organizations had grown by leaps and bounds. They were now in the hands of a few central-banking institutions located in each nation's capital, and were politically subservient to the government. A government was able to obtain whatever loans it needed for its own purposes or for a foreign government that it wanted to support. As one consequence of this, a substantial part of

France's wealth migrated to Russia and was lost there.[5] Similarly, the population of the Central European states turned over a large part of its wealth to the state and local governments in the form of loans; they will never be repaid. Even today, after all the bitter experiences of the last decade, Soviet Russia is receiving long-term credits from foreign suppliers, and we may yet see a large European or even American loan extended to the Soviets.

Large loans were the mainstay of national governments and local administrations in undertaking sweeping nationalization and municipal ownership. Through this method, national and local government agencies acquired or built railroads, streetcars, water works, and electrical works (for lighting). By the same avenue, they even acquired breweries, commercial bakeries, theaters, hotels, inns, etc. These entrepreneurial activities by governments have been an unmitigated disaster. The old fable about Midas has been turned on its head; whatever gold governments touched turned into dust. In an instant, flourishing enterprises were in need of subsidies. The governments could not even manage to make some money from the sale of leftover military supplies and state-owned weapons plants. Everywhere, and not just in Germany and Austria, demobilized goods were disposed of in the most wasteful manner.

It is inconceivable that this system of government-owned enterprises can be maintained in the long run. It is unimaginable that taxes will be collected to cover the deficits of these public enterprises. That may have been possible as long as there were only a few public enterprises of this sort, but with their increasing number it is no longer feasible. There is only one remedy for this problem. Governments and local agencies must sell off all these enterprises and turn them over to private entrepreneurs who will know how to run them at a profit. This solution, which is the only realistic option, runs counter to the strong socialist convictions of our time and the special interests of those who are employed in these enterprises. People do not want to completely abandon the principle of socialization, irrespective of the fact that it has failed wherever it has been applied.

Hence there are the many attempts to carry through various reforms,

5 [By 1914, before the beginning of the First World War, French foreign, long-term investment in Russia was 11.3 billion francs, out of a total of long-term investments of 27.5 billion francs in Europe and 45 billion francs worldwide. On February 10, 1918, the new Soviet government officially repudiated all foreign debts accumulated by both the former imperial Russian government and the provisional government that was in power from February to November 1917. — Ed].

while circumventing the only really effective solution. Commercialization of public enterprises has been advocated, but this is nothing more than a cheap slogan. It is perfectly true that these enterprises lack business leadership. But business leadership is not something external that can be injected into public enterprises. Business leadership—or in the case of joint-stock companies the representatives that operate them on behalf of the owners—implies that profit and loss is borne by the owners. Civil servants or agents of the state or the local municipalities are always subservient to the control of government authorities, parliamentary committees, etc. No matter how conscientious and educated they may be, they will always remain bureaucrats. As long as public enterprises have a monopoly position, they can conceal their mismanagement through accounting gimmicks. But where public enterprises must compete in the open market, they cannot resort even to this expedient. The state and local governments simply cannot afford the luxury of engaging in public enterprises. The reason that the Western powers, and England in particular, have sounder finances than the Central and Eastern European states is not their greater wealth but the fact that they run fewer public enterprises and above all that they have no public railroads.

It was a mistake to start out by reducing the number of public servants as a means of restoring sound public finances.[6] It would have been much wiser to have started with the elimination of useless government programs, and above all by eliminating public enterprises.

In the last analysis it is the doctrine that the state can spend what it wants irrespective of its revenue that must bear the blame for the great inflation of the war and postwar periods. Governments take it for granted that when they are unable to acquire money through other means, they can resort to the printing of new money. It was hard enough to persuade public opinion that this system must very quickly lead to a total collapse. Today this fact needs little emphasis; the struggles with inflation are vivid in everyone's memory.

Germany and Russia are among the states that allowed inflation to run its course to the bitter end. Other states, Austria and Hungary among them, stopped just short at the rim of the abyss. Still others, such as France and

6 [In 1922, the federal chancellor of Austria, Monsignor Ignaz Seipel, arranged for a $126 million loan from the League of Nations to assist in the financial and monetary reconstruction of the country. One of the stipulations under the loan agreement was that eighty thousand government workers would be dismissed as part of an austerity program.—Ed.]

Italy, waited until the next-to-last moment.[7] Calling a halt to an inflationary policy, however, is not sufficient in itself to restore sound finances. The expenditure side of the budget must be radically trimmed. This does not mean that cultural expenditures must be cut to the bone. It is absurd to expect to save money by cutting a research position in a medical institute, while public enterprises continue to squander billions.

The net value of publicly owned Austrian forests is estimated at 170 million gold crowns. Under state management, this enormous asset yielded a deficit of more than 3 million gold crowns in 1923, despite the selling off of a million cubic meters of timber. The balance sheet for 1924 is not yet complete, but there will probably be a 1.8 billion gold crown deficit. If the state had sold off its timberland and similar types of property —mines, salt mines, and, above all, the railroads—it would not have needed that large loan from the League of Nations. It is not true that a state like Austria cannot afford *essential* state expenditures. But it is an undeniable fact that it cannot afford the *luxury* of unprofitable public enterprises.

Everywhere, but particularly in Austria, people are talking about the crisis that has been unleashed by the attempt to restore sound public finances.[8] This is the wrong way to look at the matter. The restoration of sound state finances has not triggered the crisis. The crisis was brought to a head not by the restoration of sound state finances but by the elimination of the misleading bookkeeping that had been produced by the progressive depreciation of the crown.

This in itself is no cause for concern. To recognize a problem is the first step in solving it. As long as inflation concealed the poor performance of the public sector and the economy as a whole, the problem could easily be ignored. Today we know what is wrong and what are the remedies. All that is lacking is the will to carry them through. What is required is neither new nor easily popularized, but we know that it is effective. What is needed is frugality. The ability to economize, not the invention of new taxes, is the hallmark of a good finance minister.

---

7 [For brief accounts of the ending of the post-World War I inflations in Germany, Russia, Austria, Hungary, and France, see Leland B. Yeager, *Experiences with Stopping Inflation* (Washington, D. C.: American Enterprise Institute, 1981).—Ed.]

8 [When Mises delivered this lecture in late 1924, unemployment had risen to about 15 percent of the Austrian workforce, partly as a result of the austerity program connected with the loan from the League of Nations, described in footnote 6.—Ed.]

CHAPTER 16

Changes in American
Economic Policy[1]

The United States has become great and rich under the rule of an economic system that has put no restrictions on the free pursuits of the individual, and has thereby provided the opportunity for the country's productive powers to be developed. America's unprecedented economic prosperity is not due to the richness of the American soil; instead, it is due to an economic policy that has reflected how best to exploit the possibilities offered by the land. American economic policy always has rejected — and still rejects today — any protection for the inferior and less competitive against that which is efficient and more competitive. The success of this policy has been so great that it is hard to believe the Americans would ever have reasons to change it. No other country in the world can compare with the United States in wealth or a standard of living possessed by the vast majority of Americans that would have been considered impossible even two decades ago.

It is really astonishing, therefore, to see the sharp criticisms that are being directed against this economic policy. The existing capitalist system is criticized for not being "rational" enough, and it is believed that centralized economic planning could achieve far better results. The system is also criticized for not being sufficiently democratic because the voting public does not have any direct influence on the direction taken by production.

1 [This article originally was delivered as a lecture in German before a meeting of the Industrial Club of Vienna on November 18, 1926. It was published in the Industrial Club's proceedings newsletter for November 1926, No. 342. During the three months between March 9 to May 31, 1926, Mises had toured the United States under the financial auspices of the Laura Spelman (the Rockefeller) Foundation, visiting and lecturing in a dozen cities. — Ed.]

The experiences with state and municipal enterprises that have been undertaken in Europe as well as in the United States, both during and after the war, are not thoughtlessly brushed aside by the Americans; they calculate these things still more soberly than do Europeans. The nationalization of industry and the municipalizing of enterprises find very little support. National, regional, or municipal management of business is not wanted; the continuation of private management of enterprise is desired, but under the supervision and influence of the government.

This is considered to be particularly important in a certain number of lines of production, primarily over the entire transportation system, agricultural production, and lighting and power. Government is supposed to exert its influence through pricing regulations imposed by a rate-setting authority that oversees transportation, and lighting and power facilities. While attempts in this direction are constantly being undertaken, their results are unsatisfactory. The system is basically unworkable. Whenever the prices of the products in a particular line of production are considered important enough to be artificially held down through government compulsion, the profitability of investing capital in that sector of the economy is reduced. Investment capital shifts into other lines of production where the potentials for profit have not been hampered by government intervention. The production activities whose improvement is supposed to be fostered through such regulations are in fact badly served as a consequence of such government intervention. If the profit on invested capital is reduced as a result of holding the revenues of city transportation enterprises below the rate appropriate to market conditions, then the only result will be that capital moves to more rewarding uses in the future. The municipal transportation systems in a number of American cities are in a deplorable state precisely because these communities have prevented private companies from raising their rates.

On the other hand, the results from these experiments with municipal enterprises around the world (including the United States) have made communities in America reluctant to take over these businesses directly. The problems resulting from this system of government intervention would have been more strikingly apparent if these companies, finally after a struggle, had not always been able to obtain the rate increases they wanted. If the interventionist system was more universally and strictly enforced its inherent contradictions would be more clearly seen, and the Americans would be put in the position of having to choose between freeing the market or following the path that leads to nationalization and municipalization.

In comparing the United States with Europe, it is easily seen that economic activity in America, at least for the present, is still far less restricted and hampered than is the case in Europe. The fact cannot be ignored, however, that a strong movement is arising in America for trade unions and state governments to have a greater influence over economic life, and that this movement has support both in the economics literature and in the general news media. And in this respect there is no real difference among the political parties. The La Follette party was, perhaps, the most prominent one when this movement began.[2] But today both major parties, the Republicans as well as the Democrats, are ready to undertake even very radical steps in this direction in order to win the votes of the electorate.

If in the future American production fell upon hard times because of a fall in foreign sales, it is possible that with the support of the votes of farmers and the urban masses, an economic policy will be instituted that is fundamentally different from America's traditional one. The ideas that have dominated European economic policies for several decades will then be transplanted to the United States.

There can be no doubt that the results America would achieve from such a policy would be no better than what it has "achieved" in Europe.

---

2 [The "La Follette party" refers to the political movement originally organized in Wisconsin by Robert M. La Follette (1855–1925). He served as governor (1901–06) and then U. S. Senator from Wisconsin (1906–25). He ran as the presidential candidate for the Progressive party in 1924. La Follette was considered a leading feature in the Progressive movement, arguing for greater government regulation of business, especially in the railroad industry. —Ed.]

CHAPTER 17

Commercial and Bureaucratic Business Management[1]

Commercial business management reflects the nature of private enterprise, while bureaucratic business management is in line with the nature of officialdom, which administers the affairs of the state. The commercial enterprise has as its compass nothing except the profitability of its business. The entrepreneur of a private firm gives the employees, to whom he transfers various independent tasks, one single instruction: to strive for the maximization of profit. In this directive is contained all that he has to say to them, and the system of accounting is then able to determine easily and readily to what degree the instruction has been fulfilled.

The manager of a public agency or bureau finds himself in a completely different situation, since the success or failure of official activities cannot be evaluated by the same bookkeeping and auditing methods. He can give his subordinates orders about what they are expected to do, but he cannot check to see whether the resources that they spent to achieve this result are in proper relationship to the goal. If he is not omnipresent in all the agencies and bureaus under his supervision, then he is not able to judge whether or not the same result could have been accomplished with a smaller expenditure of labor and material resources. Since an arithmetical assessment in the same form as commercial bookkeeping is impossible for the determination of this relationship between ends and means, the manager of a bureaucratic organization must supply his subordinates with instructions for the carrying out of the duties for which they are responsible.

---

1 [This article originally appeared in German in the *Wochenschrift Niederösterreichischen Gewerbevereins* (February 13, 1930). It outlines themes in contrasting business and bureaucratic management methods that Mises later developed in greater detail in his book, *Bureaucracy* (Spring Mills, Pa.: Libertarian Press, [1944] 1985).—Ed]

In these instructions provisions are made, in a schematic way, for the carrying out of the ordinary and routine operation of the public enterprise. But for all extraordinary situations, before expenditures can be made, the superior authority's approval must be obtained. This may be a sluggish and inefficient procedure, but it is the only one possible in these circumstances. After all, if every subordinate agency, department, branch-office were given the right to make those expenditures that were considered necessary, then the administrative costs would rise without limit. We cannot ignore the fact that this system is highly defective and very far from being satisfactory. Consent is frequently given to superfluous expenditures and many needed expenditures are not permitted, precisely because, given the nature of the bureaucratic apparatus, it is unable to adapt to changing circumstances as readily as can the commercial sector.

But even from the economic point of view, and in spite of all its faults, the method of bureaucratic management is to be preferred to any other organizational method for the execution of the activities of the government; it is alone in keeping with the character of the constitutional state. If nowadays the bureaucratic style of management is criticized in its entirety, this is only because commercial enterprises have been transferred into the hands of public administrators, which has deflected the bureaucracy from its original domain of responsibility into the area of having to manage the economic activities of the society. Seeing the adverse influence of bureaucracy on the success of normal business activity, people now wish to "commercialize" these public enterprises. It is an absolute and complete mistake to think that the "commercial" is a form of organization that can simply be grafted onto the business of government in order to debureaucratize it. The reason is that public enterprises operate not merely to earn profits but to pursue other goals as well. That is precisely the reason why these enterprises are supposed to be in public hands.

But if the achievement of goals other than the maximization of profits became central to the management of the enterprise, then profit maximization no longer guides the enterprise and bureaucratic methods are introduced. Thus we observe today that in every country even many enterprises that are still in private hands are being "bureaucratized." This bureaucratization does not have its origin in the size of the enterprises, as the public sometimes supposes. There are very large companies that are not bureaucratized at all, and there are much smaller ones that are scarcely any different from a government office. What leads to bureaucratization in these companies is that, either from within the enterprise or because of external pressures from the side of politics, they stop considering themselves as merely commercial enterprises concerned simply with "business." Especially easily inclined in this direction are those companies that are granted monopoly status through one or another type of government measure.

The general censure that the bureaucratic system receives among the public completely misses the point when it criticizes bureaucracy per se, i.e., the adherence to rigid rules and the formalism of governmental administration. This censure, however, is completely justified when it rejects the bureaucratization of business enterprises. In the criticisms that are encountered about the bureaucratic management of public enterprises, we can perceive the first indication of an incipient retreat from the high esteem that has characterized the nationalizing and "municipalizing" activities of recent decades. People are now demanding that these enterprises be "commercialized." If it is finally recognized that the ideal of commercial business management can only be achieved in private enterprises and that every public enterprise must, of necessity, be bureaucratic, then it will also be recognized that reform of the management of public affairs cannot stop at "commercialization."

PART II

The Political Economy of the Great Depression (1931–36)

CHAPTER 18

The Economic Crisis
and Capitalism[1]

It is almost universally asserted that the severe economic crisis under which
the world presently is suffering has provided proof of the impossibility of
retaining the capitalist system. Capitalism, it is thought, has failed; and its
place must be taken by a better system, which clearly can be none other
than socialism.

That the currently dominant system has failed can hardly be contested.
But it is another question whether the system that has failed was the capitalist system or whether, in fact, it is not anticapitalist policy—interventionism, and national and municipal socialism—that is to blame for the
catastrophe.

The structure of our society rests on the division of labor and on the
private ownership of the means of production. In this system the means of
production are privately owned and are used either by the owners themselves—capitalists and landowners—for production, or turned over to
other entrepreneurs who carry out production partly with their own and
partly with others' means of production. In the capitalist system the mar-

---

1 [This article originally was published in German in *Neue Freie Presse*, No. 24099 (October 17, 1931), in a column called "The Economist." Mises delivered as a lecture in February 1931 a more detailed and complementary analysis of the causes, consequences, and
cures for the Great Depression; see "The Causes of the Economic Crisis: An Address," in
Percy L. Greaves, ed., *On the Manipulation of Money and Credit* (Dobbs Ferry, N.Y.: Free
Market Books, 1978), pp. 173–203. For an exposition of the Austrian theory of the business
cycle in the context of the causes and cures of the Great Depression, and in contrast to the
Keynesian analysis, see Richard M. Ebeling, "The Austrian Economists and the Keyne-
sian Revolution: The Great Depression and the Economics of the Short-Run," in Richard
M. Ebeling, ed., *Human Action: A 50-Year Tribute* (Hillsdale, Mich.: Hillsdale College
Press, 2000), pp. 15–110.—Ed.]

ket functions as the regulator of production. The price structure of the market decides what will be produced, how, and in what quantity. Through the structure of prices, wages, and interest rates the market brings supply and demand into balance and sees to it that each branch of production will be as fully occupied as corresponds to the volume and intensity of the effective demand. Thus capitalist production derives its meaning from the market. Of course, a temporary imbalance between production and demand can occur, but the structure of market prices makes sure that the balance is reestablished in a short time. Only when the mechanism of the market is disturbed by external interventions is the effect of market prices on the regulation of production prevented; they are disturbances that no longer can be remedied by the automatic reactions of the market, disturbances that are not temporary but prolonged.

For two generations now, the policies of European nations have been based on nothing else other than preventing and eliminating the function of the market as the regulator of production. By tariffs and trade-policy measures of other sorts, by legal requirements and prohibitions, by the subsidization of uncompetitive enterprises, and by the suppressing or throttling of companies that offer unwelcome competition for the spoiled children of the government through the regulation of prices, interest rates, and wages, the attempt is made to force production into directions that it would not otherwise have taken. Under the protection of tariffs, which destroy the unity of the world market, production is deflected from more profitable lines of production; cartels arise that are intent on preserving even the least efficient companies and whose artificial support often only leads to the result that investment activity is guided into the wrong directions.

Anticapitalist policy has been most disastrous in the labor market. When wage rates are formed on the unhampered market, all workers find employment and all entrepreneurs find the workers they need. That unemployment occurs not merely as a temporary phenomenon of negligible importance but as a long-lasting phenomenon is ascribable to the fact that governmental economic policy supports the efforts of the trade unions to establish the wage level higher than the rate which can be supported by the state of the capital supply and the productivity of labor without any capital consumption. At the wage level insisted upon by the unions, only a part of the workers can find employment.[2]

2 [For Mises's more detailed discussion of the causes of unemployment, see Ludwig von Mises, *Human Action: A Treatise on Economics* (Irvington-on-Hudson, N.Y.: Foundation for Economic Education, 4th rev. ed., 1996), pp. 592–600.—Ed.]

As long as financial support is allocated to the unemployed from public funds and as long as workers who are not prepared to work for wages less than those demanded by these unions are protected by the use of force on the part of the unions, then the artificially high wage level will continue and be protected against the competitive pressure of unemployed workers seeking employment. But, then, unemployment will also continue to spread more and more. In spite of what the dominant and official opinion behind interventionist doctrine customarily claims, unemployment relief is not at all a measure for the mitigation of the distress caused by unemployment. It is rather a link in a chain of causes that produce unemployment as a lasting and massive phenomenon.

It is usually considered a paradox that goods lie around unsold while people have a need for these goods and that unemployed people are on hand when there is still much work to be done in the world. The expressions "unsalability" and "unemployment" evoke very mistaken conceptions of the reality that they are supposed to designate. "Unsalability" does not mean that the goods simply cannot be sold but only that they cannot be sold at a price that covers the costs of production. These goods should not have been produced because another, relatively more urgent need was not yet satisfied. "Unemployment" does not mean that the worker cannot find work but only that he cannot receive the wage he demands for the work that he is willing and capable of performing.

Unprofitability of the enterprise, unsalability of the goods, and unemployment are price phenomena that arise from preventing the market from functioning as the guide and regulator of production.

Under the influence of the ideology of socialism, which today affects all thinking on economic policy, numerous enterprises have been taken out of the hands of entrepreneurs and capitalists, and put in the hands of governments and public administrations. In almost all cases these public administrations have proved to be a failure; the majority of these enterprises require more or less large subsidies from taxes, since they operate at a considerable financial loss. To raise the money for this purpose and for subsidies of every sort, including unemployment relief—which calls for the greatest expenditure—taxes are increased again and again. These taxes have long since attacked not only income but also a not inconsiderable part of capital. The most prominent characteristic of the present reigning economic system [of interventionism] is that it consumes capital.[3] The

3 [On the process of capital consumption due to various government policies, see Ludwig von Mises, *Nation, State and Economy* (New York: New York University Press, [1919]

capitalist economy has an inherent tendency to increase the stock of capital. The system of state interventionism and state socialism, in contrast, leads to capital consumption.

Since, on the unimpeded market, wages rise as the supply of capital increases, the end result of a policy that leads to capital consumption necessarily has to be a fall in the level of wages and consequently a worsening of the living standard of the masses. In the long run, trade-union policy cannot alter this outcome. Of course, it can keep the wage rate artificially high for a period of time by the use of those measures that are euphemistically called "union methods." But not only do they produce unemployment; the higher wages lead to capital consumption and thereby make serious wage reductions eventually necessary. Artificially increased wages will be paid for directly in the cost of capital and indirectly, later on, in the cost of living of the working masses. Capital consumption means, precisely, that the present consumes more than it ought to consume at the expense of the future.

This severe economic crisis did not arrive unexpectedly. That interventionist economic policy would have to lead to this consequence was predicted by economists. The advocates of interventionist and socialist economic policies would of course not stop in the pursuit of their aim; in their naive misunderstanding of the interconnectedness of economic phenomena, they were always proud when they succeeded, against the warnings of economics, in imposing one of their demands. They rejoiced at the victory that they thought they had achieved over economics, and they did not see the catastrophes to which their policy was leading.

Our economy has long since ceased to be liberal and capitalist. Decades ago the intellectual leader of English socialism, Sidney Webb, now Lord Passfield,[4] declared with satisfaction that socialist theory was

---

1983), pp. 160–63; Mises, *The Theory of Money and Credit* (Indianapolis: Liberty Fund, 3rd revised ed., [1924; 1953] 1980), pp. 234–37; Fritz Machlup, "The Consumption of Capital in Austria," *The Review of Economic Statistics* (January 15, 1935), pp. 13–19; and F. A. Hayek, "Capital Consumption," [1932] in Roy McCloughry, ed., *Money, Capital and Fluctuations: Early Essays by F. A. Hayek* (Chicago: University of Chicago Press, 1984), pp. 136–58.—Ed.]

4 [Sidney Webb (1859–1947) was an early member of the British Fabian Society, which called for the achievement of socialism through incremental legislation. He was also a prominent intellectual force in the British Labor party, having written in 1918 the famous "Clause Four" in the Labor party program that called for the nationalization of the means of production. In 1935, he co-authored with his wife, Beatrice, *Soviet Communism: A New*

nothing other than the conscious and determined recognition of trade-union principles, which in large part were already being followed unconsciously, and that the economic history of our time was nothing other than an almost uninterrupted enumeration of the progress of socialism. Since then, the influence of the socialist parties has considerably strengthened, and the interventionism of governments has penetrated everywhere. The academic socialist economists assert over and over with special satisfaction that we live in the age of a "regulated economy"; and trade unions boast about the fact that in all things they have an important, if not the decisive, voice.

Today we are harvesting the fruits of this "victory over economics." Interventionism has led to the results that economists expected. Not capitalism but the political economy of interventionism, statism, and socialism, which has been at the helm for decades, has failed. Even more state interference, socialism, planned economy, or state-capitalism cannot help us, only the understanding that a raising of the standard of living can be effected only through more employment and through the formation of new capital.

The crisis has its starting point in mistaken economic policy. It will not end until it is recognized that the task of governments is to create the necessary preconditions for the prosperous operation of the market economy, and not to squander more on foolish expenditures than the industry of the population is able to provide. That means, however, that we must give up the anticapitalist policy that has reigned in Europe for decades. No other "plan" can lead us out of the crisis.

Civilization?, in which he predicted that the Soviet system of central economic planning would eventually spread around the rest of the world. In 1929, he was granted the title Baron Passfield. —Ed.]

CHAPTER 19

The Gold Standard and Its Opponents[1]

I   The Advantages of the Gold Standard

The importance of the gold standard for the domestic market lies in the fact that it makes the structure of the purchasing power of the monetary unit independent of changes in the policy views of governments and political parties concerning the value of money. Tying the value of the currency to the value of gold erects a dam against all endeavors to benefit particular sectors of the population at the expense of other sectors through the use of monetary policy. In dealings between nations, the gold standard eliminates the disturbances that foreign-exchange fluctuations bring with them for the trading of goods and the movement of capital. It establishes very narrow boundaries for the rates of exchange between currencies, so that there is no need for all the disruptive calculations over premiums on imports and exports arising from changes in the foreign-exchange rates.

The value of money is not "stable," of course, under the gold standard. But "stable value" is, after all, a vague and imprecise concept.[2] Only a stationary economy, in the strictest sense of stationary, in which everything remains exactly the same tomorrow and the day after tomorrow as it was yesterday and the day before yesterday, would have unchanged prices and

---

1 [This article was first published in German in two parts in the *Neue Freie Presse*, Nos. 24168 & 24171 (December 25 & 30, 1931), in a column called "The Economist."—Ed.]

2 [See Ludwig von Mises, "Monetary Stabilization and Cyclical Policy," [1928] in Israel M. Kirzner, ed., *Classics in Austrian Economics: A Sampling in the History of a Tradition*, Vol. 3 (London: William Pickering, 1994), pp. 48–54; and Mises, *Human Action: A Treatise on Economics* (Irvington-on-Hudson, N.Y.: Foundation for Economic Education, 4th rev. ed., 1996), pp. 219–23.—Ed.]

consequently a money with a stable purchasing power. The achievement of the gold standard is that it frees the purchasing power of the monetary unit to a greater degree from the influence of political factors that can affect a currency than would be the case under any other conceivable and realizable monetary system.

II   *Inflationism versus the Gold Standard*

The gold standard has sometimes been opposed because gold production has been considered too plentiful, leading to the objection that the gold standard would result in a continual rise in prices and corresponding decreases in the purchasing power of the monetary unit that would only bring grief to creditors on the market. The best known representative of this idea is the American economist, Irving Fisher.[3]

The overwhelming majority of the opponents of the gold standard, however, start from the opposite point of view. They reject the gold standard because they want higher prices and lower interest rates through larger increases in the quantity of money than is possible under the gold standard. Under the gold standard, the increase in the money supply is determined by the amount of gold production (minus the quantity flowing into industrial uses). In a word, these opponents of the gold standard want inflation.

If all other prices remain more or less unchanged while the price of one commodity, say, coal, rises, this means an advantage for the owners of coal mines. But what if it is brought about by an increase in the quantity of money that raises all prices? If in the wake of this inflation the rises in prices all took place simultaneously and the prices of all goods and services increased proportionally, they would bring with them no further social rearrangements—except for disadvantages to creditors and advantages for debtors. Since, however, as economic theory has irrefutably proven, price increases inevitably do not occur all at the same time in the entire economy, nor do the prices of all goods and services rise to the same extent, they definitely do cause various social side effects. The sectors that bring to market those goods and services whose prices rise at the beginning of the process gain from the changes in the purchasing power of money. For

3 [See Chapter 14, "The Return to the Gold Standard," footnote 19.—Ed.]

a period of time, they sell at a higher price, while they are still able to purchase goods and services for their own use at lower prices that still correspond more to the purchasing power of money before the inflation. If the inflation comes to a halt, then wages and the prices of the various goods even out to a certain degree. But the gains obtained and the losses suffered in the course of the inflationary process are never made up for.[4]

It is understandable, therefore, that particular sectors demand inflation from the standpoint of their own special interests. *What is not understandable is that people believe that they can also defend inflation from the viewpoint of the nation as a whole.*

III   *The Gold Standard and Interest-Rate Policy*

The strongest objection that is made against the gold standard is that it leads to a rise in interest rates. In capital-exporting countries this claim is not unfounded. The gold standard is, of course, not the only prerequisite for the international traffic in capital; but it is one of the most important. If there were no gold standard, the granting of loans abroad would be made difficult or even impossible, which would lead to a rise in interest rates in the capital-poor countries and to a fall in interest rates in the capital-exporting countries. It is therefore evident that, in the countries dependent upon attracting foreign capital, maintaining the gold standard does not result in making credit more expensive but instead makes it cheaper. Hence all objections that are raised against the gold standard from this point of view, at least in Central and Eastern Europe, are completely unfounded.

But people are unwilling to understand this argument. Instead, they think that only the gold standard prevents the central banks from being freed from the principles governing the international currency market, which would enable them in their discount policies then to provide cheap

---

4 [On Mises's theory of the inherent non-neutrality of money, see Ludwig von Mises, *The Theory of Money and Credit* (Indianapolis: Liberty Fund, 3rd rev. ed., [1924; 1953] 1980), pp. 160–68 and 225–46; "Monetary Stabilization and Cyclical Policy," pp. 45–62; "The Non-Neutrality of Money" [1938] in Richard M. Ebeling, ed., *Money, Method and the Market Process: Essays by Ludwig von Mises* (Norwell, Mass.: Kluwer Academic Press), pp. 68–77; and *Human Action*, pp. 398–432. —Ed.]

money for loans in the domestic market. This idea is also erroneous. Even in an isolated nation, which has no economic relations with the rest of the world, it would not be at the discretion of the central bank to set the minimum lending rate without regard to the structure of interest rates on the unhampered money market.

Temporarily it is, of course, possible, by means of credit expansion — that is, by increasing the supply of fiduciary media[5] — to undercut market-established interest rates and thereby bring about a general reduction in interest rates. By use of this method, which in fact has been repeatedly tried, it is undoubtedly possible to generate an economic upturn. But sooner or later the expansion of credit must come to a halt; it cannot be continued unendingly. The progressive expansion of the quantity of money leads to a progressive rise of prices.

But inflation can continue only so long as public opinion persists in thinking that it will cease in the foreseeable future. Once the conviction has been established that inflation will not stop, panic breaks out.

The public starts to discount the value of money in expectation of future increases in the prices of goods, resulting in prices shooting up with great volatility. People move away from using the money that has been undermined by the increase in the quantity of the currency, and shift into foreign currencies, ingot metal, material assets, and barter; in short, the currency collapses.[6]

It is not due to the gold standard that consideration of relationships with foreign countries as well as past experiences with economic crises has led central banks to stop expanding credit long before these extreme consequences have occurred. Ending the inflation has often been forced upon central banks because of legal restrictions and limits on the right to issue

5 [In Mises's terminology, "fiduciary media" refers to "money substitutes" that are meant to be claims to a commodity money in the form of bank notes or checks that are believed to be redeemable on demand at the banking institution that has issued them, but which are not, in fact, 100 percent backed by commodity-money reserves at the issuing institution. See Mises, *The Theory of Money and Credit*, pp. 63–76 & 239–404; and *Human Action*, pp. 432–44. — Ed.]

6 [On the process by which a money increasingly becomes worthless due to rising inflationary expectations on the part of the money-holding public, in the context of the Great German Inflation of the early 1920s, see Ludwig von Mises, "Stabilization of the Monetary Unit — From the Viewpoint of Theory," [1923] in Percy L. Greaves, ed., *On the Manipulation of Money and Credit* (Dobbs Ferry, N.Y.: Free Market Books, 1978), pp. 5–16. — Ed.]

notes and grant credit. In any case, a policy of increasing the supply of credit would finally have to come to an end, either sooner due to a reversal in banking policy, or later through a catastrophic monetary collapse. But the sooner the policy of credit expansion is reined in, the less is the damage caused by the artificial economic situation in the form of misdirected entrepreneurial activity and capital malinvestment. And the milder also will be the economic crisis and the shorter will be the consequent period of an interruption of business and general pessimism. Rather than being considered a disadvantage, it should be viewed one of the merits of the gold standard that its unconditional adherence makes the central banks alert in a timely way to the fact that in their interest-rate policy they may have entered upon paths which must inevitably lead through an artificial upturn to an inevitable crisis.[7]

A permanent lowering of the interest rate can only be the outcome of increased capital formation, never the result of any technical banking measures. Attempts to achieve a long-term lowering of interest rates by expanding the circulation credit of the banks ineluctably result in a temporary boom that leads to a crisis and to a depression.

IV The Gold Standard and the Balance of Payments

One of the most stubborn errors regarding the gold standard is the idea that a poor country is not in a position to maintain the gold standard. But the gold standard has absolutely nothing to do with the greater or lesser wealth of a country. Every country, whether rich or poor, can have a well-ordered currency if it abstains from triggering the working of Gresham's Law[8] (according to which good money is driven out by bad), avoids the

7 [On Mises's theory of the business cycle due to credit expansion that temporarily lowers the market rate of interest, see Mises, *The Theory of Money and Credit*, pp. 377–404; "Monetary Stabilization and Cyclical Policy," pp. 65–95; *Human Action*, pp. 538–86 & 780–803. For a presentation of the Austrian theory of the business cycle in contrast to Keynesian economics, see Richard M. Ebeling, "The Austrian Economists and the Keynesian Revolution: The Great Depression and the Economics of the Short-Run," in Richard M. Ebeling, ed., *Human Action: A 50-Year Tribute* (Hillsdale, Mich.: Hillsdale College Press, 2000), pp. 15–110.—Ed.]

8 ["Gresham's Law" was named for Sir Thomas Gresham (1517–79), financier and advisor to Queen Elizabeth I. In a proclamation dated September 27, 1560, Gresham warned that since the government had fixed the exchange rate between gold and silver at a level dif-

excessive issuing of paper money, and refrains from artificially lowering the interest rate through large increases of fiduciary media. Money has never flowed out of countries that have had only metallic currency; it remains there precisely because of trade.

The idea that governmental efforts and interventions are required to protect a country from losing its currency to foreign nations turns things completely upside down.

Only if politics intervenes in the money market, with attempts to reduce interest rates artificially, can a situation come about that leads to the disappearance of gold and the foreign exchange redeemable in gold under the gold-exchange standard.[9] The belief that a country with an unfavorable balance of payments is not in a position to maintain a well-ordered currency is equally absurd. As in every balance sheet, so also in the balance of payments: The two sides of the ledger must be equal. Except for the gold-producing countries, this coincidence of the credit and debit sides is covered by the exportation of gold only if banking policy in the exporting countries attempts to maintain an artificially low interest rate.

England did not give up the gold standard because an unfavorable balance of payments made it necessary, but because the Bank of England held on to the policy of low interest rates and would not give up this policy; that is what drove gold out of the country. It is said that the mechanism of the gold standard did not work in England any more. That is best refuted by the fact that England dropped the gold standard with a bank interest rate of 4.5 percent.[10] If it had been willing to maintain the gold standard,

---

ferent from the market rate, the more undervalued coins were sure to be exported. In other words, the bad (overvalued) money would drive out the good (undervalued) money. —Ed.]

9 [Under a "gold exchange standard," a national central bank deposits part of the gold that is meant to serve as the reserves backing its own currency with another central bank, and holds that other central bank's currency as a reserve behind its own currency. —Ed.]

10 [On September 21, 1931, the Bank of England suspended payment in gold on demand for its currency, under the threat of heavy withdrawals of gold by other countries. See Frederic Benham, *British Monetary Policy* (London: P. S. King, 1932), pp. 9–10: "On May 14th, immediately after the collapse of the [Austrian bank] Kredit Anstalt, the Bank Rate was actually lowered from 3 to 2.5 percent. It was not changed until July 23rd, when at last it was raised to 3.5 percent. During the last week of July the Bank of England lost over 25 million pounds in gold. On July 30th the Bank Rate was again raised, but only to 4.5 percent. Great Britain had always advocated a high Bank Rate as the remedy for a financial crisis and a drain of gold. She had been on the gold standard, in effect, for over two hundred years, with only two breaks—one during the Napoleonic wars and one during the last

then it would have had to follow the same discount policy it had always followed since the Peel Act.[11] England gave up the gold standard; the gold standard did not give up England.

The pessimism that the structure of our balance of payments arouses is not justified. It is not true that the deficit in the trade balance was the causal factor and that we took out foreign loans in order to cover a part of this deficit. It was the foreign borrowings in the first place that created a balance-of-trade deficit of a corresponding size. The equivalent value of the loans can come in no other way than in the form of goods. If we had not wanted to accept foreign loans, then fewer foreign goods, equivalent to the amount of these loans, would have been imported or more would have been exported. The deficit in the trade balance means something different in every individual case. It can mean acceptance of credits from abroad; it can also mean that payments are made from abroad in other ways, for example, by tourism, by transit trade, or by interest on loans.

Good banking policy makes well-ordered currency relationships possible. Bad banking policy jeopardizes the currency. That interest rates in Central Europe are extraordinarily high is the long-term consequence of the capital-consuming policies that have been pursued with veritable fanaticism for two decades. This evil cannot, however, be remedied by banking-policy trickery. All that the policy of artificially lowering the rate of interest can achieve is destruction of the currency.

V   The Unequal Distribution of Gold

In recent years the monetary portion of the world's stock of gold has accumulated to a considerable extent in the United States and in France. We customarily speak about this as if it were a matter that is independent of the currency policies of various nations. But in reality this concentration of gold in a few countries is the result of that policy of artificially lowering the rate of interest, of which we spoke above. The United States and France, and a few additional smaller nations, have participated in this policy only hesitantly and with reluctance. The gold that the other nations

---

war [World War I]. Now for the first time in her history she suspended gold payments in time of peace and with a Bank Rate of 4.5 percent!"—Ed.]

11 [See Chapter 2, "On the Currency Question," footnote 5.—Ed.]

have driven out had to accumulate with them. Neither France nor the United States has desired this situation.[12] Least of all it has been sought by the capitalists of these countries, who would of course prefer higher interest returns on their capital abroad, and who would, therefore, regret that the movement of capital is interrupted in this way. If all those countries that today believe that they can reduce interest rates permanently, without bringing about all those undesired consequences referred to above, would give up this policy, then a part of the gold that is concentrated in the United States and in France would flow back again.

VI   Conclusion: The Gold Standard or Inflation

One must keep it clearly in mind that economic policy can only choose between the retention of the gold standard—the question of whether a pure gold standard or the gold-exchange standard need not be considered at this point—or inflation. If one does not wish to follow a policy of constantly rising prices for goods and rates of exchange, then one must refrain from all attempts at lowering the rate of interest other than through the promotion of capital formation at home and the attraction of foreign capital. It is undeniable that an artificial lowering of bank interest rates can produce an economic boom. But it is equally incontestable that this path leads very quickly to a crisis. This crisis will be all the more difficult and detrimental the longer the period during which a misguided interest-rate policy has been followed and the further away interest rates have been pushed from the rates that would have been formed on the market in the absence of an expansionary credit policy.

Every country, even the poorest, can preserve the gold standard; and every country, even the very poorest, must preserve the gold standard. For only the gold standard makes it possible for poor countries to develop their productive capabilities by attracting foreign capital.

12 [Between 1918, at the time of the end of the First World War, and 1931, when Mises wrote this article, the gold reserves of the United States had increased from 2.6 billion to 4 billion; French gold reserves during this same period increased from 664 million to 2.7 billion.—Ed.]

CHAPTER 20

The Myth of the Failure of Capitalism[1]

It is almost universally argued nowadays that the economic crisis of the last few years means that the end of capitalism has arrived. Capitalism has allegedly failed. Being incapable of performing its economic function, humanity has no other choice, if it is not to perish, than to make a transition to the planned economy, to socialism.

This is by no means a new idea. The socialists have long maintained that economic crises are the necessary outcome of the capitalist mode of production, and that the reoccurrence of crises can be permanently brought to an end only through a transition to socialism. If at present these assertions are championed with greater emphasis and find a louder echo in public opinion, it is not because the present crisis is more severe and has lasted longer than its predecessors. Rather, it is due to the fact that public opinion is far more extensively dominated by socialist views than in previous decades.

I

Before political economy came into existence, it was believed that anyone with power and the determination to use it could do whatever he wanted. But even though the power of those in authority was considered to be un-

1 [This article was originally written in German and appeared in *Der Internationale Kapitalismus und die Krise. Festschift für Julius Wolf zum 20. April 1932* [International Capitalism and the Crisis. Essays in Celebration of Julius Wolf on April 20, 1932]. Julius Wolf (1862–1927) taught in Zurich, Breslau, and Berlin. He was a critic of socialism and Marxism. He published *The System of Social Policy: Socialist and Capitalist Order* (1892) and

182

limited and omnipotent, the priests would admonish the rulers to show moderation in the use of their power for the sake of the salvation of their souls.

This view was destroyed with the founding of sociology and the work of a large number of great intellects, among whom the names of David Hume and Adam Smith shine most brightly. It was discovered that social power is something moral and intellectual, not something material or "real," in the vulgar meaning of the word, as had been thought. And it was realized that there is an inevitable unity to market phenomena that even power cannot undermine. It was discovered that in the social arena there is something at work that even the one holding power cannot bend and to which, in achieving his ends, he must conform no differently than in submitting to the laws of nature. In the entire history of human thought and the sciences, there has never been a greater discovery.[2]

Beginning with the recognition of the laws of the market, political economy demonstrates the effects that result when political power and force interfere with the functioning of the market. The isolated intervention is unable to attain the ends for which it is introduced by the authorities; it leads to consequences that are undesirable even from the perspective of those in power. Thus, even from the interventionist's point of view, the effects are useless and harmful. This insight leads to the conclusion that if one is to arrange his actions in accordance with the lessons of scientific thought—and we think about these things not only for the sake of knowledge but to manage our affairs better to attain the ends we desire—then he must reject interventionism as superfluous, useless, and harmful, just as liberal doctrine shows it to be.

It is not that liberalism wants to introduce value judgments into scientific analysis; it merely wants to use the results of such analysis to better arrange the society so our ends may be more efficiently attained. Political parties, after all, do not differ about the ultimate ends for which they wish

---

Economics as an Exact Science (1908). His professional interests then turned to the subject of sex, and he wrote *The Rationalization of Sexual Life* (1912) and "The Science of Sex and the Science of Culture" (1915). He also wrote on the topic of population growth, developing a modified version of Malthus's theory.—Ed.]

2 [On the unique contribution of the Classical economists and their concept of social and economic order, see Richard M. Ebeling, "How Economics Became the Dismal Science," in Richard M. Ebeling, ed., *Economic Education: What Should We Learn About the Free Market?* (Hillsdale, Mich.: Hillsdale College Press, 1994), pp. 51–81.—Ed.]

to apply economic policy. They differ only about the means best suited for the attainment of those common ends. The liberals are of the opinion that private ownership of the means of production is the most effective way to generate wealth for all. They consider socialism to be unworkable and the system of interventionism, which supposedly stands midway between capitalism and socialism, to be unable to achieve the ends desired by its proponents.

The liberal perspective has met bitter opposition. But the opponents of liberalism have failed in their attempt to refute its underlying theory and its practical application. They have used evasion instead of logical argument in an effort to protect themselves from liberalism's crushing criticisms of their own plans. The socialists avoid criticism by claiming that Marxism has banished any investigations concerning the organization and the effectiveness of a socialist society; they continually exalt the socialist state of the future as a paradise on earth, but they refuse to enter into any discussion of the details of their plan. The interventionists have chosen a different technique. On totally inadequate grounds, they challenge the universal validity of economic theory. Not being in a position to logically combat economic theory, they merely refer to a "moral pathos," which had already been spoken about in the invitation to the founding meeting of the *Verein für Sozialpolitik* in Eisenach.[3] They confront logic with moralizing, theory with resentment, and argument with reference to the power of the state.

Political economy predicted the consequences from interventionism and from state and municipal socialism exactly as they have occurred. All of its

3 [The *Verein für Sozialpolitik* (the Association for Social Policy) was founded in 1872 by a group of German economists, historians, and political scientists opposed to both the free-market policies associated with British Classical economics and the ideas of revolutionary socialism. While accepting much of the socialist critique of capitalist society, these German social scientists advocated what they called State Socialism and the welfare state. Their ideal was a paternalist system of social insurance and government regulation of industry and trade by the imperial German government. They said economic and social policy was to be guided by expediency and pragmatism, and not by any general and universal principles concerning man and the social order. See Eugen von Philippovich, "The Verein für Sozialpolitik," *Quarterly Journal of Economics* (January 1891), pp. 220–37; and Richard M. Ebeling, "The Political Myths and Economic Realities of the Welfare State," in Richard M. Ebeling, ed., *American Peristroika: The Demise of the Welfare State* (Hillsdale, Mich.: Hillsdale College Press, 1995), pp. 3–38, for a brief history of the origin of the German welfare state and the German economists and historians who advocated it.—Ed.]

warnings were ignored. For fifty or sixty years the countries of Europe have followed an anticapitalist and antiliberal policy. More than forty years ago Sidney Webb (Lord Passfield) wrote: "... it may now fairly be claimed that the socialist philosophy of today is but the conscious and explicit assertion of principles of social organization which have been already in great part unconsciously adopted. The economic history of the century is an almost continuous record of the progress of socialism."[4] This was written at the beginning of this development and in England, where liberalism was able to withstand anticapitalist economic policies the longest. Since then, interventionist policy has made great advances. The widely held view nowadays is that we live in the age of the "regulated economy"—as a step on the way to the blessed socialist society that is to come. And now that precisely everything that economics had predicted has come to pass, now that the fruits of anticapitalist economic policy have become clear to see, the cry is everywhere heard: This is the downfall of capitalism, the capitalist system has failed!

Liberalism is not responsible for any of the institutions that reflect the economic policies of our day. Liberalism was opposed to the nationalization of enterprises and municipal projects that are now shown to be a catastrophe for the public budget, as well as a source of filthy corruption. It was against denying protection for non-striking workers and placing the power of the state in the service of the trade unions. It was against unemployment compensation, which turns unemployment into a permanent and mass phenomenon. It was against social insurance, which turns the insured into grumblers, malingerers, and neurasthenics.[5] It was against tariffs (and by implication against cartels) and restrictions on the freedom

4 Sidney Webb, "Historic," in George Bernard Shaw, ed., *Fabian Essays in Socialism* (Garden City, N.Y.: Doubleday, [1890] 1965), p. 47. [Sidney Webb (1859–1947) was one of the most influential members of the Fabian socialist movement, which was dedicated to the gradual, nonrevolutionary transformation of Great Britain into a socialist society. He was one of the founders of the London School of Economics in 1895. In the 1930s, he and his wife and intellectual partner, Beatrice, wrote lengthy defenses of the Soviet experiment under Stalin.—Ed.]

5 [For a brief account of the origin and consequences of the German national health-insurance program, from its founding under Bismarck through the Weimar Republic before Hitler came to power, see Richard M. Ebeling, "National Health Insurance and the Welfare State," in Jacob G. Hornberger and Richard M. Ebeling, eds., *The Dangers of Socialized Medicine* (Fairfax, Va.: Future of Freedom Foundation, 1994), pp. 25–37.—Ed.]

of movement.[6] It was against taxation and inflation. It was against military armaments, against colonial acquisitions, against the repression of minority-speaking populations, against imperialism, and against war. It put up a stubborn resistance against the policies that resulted in capital consumption.[7] And liberalism did not create the armed party troops that are only waiting for a favorable opportunity to start a civil war.[8]

6 [See Ludwig von Mises, "The Freedom to Move as an International Problem," [Christmas 1935] in Richard M. Ebeling and Jacob G. Hornberger, eds., *The Case for Free Trade and Open Immigration* (Fairfax, Va.: Future of Freedom Foundation, 1995), pp.127–30. —Ed.]

7 [In 1930, Mises collaborated with Richard Schüller, Edmund Palla, and Engelbert Dollfuss in a study on the form and degree to which capital consumption had occurred in Austria, *Bericht über die Ursuchen der wirtschaftlichen Schwierigkeiten im Österreich* [A Report on the Causes of the Economic Difficulties in Austria] (Vienna: 1931). See also Fritz Machlup, "The Consumption of Capital in Austria," *The Review of Economic Statistics* (January 15, 1935), pp. 13–19, especially p. 13, n. 2: "Professor Ludwig v. Mises was the first, so far as I know, to point to the phenomenon of consumption of capital. As a member of a committee appointed by the Austrian government...he also emphasized comprehensive factual information"; and Nicholas Kaldor, "The Economic Situation in Austria," *Harvard Business Review* (October 1932), pp. 23–34.—Ed.]

8 [In Germany during this time, both the Communist party and the National Socialist party (the Nazis) had organized, armed followers ready to use violence in street battles with their political enemies and for intimidating demonstrations of force. Hitler's were known as the Storm Troopers, or Brown Shirts. See Ludwig von Mises, *Omnipotent Government: The Rise of the Total State and Total War* (Spring Mills, Pa.: Libertarian Press, [1944] 1985), pp. 207–10:

> Both the nationalist Right and the Marxian Left [in Germany] had their armed forces. ... Their members were people who had their regular jobs and were busy Monday to Saturday noon. On weekends they would don their uniforms and parade with brass bands, flags, and often with their firearms. They were proud of their membership in these associations but they were not eager to fight; they were not animated by a spirit of aggression. Their existence, their parades, their boasting, and the challenging speeches of their chiefs were a nuisance but not a serious menace to domestic peace.... But [Hitler's] Storm Troopers were very different from the other armed party forces both of the Left and the Right. Their members were ... jobless boys who made a living from their fighting. They were available at every hour of every day, not merely on weekends and holidays. It was doubtful whether the party forces—either of the Left or the Right—would be ready to fight when seriously attacked. It was certain they would never be ready to wage a campaign of aggression. But Hitler's troops were pugnacious; they were professional brawlers. They would have fought for their Führer in a bloody civil war if the opponents of Nazism had not yielded without resistance in 1933.

In Austria at the same time, the "armed party troops" were made up of three groups. The *Heimwehr*, or Home Defense Force, had come into being shortly after the end of the First

II

The argument used for making capitalism responsible for at least some of these things is based on the idea that entrepreneurs and capitalists are no longer liberals but have become interventionists and statists. The state-

---

World War in local communities, especially in the provincial and rural areas. Their original purpose was to defend the border areas when the political boundaries of the new Austria were uncertain and invading forces threatened border communities. But they soon became a well-organized private army that in the early 1930s had almost 50,000 trained and uniformed men. They served as the private military force behind the Christian Socialists. The *Schutzbund*, or Protection League, was organized in opposition to the *Heimwehr* as the private military arm of the Social Democratic Party. In the early 1930s, a third private army joined them, the Brown Shirts, serving as the strong-arm organization for the Austrian Nazi movement. From the early 1920s, the *Heimwehr* and the *Schutzbund* were well-trained and organized, and equipped with uniforms, rifles, and ammunition. They had camps and clubhouses, and regularly engaged in field maneuvers throughout the country. When the two groups would encounter each other during these training sessions, they often entered into actual battles. In July 1927, fierce fighting broke out between them and the Austrian police and government troops in the streets of Vienna, after a serious gun battle between them in the Austrian countryside earlier that year. See Ludwig von Mises, *Notes and Recollections* (South Holland, Ill.: Libertarian Press, [1940] 1978), pp. 88 & 90:

> It was even more significant that the Social-Democratic Party had at its disposal a Party Army that was equipped with rifles and machine guns—even with light artillery and ample ammunition—an army with manpower at least three times greater than the government troops, such as the Federal Forces, state and local police.... The Social-Democratic Army, officially called the "Organizers," [*Ordner*] conducted open marches and field exercises which the government was unable to oppose. Unchallenged, the Party claimed the "right to the street."... The terror caused by the Social-Democrats forced other Austrians to build their defenses. Attempts were made as early as winter 1918–1919. After various failures, the "Home Guard" [*Heimwehr*] had some organizational success.... I watched with horror this development that indeed was unavoidable. It was obvious that Austria was moving toward civil war. I could not prevent it. Even my best friends held to the opinion that the force (actual and potential) of the Social-Democratic Party could be opposed only by violence. The formation of the Home Guard introduced a new type of individual into politics. Adventurers without education and desperados with narrow horizons became the leaders, because they were good at drill and had a loud voice to give commands. Their bible was the manual of arms; their slogan, "authority." These adventurers—petty *Il Duces* and *Führers*—identified democracy with Social-Democracy and therefore looked upon democracy "as the worst of all evils." Later they clung to the catchword, "corporate state." Their social ideal was a military state in which they alone would command.

—Ed.]

ment is correct, but the conclusions drawn from it are wrong. These conclusions are based on the completely untenable Marxist view that entrepreneurs and capitalists safeguarded their special class interests through the use of liberalism during the heyday of capitalism, but now, in the late and declining period of capitalism, they protect their interests through interventionism. Thus it is supposedly shown that the "regulated economy" under the system of interventionism is an historically necessary economic arrangement for that phase of capitalism in which we presently find ourselves. But the idea that Classical economics and liberalism were the ideology (in the Marxist meaning of the word) of the bourgeoisie is one of Marxism's many absurd doctrines. If entrepreneurs and capitalists thought like liberals in the England of 1800 and think like interventionists, statists, and socialists in the Germany of 1930, the reason for this is that even entrepreneurs and capitalists are in the grip of the ruling ideas of the time. Entrepreneurs had special interests that could have been safeguarded by interventionism and harmed by liberalism in 1800 no less than in 1930.

Nowadays the great entrepreneurs are often referred to as "economic leaders." Capitalist society knows no "economic leaders." The characteristic difference between a socialist economy and a capitalist economy lies precisely in the fact that the entrepreneurs and the owners of the means of production follow no other leadership than that of the market. The custom of referring to the directors of large enterprises as economic leaders signifies that today one generally achieves these positions not through economic success but by other means.

In the interventionist state it is no longer of crucial importance for the success of an enterprise that the business should be managed in a way that it satisfies the demands of consumers in the best and least costly manner. It is far more important that one has "good relationships" with the political authorities so that the interventions work to the advantage and not the disadvantage of the enterprise. A few marks' more tariff protection for the products of the enterprise and a few marks' less tariff for the raw materials used in the manufacturing process can be of far more benefit to the enterprise than the greatest care in managing the business. No matter how well an enterprise may be managed, it will fail if it does not know how to protect its interests in the drawing up of the customs rates, in the negotiations before the arbitration boards, and with the cartel authorities. To have "connections" becomes more important than to produce well and cheaply.

So the leadership positions within enterprises are no longer achieved by men who understand how to organize companies and to direct production in the way the market situation demands, but by men who are well thought of "above" and "below," men who understand how to get along well with the press and all the political parties, especially with the radicals, so that they and their company give no offense. It is that class of general directors that negotiate far more often with state functionaries and party leaders than with those from whom they buy or to whom they sell.

Since it is a question of obtaining political favors for these enterprises, their directors must repay the politicians with favors. In recent years, there have been relatively few large enterprises that have not had to spend very considerable sums for various undertakings in spite of it being clear from the start that they would yield no profit. But in spite of the expected loss it had to be done for political reasons. Let us not even mention contributions for purposes unrelated to business—for campaign funds, public welfare organizations, and the like.

Forces are becoming more and more generally accepted that aim at making the direction of large banks, industrial concerns, and stock corporations independent of the shareholders. Statist writers have hailed this politically motivated "tendency of big enterprise to socialize itself," i.e., to let interests other than regard for "the maximum profit for the shareholders" guide the administration of the enterprise.[9] In the reform of the German securities law, efforts have already been made to make the interests of the shareholder subordinate to the interest and welfare of the enterprise, namely, to "its intrinsic and permanent economic, juridical, and sociological value and its independence from the shifting majorities of changing shareholders."[10] The directors of large enterprises nowadays no longer think they need to give any consideration to the interests of the shareholders, since they feel themselves thoroughly supported by the state and that they have interventionist public opinion standing behind them.[11]

---

9 John Maynard Keynes, "The End of Laissez-faire," [1926] in *Essays on Persuasion* (New York: W. W. Norton, 1963), pp. 314–15.

10 Richard Passow, *Der Strukterwandel der Aktiengesellschaft im Lichte der Wirtschaftsenquente* [The Changing Structure of Joint-Stock Companies in Light of Public Hearings on the Economy] (Jena: Gustav Fischer, 1929), p. 4.

11 [On the extent of government intervention, regulation, and control in the German economy in the 1920s and early 1930s when Mises wrote this article, see Gustav Stolper, *German Economy, 1870–1940* (New York: Reynal & Hitchcock, 1940), pp. 198–220. See especially pp. 219–20:

In those countries in which statism has most fully gained control—for example, in the successor nations of the old Austro-Hungarian monarchy—they manage the affairs of their corporations with about as little concern for the firm's profitability as do the directors of public enterprises. The result is ruin. The theory that has been cobbled together says that these enterprises are too big to allow them to be managed simply in terms of their profitability. This is an extraordinarily convenient idea, considering that renouncing profitability in the management of the company leads to the enterprise's insolvency. It is fortunate for those involved that the same theory then demands state intervention and support for those enterprises that are viewed as being too big to be allowed to go under.

III

It is true that socialism and interventionism have not yet succeeded in completely destroying the capitalist economy. If things had already gone that far, we Europeans, after centuries of prosperity, would again experience what hunger means on a large scale. But we still have enough capitalism around us that new industries come into existence and the existing ones continue to improve and expand their productive facilities. All the economic progress that has been made and is being made comes from what still remains of the capitalist economy in our society. But capitalism is constantly undermined by government intervention and must hand over

---

When at last it became apparent that this state intervention in the shape it had achieved at the height of the prosperity period [of the 1920s] was powerless to prevent the outbreak of the most disastrous economic crisis in German history, the full responsibility for the economic decline was blamed on the "system"—that is, the Weimar democracy. But paradoxically enough, it was not the system of state intervention as such that was blamed by the opposition. This system was much too deeply rooted in the German political and economic history of the last few centuries. On the contrary, the general popular feeling pressed the demand that this very imperfect and incomplete system of state interventionism be superseded by one more nearly perfect and complete. This was the content of the "anticapitalistic yearning" which, according to the National Socialist slogan of the day, pervaded the German nation....This explains why the opposition against the National Socialist dictatorship was much weaker in the field of economics than in the political and cultural field. The road to the totalitarian state had been well laid out. The National Socialist government needed but to utilize for its own aims the instruments of state power forged by its predecessors.
—Ed.]

in taxes a very considerable portion of its profits to cover the deficits of inefficient public enterprises.

The crisis from which the world is suffering today is the crisis of interventionism and of national and municipal socialism; in short, it is the crisis of anticapitalist policies. Capitalist society—there is no difference of opinion about this—is governed by the workings of the market process. Market prices bring supply and demand into balance and determine the direction and extent of production. The capitalist economy gets its meaning from the market. If the function of the market as regulator of production is permanently undermined by an economic policy that attempts to set prices, wages, and interest rates other than in the way the market forms them, then a crisis will surely occur.

It is not Bastiat,[12] but Marx[13] and Schmoller[14] who have failed.

12 [Frederic Bastiat (1801–50) is often considered one of the most effective critics of all forms of government intervention and socialism in the first half of the nineteenth century. With clear logic combined with biting sarcasm he demonstrated the contradictions and absurdities in all forms of protectionism and restrictions on free competition. He also argued that in the free market, the interests of individuals were brought into harmony for mutual betterment.—Ed.]

13 [Karl Marx (1818–83) was the most influential socialist writer of the last one hundred and fifty years. His theory of scientific socialism and class conflict became the basis for the Communist revolutions and dictatorships of the twentieth century.—Ed.]

14 [Gustav von Schmoller (1838–1917) was a prominent University of Berlin economist in imperial Germany who led the "Socialists of the Chair" and who defended and glorified Prussian and military power. He was a leading member of the German Historical School, which rejected abstract, deductive theorizing in economics for detailed historical studies from which it was hoped empirical laws of economics might be discovered. He also was a strong advocate of the German welfare state and regulation of industry and trade in the name of the national interest. He was one of the founders of the *Verein für Sozialpolitik*.—Ed.]

CHAPTER 21

Interventionism as the Cause of the Economic Crisis

A *Debate Between Otto Conrad and Ludwig Mises*[1]

Remarks by Dr. Otto Conrad

In his lecture on "The Causes of the Economic Crisis,"[2] Ludwig Mises makes use of his well-known *Critique of Interventionism* for an explanation of the economic crisis.[3] This explanation culminates in the following sentences: "With the economic crisis, the breakdown of interventionist economic policy becomes apparent. . . . The capitalist social order acquires meaning and purpose through the market. Hampering the functions of the market and the formation of prices does not create order. Instead it leads to chaos, to economic crisis."[4]

No doubt this is correct. An economic crisis is characterized by a prolonged and severe imbalance between supply and demand. Such an imbalance is impossible if prices and wages are flexible, i.e., if they are not prevented from rising and falling according to the conditions of the market. If prices (and wages) can rise when demand is dominant and fall when supply is dominant, then supply and demand always have to come back into balance. If, on the other hand, prices are kept too low, e.g., as in the

1 [This chapter contains an exchange, originally written in German, between Otto Conrad and Ludwig von Mises that appeared in the *Jahrbucher für Nationalökonomie und Statistik* (1932).—Ed.]

2 [Ludwig von Mises, "The Causes of the Economic Crisis: An Address," [1931] in Percy L. Greaves, ed., *On the Manipulation of Money and Credit* (Dobbs Ferry, N.Y.: Free Market Books, 1978), pp. 173–203.—Ed.]

3 [Ludwig von Mises, *Critique of Interventionism* (Irvington-on-Hudson, N.Y.: Foundation for Economic Education, [1929] 1996).—Ed.]

4 [Mises, "The Causes of the Economic Crisis," pp. 201–2.—Ed.]

case under rent controls, then supply falls short of demand and a shortage arises; if prices are held too high, then demand falls short of supply and the economy cannot fully develop its productive potentialities. In light of this, I, too, attribute the economic crisis to the continuation of excessively high prices and wages.[5] This being a case of a disruption of the normal self-adjustment process, different from a cyclical downturn, I refer to it as an "economic paralysis," to distinguish it from the customary expression, an "economic crisis."

And based on what has been said, with regard to the ultimate cause behind an economic paralysis there is complete agreement between Mises and myself. We both find the cause for this paralysis in the impediments standing in the way of a downward movement in prices and wages. But as to the question of who is driving prices and wages up or prevents them from falling, we have widely different opinions. Mises assigns responsibility for the economic paralysis to the *state* because of its tariffs and taxes, its social and pricing policies, and to the *working class* because of its wage policy. *Mises says not a single word about the entrepreneur and his pricing policy.* In my opinion, *the entrepreneur has a leading role* in promoting interventionism. The entrepreneur substantially contributes to increases in prices and puts great obstacles in the way of necessary price reductions. It is worth looking into the reasons behind Mises's complete disregard of the interventionism of the entrepreneurs because it provides the opportunity to correct the errors of many other theorists, besides just Mises.

There are three aspects to this problem that should be mentioned.

1. Mises uses a vague and incomplete concept of monopoly.

2. Mises is confused about the prerequisites for the integration of unemployed workers into the economic system.

3. Mises is confused about the repercussions of "rationalization" for the demand for labor.

I ❧❧❧

Mises's starting assumption is that the price that is formed on the unhampered market reflects a state of equilibrium in which price and costs coincide. Mises calls this price the "natural" price; he sees it as the price that

5 [Otto Conrad, *Absatzmangel und Arbeitslosigkeit als Dauerzustand* [Depressed Sales and Unemployment as a Permanent Condition] (Vienna/Leipzig: Holder-Picher-Tempsky, 1926); and *Der Mechanismus der Verkehrswirtschaft* [The Mechanism of the Economics of Commerce] (Jena: Gustav Fischer, 1931).—Ed.]

is regularly formed on the market. The natural price is the price that is most advantageous for the consumer. Mises speaks of an inescapable force inherent in the capitalist system that compels entrepreneurs and capitalists to use their productive facilities and work forces in a way that most abundantly satisfies the wants of the consumer, given the social and technological circumstances. The *competition* of the market sees to it that those entrepreneurs and capitalists who are not equal to the task lose their dominant position in the production process. The market forces the entrepreneur to manage his business in such a way that in earning the greatest profit he serves the needs of the consumers in the *best and least expensive way*.[6]

These assertions hold, Mises says, under the presumption that competition is unrestrained and therefore unhampered in its operations. It is the pressure of competition that keeps the price at the level of costs. All efforts to push the price above cost and to maintain it there accordingly must prove futile. As a result, any interventionism on the part of the entrepreneur, which might be aimed at ratcheting up prices, is also excluded. Equally impossible is any artificial lowering of the price below the "natural" level because then the price would no longer cover costs and production would be shut down. Mises is quite right, therefore, when he concludes that all attempts to lower the natural price through price controls and other interventionist pricing policies are pointless and nonsensical.

But all of this takes the idea of unrestrained competition as an assumption. The question arises as to whether or not competition in our economy is normally unrestricted, as Mises assumes, and therefore whether the customary, regular market price is the natural price, at which costs and price coincide. Mises does not overlook the fact that there are deviations from the natural price; but he sees this as a problem only in the case of monopoly prices, and he makes the assertion that the amount of monopoly in our contemporary economy is relatively small. "Twist and turn the monopoly question as one may, one always comes back to the fact that monopoly prices are possible only where there is control over natural resources of a particular kind or where legislative enactments and their administration create the necessary conditions for the formation of monopolies."[7] According to Mises, these are the only cases in which permanent

---

6 [Mises, "The Causes of the Economic Crisis," pp. 176–77.—Ed.]

7 [Ludwig von Mises, *Liberalism: The Classical Tradition* (Irvington-on-Hudson, N.Y.: Foundation for Economic Education, [1927] 1996), p. 95.—Ed.]

deviations from the natural price are possible. Like most theorists, Mises distinguishes between only *two* kinds of market relationships: competition, under which the price tends to coincide with the costs; and monopoly, under which competition is excluded. In the context of these two headings, it is understandable that Mises considers the natural price as the one that is usually formed on the market.

In contrast to this, I demonstrated many years ago that there are *three* kinds of market relationships: *free* competition, *restricted* competition, and the *exclusion* of competition. Only in the case of free competition do price and costs coincide. Between free competition and the exclusion of competition there is a whole series of different gradations of *restrictions on competition*, which make it possible for the entrepreneur to hold the price more or less high above costs, according to the degree of the restriction on competition. In the case of the exclusion of competition the entrepreneur is in a position to arbitrarily set the price within certain limits.[8]

Mises leaves out of consideration all cases of restrictions on competition, under which the price is maintained above costs and the natural price does *not* come into existence. At the same time he considerably underestimates the extent of monopoly.

A first group results from *natural* restrictions on competition, among which land monopolies are the most important; Mises also mentions them. These result not only from the wealth and resources of the land but also from the control of land in favorable locations, where the more favorable locations depend upon the most diverse set of circumstances.

The second group results from *artificial* restrictions on competition, under which the flexibility of prices is prevented by price agreements. Under this heading are the numerous price agreements in industry and commerce, in the transportation system, among the banks and insurance companies, and regardless of whether they take the form of rigid cartels or something less formal. Mises also considers cartels to be monopolies. But he insists that, with very few exceptions, cartels owe their existence to the interventionist policy of government, and not to any inherent tendencies

---

8 I consider it appropriate to put "restrictions on competition" and the "exclusion of competition" together under the name of "monopoly" and then contrast *all* cases of *unfree* competition with free competition. I think this terminology is justified by the fundamental distinction that exists between price formation in free competition and price formation under which there appears even a single restriction on competition. This distinction is fully justified in my book, *Der Mechanismus der Verkehrswirtschaft*, pp. 260 ff. and particularly, p. 281 ff.

in the free economy.[9] We shall leave unanswered the question as to what degree the formation of cartels is dependent upon tariff protection. We shall assume that, with the elimination of customs barriers, cartels would disappear. The question still remains, however, as to *with whom* do tariff policies favoring cartels originate. It is easily seen that governments do not force tariffs on the entrepreneurs but rather it is the entrepreneurs who demand the tariffs, using any means available. The blame for interventionist policy is, then, not to be placed on governments but on the entrepreneurs. This is even more the case when the cartels not only try to keep prices high in their own area of production but try to influence the prices formed at the higher stages of production as well. Such artificial limitations on competition relate not only to cartels but also to all other kinds of pricing agreements, above all in the retail business. That the fall in raw-material prices has not affected the prices for manufactured goods, that a large gap exists between wholesale and retail prices and between factory and sale prices, all demonstrate in the clearest way today that the resistance to price reductions by the entrepreneurs has been very successful. Nowhere is to be seen that ineluctable pressure to satisfy the needs of the consumers in the best and most inexpensive manner, which Mises claims entrepreneurs must do under competition.[10]

A third group results from limitations on competition having nothing to do with the natural scarcity of certain essential resources or cartel agreements or legal restrictions, but from what I call *de facto* restrictions on competition. They arise from those numerous cases in which certain enterprises acquire a monopoly position due to the fact that they are designed from the start to meet the entire demand in a market. Examples would be the post and telegraph, telephone service, the railroads, highways, and inland navigation, the gas and electric works, water distribution systems, and in smaller cities also slaughter houses, warehouses, theaters, concert halls, bathing installations, etc. It would not be profitable for a second, competing enterprise to appear in these markets. Competitive pressures do not

---

9 [Mises, *Critique of Interventionism*, p. 40. — Ed.]

10 In a significant study of recent price conditions in Austria, the director of the Austrian Institute for Business Cycle Research, Dr. Oskar Morgenstern, concluded, on the basis of very instructive data, that not only monopolists but the ordinary entrepreneur as well has the ability within broad limits to determine the market price independent of demand. See "Die Preise im Konjunkturzyklus [Prices in the Business Cycle]," *Österreichischer Volkswirt* (September 26 & October 3, 1931).

exist in these instances, and the prices of these enterprises can be kept high above their costs. Mises, of course, will not admit that this is true even with regard to the railways. He writes: "A few decades ago people used to speak of a transportation monopoly. To what extent this monopoly was based on the licensing system remains uncertain. Today people generally do not bother much about it. The automobile and the airplane have become dangerous rivals to the railroads. But even before the appearance of these competitors the possibility of using waterways already set a definite limit to the rates that the railroads could venture to charge for their services on several lines."[11] In reply to this, no monopolist can raise his price without limit. Our problem does not concern the question of whether a price could be raised without limit. It is about whether the price can be maintained above its natural level. And this is to be answered in the affirmative with regard to the railroads as well as to all other *de facto* restrictions on competition.

Now, finally, as far as *legal* monopolies are concerned (design and trademark protection, author and inventor protection, privileges and franchises), Mises designates them all as products of government intervention. He wishes to combat them by abolishing all these legal restrictions, after which the problem will disappear. This is only partially correct. Among the legal monopolies are franchises, including the aforementioned *de facto* monopolies (transportation firms, gas and electric works, etc.). The franchise is a way for the government to exercise an influence on the prices set by these enterprises, to assure against the reckless exploitation of their monopoly position. The intervention of the government is present in these cases to curb the interventionism of the entrepreneurs. Consequently, ending government intervention in this area would by no means eliminate the monopoly problem. Legal monopoly would simply be replaced by *de facto* monopoly, which thereafter could be exploited without restraint.

Out of all of these numerous restrictions on competition, Mises recognizes only natural and legal monopolies, and he regards the latter as obviously avoidable. Given this perspective, it is understandable that Mises overlooks the interventionism of the entrepreneurs. In all cases in which a restriction on competition or a monopoly can be taken advantage of, *the entrepreneur* is the interventionist. He keeps the price above his costs and sets the price differently from how it would have been formed on the unhampered market. The entrepreneur commits a pricing-policy interven-

11 [Mises, *Liberalism*, p. 94.—Ed.]

tion in the sense in which Mises defines it.[12] Mises could not have over-looked this if he had not defined monopoly the way he did. He curtly dis-misses the term "free competition" as a foggy phantom;[13] but without it the cases of restricted competition cannot be clearly grasped. If Mises had devoted more time to observing the actual conditions of competition in the economy today and given more attention to the literature concerning it, it would not have escaped him that the "natural" price coinciding with costs is *a rare exception* and not the rule. He would have seen that the inter-ventionism so vigorously combated by him is practiced not only by public bodies and by the labor force, but also and above all by the entrepreneurs.

II ❧❧❧

The foregoing remarks do not completely explain all the misunderstand-ing there is about the true state of things. An essential role is played here by something about which Mises is not sufficiently clear. This concerns the conditions for *the process of integrating unemployed workers into the economic system.*

"For the entrepreneur," says Mises, "the employment of workers is part of doing business. If the wage rate drops, the profitability of his enterprise rises, and he can employ more workers. So by reducing the wages they seek, workers are in a position to raise the demand for labor."[14] Is this cor-rect? Adding men to the work force is really only possible if it is assured that the increased production of these workers can be sold. That presupposes the expansion of demand in proportion to the output of the enterprise. But how can demand be expanded merely because the business becomes more profitable? The entrepreneur does not use the increased profit provided by the wage decrease to buy more of the production of his own plant!

One sees that Mises is not fully aware of the requisite condition under which a wage decrease leads to new hiring in the work force. The neces-sary condition is for the wage decrease to find expression in a lowering of the price of the product. Only if the price falls can that expansion of de-mand occur, which assures a market for the increased production result-ing from employing newly hired workers. If, on the other hand, the

---

12 [Mises, *Critique of Interventionism*, p. 7: "Price intervention aims at setting goods prices that differ from those the unhampered market would set." — Ed.]

13 [Ibid., pp. 34–35. — Ed.]

14 [Mises, "The Causes of the Economic Crisis," p. 186. — Ed.]

entrepreneur retains the savings in labor costs for himself, then no expansion of demand occurs and no new workers can be employed. Without an increase in buying power an expansion of demand, of production, and of the labor supply is impossible. But buying power can be increased only by a cut in prices. No doubt the lowering of his wages is the only means the worker has at his disposal for increasing his labor opportunities. But this only works indirectly in that it makes the entrepreneur's business more profitable and so enables him to be in a position to lower his selling price. If the entrepreneur does not do this, then the wage cut fails in its purpose, and an expansion in the demand for labor does not occur.

For more workers to be employed it is not enough that the businesses are more profitable. The entrepreneurs must use this increased profitability to bring down their selling prices. Because Mises overlooks this, he objects to "the demand that the reduction of prices be tied to reduction of wages."[15] In his eyes, healing the economic paralysis only requires a reduction in wages, the reduction in prices is not important. That is the *second* reason why the entrepreneur is not mentioned among the factors that Mises considers responsible for economic paralysis. It is up to the entrepreneur, not the worker, to reduce prices. If, like Mises, one regards a reduction in prices as something unimportant for the economy's recovery, then every inducement naturally slips away to make the entrepreneur co-responsible for the economic paralysis. But actually it is the rigidity of prices, and only indirectly the rigidity of wages, that causes economic paralysis. The level of the prices of goods is decisive in creating the buying power for the consumers. If, as Mises quite correctly emphasizes, the consumer is the real master of the economy because his demand for various quantities of goods determines what gets produced in the individual lines of production,[16] then everything depends upon putting consumers in the position to be able to buy more goods than before. But that is only possible if the prices of goods decrease.

III ❧❧❧

The same confusion as that regarding the effects of wage pressures on the demand for labor appears in Mises's discussion of the *effects of rationalization on labor demand.* "Workers released by the introduction of indus-

---

15 [Ibid., p. 191.—Ed.]
16 [Ibid., pp. 176–77.—Ed.]

trial technology find employment in other positions. The ranks of newly developed branches of industry are filled with these workers. The additional commodities available for consumption, which come in the wake of 'rationalization,' are produced with their labor. Today this process is hampered by the fact that those workers who are released receive unemployment relief and so do not consider it necessary to change their occupation or the place of work in order to find employment again."[17] Rationalization increases the productivity of labor. Therefore the same quantity of goods can be produced with a smaller workforce or a greater quantity of goods can be produced with the same number of workers. Mises then assumes without further consideration that this increase in goods actually will be produced. In his opinion the released workers will find employment again if only they are willing to change their line and place of work.

But for this increase in goods actually to be produced the *sale* of the increased product must be assured, and that is the case only if a *moderation in the price* goes hand in hand with the increase in production. Greater quantities of goods can find buyers only at lower prices. So besides the willingness of the workers to change their place and type of work, a *second* precondition also must be fulfilled if the released workers are to find employment again. The savings in labor costs brought about by rationalization must be joined with reduction in prices. If this does not occur, if the entrepreneurs keep the profits resulting from rationalization, then prices will not be lowered, no more goods can be sold than before, and therefore no more goods can be produced than before. So then—as a consequence of rationalization—the *same* quantity of goods is produced with *fewer* workers and the redundant workers become permanently unemployed.

The Interventionism of the Entrepreneurs?
Reply to the Preceding Remarks of Otto Conrad
by Ludwig Mises

I ❧❧❧

A large segment of public opinion looks upon economic events exactly as Conrad does in the foregoing comments, with the eyes of the public prosecutor looking for the guilty parties who need to be punished. Conrad be-

17 [Ibid., p. 193.—Ed.]

lieves that he must pronounce entrepreneurs of being guilty of interventionism, and he censures me because I have failed to do this. But my view of the matter is completely different from Conrad's. I am an economist, not a preacher of morality who wishes to judge, avenge, and punish. I do not look for guilty parties but for causal connections. And if I speak of interventionism, I am not making accusations against the "state" or against "labor." I only attempt to point out to what consequences a system, a policy, an ideology must necessarily lead. Before I used the term "interventionism" and precisely defined it conceptually, the expression was alien to most German writers.[18] Today it is in general use; even the *Handwörterbuch der Staatswissenschaften* [The Encyclopedia for the Social Sciences] hastens to include an article on "State Interventionism" in a supplementary volume to its latest edition. When an expression becomes popular, it easily loses the conceptual exactness that alone makes it appropriate for scholarly investigations. This has also happened to the term "interventionism." Otherwise Conrad probably would not have been able to say that entrepreneurs practice interventionism.

Entrepreneurs, capitalists, landowners, and workers are participants in the market, and they demand prices for their services. The consumers answer these price demands through their buying or abstention from buying on the market. From this interaction there results the market, on the basis of which supply and demand are brought into balance. Through the process of price formation the market performs its function as regulator of production. It gives direction to all the activities of a society based upon the

---

18 [Mises, *Critique of Interventionism*, pp. 1–2 & 4:

Interventionism is a limited order by a social authority forcing the owners of the means of production and entrepreneurs to employ their means in a different manner than they otherwise would. . . . Interventionism seeks to retain private property in the means of production, but authoritative commands, especially prohibitions, are to restrict the actions of private owners. . . . Particular orders may be quite numerous, but as long as they do not aim at directing the whole economy, and replacing the profit motive of individuals with obedience as the driving force of human action, they may be regarded as limited orders. . . . We must distinguish between two groups of such orders. One group directly reduces or impedes economic production (in the broadest sense of the word, including the location of economic goods). The other group seeks to fix prices that differ from those of the market. The former may be called "restrictions of production"; the latter, generally known as price controls, we are calling "interference with the structure of prices." . . . [I]nterventionism . . . does not seek to abolish private property in production; it merely wants to limit it . . . [I]t seeks to create a third order: a social system that occupies the center between the private-property order and the public-property order.

—Ed.]

private ownership of the means of production and the division of labor. If the process of price formation on the market is impeded by commands that proceed from coercive governmental authorities, then we speak of a price-interventionist policy.[19] It would be completely meaningless also to talk of interventionism where there is nothing more than market participants who demand prices that are "too high." If the price demands of the sellers are consistent with the condition of the market, then from the standpoint of scientific consideration they cannot be labeled as being "too high." If, however, they do not correspond to the condition of the market, then they will produce those consequences that the mechanism of the market must always bring about. A portion of the goods brought to market cannot be sold, and from this there will develop consequences that finally bring down the market price to that point corresponding to the condition of the market.

When Conrad criticizes me for speaking of the wage policy of the workers but ignoring the pricing policy of the entrepreneurs, he fails to recognize the fundamental difference that exists between these two. Labor unions exercise physical force against strike breakers with the indulgence of the government; entrepreneurs cannot proceed in the same way against competitors, since at least a little bit of liberalism is still in effect. The unemployed are supported from public funds; presently in Europe, unsold goods are not yet bought up with public funds and destroyed (as they do with coffee in Brazil).

There are efforts at work to raise prices through credit expansion. Conrad will, however, scarcely wish to claim that I have not emphasized sharply enough the consequences from an expansion of circulation credit and in general from inflation of every kind. For many long years I stood all alone among German writers in defense of the theory of circulation credit and its explanation of economic crises; today the theory is generally accepted.[20] And in my work referenced by Conrad, I have referred to the policy of governments that buy up goods with public funds in order to maintain high prices as a form of unemployment assistance.[21]

19 [Ibid., pp. 7–11.—Ed.]

20 [Ludwig von Mises, *The Theory of Money and Credit* (Indianapolis: Liberty Fund, 3rd rev. ed., [1924; 1953] 1980); and "Monetary Stabilization and Cyclical Policy," in Israel M. Kirzner, ed., *Classics in Austrian Economics: A Sampling in the History of a Tradition* (London: William Pickering, 1994), pp. 33–111.—Ed.]

21 [Mises, "The Causes of the Economic Crisis," pp. 193–95.—Ed.]

II ❧❧❧

Conrad denies that wage reductions must bring about the increased employment of workers. If, according to him, wage reductions do not bring a decrease in prices, because the entrepreneur keeps for himself the savings in labor cost, then no expansion in demand results, and no additional workers can be employed. Now, in my opinion, no economist can concede that entrepreneurs are able to maintain high prices arbitrarily. Whoever considers that to be possible denies the interdependency between market prices, which forms the starting point of all economic investigations and without which all economic discussion would be nonsensical. If the participants in the market were "free," in the sense that market prices depended exclusively upon their own conduct, then it would be justifiable to replace catallactics[22] with moral theological discourse like that of the medieval churchman or of the ethical school of political science. Only if one takes the viewpoint of those who are not economists—a viewpoint with which I am not going to argue *here*—does it make any sense to blame entrepreneurs because they don't lower prices enough. The preacher of morality says to the entrepreneurs, "Lower prices so that others are not harmed." The economist knows that if they demand more than is consistent with the state of the market, a part of their goods will be unsalable; they, therefore, must either reduce the prices they are demanding for their goods or lose their positions as entrepreneurs.

But for the moment, let us accept Conrad's viewpoint and assume that the entrepreneurs keep entirely for themselves the profit resulting from the reduction in workers' wages or from the improvement in the methods of production by keeping prices at the old level. Conrad thinks that in the case of a reduction in wages no additional workers are employed, and in the case of industrial rationalization workers will become unemployed because no market can be found for the increased production. After all, greater quantities of goods can only find buyers at lower prices.

Let us consider this. If the increase of income that occurs due to the reduction in wages or from the development of new technology is not of any advantage to the workers but only to the entrepreneurs, then the entrepreneurs become richer. Their income rises by precisely that amount which they have withheld from the workers, meaning that they can now

22 ["Catallactics" is the Greek word for "exchange." It also means "to turn from enemy into friend."—Ed.]

either consume more or invest more. All underconsumption theories founder on the understanding that the "too little" which the "exploited" receive must have been transferred to the "exploiters," and the latter must either consume it or invest it. Of course, under these conditions production would have to move in another direction; fewer articles of mass consumption would be produced, and there would be more available for the consumption of the upper classes as well as for investment in more means of production. But, and this alone is important for us in this connection, it cannot be shown how this disadvantage for the masses could disrupt the market in the sense that unemployment would have to arise.

Entrepreneurs do not have it in their power, as Conrad seems to think, to raise prices as much as they like. But if they could do so, they certainly would not be able to make unemployment a permanent phenomenon.

III ❧❧❧

Socialist writers today especially try to support their demand for replacing the capitalist social order with the socialist one by claiming that capitalist society has an inherent tendency leading toward the progressive cartelization and pooling of enterprises. I believe I have provided proof that cartelization and pooling, excepting in special cases that I have delineated precisely, are a result of protectionist policies and other state intervention.[23] They owe their origin to interventionism, not to any emerging tendency operating in the unhampered market economy. If we had free trade everywhere today, then the formation of cartels and trusts would play a very insignificant role. Conrad chooses not to go into the question of whether and to what degree tariff protection is really essential as a precondition for the formation of cartels; he is ready to assume that cartels would have to disappear when customs barriers did. But entrepreneurs advocate protective tariffs, and therefore, according to Conrad, "the blame for interventionist policy should then not be placed on governments but on the entrepreneurs." Entrepreneurs are always ready to take advantage of any limitation on competition or from a monopoly. "Interventionists," that is, adherents of interventionist economic policies, are, with the exception of a few economists, all of our contemporaries. I have often stressed this most emphatically, and I have never maintained that the entrepreneurs were

23 [Ludwig von Mises, *Socialism* (Indianapolis: Liberty Fund [1951] 1981), pp. 344–51. —Ed.]

not also interventionist-minded. The entrepreneurs' desires can, however, only be implemented if the coercive authorities in society seek to carry them out.

Customs duties deflect production from places possessing more favorable conditions for production to places having less favorable conditions for production; they therefore reduce the productivity of human labor. By bringing about a series of further conditions, customs duties make it possible for the entrepreneurs to obtain higher, monopoly prices instead of competitive prices. Protectionism therefore decreases the overall output of the labor of society and brings about shifts in income. But it cannot be maintained that it prevents the adaptation of the economy to the situation created by the existence of a tariff barrier. Only if the economy is prevented from adapting do those disturbances arise that both Conrad and I have in mind.

IV ❧❧❧

One of Conrad's fundamental errors lies in his views concerning the consequences of restrictions on competition. Restrictions of any sort on competition—included among production-intervening policies, according to the terminology that I introduced[24]—diminish the social product, but they do not disrupt the functioning of the market. If the government orders that only the beneficiaries of its special privileges may practice a certain profession, e.g., that women cannot be employed for night work, or that foreign goods can either not be imported at all or only upon payment of a tariff, then no doubt all of this influences the concrete configuration taken on by the prices of the market. But the market brings supply and demand together through changes in prices. To use Conrad's expression, no economic paralysis occurs.

Hence the widely held view that only under free competition can the market work as the regulator of production is completely false. Liberalism demands freedom of competition because it expects from it the greatest possible productivity from the labor of society. But the fact that antiliberal policies restrict competition is not a rational argument for further government intervention, with the word "rational" meaning the purposes in mind of the initiators of the original intervention. If competition

---

24 [Mises, *Critique of Interventionism*, pp. 5–7.—Ed.]

has been restricted and if as a consequence prices have risen, then a price-interventionist policy that is meant to bring prices back down to where they were before will work no differently than they would have worked in reference to prices that had been formed under free competition.

Only with regard to monopoly prices—using this term in its legitimate and strict catallactic meaning—the situation is different. The difference between the higher monopoly price and the lower competitive price is open to government for intervention.[25] But in the overwhelming number of cases referred to by Conrad, monopoly does not exist in this meaning—the only logical meaning—of the term.

Conrad refers to the "large gap between wholesale and retail prices and between factory and consumer prices" in order to prove the success that entrepreneurs have had with their resistance to every reduction in their prices. But he seems to have forgotten that this resistance can only be successful where—as in Germany and most especially in Austria—a specific, middle-class-oriented government interventionist policy makes it successful.

V ❧❧❧

Conrad has never correctly understood the theory of imputation,[26] or in general the whole body of modern economics, because he always wants to assign some moral meaning to it. Intentionally, subjectivist doctrine is completely value-free. It makes no ethical judgments and has never in the least declared that wages "should in some sense be proportionate to the labor performed." All it says is that at the "static," i.e., the equilibrium, wage all those who want to work can find employment and all employers who are looking for workers are able to find them—and that at any higher wage rate unemployment must occur.

In all of his writings and in his remarks above, Conrad shows that he is of the opinion that the capitalist order, which rests upon the private ownership of the means of production, can only function "properly" if entrepreneurs and workers are controlled by certain rules of conduct, the

25 [Ibid., p. 105.—Ed.]

26 [The theory of imputation attempts to demonstrate the process by which the value of a finished product on the market is reflected back into the relative values of the factors of production utilized in its manufacture.—Ed.]

observance of which cannot be automatically guaranteed in the market. Therefore inappropriate conduct, namely conduct that leads to "economic paralysis," may be constantly practiced.

Considering the fact that Conrad refers to himself as an opponent of state interventionism—believing as he does that state interventionism leads to "economic paralysis"—it would seem that, implicitly, he would reject the idea that the state can force entrepreneurs and workers to observe some type of "proper" conduct. However, Conrad only opposes interventionism, and the use of those policy instruments, that he considers inappropriate. He actually demands the most rigorous interventionism. "The industrial corporations, the chambers of commerce and industry, the associations of entrepreneurs, etc., may control prices, and the authorities must intervene with inexorable severity against every entrepreneur who raises prices excessively."[27]

Given these circumstances, it is difficult to understand why Conrad approves of my *Critique of Interventionism*. What he proposes is really nothing other than interventionism. The theoretical starting point for his train of thought is the notion that, in the economic order that is based on the private ownership of the means of production, prices are not determined by the underlying economic data. Therefore, market prices can and must be brought to their "correct" position by some sort of "well-intentioned" and "well-informed" courts of justice. If one shares this opinion—and it cannot, of course, be rejected out of hand without the type of thorough reflection that is done in economic *theory*—then one may openly declare that economic *theory* is impossible. One is then practicing ethics and not value-free science, and one can only hope for an enlightened regime whose interventions will lead the market along the "correct" path.

---

27 [Otto Conrad, *Der Abbau der Preise* [The Reduction of Prices] (Vienna, 1932), p. 16. —Ed.]

CHAPTER 22

Planned Economy and Socialism[1]

Those who recommend the planned economy as a new type of economic order, one that is fundamentally different from previous economic systems, make the objection that under a capitalist system economic activity takes place without a plan, and it is this "planlessness" that is to blame for the severe depression from which the economy is presently suffering. This objection of a presumed planlessness, however, ignores the fact that forces are at work in the capitalist social order that give a rational direction to all economic activity and thus assure the system's success.

No entrepreneur can produce anything other than what consumers are willing to buy without exposing himself to the danger of serious losses and economic bankruptcy. Entrepreneurs and capitalists are forced to manage their productive enterprises and their labor forces—given their supplies of capital and the state of technology—in such a way that the needs of the consumers are as fully satisfied as is possible. It is therefore a mistake to refer to the capitalist system of production as an economy for profit in contrast to a planned economy as an economy designed to satisfy needs.

The Market

In the final analysis, in a capitalist economy it is the wants of the consumers that decide the amount and the direction of production, precisely because entrepreneurs and capitalists must be focused on the profitability

---

1 [This article originally was published in German in *Neues Wiener Tagblatt*, No. 78 (March 19, 1933).—Ed.]

of their businesses. Entrepreneurs try to supply those goods whose sale promises them the highest possible profit. But it is the market that decides where profits are earned and losses suffered. If consumers demand more of a product, then its price rises; if they demand less, then the price falls. If entrepreneurs produce only those goods whose sale promises to bring them profits, then that means they are following the wishes of the consumers. It is the market, therefore, that directs a capitalist economy, based on the private ownership of the means of production. The changing prices of the market bring supply and demand into equilibrium. The market price—called the "natural price" by the Classical economists and the "static price" by modern economists—finds its level at a point at which no prospective buyer who is ready to pay the market price leaves the market unsatisfied, and no prospective seller who is willing to accept the market price leaves the market with unsold goods.

Disruptions of the Market by Interventionist Intrusions

The disruptions from which the world's economy has been suffering for years are to be attributed directly to the fact that the functioning of this market mechanism has been interrupted. This is most obviously the case with that most disturbing symptom of the economic crisis: persistent mass unemployment. Due to labor-union action, wages have become rigid. They have succeeded in having part of the work force employed at wages higher than would have existed on an unhampered market. The other side of this success is represented by the continuing unemployment of a growing number of qualified workers. At the "natural" or "static" wage level that is formed on the unhampered market, entrepreneurs are able to find all the workers that they are seeking and for which they are willing to pay; and all qualified workers who are willing to work for this wage are able to find employment. However, if wages are set at a level higher than the market-determined wage, due to the government-supported policies of the labor unions, then only a part of the work force finds employment.

The disruptions of the economic order, therefore, are not to be ascribed to any inability of the market economy to properly manage its production possibilities. Instead, it is precisely the intrusions of interventionist policy that prevent the attainment of an equilibrium situation.

A *Planned Economy Is a Controlled Economy*

The advocates of a planned economy correctly recognize that interventionist policy is unworkable because it leads to consequences for which no one would wish: the consumption of capital, the long-term unemployment of millions, and a growing imbalance between production and consumption. But the means that they propose for alleviating this situation are impracticable. They recommend that every form of economic activity be subjected to the systematic planning of one central authority. This is the same program the socialists refer to as "socialization" and that the Communists call "bolshevism." The socialists and Communists have also used the argument about the supposed planlessness of the capitalist system — which they call the anarchy of production — as the primary point in favor of their alternatives. And, like the proponents of the planned economy, the socialists and Communists also claim that they are not proposing the governmentalization of the economy. Instead, they propose nationalization, or turning over the means of production to the workers.

But this is merely playing with words. The unified systematization of all economic activity, which planned economy, socialism, and Communism all strive for in the same way, can only be achieved if the state's social apparatus of control stands behind the plan, supports it, and elevates the plan to the status of a compulsory system. If this were not done, then each individual would be free to act differently than the manner in which the plan prescribes. Entrepreneurs could produce other things and sell at other prices than anticipated in the plan; workers could seek positions other than the ones to which the plan wants to assign them.

The systematization of the planned economy can, therefore, only be brought about through a decree of the state; those who would act in conflict with this decree must be forced into compliance by the apparatus of control that is given the assignment of enforcing the commands of the state. Only those who have not thought the problems through to their logical conclusion can maintain that a planned economy is not a controlled economy.

It is also a mistake to think that one can perceive a presumed difference between a planned economy and socialization, which supposedly lies in the fact that a planned economy leaves more room for individual initiative than does a socialist order. Individual initiative precisely means that the entrepreneur does what, according to his own lights, will best meet the wants of the consumers. But if the entrepreneur is not free to decide what and how to produce as he considers best from the perspective of his interest in earning profits, if instead he is instructed to obey the plan—which prescribes for him what and how he is to produce and at what price he must offer the product—then all his initiative is stifled. He may remain an entrepreneur in name; but in fact in a planned economy, although perhaps privileged in his personal income, he becomes a high-ranking civil servant in the general economic apparatus of the government. Nothing more will be left to his own initiative than is left, for example, to the manager of a factory in the Soviet State.

Economics has shown that no socialist system can work because under it, it is impossible to anticipate the outcome of a future undertaking and subsequently to determine through accounting methods the resulting outcome. The method of economic calculation that is used in a capitalist society, and without which all business and economic rationality as well as all technological evaluation would be unfeasible, assumes the use of money and the existence of a market for what is produced. In a socialist society these assumptions are missing; hence there could be no real economic activity in our sense of the word, and it would be thoroughly impossible to carry out roundabout processes of production.

The fact that certain nationalized undertakings are possible in a society which otherwise rests upon the private ownership of the means of production, and that in particular regions of the world socialization has been undertaken at the national level while the capitalist system is retained in the other parts of the world, does not diminish the probative force of this decisive argument. These state enterprises within a capitalist Europe, and the Soviet regime within the wider capitalist world, can base their economic calculations on the prices that are formed on capitalist markets. Soviet Russia lives not only materially on the support of the capitalist world that has "invested" capital in Russia; what is even more important, it bases its own economic calculations on the market prices of capitalist society. There is no such thing as socialist economic calculation, and there never can be; that is to say, socialism is unworkable.

A Planned Economy and Entrepreneurship

All of this also holds true for a planned economy. A planned economy differs from socialism only in that the managers not only are formally reduced to the status of civil servants, they also descend physically into the position of bureaucrats who are put at the head of departments of the centralized planning agency. And as the great Italian economist, Vilfredo Pareto,[2] emphasized, weak and subservient managerial types of the second and third generation, who do not understand how to manage their inheritance and who have lost their self-confidence because of the failures they have suffered, find the planned economy particularly attractive. These weak heirs of capitalist wealth numerically predominate in the managerial class everywhere in the interventionist system, and it is easily understood why the idea of a planned economy finds support in these circles.

Socialism by Another Name

The planned economy is not a defense against socialism; on the contrary, it is the only way in which socialism can still operate in Central Europe today. The Bolshevik experiments in Russia, the inefficiencies made obvious under socialist leadership in the decade and a half that has passed since the war, and the corruption that has been connected with all attempts at socialization, have shaken the trust of public opinion in socialism wherever it appears openly under this name. Under the new name of the planned economy, the system that was discredited under its old name now finds new adherents. If experiments with the planned economy should end up being carried out on a large scale in one of the industrialized states of Central Europe, people would soon experience a frightful disillusionment.

One cannot combat a mistaken principle, which is what socialism is, by trying to put it into effect under a different name. If one wants to prevent the downfall of European civilization, then one must decide to openly and honestly come forward against all forms of socialization of the means of production. Neither socialism nor a planned economy can overcome the great economic crisis; this can only be achieved through the radical renunciation of interventionist economic policy.

2 [Vilfredo Pareto (1848–1923) was one of the leading Italian mathematical economists of the first half of the twentieth century. His *Manual of Political Economy* (1906) developed the theory of general equilibrium and indifference-curve analysis. He was an economic liberal and a strong opponent of socialism. Critical of favoritism and privilege under democracy, he was falsely accused of being profascist after Mussolini came to power in Italy. Pareto also was a prominent sociologist, his major work being A *Treatise on General Sociology* (1916); one of his contributions to sociology was a theory of the rise and fall and circulation of elites in society. He taught at the University of Lausanne in Switzerland from 1893 until 1900, when he inherited a fortune. In 1901, his wife ran away with their cook and he was left with his large menagerie of cats. —Ed.]

CHAPTER 23

The Return to Freedom of Exchange[1]

1   General Observations

Countries do not put themselves in a situation in which they would be tempted to adopt those measures covered by the term "foreign-exchange control" if they do not resort to inflation or attempt to use credit expansion as a means of reducing interest rates below those that would prevail on the money market free of intervention by the note-issuing central bank. This has been shown not only in an indisputable way by economic theory, but it has been confirmed by the entire monetary history of Europe and America.

It is a mistake to believe that an "unfavorable" balance of payments or a negative balance of trade must necessarily lead to the depreciation of a country's currency. Holding such a view means to forget that the debit items of the balance of payments are always balanced by the credits, and that imports are always paid for by exports (in the broadest meaning of these two terms). An increase in imports is possible only if its equivalent value is covered by an increase in merchandise exports, or a greater quantity of services rendered abroad, or additional loans that are contracted, or by other similar means.

The view that loans are contracted to cover a deficit in the balance of trade is the opposite of the way things really are. When a country contracts a foreign debt, its trade balance becomes negative by an amount equal to that of the loan. On the other hand, the payment of the interest and amor-

---

1 [This article was originally delivered as a lecture at the Vienna Congress of the International Chamber of Commerce on May 30, 1933. It appeared in *Minerva Bancaria: Revista Mensile* (June 1933), published in Venice, Italy. It is translated from the Italian.—Ed.]

tization fees on the loan makes the trade balance positive by the same amount.

The theory according to which the rate of exchange depends on the state of the balance of payments or the balance of trade is mistaken because it does not consider that any change in the quantity of foreign loans or in imports and exports is not possible if there are no price differentials that make them profitable. It is true that prices are established daily on the basis of the current state of the balance of payments; but this, in turn, results from the prices and price differentials that dictate the purchases and sales that are worth undertaking.

It is also mistaken to distinguish between essentials and nonessentials. It is argued that because essentials have to be imported at any cost, a country that has to import essentials but only exports nonessentials will constantly experience a fall in the value of its currency. It is forgotten that the greater or lesser need for these various products is already captured in the volume and intensity of the demand for them at the prices at which they are purchased.

However great may be a country's need for foreign manufactured goods, raw materials, or foodstuffs, these cannot be obtained if that country is unable to pay for them. To import more, it must export more. If that country is unable to export finished or semifinished goods, but will not or cannot give up its imports, then it must go into debt.

Only if a country's central bank pursues a policy of artificially lowering the rate of interest below the rate that would be established by the free market can the rate of foreign exchange rise, which would automatically limit imports and stimulate exports, and therefore set in motion a reverse movement bringing the exchange rate back to its former level. However, if inflation is occurring, and domestic prices are rising, imports will not be restricted by the rise in the rate of exchange, exports will not be stimulated, and a reverse movement will not counter the worsening exchange rate.

The cause of the exchange rate's depreciation is always to be found in inflation, and the only remedy for fighting it is a restriction of fiduciary media and bank credit. The crucial mistake during the war and in the early postwar years was to ignore this truth and to try to combat the monetary depreciation by restricting foreign-exchange markets rather than ending the inflation. It is disturbing to see the same error being committed once again.

2   The Reasons Behind the Reintroduction of Foreign-Exchange Controls

National political considerations persuaded a number of governments since the spring of 1931 once more to resort to an increase in their currencies. Faced with the choice of either allowing a number of banks and other large enterprises to fail or helping them by expanding the currency, they have chosen the second solution. They have increased the quantity of paper money in circulation, thus initiating a process that had to lead to a depreciation of their currencies.

There is no point in criticizing the policy that has been followed or to blame the people who were responsible for it. We will only note that there were and are only two possibilities. Either the policy is resisted that puts the currency at risk through setting interest rates below the rates reflecting actual market conditions, or a policy of credit expansion is followed, which inevitably leads to monetary depreciation. There can be an attempt to stabilize the domestic level of prices, as has been done in England, but in that case depreciation in the currency's exchange rate could not be avoided. On the other hand, the goal can be to maintain the foreign-exchange rate and allow domestic prices to participate in the general decline in prices experienced on the world market. The two goals cannot both be achieved at the same time.

There is now a better appreciation of the benefits from stable exchange rates in comparison to the serious consequences from a depreciation of the exchange rate and the even greater negative effects resulting from foreign-exchange control. It is therefore doubly necessary to remember that maintaining stable exchange rates is incompatible with the pursuit of these other domestic economic policy goals.

3   The Effects of Foreign-Exchange Control and the Conditions Necessary for Its Abolition

The expression "foreign-exchange control" generally includes a variety of measures aimed at a number of policy goals. Much confusion has been created by not having kept these different measures distinct.

In the first place, foreign-exchange control must be evaluated in terms

of whether or not the government wants to maintain the legal, but fictitious, rate of foreign exchange.

a) *Control of foreign exchange with the maintenance of a fictitious exchange rate.* There are some countries (Austria and Hungary) that have a
policy that refuses to admit that there has been a depreciation in their currency, and maintain their foreign-exchange rate below the market rate.[2]
Its primary purpose is to further domestic policy goals, and it is only sec-
ondarily concerned with issues of international trade. Through its use
some social groups have been deprived of their wealth in the form of foreign exchange, and all creditors who have contracted for payment in gold
or foreign currency are harmed since payment in gold or foreign currency
has been replaced with payment in depreciated paper money. Conversely,
those who have benefited are the domestic debtors who were supposed to
pay in gold or foreign currency, as well as all those who have been able to
obtain a foreign currency at a price below the unhampered market rate.

It may be officially stated in these countries that the purpose behind
foreign-exchange control is to stimulate exports and discourage imports.
But, in fact, the system actually produces the opposite effect; imports are
stimulated and exports are hindered. The obligation imposed on exporters
to remit to the Exchange-Control office all or a part of the proceeds from
their foreign sales is equivalent to a tax on their exports. And the allocation
of foreign exchange among importers at this below-market fixed exchange
rate is equal to a premium on imports.

It is absolutely correct if, in these countries, a shortage of foreign exchange is reported. But such a shortage necessarily results from setting a
maximum price for their currencies not corresponding to the conditions on
the market. In order to avoid losses, everyone tries not to remit foreign currency to the Exchange-Control office. It is not required to explain the
process by which there occurs the shortage of foreign currency; it's the
same process described by Gresham's Law.[3]

b) *Control of foreign exchanges without fixing a rate of exchange different for the market rate.* If, as has been done in England, all attempts to

2 [On the introduction of and consequences from exchange control in Austria, Hungary,
and Germany in the 1930s, see Howard S. Ellis, *Exchange Control in Central Europe*
(Cambridge, Mass.: Harvard University Press, 1941); and Oskar Morgenstern, "The Removal of Exchange Control: The Example of Austria," *International Conciliation*, No. 333
(October 1937), pp. 678–98. —Ed.]

3 [See Chapter 19, "The Gold Standard and Its Opponents," footnote 8. —Ed.]

impose a rate of exchange on the foreign-exchange market is abandoned, the Exchange Control becomes a purely neutral institution from the standpoint of commercial policy. But in most instances this is not the case.

The theory that exchange-rate depreciation results from the status of the balance of trade is often invoked as a rationale for restricting or prohibiting imports. Limiting and even prohibiting the importation of more than a certain quantity of goods and ignoring contractual obligations is justified by citing the conditions of the moment. Meeting these obligations, therefore, becomes impossible. Furthermore, since payment is only authorized for certain categories of imported goods, the Exchange-Control office ends up allocating foreign exchange for only particular imports and not for others. It is difficult to say which of these two methods is more harmful to foreign trade. It is certain that, sooner or later, both end up severely hampering international trade.

Separate from trade policy, the Exchange Control also—in fact, primarily—serves the furtherance of credit policy in various countries. Both in the countries that officially maintain a rate of exchange different from the market rate and in those that do not, the purpose behind the foreign-exchange control is to prevent foreign creditors from withdrawing funds and putting their debtors into difficulty. By forbidding debtors from making payments they owe abroad, they are freed from the consequences usually connected with default on a loan.

4 Exchange Control and Bank Insolvency (The Problem of Short-Term Credit)

The primary problem behind the foreign-exchange controls comes from the fact that a number of European banks have invested long-term the equivalent of the short-term credits that have been extended to them from abroad, with no ability to pay on their part being anticipated in the near future. These banks are not in a position to fulfill obligations to their creditors to pay on demand or on short notice. It is the most difficult problem confronting these European banks today. Foreign-exchange control enables these banks to use the government's restrictions as a way to avoid making their repayments abroad. But this does not resolve the underlying problem, it merely postpones it. This problem, however, must be resolved; otherwise a restoration of international relations in these as well as in credit matters in general cannot be restored.

Foreign-exchange control allows these banks to contact their creditors and temporarily arrange moratorium agreements. But these agreements do not provide a definitive solution. But a definitive solution must be found in order to restore the credit system and its functioning again in a normal manner. This is one of the principal conditions necessary for bringing an end to the world economic crisis.

The restructuring of the insolvent banks must therefore precede the abolition of foreign-exchange control. The banks whose balances are in severe deficit must be liquidated, and the losses that have occurred must be recognized as complete losses. It is useless to postpone the liquidation of these enterprises. The losses will only be made greater by delaying a final settling of accounts. Fortunately, the balances of the majority of the banks in question are not bankrupt but only insolvent. These banks would be in a sound condition if the maturity dates of their own debt obligations coincided with the dates when they received claims owed to them. It is necessary to make every effort to reach an arrangement through agreements between these banks and their foreign creditors, in collaboration with the governments of the various countries involved as well as with international organizations (the League of Nations, the Bank of International Settlements, the International Chamber of Commerce). This is all the more feasible considering that it is not in the interest of creditors that the banks in which they have placed their capital should fail and suffer further losses, only adding to the harm to themselves in the process. These arrangements should be initiated and carried out as soon as possible. Once they are, there will no longer be any obstacles, from this source, to delay the abolition of foreign-exchange control.

It would be superfluous, in this regard, to provide special legislation requiring that banks maintain their own liquidity in the future. The banks will do this in their own interest, particularly if it is clear that any bank that poorly manages it own affairs can have no hope of being kept afloat by government intervention at the expense of the rest of society.

5   Foreign-Exchange Control
and Long-Term Indebtedness

Long-term indebtedness, unlike short-term indebtedness, is not closely connected with the problem of foreign-exchange control. The fact that certain countries, certain public enterprises, and various industrial and agricultural private companies are not capable of meeting their long-term obligations is an aspect of the present economic crisis that requires a prompt remedy.

The delays in straightening out the general economic situation have had very serious consequences. Allowing enterprises that have contracted long-term debts and are unable to repay or amortize them to appeal for foreign-exchange control has delayed the economic recovery and the normalization of the relations between these enterprises and their creditors. Far from being in any way beneficial, this has suspended a solution to the problems, re-created unease, and retarded a return to a normal state of affairs.

Even more difficult than the problem of long-term debts owed by private enterprises is the problem of long-term obligations incurred by public enterprises, central governments, provinces, and cities. The ease with which these entities were able to contract debts led them to borrow capital to a degree far out of proportion with their ability to pay. Even if the fall of prices had not so greatly aggravated their debt burden, their situation would still not be much better. Public enterprises contracted debts far exceeding their ability to pay.

The worst solutions to the problem of long-term indebtedness are: currency depreciation through inflation; requiring the service and amortization of previous debts only in the national currency; making the foreign creditor accept payment only in the national currency; and restricting or prohibiting the transfer of the debt payments abroad except in those cases where the foreign creditor, thanks to international agreements, enjoys a position that protects him from national legislation. In this way the debtor can, it is true, temporarily alleviate his own situation. But such a temporary advantage will be paid for dearly with the breakdown of international credit relations.

These relations are, in fact, already paralyzed. The servicing and amortization agreed to by contractual obligations on old credits are only being partially paid; and new credits are available only to a limited extent or not at all. It is a situation that, in the long run, neither creditor nor debtor countries can endure. Consequently, nothing seems more urgent than an agreement between creditors and debtors for a new arrangement concerning conditions of payment (always with the collaboration of the international organizations that are able to facilitate these difficult negotiations) that will make it possible to fulfill the commitments agreed to in the contracts.

6   Exchange Control and the Balancing of Public Budgets

In some countries there is a connection between the unfavorable conditions in their public finances and exchange control, especially since these countries are tempted to initiate inflation and endanger their currencies. It should be urgently recommended that all states balance their budgets without any further recourse to the issuing of paper money. Nevertheless, even if they undertake a depreciation of their currency, they must not assume that this implies the right to institute legal restrictions on foreign trade or to prohibit the payment of foreign debts.

7   The Control of Exchanges and the Problem of Unemployment

To relieve unemployment it is constantly recommended that jobs be created through the expansion of credit or the issuing of bank notes. Since these proposals call for a rise in prices through international inflation, they should be discussed in connection with a reestablishment of the gold standard and the setting of the price level, not in reference to foreign-exchange control.

As far as the issue of foreign-exchange control touches on this problem, it is enough to remember that any country that resorts to inflation, either by expanding credit or by issuing bank notes, and regardless of whatever name under which it is done, must necessarily bring about an increase in the price of foreign currencies as expressed in its national currency. And in those conditions there is no way to prevent such an increase by a system of exchange control.

8   Conclusions[4]

1. In a country in which bank notes and credit are being expanded, foreign-exchange control cannot prevent the exchange rates from worsening. And

4 [Other undesirable effects from foreign-exchange controls were also emphasized by Mises. See "Noninflationary Proposal for Postwar Monetary Reconstruction," [1944] in

vice versa, in countries in which neither bank notes are being issued nor credit expanded, exchange control is unnecessary in order to insure the stability of exchange rates.

2. The effect of exchange control is to hinder international trade to a degree far exceeding anything ever done to hinder it through customs duties and even by import prohibitions. Since the reestablishment of exchange control in various countries (that is, since the summer of 1931), international trade has suffered more than during the entire half-century of protectionist policies that preceded it. If the exchange control is maintained, we risk seeing international trade relationships fall into chaos, rendering illusory all the facilitation of trade obtained from treaties and international agreements.

3. There is no doubt that the exchange control must be abolished as soon as possible.

4. A precondition for the abolition of exchange control is solving the problem of short-term indebtedness. It is necessary that agreements be concluded between creditors and debtors for the postponement of the maturity dates of short-term debt so the debtor may be able to make repayment in stages without impairing his financial position or the state of his business.

5. A necessary condition for the return to the freedom of foreign-exchange transactions is the negotiating of a new settlement relating to the problem of long-term debts.

6. The abolition of exchange control is a precondition for the return

---

Richard M. Ebeling, ed., *Selected Writings of Ludwig von Mises, Vol. 3: The Political Economy of International Reform and Reconstruction* (Indianapolis: Liberty Fund, 2000), p. 95:

> At any rate, foreign exchange control is tantamount to the full nationalization of foreign trade. . . . Where every branch of business depends, to some extent at least, on the buying of imported goods or on the exporting of a smaller or greater part of its output, the government is in the position to control all economic activity. He who does not comply with any whim of the authorities can be ruined either by the refusal to allot him foreign exchange or to grant him what the government considers as an export premium, that is, the difference between the market price and the official rate of foreign exchange. Besides, the government has the power to interfere in all the details of every enterprise's internal affairs; to prohibit the importation of all undesirable books, periodicals, and newspapers; and to prevent everybody from traveling abroad; from educating his children in foreign schools; and from consulting foreign doctors. Foreign exchange control was the main vehicle of European dictatorships.

—Ed.]

to normal business transactions and communications among countries. Moreover, in order to maintain freedom of foreign-exchange transactions it is necessary that the barriers to trade resulting from bans on imports and prohibitive customs duties be terminated.

7. In order to reestablish normal international credit relations, it is necessary that restrictions on foreign-exchange transactions be abolished, and that international agreements be made that will make a return to such measures impossible in the future. Only by reestablishing normal relationships in matters of extending credit will it be possible for poor countries to obtain the capital and the means that they need to put their economies back in order, as well as once again to become active members in the international economic community.

CHAPTER 24

Two Memoranda on the Problems of Monetary Stabilization and Foreign-Exchange Rates[1]

I On New Technical Arguments for Postponing Stabilization

A ❧ HOW TRUE IS THE THEORY THAT FOREIGN TRADE IS STIMULATED BY FLUCTUATING PARITIES?

Fluctuations in the exchange ratio between a country's national currency and foreign currencies affect the conditions of foreign trade until prices, wages, and interest rates have fully adjusted and a new equilibrium has been established. They influence foreign trade only for a limited time, and not permanently. Their effect is in the short run, not in the long run.

Some authors used to denounce this opinion as old-fashioned doctrinairism and believed that modern experience has proven that both the stimulating effects of a rise in foreign exchange and the paralyzing effects of a fall of foreign exchange may last indefinitely. Of course, the Classical economists proved that monetary fluctuations influence foreign trade only in the short run. But the opposite view is the older concept. It was maintained by seventeenth-century mercantilism, and since then by all friends of depreciation, especially by the European and American bimetallists in the last decades of the nineteenth century. In vain, great efforts have been

---

1 [The following article contains Mises's response in the form of two memoranda to a series of questions submitted to a group of experts concerning aspects of monetary policy and foreign-exchange rates. He wrote them in February 1936. They originally were published in *The Improvement of Commercial Relations Between Nations and the Problems of Monetary Stabilization* (Paris: International Chamber of Commerce, 1936).—Ed.]

devoted to refuting the validity of the Classical doctrine. Its logic is above all criticism. It is an irrefutable economic proposition.

It is incorrect to say that the conditions assumed by the orthodox theory no longer exist and that therefore its conclusions are not applicable to the present situation. Conditions have changed and the economic world is very unlike what it was a hundred or a hundred and fifty years ago. But the elementary conditions presupposed by the Classical doctrine have not been touched by these changes. They exist as long as there are prices, markets, and the international transfer of commodities. It is not true to say that the conditions assumed include free trade between nations. Trade barriers like our own divided the world in which the Classical economists lived. It was just this fact, that there are checks, both natural and institutional, to the transferability of capital, labor, and commodities from country to country, that made them discriminate between home trade and foreign trade.

What has changed is neither the conditions assumed by the orthodox theory nor the fact that there are trade barriers between nations, but the appreciation of the effects of foreign-exchange fluctuations.

First of all, there is the problem of wages and unemployment. In many countries wages did not fall as low as the depressed state of trade required. The salaries and wages of public servants in some countries are too high relative to public revenue. It seems impossible to restore budgetary equilibrium except by a reduction of the payroll. In trade and industry, wages in some countries are too high in comparison to the prices at which the products can be sold. The rigidity of wages has so far been successful, as real wages did not fall in the years of the slump. But on the other hand, with falling prices and unchanged nominal wages, the volume of unemployment increased as entrepreneurs were unable to employ the same number of hands as before.

It is obvious that the proposals to do away with the rigidity of wages are very unpopular. But it is not fair to charge those who see no other means of escape with the accusation of hardheartedness. Those who prefer devaluation of the currency also aim, ultimately, at a reduction in real wages. All the proposals in favor of devaluation are based upon the tacit assumption that nominal wages will remain unchanged, and that with rising prices for commodities real wages will drop. Of course, they do not expressly mention this point. But when speaking of reductions in costs they mean nothing other than a reduction both in gold wages and in commodity wages while nominal wages remain unchanged at least for some time following the devaluation of the currency. The reduction in the costs

of production that is meant to stimulate exports is to a large extent a reduction in the cost of labor.[2]

It is true, the friends of devaluation assume that prices, especially retail prices, will for some time remain unchanged. But this is a fallacious
assumption. If the prices on the world market remain unchanged, then

2 [In February 1936, at the very time that Mises was criticizing devaluation as a roundabout
method to bring about a decline in real wages through a rise in prices while nominal (or
money) wages are presumed to remain the same, there appeared John Maynard Keynes's
The General Theory of Employment, Interest and Money (Cambridge: Cambridge University Press, [1936] 1973). Keynes justified using just such a method for reducing real wages
on the rationale that "[i]n fact, a movement by employers to revise money-wage bargains
downward will be much more strongly resisted than a gradual and automatic lowering of
real wages as a result of rising prices" (p. 264). But already in 1931, Mises had pointed out
in his monograph, "The Causes of the Economic Crisis: An Address," (in Percy L. Greaves,
ed., *On the Manipulation of Money and Credit* (Dobbs Ferry, N.Y.: Free Market Books,
1978), pp. 199–200):

> Only one argument is new, although on that account no less false. This is to the
> effect that the higher than unhampered market wage rates can be brought into
> proper relationship more easily by an inflation. This argument shows how seri-
> ously concerned our political economists are to avoid displeasing the labor
> unions. Although they cannot help but recognize that wage rates are too high
> and must be reduced, they dare not openly call for a halt to such overpayments.
> Instead, they propose to outsmart the unions in some way. They propose that the
> actual money wage rate remain unchanged in the coming inflation. In effect,
> this would amount to reducing the real wage. This assumes, of course, that the
> unions will refrain from making further wage demands in the ensuing boom and
> that they will, instead, remain passive while their real wage rates deteriorate.
> Even if this entirely unjustified optimistic expectation is accepted as true, noth-
> ing is gained thereby. A boom caused by banking policy measures must still lead
> eventually to a crisis and a depression. So, by this method, the problem of low-
> ering wage rates is not resolved but simply postponed.

Again, in 1945, Mises noted in his essay "Planning for Freedom":

> If in the course of an inflation the rise in commodity prices exceeds the rise in
> nominal wage rates, unemployment will drop. But what makes unemployment
> shrink is precisely the fact that real wage rates are falling. Lord Keynes recom-
> mended credit expansion because he believed that the wage earners will acquiesce
> in this outcome; he believed that "a gradual and automatic lowering of real wage
> rates as a result of rising prices" would not be so strongly resisted by labor as an at-
> tempt to lower money wage rates. It is very unlikely that this will happen. Public
> opinion is fully aware of the changes in purchasing power and watches with burn-
> ing interest the movements of the index of commodity prices and of cost of living.
> The substance of all discussions concerning wage rates is real wage rates, not nom-
> inal wage rates. There is no prospect of outsmarting the unions by such tricks.

See Mises's *Planning for Freedom and Sixteen Other Essays and Addresses* (South Holland,
Ill.: Libertarian Press, 1980), p. 14.—Ed.]

wholesale prices for all imported raw materials and foodstuffs go up due to the devaluation, and then retail prices will have to rise too. There may be a time lag between the rise in wholesale prices and the rise in retail prices, but in the end an adjustment takes place.

There are still more items in the bill of costs. There is especially the burden of debts and the payment of interest. Devaluation means, in the first place, an alleviation of the debts. But the creditors, to whose disadvantage this measure works, are not the rich. In former times the creditors were generally the rich, and the debtors the poor. In our age of bonds, savings deposits, and insurance, things are different. The creditors belong mostly to the salaried and wage-earning classes. The sums credited are the poor man's portion of the national wealth. They represent the nonconsumed portion of labor's income, they are labor's reserves for the days of unemployment, sickness and old age, for the bringing up of children and for the support of the widows. The debtors are mostly the entrepreneurs and the capitalists, who own the shares of the corporations, and the landed proprietors and the farmers.

As far as devaluation reduces costs by reducing the burden of debts, it shifts income from the most numerous class of modern society to the relatively small group of proprietors and entrepreneurs. The policy of devaluation, which owes a great deal of its popularity to the humanitarian point of view that condemns a cut in wages—of course, nominal wages—does not only fail in attaining wage stability; it impairs, besides, the situation of the less wealthy classes by reducing their savings.

The stimulus that rising prices for foreign exchange give to the export trade is to some extent due to the fact that for a period of transition and adjustment entrepreneurs are ready to sell the imported raw materials that are contained in the manufactured goods for less than their world price. The manufacturer has bought these raw materials by paying or borrowing a sum of local currency. If the prices, in terms of local currency, that he obtains for his product give an adequate allowance for this sum, he does not mind that the same amount of local currency now means less in terms of foreign exchange and that he will not be able to get for it the same quantity of imported raw materials.

The encouragement that export trade gets from devaluation is due to something like a subsidy received at the expense of all classes connected with foreign trade. Labor contributes by a cut in real wages, creditors by the reduction in their claims, entrepreneurs by losing a part of their capital in selling at prices too low for the replacement of the materials used. Whereas in general an increase in exports means at the same time a corresponding increase in imports, it is different when the increase in exports is due only to a depreciation of the currency. On the one hand, the sums received for the exported goods do not increase in the same proportion as the quantity exported, and therefore the exporting country does not get the additional means for an adequate increase in imports. On the other hand, depreciation makes imports more difficult as there is a time lag between the rise in the foreign exchange and the rise in the home prices of the imported goods. The stimulating effect is limited to exports; imports are more hindered than encouraged.

It may be doubted whether the economists of a country that has depreciated its currency may look with satisfaction on the increase in exports due to the depreciation. Their countrymen are selling more abroad, but they are not adequately rewarded for the additional exports. In the big inflations of the postwar period, people used to denounce these additional exports as a "selling off" and reproached the foreigners for taking advantage of the distressed state of their currency.

On the other hand, the countries whose imports are increasing from the areas with a depreciated currency are not prepared to accept this inflow of goods. That these goods are cheaper than those manufactured in their own country and that they are sometimes sold at prices that do not make sufficient allowance for the replacement of raw materials used in their production makes the importing country consider the transaction as an act of dumping. Measures to restrict such additional imports are proposed and very often adopted. In this way (under the present conditions of a general dislike for imports), the encouragement of exports due to the upward movement in the price of foreign exchange does not lead to an upheaval but rather to a further restriction in foreign trade.

Confining their reasoning only to their own policy, nations see in a nonstabilized currency system, and in the opportunities for depreciation that it affords, a means to increase exports and fight against imports. What they like to ignore is that the increase in exports due to monetary conditions arouses in foreign nations the tendency to use repressive measures to restrict imports.

It cannot be denied that for a limited time a country's exports are stimulated by a rise in foreign exchange. In this respect the belief that fluctuating parities stimulate foreign trade is founded on fact. On the other hand, the instability of the currencies of many countries, just because it artificially stimulates their exports, increases in other countries the inclination to make trade barriers higher and more effective.

B ❧ What is the case for and against the view that competitive exchange depreciation is deflationary?

Depreciation means for a time increased exports and reduced imports. It enables a country for a time to undercut world-market prices and thereby to aggravate the tendencies working for a decline in the prices of the goods exported. On the other hand, the consumer whose income, in terms of foreign exchange or gold, did not increase at all or not to the same degree as the price of the foreign exchange went up, can no longer afford to buy the same quantity of imported goods. Imports are decreasing because the consumption of imported goods drops. In this respect, the belief that the depreciations that have taken place in the last five years contributed to the fall in prices on the world market is well founded.

However, the importance of this factor should not be overrated. There have been other stronger tendencies working for the fall in gold prices.

C ❧ Should we accept the view that wider "gold-points" will enable a restoration of a stability in exchange?

D ❧ The case for and against "flexible" parities.

It seems advisable to combine the answer to question C with the answer to question D, as the former concerns only a special case of what has to be more generally discussed under question D.

A gold standard with flexible parities would mean something radically different from the old gold standard. It would transfer to the government or to some special board the power to fix and alter the price of gold and foreign exchange. The working of the system would be entirely dependent on the use the authorities make of the power given to them. They might believe that the best policy was not to use the right to change the parity at all and to let the parity, once it was adopted, last permanently. It is, however, more probable that they would have other views on the expediency of bringing about a change in the parity and that they would try to make the country independent of the situation on the world market.

The only point on which the opinion of all political parties in all countries has always been unanimous is the condemnation of a high rate of interest. And since people believe—in spite of the teachings of economics and the experience to be learned from the history of banking—that banks have the power to reduce the rate of interest by credit expansion not only for a short period of time but permanently, there will be a general bias for a policy of cheap money, i.e., for low rates of interest. The public will find no harm at all in a policy tending to stimulate business and making prices and wages go up as the result of granting additional credit. They will prefer easy money and rising prices to the maintenance of the established parity. They will try to profit as much as possible from the faculty afforded by the system of flexible parities.

When in the last five years many countries devalued their currency in order to prevent a further fall in prices on their home market, to avoid a rise in the rate of interest, and to give a stimulus to export trade, the measure has been considered as an exceptional one that should be employed only once and never again; it is said to be an emergency expedient justified by the unparalleled event of the heaviest slump in the world's history. It is doubtful whether people were right in this assumption. It seems very probable that, unless there is a radical change in current beliefs concerning monetary policy, nations in the future will again take recourse to the comfortable expedient of devaluing the currency. The situation in which some people believe that prices and interest rates are too high, that real wages should be reduced, and that the export trade needs an encouragement will surely occur again. Public opinion will then ask for a new devaluation, and the government will find no valid reason to oppose such desires.

Even if the country's currency has been stabilized and a new parity has been promulgated without the intention to go off it again, one day or another things may be different. But under a regime of flexible or movable parities, repeated devaluation will be considered as a regular expedient. The enactment of flexible parities already includes a program for new and repeated devaluations.

Flexible parities mean full power for the executive to alter or fix the price of foreign exchange. Wide gold points limit this faculty by fixing two points that should not be exceeded.[3] Compared with a system of boundlessly fluctuating parities it means a closer approach to stability. However, it would not at all make the restoration of stability easier to attain. As soon as the price of foreign exchange has reached the upper gold point, the central bank or the exchange equalization fund would have to follow exactly the same policy to prevent a further rise; i.e., they would have to follow the rules of the orthodox gold standard.

---

3 [The "gold points" represented the upper and lower limits of fluctuations of a country's foreign-exchange value under the gold standard, beyond which it would be profitable to either export gold out of or import gold into the country.—Ed.]

E ❧ What are the lessons of the various exchange equalization funds?[4]

The most difficult problem that reserve policy has to handle today are the precarious conditions of the banking system in times of monetary and political instability. It is obvious that capitalists are anxious to avoid as far as possible losses caused by devaluation. They therefore hold big balances with the banks of those countries whose currency they consider more stable than the currency of their own country. That foreigners used to entrust large sums to the banks of Great Britain, France, Switzerland, and the Netherlands is under the present conditions more of a disadvantage than an advantage for the credit and currency situation of these countries. When the foreign depositors believe that the country's currency will drop in respect to gold, they wish to transfer their deposits to countries whose currency is supposed to be for the time being more stable in respect to gold. The banks are of course not able to pay back at once a great amount of the deposits received. If the central bank were to leave them without assistance they would have to suspend payments. But if the central bank provides them with the notes needed for the repayment of the deposits, then the additional issue of large amounts of bank notes, which are immediately used for buying gold or foreign exchange, makes the foreign exchanges go up rapidly. No bank reserve and no exchange equalization fund can stand such a sudden attack.

It is obvious that the proposals for a devaluation of a country's monetary unit that are recommended by influential political leaders frighten the public. It is not correct to say that the attacks of speculators endanger monetary stability. It would be more correct to say that the continuous discussions on the advisability of devaluation induce depositors, both natives and foreigners, to withdraw deposits and to buy foreign exchange, and that it's this buying that makes foreign exchange go up.

A successful reserve policy cannot be limited to the appropriate ad-

4 [An exchange equalization fund was meant to serve as a "buffer" supply of gold or foreign assets, which would enable a government to resist variations in its currency's foreign-exchange rate (a) by buying all of its currency offered for sale on the foreign-exchange market at the established rate of exchange, if there were speculative selling of its currency, and (b) by selling its currency in any amount demanded on the foreign-exchange market at the established rate of exchange, if there were speculative buying of the currency. The funds set aside for this purpose were considered at best sufficient to fight off short-term fluctuations in the country's exchange rate.—Ed.]

ministration of the bank's reserves and of an exchange equalization fund. What is needed is to put an end to the uncertainty concerning the future conduct of monetary policy. It is intolerable that governments and parliaments hesitate for years between the maintenance of the present parity and a new devaluation.

II   On Exchange Stabilization and the Problem of Internal Planning

Monetary instability is never the immediate outcome of an economic or political situation; it is always the monetary policy that leads to depreciation and instability, and not the economic, financial, and political conditions of a country. When a government—let us say in time of a big war—takes recourse to inflation, its rulers believe that under existing conditions issuing additional notes is the best way or at least the less detrimental way to provide for the financial means that are required. They prefer inflation to an increase in taxation, to borrowing, and to reducing expenditure, either because they believe the harm done by inflation is small when compared with the drawbacks of higher taxes, loans, or reduction of expenditures or because they are not familiar with the fact that an increase in the quantity of notes in circulation must lead to a fall in purchasing power.

That in the last several years the governments and parliaments of some countries went off the gold standard was due to a change in the current opinions about the ends after which monetary policy has to strive. The nineteenth century's monetary policy was guided by the idea that, for the sake of international trade, stability of the foreign exchanges had to be considered as the foremost goal. To avoid instability of foreign exchanges one resorted to the gold standard, which it was expected would be sooner or later adopted by all commercial nations.

The radical change undergone in the last thirty years in these opinions cannot be better characterized than by contrasting Georg Knapp[5] and John Maynard Keynes.[6]

5 [See Chapter 5, "On the Actions to Be Taken in the Face of Progressive Currency Depreciation," footnote 17.—Ed.]

6 [John Maynard Keynes (1883–1946) was the most influential British economist of the twentieth century, arguing for activist monetary and fiscal policy to stabilize economy-wide fluctuations in employment and output.—Ed.]

Knapp was a statist, a protectionist, a sworn foe of every kind of freedom. Nevertheless, in 1905, in his well-known book,[7] which may be styled the manifesto of the Great German Inflation, he designates the aim to which a country's monetary policy should be directed to be the maintenance of the stability of foreign exchanges for the benefit of foreign trade. Eighteen years later, Keynes, who at the time at least still considered himself a liberal and a free trader, announced in his *Tract on Monetary Reform* that more important than the maintenance of the stability of foreign exchanges is the stability of the domestic price level.[8] Even the German conservative antagonist of private enterprise considered stability of foreign exchange as the foremost aim of monetary policy in prewar times, and after the war even the British liberal and advocate of freedom condemned it. Nothing proves better the contrast between the prewar and postwar mentality.

Nor would it be justified to call the goal of planning and for national self-sufficiency a product of the depression. On the contrary, the heaviness of the slump and its long duration are to a great extent due to the fact that governments postponed recovery by their interference into domestic and foreign trade. There are two views on the policy that should be adopted for the sake of a betterment of economic conditions. According to one of these opinions, only a return to a more liberal system would bring the end to the depression. According to the other opinion, the only remedy is to be found in more government interference, in more planning, and in a closer approach to self-sufficiency. Some statesmen used their public speeches, lectures, and articles to recommend the liberal way. But what is really done in most of these countries is just the contrary. From day to day, there is more government interference and less room for the manifestation of private initiative.

We have to realize the fact that the economic ideas that are current today among statesmen and politicians consider every import as a mischief, and believe that every measure that succeeds in keeping out some foreign product from the domestic market to be extremely advantageous. It is true every nation wishes to increase exports and to have more foreign

7 [Georg Friedrich Knapp, *The State Theory of Money* (Clifton, N.J.: Augustus M. Kelley, [1905] [1924] 1973), pp. 274–79. The referenced section of his book is subtitled, "The Stable Exchange as the Ultimate Goal."—Ed.]

8 [John Maynard Keynes, *A Tract on Monetary Reform* (New York: Harcourt, Brace, 1924), pp. 167–77. The referenced section of his book is subtitled, "Stability of Prices versus Stability of Exchange." Keynes explains that "[o]ur conclusions up to this point are, therefore, that, when stability of the internal price level and stability of the external exchanges are incompatible, the former is generally preferable" (p. 177).—Ed.]

tourists visiting the country. But on the other hand, every nation makes imports more difficult, not only by tariffs but by the efficacious weapons of the quota system, and puts obstacles in the way of its citizens wishing to travel abroad. The volume of foreign trade and of tourism is falling continuously. There is hardly a country in the world that has not in these last five years progressed a good deal on the way to national self-sufficiency.

As long as nations were not yet inspired by a general dislike for all kinds of imports and for all transactions that make money go out of the country, they recoiled from a monetary policy of insulation and isolation. The gold standard is an international standard. In the era of liberalism and free trade it was the gold standard's glory to be an international standard. In our days of statism, interventionism and autarky, it is its disgrace. Rising prices of foreign exchange, once presumed as disadvantageous because of their repercussions on foreign trade, are today just for the same reasons considered as highly recommendable.

It would be possible to isolate a country almost absolutely from the world market and to keep it from the international division of labor, and nevertheless to maintain the gold standard and fixed parities. How far such a policy can go depends on the power of the nationalist ideology. If a government succeeds in persuading its citizens that autarky and its corollary, less supply of commodities, are—for some metaphysical and military reasons of independence—preferable to wealth based on international exchange of commodities and services, there are no more checks on the erection of Chinese walls around the country. The maintenance of the gold standard would be incompatible with such a policy. The gold standard would, of course, have lost under such a *raison d'être*. But national self-sufficiency is possible even with an international standard.

There are considerations of a different kind that seem to recommend a policy of devaluation. If the government wishes to make prices go up and to alleviate the burden of debts, it takes recourse to devaluation. As far as debts are concerned, the result obtained is final. But it has been explained in the remarks above that the effect on the price system can be achieved only for a limited time, and that devaluation is not the way to make prices, wages, and interest rates on the domestic market permanently free from the repercussions of the situation on foreign markets.

The policy of monetary instability and fluctuating parities is more the corollary than a substitute for a policy of total planning. The nationalization of foreign trade, the most radical means for the control of dealings with foreign countries, would be able to isolate a country much more effectively than any system of unstable currency.

PART III

Austrian Economic Policy and the Great Depression (1927–35)

CHAPTER 25

The Balance Sheet of Economic Policies Hostile to Property[1]

The time has come to draw up a balance sheet of the economic policies of the last few years. The stabilization of the currency is now far behind us, foreign credits are nearly exhausted, and the various direct and indirect consequences of the crisis of 1921 have already been overcome. The financial balance sheets of Austrian enterprises, which have been published in recent years, make it possible on the basis of solid data to form a picture of the effects on the country due to the war and the wartime economy, the peace treaty and the dismemberment of the Austro-Hungarian economic area, the inflation and the economic policy of the postwar period.

The picture that the financial balance sheets offer is not an encouraging one. A large part of Austria's banking and industrial capital has been lost. The banks and the great industrial enterprises have been viewed as a financial reservoir from which could be drawn all the funding thought necessary for meeting the expenditures of a variety of extremely expensive social and economic policies.

It is now clear what perceptive people had long known and said was true: that resources were being provided from capital and not from the proceeds of the enterprises. A political system that rests upon the consumption of the productive capital of the nation lacks stability, even if the ballots of millions of voters support it. The most important and most urgent change that must occur, therefore, is the elimination of all those taxes and duties that are taken out of the capital of the economy rather than the income of the citizens. But this goal can only be reached if the strictest parsimony is practiced in public finances.

1 [This article was first published in German in *Wochenschrift des Neiderösterreichischen Gewerbevereins* (January 20, 1927).—Ed.]

If we consider the national budget proposal for 1927, which concludes with a deficit of 135 million schillings, we find that this loss is completely attributable to the unfavorable results of the management of national enterprises and the railroads. The deficit of the Post and Telegraph Office and the railroads estimated in the budget amounts to 170 million schillings, or about 35 million schillings more than the total national deficit. The deficit of these two groups of national enterprises is more than twice as large as the entire expenditure budgeted for national defense; it is even somewhat larger than the entire profit of the tobacco monopoly, and is almost as great as the earnings of the Association for Commerce, Trade, and Industry and the income tax taken together. Hence, there is no prospect that the deficit caused by these government enterprises will be made to disappear.

Not even the national forest administration understands how to conduct public management without a loss. The roughly 400,000 hectares of national forest appear in the national budget with a loss of a half million schillings, and the national mountain administration with a loss of about 1.8 million schillings.

If one considers what enormous sums have been extracted from the nation's wealth through the failure of publicly managed enterprises and through the failure of the Postal Savings Office, one can pretty well judge how completely different our national finances would be today if the national agenda were restricted to the more limited responsibilities of government. The economic failure of all public enterprises is, however, not a peculiarity of the Austrian government. Public enterprises have failed all over the whole world. The finances of every single European and non-European nation are in as much or greater disorder as the government concerned has gone farther into the field of the management of business enterprises. In view of this fact, it sounds like a mockery that only a few years ago the further expropriation of private enterprises was recommended in all earnestness for the relief of financial distress and that this policy is still looked upon by wide circles as the highest wisdom in financial policy. The real root of all of our finance difficulties lies precisely in the existence of these public enterprises; in order to cover their operational losses the private sector must be taxed enormously.

Another effect resulting from the economic policy of the postwar period is the decline in the proceeds that the public treasury received from the taxation of urban residential rents. Before the war the nation, the provinces, and the municipalities received almost as much from urban rental properties as the landlord received. Already before the war, housing was 50 percent "socialized." Hence political protection for the renter has caused a huge loss in public finances. In 1913 the total tax on rental income in the region of the city of Vienna was 128 million gold crowns or 184 million schillings. The proceeds from the residential-construction tax, which is, moreover, being introduced for a special purpose, amounts to only 38 million schillings.

For years two radically wrong ideas have dominated our theory of taxation and, unfortunately, also our taxation policy. One idea teaches that the public budget should not regulate expenditures in accordance with the amount of tax revenue but, on the contrary, that tax revenue should be in accordance with expenditures. The other idea claims that taxation must not touch the property and entrepreneurial activity of the mass of the population. These two principles should be held responsible for the enormous rise in public expenditures and tax burdens. Many taxes are defended by the claim that public works, which are paid for from tax money, give business to industry and reduce unemployment. It is forgotten, however, that on the opposite side of the expenditures out of public funds there stands a decrease in the expenditure of the private sector by exactly the same amount that is taken from it through taxation.

Our international trade balance is in deficit. In and of itself a balance-of-trade deficit is not necessarily a bad thing. It all depends on how the deficit in the balance of trade is compensated for in the balance of payments. If, year in and year out, a country has tax and dividend payments to draw from abroad and receives their value in imported goods, then the deficit in the trade balance is not an indication of distress and a poor state of business but instead an indication of prosperity and wealth. But if a country like Austria pays for the deficit in its balance of trade by increasing its indebtedness abroad and by exporting securities, then the adverse trade balance means the consumption of capital. Therefore we must, at all costs, strive to improve our balance of trade; i.e., we must export more goods and import less. But this can be achieved only if industrial costs of production are reduced. Aside from any immediate changes in our international trade policy, there is no other way effectively to reduce the importation of manufactured products on the domestic market and to increase the sale of Austrian products abroad than to lower the costs of production.

But not all the costs of the factors of production in the Austrian economy can be influenced by measures involving changes in domestic economic policy. We have to pay the world-market prices for the raw materials and primary products that we need to import from other countries. As a capital-poor country we must draw upon foreign capital; the state of the foreign money and capital markets, upon which the interest rates we have to pay is dependent, is not subject to the influence of Austria. Reductions in the costs of production only can be effected through a lowering of domestic wages or taxes. If we cannot succeed in reducing taxes and the social burdens that the private production sector has to bear, then wages will inevitably have to go down or unemployment will have to go up.

The reduction of the tax burden on our enterprises is therefore in the interest of all sectors of the population, not only in the interest of businessmen but also and especially in the interest of the labor force. Nothing is more erroneous than the dominant view in Austria today that the question of any radical revision of our public finances and a reduction in tax burdens concerns only businessmen and proprietors. The financial situation of a society may provide ever-so-beautiful cash earnings; but if it undermines the necessary conditions for the nation's economic productivity, it is a policy of decline and destruction that must be opposed with all possible strength.

CHAPTER 26

Adjusting Public Expenditures to the Economy's Financial Capacity[1]

I

Year after year, the Federation, *Länder*[2] [provinces], and municipalities have been increasing the taxes that they exact from the badly shaken Austrian economy. From 1925 to 1929, the total of Federation, provincial, district, and municipal taxes increased from 1,419 million schillings to 1,865 million schillings, an increase of 31.4 percent, or nearly equal to 8 percent per year. In direct federal taxes alone, the increase was even greater; during this period its revenue grew from 285 million schillings to 385 million schillings, for an increase of 35 percent. According to the intentions of the people in government, this trend in tax increases has not reached its end. The federal budget, as well as the budget of the city of Vienna, is anticipating further, very significant increases.

1 [Section I of this article was originally delivered in German as a lecture before the Industrial Club of Vienna on December 1, 1930. The Industrial Club published it in their proceedings newsletter on December 10, 1930 (No. 351). Section II of this article is comprised of Mises's additional remarks at the conclusion of a general discussion of the topic at the Industrial Club's next meeting. These were published in their newsletter in January 1931 (No. 352). Some of the proposals that Mises makes for reforming and redesigning the political and administrative structures of Austria were developed by him in a wider context ten years later in his 1940 monograph, "A Draft of Guidelines for the Reconstruction of Austria," in Richard M. Ebeling, ed., *Selected Writings of Ludwig von Mises, Vol. 3: The Political Economy of International Reform and Reconstruction* (Indianapolis: Liberty Fund, 2000), pp. 133–68.—Ed.]

2 [The "Länder" refers to the provinces into which Austria was divided. They each had a great deal of administrative autonomy separate from the federal Austrian authority in Vienna. At the same time, the municipality of Vienna was also jurisdictionally a "Land" independent of the federal government.—Ed.]

The population takes it for granted that public expenditures will go up every year by a few percent. The federal government has already reached an annual rate of increase of almost 10 percent. It is obvious that this cannot continue at the present pace, because the economic crisis can be expected to make itself felt in the future in the form of a sharp reduction in tax receipts. In this context, we must take into account that a large number of the municipalities are heavily in debt and the situation of the public (i.e., state-run) enterprises is visibly getting worse. Even if the state's expenses were not increased, we have to face the fact that in the coming years, the administrative operations of the Federation, the provinces, and the municipalities will yield considerably less tax revenue.

How could it come to this, and how is this going to end?

The errors in our fiscal policy stem from the theoretical misconceptions that dominate public opinion about financial matters. The worst of these misconceptions is the famous, and unfortunately undefeated, idea that the main difference between the state's and the private sector's budget is that *in the private sector's budget expenditures have to be based on revenues, while in the public sector's budget it is the reverse, i.e., the revenue raised must be based on the level of expenditures desired.* The illogic of this sentence is evident as soon as it is thought through. There is always a rigid limit for expenditures, namely the scarcity of means. If the means were unlimited, then it would be difficult to understand why expenses should ever have to be curbed. If in the case of the public budget it is assumed that its revenues are based on its expenditures and not the other way around, i.e., that its expenses have to be based on its revenues, the result is the tremendous squandering that characterizes our fiscal policy. The supporters of this principle are so shortsighted that they do not see that it is necessary, when comparing the level of public expenditures with the budgetary expenditures of the private sector, not to ignore the fact that enterprises cannot undertake investments when the required funds are used up instead for public purposes. They only see the benefits resulting from the public expenditures and not the harm the taxing inflicts on the other parts of the national economy.

The second questionable principle is the preference for direct taxation—those taxes that are assessed on "property"—over indirect consumption taxes. Over many years, the inflammatory rhetoric of the Social Democrats has succeeded in spreading the view that taxes on commodities of mass consumption should be opposed, but that *levying "taxes on property" does not affect the interests of the workers.* The leaders of the Social Democratic party always talk about "gifts" for entrepreneurs whenever property-tax reductions are proposed. In reality the situation is quite the opposite. Property taxes impede the creation of capital. And when the taxation of enterprises goes too far, it results in the consumption of capital. To a large extent, this has been the case here in Austria for the last eighteen years. Capital consumption is detrimental not only for the owners of property but for the workers as well. The more unfavorable becomes the quantitative ratio of capital to labor, the lower is the marginal productivity of the work force, and, consequently, the lower are the wages that can be paid. That the Austrian economy is only able to compete and survive on the basis of the relatively low wages that are paid today is primarily due to the fact that very significant amounts of the capital belonging to Austrian entrepreneurs have been eaten up during the past eighteen years.

The view that levying taxes on property in any amount does not affect the interests of the masses is just one of the steps leading to the demagogic and false doctrine that it is safe to burden the state with any amount of costs. We see that when this type of thinking is dominant, unlimited demands are made by all and sundry for access to public monies. It is as if the state's coffers were like Lady Fortuna's moneybag into which the finance minister could put his hand, again and again, without ever depleting it.

In any case, we Austrians have arrived at the limit of our financial capacity. But the federal budget for 1931 and the budget of the city of Vienna do not take any notice of this; they count on increasing their revenues even further and believe, therefore, that they can continue to increase their expenditures.

Whenever there is any talk about decreasing public expenditures, the advocates of this fiscal spending policy voice their objection, saying that most of the existing expenditures, as well as the increases in expenditures, are inevitable. Any notion of applying the concept of austerity to the machinery of the public sector is to be rejected. What exactly does "inevitable" mean in this context? That the expenditures are based on various laws that have been passed in the past is not an objection if the argument for eliminating these laws is based on their damaging effects on the economy. The metaphorical use of the term "inevitable" is nothing but a haven in which to hide in the face of an inability to comprehend the seriousness of our situation. People do not want to accept the fact that the public budget has to be radically reduced.

The federal government (though not the provinces and municipalities) has undertaken extensive savings in the last few years by dismissing a number of public servants. But, unfortunately, it was forgotten that if a *dismissal of public servants* is to be financially effective in the long run, it has to be preceded by a *reduction in public responsibilities and by administrative reform.* Our administration continues to be overloaded with duties it has to perform, which in other countries do not require the involvement of public executive bodies.

An especially striking example is the *Probate Examining Office.* Already decades ago, the master of Austrian jurisprudence, Josef Unger,[3] contended that this superfluous institution should be eliminated. Since then, both lawyers and the business sector have repeatedly demanded its elimination. Some twenty years ago, the Austrian Chamber of Commerce spoke out against the continuance of the Probate Examination, and even the judges themselves would like to see this function disappear from their area of responsibility. Nevertheless nothing was changed; we continue to endure this superfluous institution, which causes unnecessary costs to both the state and the citizenry.

Financially much more aggravating is the degree of administrative duplication. Once there was some political justification for the coexistence of the imperial-royal or sovereign administration and the autonomous administration, even though it was never justifiable from the economic viewpoint.[4] But since the coup it does not make any political sense whatsoever any more. The formerly sovereign administration and the formerly autonomous administration are now fused into one by the fact that in November 1918 the area of activity of the imperial-royal head of the government, appointed by the emperor, was given to the governor of the province, who is elected by the provincial parliament. Nevertheless, the fusion of the autonomous and sovereign administrations that, already decades before the coup, had been deemed to be necessary was implemented only in part.

I will cite here two especially pertinent examples regarding the fiscal administration. *Real estate sales* are taxed via the state property-transfer fee that, according to the reasons for its introduction in 1850 as published in the Royal Law Gazette, is considered to be a tax on capital appreciation. But, additionally, the same transfers also become subject to the au-

3 [Josef Unger (1828–1913) was considered one of Austria's leading philosophers of law and legal practice. — Ed.]

4 [See Chapter 9, "Vienna's Political Relationship with the Provinces in Light of Economics," footnote 7. — Ed.]

tonomous capital-appreciation tax. The two levies, seeing that they exist independently of each other, should at least be assessed and collected by the same office. In reality, however, the state property-transfer fee is assessed by the state's fee assessment offices and the capital-appreciation tax by independent autonomous authorities and bodies. The taxable person has to contact both entities for each transfer, and both entities require, separately, the assistance of the Title Registration Court. It would be rather difficult to come up with a more inefficient and costly procedure. Another example is social security and wage-deducted income tax. *Employee and worker income* is taxed on the basis of two completely different principles. Here as well, the federal and the autonomous fiscal bodies exist side by side, without any connection between them whatsoever, and they independently negotiate with the assessor, using him to assist with collection and transfer. Nothing would be easier—even if the two levies were to continue—than to turn over the collection of the social-security tax as well as its transfer to the federal agencies in charge of the income-tax administration.

Perhaps the most blatant and irritating case of superfluous double administration can be found in the case of the *Wiener Gemeindewache* [Vienna Municipal Guard], as it lacks even the excuse that its existence was attributable to the old institutions. It is well known that the creation of the Municipal Guard came about due to a momentary need of party politics.[5] Vienna's budget for 1931 lists the expense for this most superfluous of all institutions at 4.25 million schillings.

But leaving completely aside the double administration that is more than amply described by the preceding examples, it can clearly be seen that our entire *administrative organization is hypertrophic.* If perhaps not in the administrative *de facto* sense, then certainly in the organizational

5 [In January 1927, a child was killed during a battle between the *Heimwehr* (Home Defense Force) and the *Schutzbund* (Protection League), the respective private armies of the Christian Socialist and Social Democratic parties, outside Vienna in a village near the Hungarian border. Two Christian Socialist members of the *Heimwehr* were arrested, tried, and found not guilty in July 1927. The Social Democrats called a general strike in Vienna, which soon resulted in mobs, led by known Communists, burning down the Palace of Justice, preventing the fire brigade from putting out the fire, and rampaging through the streets destroying private businesses. The armed city police was called in to put down the violent disturbances, resulting in the death of eighty-four people. In response, the Social Democratic mayor of Vienna, Karl Seitz, declared that the city police were incompetent. He proceeded to form his own *Wiener Gemeindewache*, recruited from the *Schutzbund*, as an alternative and parallel city police force with its own secret service. It remained active and financed out of tax revenues of the Vienna city government until 1934.—Ed.]

sense, we have *four authorities*: the municipal administration, the district administration, the provincial government, and the federal government. Each of the five smaller federal provinces has a population ranging between 140,000 and 370,000 people. Apart from its provincial government —with its complete, large apparatus—each of these provinces has a fully trained district administration; there is a total of six town districts and thirty head district staffs in these five provinces, and there cannot be any doubt that this goes much too far.

Comparisons with situations abroad cannot be counted as entirely applicable because the administrative setup here is different from that in other countries. However, it is possible to determine that, regarding their size, but more than anything else regarding their number of inhabitants, each of the five provinces is not much larger than the administrative district that functions immediately above the municipal level in many foreign states. Since for political reasons there can be no thought of eliminating the provincial office, then the head district staff should be eliminated, and the municipal administration should be placed directly under the authority of the provincial government. This type of reform is indicated by geographic, technical, and administrative policy viewpoints. It should be mentioned that the subdivision into provinces and district administrations was not tailored to serve the small provinces of present-day Austria, but primarily was designed for the larger administrative areas of the old Austro-Hungarian state, e.g., Bohemia, Moravia, and Galicia.

Furthermore, one has to take into account that an enormous revolution has occurred in the transportation sector. Nowadays it is easier to reach the capital from the remotest village than it was to get to the district town only a few years ago. When Alexander Bach[6] created this administrative organization, there were hardly any railway lines crossing the country, only bad roads; there were no automobiles, no bus lines, no telephones, and only here and there a postal and a telegraph office. The ease with which the provincial capital as well as the federal capital can be reached, as well as a certain tendency inherent in the Austrian people to circumvent the official line of authority, has resulted in the custom that citizens, peasants, and workers go directly to the provincial government, and even the federal government, with the most insignificant matters. Many matters are being processed only pro forma by the staff at the district headquarters,

6 [Alexander Bach (1813–93) served as minister of the interior in the 1850s, and is best known for having liberated the peasants of Hungary.—Ed.]

whereas the authorities higher up on the hierarchical ladder do the actual processing. There is an unmistakable trend to bypass the lower authorities, even in the more recent administrative policy decisions.

A particularly characteristic case that could be mentioned is the recently issued ordinance regarding the obligation to obtain a license for commercial cattle and meat sales in Vienna, and putting the country's highest administrative office officially in charge of granting these licenses.

It is taken as a given that special and local interests will rebel against the endeavor to eliminate the staffs of the district headquarters. But one of the authorities will have to go and the district headquarters' staff is the most dispensable. Furthermore, one also has to take into account that the political-administrative post of the district head has ceased to exist in the republic. Formerly it was the body of the sovereign government that was in charge of supervising municipalities and the population. But such a job is not compatible anymore with the ideas of a democratic state.

The reform could be first implemented in the five smaller provinces. If it were successful there, then it might be extended to the larger federal provinces, where it might seem expedient to replace the staffs of the district heads with county commissioners' staffs whose administrative districts would have to combine several of the former political districts. It is understood that in view of East Tyrol's special circumstances a special administrative entity should be kept in place there, and that the situation concerning commercial traffic requires special arrangements as well. In the interest of streamlining the administration and reducing its costs, it would also be welcome if the reform made it possible to combine a number of smaller communities into larger ones.

The simplification of the *fiscal administration* should be similarly handled. An important precondition has been met with the measures for simplifying the assessment of the general sales and income tax on small commercial and trading operations. If it is possible to have the personal income tax in several municipal districts of Vienna assessed by a *single* public office, then it follows that it would also be possible to have a *single* office assess the much simpler—and much less revenue-yielding—personal income tax in the smaller federal provinces.

Radical reforms also have to be implemented in the *administration of the Department of Justice.*

As the Justice Ministry's official in charge recently advised, there is one judge per 4,847 citizens in Austria; in Sweden that ratio is one per

7,600 inhabitants, in Norway one per 8,300, in Italy one per 9,770, in Denmark one per 13,300, and in France 20,000. Even if we do not take into account France and Denmark, we have twice as many judges as those economically much stronger countries. In Germany there is one judge for every 6,651 inhabitants; this means that we have about 40 percent more judges than the German Reich. It should be mentioned that the German justice administration is preparing a reform—with approval of the German judges—for the purpose of considerably lowering expenditures on the judiciary. Our Ministry of Justice is also planning some reforms to reduce the number of judges. Surprise! This endeavor has met with resistance from our judges.

There is not a single area within our domestic administration where it would not be advisable to implement extensive reforms, which would not only result in savings but, at the same time, also lead to better service by adapting to the requirements of a modern economy. It is a tragic mistake on the part of some of our civil servants that they believe they have to fight such reforms. They do not realize that a reduction in the number of civil servants is the prerequisite for increasing their individual incomes.

But none of the austerity measures in the government administration are to any avail as long as public enterprises are run at a deficit. *A solution to the political and economic circumstance of the day will not be found in the government administration or in the state-owned enterprises.* Some of these enterprises are clearly in the red, whereas others are able for a time cleverly to cover their operational shortfalls to one degree or another. This situation is untenable in the long run. It must be understood that not even the public authorities are able to continue to run unprofitable enterprises. If these enterprises are in fact unprofitable, or if the government administration does not know how to make them profitable, then they should be gotten rid of by being sold to the private sector. If there is no way to make them profitable, well then, they should be shut down.

To continue operating unprofitable businesses represents an *indirect subsidy* for some interested parties and, therefore, its effect is on a par with any other subsidy policy. It really does not require any further explanation that the *direct subsidizing* of businesses ought to be condemned in whatever form it is carried out. Who really should be subsidized? After all, the subsidies are not paid for by the state; in the end, they are paid for by the market economy. This country's agriculture is subsidized, or rather its farmers are, and it is a fact that the less the individual farmer produces, the larger the amount of a subsidy he receives. And why not subsidize the textile industry, where the conditions are no less critical than in the agricultural sector, and why not some other industries as well that have to overcome great difficulties? If the criterion of a "hardship" is considered to be sufficient grounds to be entitled to a subsidy out of public monies, then probably most of the branches of production will be able to request such entitlements.

The politics of open and hidden subsidies show up most clearly in that particular way of thinking that has lost sight of the interdependence that exists between state revenues and expenditures. *One line of production can be subsidized only at the expense of all other industries, as well as of other departments of the state.* The amount being used to subsidize one particular industry will then not be available for any of the others. This is the same situation as that concerning the effectiveness of unemployment benefits and public works in general; they do not succeed in providing what is popularly called "new job opportunities," they only shift job opportunities from one economic sector to another.

Austerity measures could not be pushed through as long as it still seemed possible to cover a significant portion of public expenditures through a "tax on property." The demagogic notion that the interests of the masses are not affected by assessing high taxes on property seemed to justify any and all public expenses. But by now we have brought the consumption of capital to the point where it is impossible to ignore the connection existing between a lack of capital and large-scale and desperate hardship.

Corporate taxes, as well as the income tax, have to be cut, because if they are kept at their present high level, they impede industrial production and allow unemployment to grow at the speed of an avalanche. In whatever way the political situation may develop, fiscal policy in coming years must be directed at cutting taxes on property and shifting the state's budgetary source to taxation of the general population. Possibly it will then be easier for public opinion to understand the connection between revenues and expenditures, and thriftiness will be back in favor once again. Over the last several years it seemed that the entire purpose of our fiscal policy was to invent new taxes and even to more strictly apply existing ones. In the coming years the Public Budget Administration will have a far more difficult task — namely, to get along on less in order to adjust public expenditures to the financial capacity of an impoverished economy.

II

The problem of reforming the administration and making the required budgetary savings must not be handled in a way that leads to the question, who to "blame" for the present state of affairs? This is not about finding culprits that should be punished, but about determining the nature of the illness and the means to cure it, and then to take all measures that the cure requires. It would be especially inappropriate to fabricate a conflict between the civil servants and the population. The reform will not be successful without the help of the civil service, and its implementation is as much in the interest of the civil servants as in the interest of the rest of the population. If the principle is stated as, "Fewer but better paid and, therefore, more efficient civil servants," nothing can be misconstrued as inherently detrimental to the civil servants.

The goal cannot be achieved by timidly and fearfully shying away from any major reform. The fear that any reforms might be too radical does not apply. Reforms are inevitable. Especially for the person who wishes to conserve and not destroy what already exists, the task is to implement any reforms in a careful and determined manner while there is still time, and not in a more subversive manner at a time of severe political and economic difficulties.

The objections are not justified that have been made against the proposal for the district directors' staffs in the five smaller provinces to be dissolved and their responsibilities transferred to the provincial government office. In many foreign countries the area and population of the jurisdictional authorities organized directly above the municipal level is not larger than the area and population of the provinces. The comment was made that the example of the Anglo-Saxon states does not apply since, supposedly, our mentality and that of the Anglo-Saxons are completely different. But the point is precisely to change this mentality of ours. We have imported many things from America in the past years and among them are probably many that surely cannot be fully endorsed; but that does not mean refusing to adopt any of America's good features.

Nobody can deny that we must take into account that the state's budgetary revenues will be significantly lower next year. But if this is admitted, then—early on—one has to think about ways to make the administrative system operate with less money. When one looks at the fiscally required expenditure cuts, all the arguments are invalid that are made in favor of merely keeping intact the present system or its individual parts that need to be eliminated.

CHAPTER 27

Foreign-Exchange Control and Some of Its Consequences[1]

Today is really the first time that the Plenum of the Vienna Chamber of Commerce has concerned itself, even if not in public, with the full range of questions relating to the management of foreign exchange. A detailed presentation of the developments and policies that have been followed until now by the National Bank can be dispensed with, since all of you are fully aware of what has transpired.[2] In connection with the problems at the Credit Anstalt, the National Bank has departed from the rules specified in the statute concerning the issuance of bank notes and has undertaken an export policy that has endangered the stability of the schilling. No doubt there have been compelling reasons for this, reasons that resulted in this policy being chosen over others. But there have been few remarks among the public and in various other discussions about the particular procedure that has been followed. From among the choices between a

---

1 [This paper was originally delivered in German at a session of the Vienna Chamber of Commerce on February 18, 1932. It has not been previously published.—Ed.]

2 [In May of 1931, one of Austria's and Central Europe's most important banks, Credit Anstalt, was threatened with collapse due to huge financial losses. A run on the bank and a rush to exchange Austrian schillings for foreign currencies resulted in the Austrian government passing a series of emergency measures between May and December of 1931. Fearful of a rapid depletion of foreign-currency reserves, in October 1931 the Austrian government instituted foreign-exchange control. Distortions, imbalances, and corruption resulting from the law led to three revisions of the law during the first year, each one loosening the controls. The exchange-control system was finally phased out beginning in 1933 and continuing into 1934, after the Austrian government received loans from a group of international sources. On the Austrian experience with foreign-exchange control, see Howard S. Ellis, *Exchange Control in Central Europe* (Cambridge, Mass.: Harvard University Press, 1941), pp. 27–73; and Oskar Morgenstern, "The Removal of Exchange Control: The Example of Austria," *International Conciliation*, No. 333 (October 1937), pp. 678–89.—Ed.]

possible devaluation, a debasement of the schilling, and a variety of other options, a decision was made in favor of the debasement of the schilling. The introduction of this policy immediately forced the National Bank, on November 23, 1931, to cease exchanging the Austrian schilling for foreign currency on demand at the legally prescribed rate of exchange, for the first time since 1923.[3] From the moment this was done, the schilling was then set free for its foreign-exchange rate to be formed on the market, and of course the price of foreign exchange rose in Vienna.

Thought was then given to various ways and means for remedying this undesirable situation. What was rejected at the time was a radical reversal of the National Bank's discount-rate policy as the only way to solve the problem. Instead, it was believed that the problem could be handled through trade policy. A solution was attempted through influencing the balance of payments and the balance of trade by means of shackling foreign trade. This method was chosen because the position was taken—and it was the decisive one—that it was absolutely essential to maintain the stability of the legally established parity value of the Austrian schilling. This was done in spite of the fact that the schilling had already lost its parity value on the market and remains a fiction today. As a result, a whole series of policy measures have been followed that have had extremely deleterious consequences. And, in turn, these have been a causal factor in bringing about a general dissatisfaction with the entire economic system during the present economic crisis, for which there has been a search to find ways to deal with the situation.

That we find ourselves on the road to a controlled economy has been considered the most important negative effect from these circumstances. Though it is often expressed in this way among the general public, I think this description of the matter is not quite accurate. Actually, the controlled economy is already the first step toward foreign-exchange control; and such control over foreign exchange can only be successful if we proceed, step by step, until we have reached a point of complete nationalization for the sake of managing our foreign trade.

The other possibility is that we undertake an anti-inflationistic policy,

3 [Under the auspices of the League of Nations, the Austrian National Bank was reconstructed following the severe inflation of the early 1920s. In July 1923 the old Austrian crown was stabilized at 70,935 crowns for one dollar on the foreign-exchange market. On March 1, 1925, a new Austrian schilling was introduced equaling 10,000 old crowns and having a value of 0.21172086 grams of gold. The schilling was made fully redeemable in gold in June of 1925.—Ed.]

a policy of restraint on the part of the note-issuing central bank. These are the only two options. On the one hand, a discount policy that holds strictly to the National Bank Statute—which has not been repealed and still exists as Austrian law—or, on the other hand, giving up the attempt to maintain the stability of our currency's value. The endeavor to get around this through the third alternative of a system of foreign-exchange control must be considered a mistake, even from the viewpoint of those who champion such regulations on foreign exchange. The proponents of these regulations, after all, maintain that all they wish to do is get past the immediate problems so economic recovery can come about in some other way.

The assertion is constantly made that the rise in domestic prices that would be expected as a result of the schilling's devaluation abroad has not come about. Even the government repeats this assertion in the press. It is, however, contradicted by the figures in the official statistics. Since this is an issue of great importance, permit me to point out that the price index of Austrian-sensitive goods that has been calculated by the Austrian Institute for Business Cycle Research already shows a 13.8 percent increase through the middle of January [1932]. It should also be noted that during this same period the schilling's value in gold on the world market has fallen considerably. We are indebted to the Austrian Institute for Business Cycle Research for these data.[4] Data published by the Federal Bureau of Statistics show that the combined index of wholesale prices stood at 114 in January [1932] in comparison to 112 in December [1931] and 105 in January of 1931. The index of food prices rose from 106 to 109 between December 1931 and January 1932 and was at 93 in January 1931. The index of industrial-materials prices rose by one point to 126 between December 1931 and January 1932, in comparison to the index's value a year ago in January 1931 at 130. It should be noted that during this same period (between December 1931 and January 1932), the reverse movement occurred on the world market.

In the area of consumption, the index of prices for small-business retail trade has also seen an increase. It is a well-known fact, and one that is always brought up by the opponents of retail trade, that a decline in wholesale prices only has its effect in reducing prices at the retail level after a period of time; this point is constantly brought up in reference to meat and

---

4 [The Austrian Institute for Business Cycle Research was founded in December 1926 with the assistance of Ludwig von Mises. It began operations in January 1927, with Friedrich A. Hayek as its first director and Mises serving as its acting vice president.—Ed.]

bread prices. But the same process also operates in the reverse direction; if prices rise at the wholesale level, there is always a time lag before the new prices have their effect in the retail trade. For a short time, but certainly not in the longer term, retail business has delayed a part of the rise in prices, but the rise in prices in fact is on its way. I have mentioned this only in order to emphasize the incorrectness of the commonly repeated claim that the domestic structure of prices is in contradiction to the foreign-exchange rate. In fact, we do have inflation. About this there can be no doubt, especially if one takes the view that a characteristic feature of inflation is the fact that domestic prices of goods and foreign-exchange rates show a different structure vis-à-vis foreign countries.

It is believed that these symptoms can be cured through the introduction of foreign-currency control. It repeatedly has been said that foreign-exchange control is not unique to Austria, but also exists in a number of foreign countries. It must be remarked in opposition to this argument that it obviously makes a great deal of difference whether or not foreign-exchange control is practiced in a country that is at the same time maintaining the fiction that its currency has not been devalued. In Germany, foreign-exchange control has been combined with the actual maintenance of redemption at the legal gold parity of the German mark; this makes it possible for German enterprises whose credits have been called in from abroad to tell their creditors that the Reichsbank has not made the necessary funds available to them.[5] That is something quite different from the foreign-exchange controls in Austria.

Related to this, I should also like to explain the manner in which clearing agreements have been forced upon us from abroad. We found ourselves in a situation similar to Hungary's when it introduced a system of foreign-exchange control a few months ago.[6] I do not want to say, of course, that Hungary can in any way serve as a model for us, since the currency condition in Hungary is without a doubt nothing short of desperate. Hungary's economic-policy situation is far more unfavorable than Austria's. In Hungary, foreign-exchange control was introduced chiefly for the purpose of paying off debts owed to Austria following the devaluation of the pengo. In this situation it was especially important for Austria to have an agree-

5 [On Germany's experience with a system of foreign-exchange control, see Ellis, *Exchange Control in Central Europe*, pp. 158–289.—Ed.]

6 [On Hungary's experience with a system of foreign-exchange control, see Ellis, *Exchange Control in Central Europe*, pp. 74–157.—Ed.]

ment that provided the possibility for old debts still to be repaid. Austria now finds itself in the same situation. The Western nations wish to conclude a clearing-agreement treaty with Austria because they want to find a method through which it would be possible to have a settlement of debts. It is expected that under Austria's foreign-exchange regulations it will be immediately possible for Austrians to make payments on debts they owe for imported goods.

Coming back to the question of foreign-exchange control, the following must be pointed out. Under the existing tariff system, the fiction that the schilling has not been devalued leads to the actual encouragement of the importation of goods into Austria. Our customs tariffs are, by law, to be paid in gold; but if the fiction is maintained that the paper schilling is the same as the gold schilling, and if we assume a 20 percent premium, then the result is that foreign goods coming into Austria are charged a 20 percent lower duty than corresponds to the legal tariff regulations.

On the other hand, this fiction acts as a restraint on exports since the Austrian exporter is required to turn over either the entire or at least a considerable part of the foreign currency earned from his export sales to the National Bank at the fixed rate of exchange prescribed by law. If at this fixed exchange rate the number of schillings received is not sufficient to pay for the same amount of domestic goods as had been previously sold abroad, then it is clear that in many cases the exporter has part of his business taken away from him. The trade statistics for the last few months confirm that exports have declined.

Another consequence of the foreign-exchange control system has been its effect on domestic consumption. The most important insight from the balance-of-trade deficit is that consumption no doubt has been too high in recent years. In Austria, the increased consumption of capital shows itself in the balance-of-trade deficit. We have not taken out foreign loans to cover the deficit in the balance of trade; instead, the balance of trade went into deficit because loans were taken out. We have not consumed capital in order to cover the trade deficit but because Austrian economic policy, trade-union wage policy, etc., resulted in enterprises having to cut into their real capital. To understand the complicated mechanism that has brought about an "eating up" of components of factories and machinery, one must go through a set of interconnecting links, the last link being the array of superfluous articles for mass consumption that has come into Austria. They would not have been imported if we had followed a different economic policy.

Our economic policy has been operated in such a way that foreign exchange has been made somewhat more plentifully available for the importation of foodstuffs in comparison to the allotment of foreign exchange for semifinished products and raw materials needed by domestic industry for the production of export goods. Foreign exchange is far less willingly supplied for the purchase of goods needed in the export industries as part of an effort to prevent a rise in the prices of and a decrease in the purchase of consumption goods. Rising prices cannot be avoided, while considerable barriers are put in the way of exporters. The data referred to earlier show that the attempt to prevent a rise in prices through the use of foreign-exchange control has not been successful. In addition, I would like to refer to a very interesting article in yesterday's *Reichpost* that mentioned without comment that our cost of living is rising, in spite of the direct efforts of the central office of foreign-exchange control to make generous allotments to prevent this from happening.

The situation today would have become quite different and far more intolerable if not for the fact that the system of foreign-exchange control is riddled with loopholes. In fact, among the many gaps under foreign exchange control the system of *certificates* is the one that makes it possible for the Austrian export industry and transportation trade still to exist.[7] Clearing agreements, on the other hand, act in part to undermine the system in that a number of goods come into the country that otherwise would not.[8] A whole group of superfluous consumer goods comes in that would not if the whole system were eliminated.

7 [In February 1932, the Austrian National Bank, in cooperation with the Vienna Chamber of Commerce, established a certificate system permitting the Chamber to issue "certificates" allowing exporters of manufactured goods to retain foreign-currency proceeds they earned from sales abroad so as to be able to have the necessary funds to purchase imported raw materials essential for continuation of production in their enterprises.—Ed]

8 [Clearing agreements were barter trading arrangements between countries under which goods were imported and exported at non-market prices and non-market rates of foreign exchange, as determined by the respective governments. In 1931 and 1932, Austria entered into such clearing agreements with Switzerland, Hungary, Italy, and Yugoslavia, and partly with France. On the introduction of clearing agreements in Austria, see Antonin Basch, *The Danube Basin and the German Economic Sphere* (New York: Columbia University Press, 1943), pp. 83–85:

It was Dr. [Richard] Reisch, the President of the Austrian National Bank, who advocated the introduction of clearing agreements. Dr. Reisch's proposal was to discontinue the usual direct method of payment between exporter and importer by means of foreign exchange and to establish cumulative accounts of the central bank of one country with the central bank of the other. The importer was to

The foreign-exchange decrees have brought about effects that often seem simply incomprehensible. The first thing to mention in this context is the question of the *export of schilling notes*. In the years from 1914 to 1922, or let us say until 1921, a considerable number of bank notes were exported abroad from Austria. The whole world—not just the business world, but the masses as well—believed that currencies would recover after overcoming the difficulties of the war and the postwar period. The common man abroad practiced currency speculation and bought and hoarded mark notes and crown notes. I offer no opinion as to whether it made any sense at that time to lift the prohibition against the export of marks. But in reality, during those years Austria lived off the fact that crown notes were exported abroad, remained there, and only came back after they had sig-

---

pay the amount due for his imported goods to the central bank of his own country in his national currency. The exporter was to receive payment from his central bank in his national currency. There would be no import difficulties or restrictions because of uncertain payment in the country of destination; foreign trade would not be burdened and subsequently reduced for reasons of foreign exchange. Dr. Reisch hoped that not only the existing volume of foreign trade would be maintained but that the system would be so flexible as actually to increase it. Very little attention was paid to the question as to how and in what time periods the balances on the cumulative accounts were to be settled. Without a satisfactory solution of this point difficulties would inevitably follow within a short time. It could equally well be foreseen that clearing agreements would develop into a system of balanced foreign trade between two given countries. Austria, which maintained an import surplus with most countries, thought, perhaps, this would work to her advantage.... It was not long before the clearing plan proved to be one more step toward the further disintegration of international trade rather than an expansion of foreign trade.

The clearing system undermined the advantages of multilateral trade because it was basically a

system of bilateral relations which attempted to balance the foreign trade between a given pair of countries. This basic feature of the entire system was the result of the fact that the proceeds of export were permitted to be used only within the buying country and only for certain purposes. Originally the scope of the agreements was confined to payment for import and export, but it was soon extended to include payment for practically every type of claim (financial, pensions, royalties). In other words all claims, balances, and amounts belonging to the residents of one country were used solely for payment in connection with the relations between the two countries in question. The principle was followed that no payment could be affected in the currency of a third country or by exporting goods to a third country. In this fashion a more or less complete bilateralism in payment between two countries evolved.

See also Ludwig von Mises, *Human Action: A Treatise on Economics* (New Haven, Conn.: Yale University Press, 1949), pp. 796–99. This section, "Remarks About the Nazi Barter Agreements," is not included in later editions of *Human Action*.—Ed.]

nificantly depreciated in value. Purely tangential reasons caused a prohibition on the export of crowns. It was included in the foreign-currency decree without hesitation. I should like to emphasize that now, unfortunately, the idea of hoarding another country's bank notes no longer exists in the world. It would be most agreeable if there were masses abroad who wanted to speculate in schillings.

The official quotation for schilling bank notes is not a crucial factor for determination of the currency's foreign-exchange value. The decisive element is the quotation for the payoff value of schilling-denominated debt in Vienna. The trade in bank notes abroad has the purpose of making the notes available to the traveler who is going to Austria. Prohibiting the export of schillings has brought about a rise in the price of bank notes. But its only effect is that foreigners feel taken advantage of by the higher price, an unpleasantness that no doubt fails to foster the goodwill upon which our foreign trade is dependent. So the prohibition on the exportation of schilling notes really has no practical meaning. On the other hand, the National Bank demanded at the time of the first foreign-exchange decree that the schilling-denominated debts (or "credits") owed to foreigners in Vienna be frozen and that a transfer of the schilling credits of foreigners —which had been acquired in a perfectly legal manner—be prohibited, as a means of preventing business from moving abroad.

The National Bank's effort at preventing schillings held abroad from returning to Austria and therefore keeping them off the market has not been achieved. The payoff values of these schilling-denominated debts in Vienna are determined on the market. But they are not treated the same as credit instruments that are normally handled through an Austrian financial institution and that are, therefore, readily accepted by everyone. They are transfers of financial claims against Austrian businessmen who, no matter how large and reliable they may be, are in practice unknown abroad. As a consequence, the actual price today for such a claim in Vienna is burdened with a discount on the exchange. It cannot be said that trading in schilling-denominated debt does not occur, because the foreign banks—insofar as they pay any attention to Austrian conditions— advise their principals continuously of the prices of these Vienna claims, and the discount amounts to 20 percent, on average. There is no point in concealing this fact since foreign newspapers report on conditions in Vienna. This whole head-in-the-sand policy is really useless, and the discount would not be nearly so large if the value of such claims could be openly negotiated. It is a completely absurd prohibition made even more absurd by the fact that Austrian banks have been forbidden to pay interest on these credits, making it impossible for foreigners to use these credits in any profitable way.

Before the fourth foreign-exchange decree went into effect, it was still possible for new schilling credits owned by foreigners to come into existence because importing for payment in schillings and exporting schillings was still permitted. That has now been forbidden, and its prohibition only can be understood in terms of this idea that the schilling should be completely withdrawn from being traded on foreign markets. This could be done only if we were in reality a rich country, and then the Austrian economy could secede from international trade and be self-sufficient.

A number of very serious doubts have emerged concerning the present foreign-exchange control policy. The Chambers of Commerce, Trade, and Industry can in no way be criticized for trying to block this government policy. On the contrary, they tried to promote it. But in the course of a month's experience this system was seen to be unworkable and leading to consequences that are extraordinarily harmful for the Austrian economy. For this reason it seems urgent that the responsible authorities [at the Chamber] must hold even more strongly to the ideas expressed in the different corporations, leading associations, and private companies, and which have already been expounded in exactly the same way in a number of Chamber sessions, smaller meetings, and sessions of the Trade-Policy Board. That is the purpose of the present session, and the questions with which the Chamber has to be occupied are therefore directed toward finding out in what way relief can be provided.

With a strong majority, the Chamber's Trade-Policy Board expressed the opinion that clearing agreements have not achieved the goal that was hoped for them. The Trade-Policy Board went so far as to demand that the clearing agreement with Hungary, the termination of which was supposed to occur on February 15, really be terminated on February 15. There is nothing more to say about this because the government has ignored this demand.

The second group of ideas around which there is fairly wide unanimity concerns ending the prohibition against foreigners purchasing new schilling-denominated credit instruments. And the third question concerns the possibility that foreigners should have control of their credits in Vienna. These old credits are estimated at between 40 to 50 million schillings.

All of these measures would only serve as a preparation for a real improvement in the situation. It is clear that a complete remedy for all of these difficulties can only come through a change in monetary and banking policy. For that is where the causes of the present situation are to be found, and that is where the bull must be taken by the horns in order to remove our difficulties. That is also probably the reason why there has occurred a change in the presidency of the note-issuing central bank.[9]

---

9 [On February 5, 1932, Dr. Victor Kienbock was appointed president of the Austrian National Bank.—Ed.]

CHAPTER 28

An Agenda for Alleviating the Economic Crisis:

The Gold Parity, Foreign-Exchange Control, and Budgetary Restraint[1]

I

The Chamber is convinced that the final goal behind all measures undertaken in the area of monetary policy must be the maintenance of the legal gold parity of the schilling and the elimination of the undervaluation of the schilling that has occurred vis-à-vis foreign money and partly vis-à-vis goods.

It is unsatisfactory for monetary policy to have as its only goal the stabilization of the value of money at around its present level. The Federation, the provinces, and the communities, the financial institutions, large enterprises, municipalities, real-estate agencies, and agricultural entities have assumed debts in gold and foreign currency. Servicing the interest and repaying the principle at a lowered rate of exchange for the schilling would impose a burden that exceeds the capacity of the debtors.

Both domestic and foreign confidence in Austrian monetary and financial management would seriously suffer if an experiment were to be attempted at lowering the gold content and purchasing power of the schilling only a few years after the reconstruction of the country's monetary system and the legal establishment of the gold parity of the schilling.[2]

Public opinion is unanimous in demanding the return of the schilling to the level of its legally established gold parity.

1 [This paper was originally delivered in German at a session of the Vienna Chamber of Commerce on March 23, 1932. It has not been previously published. —Ed.]

2 [See Chapter 27, "Foreign-Exchange Control and Some of Its Consequences," footnote 3. —Ed.]

II

The reestablishment of the legal gold parity must not be delayed until the time when the prices of all goods in general as expressed in schillings have risen into line with the decreased foreign valuation of the schilling. Otherwise the reestablishment of the gold parity would require a sharp reduction in prices, along with a period of severe adjustment.

A reduction in the number of bank notes in circulation is essential for reestablishing the legal gold parity of the schilling. The note-issuing central bank must, therefore, follow a restrictive credit policy as an unavoidable necessity, even though it may create unfortunate difficulties for the economy and impose certain sacrifices on society.

Pressure is being applied from various directions for the National Bank to "stimulate" the economy through an expansion of credit. Though these proposals seem enticing, they would be pernicious in their application. Short-run financial difficulties faced by both the public authorities and individual private enterprises can no doubt be fixed by the expansion of credit. In the longer run, however, the expansion of credit inevitably must be severely damaging for the currency and our entire economy.

There is another perspective from which restraint in the granting of credit by the National Bank also seems unavoidable. Spending is too high in both the private sector and the public budget. We are living beyond our means; we are consuming capital; we consume more than we produce, and this overconsumption shows itself most clearly in our balance-of-trade deficit. In business transactions the possibility of postponing the date for payment of debts further and further into the future finally has the effect of locking up credits that have been granted to the larger enterprises. Tightened credit conditions, which force every enterprise to exercise greater restraint in the future concerning the scale and especially also the time horizon of credits received, is a measure that is absolutely necessary for remedying the present conditions.

III

The Chamber expresses the conviction that the obvious goal of monetary policy is to end foreign-exchange control as soon as possible and to reestablish full freedom of trade in the economy. For the transition period the Chamber demands:

1. All further coerced measures must stop.

2. The regulation that has taken away foreigners' control over their schilling credits existing in Austrian financial institutions is to be lifted. This regulation was imposed because it was desired to make impossible negotiations abroad about the value of schilling-denominated debts in Vienna. The desire was that no quotation for a Vienna-based schilling-denominated debt would have a payoff value that deviated from the Austrian National Bank's officially announced rate of exchange.

This goal was not achieved. Foreigners chose to instruct their Austrian debtors who owed them schillings not to pay into their accounts at an Austrian financial institution. Instead, they disposed of these claims by consignment abroad, a procedure that cannot be forbidden to them. The prices that have been obtained in this traffic of consignments and orders for payment are published abroad and considered the correct assessment of the value of the Austrian schilling. In fact, these prices include not only a discount reflecting the schilling's value today as influenced by increases in the quantity of money in circulation, but a risk premium as well. They are discounted by the extent to which the buyer must be compensated with a risk premium that would normally not have to be paid if settlement of the debt was done through a reputable Austrian financial institution known to all in the banking community. This is the case because those against whom a claim is being made are industrial and business enterprises, which though they may be completely creditworthy are unknown in the arena of international transactions in comparison to the same way an ordinary financial institution is known. The reintroduction of normal negotiations over the payoff value of Vienna debts denominated in schillings would, therefore, probably reduce the discount in Austrian currency by several percent.

3. The prohibition on the export of bank notes must be lifted. The value of the schilling abroad is not based on the traffic in bank notes, but on the payoff value of schilling-denominated debt in Vienna. Foreigners buy bank notes, when schillings may be freely exported, primarily to satisfy the demand of those who are traveling to Austria. By suppressing the export of bank notes it has been possible to keep the rate of exchange of Austrian notes on the foreign market high above the payoff value of schilling-denominated debts in Vienna. The importance of achieving this result is extremely problematical, since it hinders foreign trade. If the foreigner calculates the schilling prices that he has to pay in Austria at the value that he had to pay for Austrian bank notes in his own country's currency, he finds prices in Austria to be too high. If exports may be sold for

schillings and if the schilling accounts of foreigners at Austrian financial institutions are decontrolled, then no reason will exist any longer to choke off the export of schillings. Then many vexatious border-control measures also can be cancelled.

4. All new measures—like the system of certificates and the permitting of so-called private clearings[3]—that facilitate the export trade and enable the importing of those foreign raw materials and semifinished products essential to production must be maintained and indeed expanded. Austria must bring from abroad a sizable portion of the foodstuffs and raw materials needed for the provision of its population and can pay for these imports only by exporting finished products, through commercial activity, and from the profits earned from foreign trade.

Every attempt at isolating the country from world commerce must have the most harmful effects. Those things imposed on us from abroad, and which cannot be prevented through any policy of our own, must be tolerated as unavoidable. What we must not do is promote our own isolation from the world market.

IV

If the European nations hope to overcome the severity of the economic crisis, they will have to change their economic policies and undertake extensive reforms throughout their respective economies. The political preconditions will have to be established to deal with the problems of disarmament, a final determination of the reparations question, and a sorting out of a variety of international-policy issues that constitute points of serious conflict. Then trade policy would be based on an appreciation of the benefits from the international division of labor, instead of the restrictive trade policies that are becoming more acute with each passing day. The financial system of Central Europe must be rebuilt. The public budget must be so restricted that government spending no longer represents a constant threat to all economic activity due to its excessive claims on society.

All these problems can only be referred to in the present context. The

---

3 [In February 1932, the Austrian National Bank permitted exporters earning foreign currency from sales abroad to sell at least a portion of their foreign-exchange holdings directly to Austrian importers of foreign raw materials, and at a rate of exchange above the official rate.—Ed.]

most urgent tasks facing monetary policy cannot wait for the resolution of these wider problems. There is only one precondition that must be demanded in this connection. This is the demand that the Federation, the provinces, and the municipalities follow a uniform policy in relation to their borrowing policies. All additional assumptions of debt must be under the control of independent public authorities.

CHAPTER 29

An International Loan as the "Breathing Room" for Austrian Economic Reform[1]

You have the official letter from the government and the bill itself in your hands. The first question, independent of all political perspectives, is determining what would be the financial effects of the loan. In the most favorable case, 300 million gold schillings will be made available to the Austrian federal government; and of this amount 100 million will be used for repaying the advance provided in that amount that is still outstanding from the Bank of England. A further amount must be used to pay back, either in its entirety or in large part, a rediscounted credit of 90 million that was provided by Bank for International Settlements in Basel.[2] If we assume

1 [This paper was delivered in German as a speech before the Vienna Chamber of Commerce on July 25, 1932. It has not been previously published.—Ed.]

2 [In June of 1931, Austria appealed for financial assistance to provide funds needed to stem the massive loss of gold and foreign exchange following the collapse of the Credit Anstalt bank in May. On June 16, the Bank of England provided a 150-million schilling credit to the Austrian National Bank. This was immediately followed by a 100-million schilling credit from the Bank for International Settlements in Basel, Switzerland. In August of 1931, the Austrian government appealed to the League of Nations in Geneva for a 250-million schilling loan. Representatives of the Financial Section of the League traveled to Vienna to evaluate the situation. On October 15, 1931, the Bank of England and the Bank for International Settlements postponed repayment of their loans. On May 9, 1932, Austria sent another appeal to the League of Nations for a loan. After Austria declared a partial moratorium on payment of its international debts, the League signed the Geneva Protocol on July 15, 1932, stating a willingness on the part of Great Britain, France, and Italy to extend a loan to the Austrian National Bank. The actual loan, in the amount of 296 million schillings (237.4 million in devalued schillings), was not transferred to the National Bank until August of 1933. It enabled the bank to repay the 100 million schillings owed to the Bank of England and the 90 million schillings owed to the Bank for International Settlements, as well as 50 million schillings still owed to the League from 1923. Later conversion of the loan to a much lower interest rate dramatically reduced Austria's

that the entire 300 million schillings will be made available, because the other countries actually provide their corresponding contributions to the loan, and if we assume that 190 million of the 300 million are actually used for the purposes just mentioned, then there remains an amount of 110 million, which will perhaps go up to as much as 150 million, actually available to the Austrian federal government. The text of the loan protocol and the declared intentions of the government exclude using this amount to cover the current budget deficit. Indirectly, however, the loan will contribute to covering the deficit since there is the obligation in the agreement to repay those short-term borrowings that the federal government had assumed for its own uses or to give support to various banking institutions.

If we keep in mind this sum of 110 to 150 million and, at the same time, recall that the Federal Transportation Department alone has a current-account debt of 83 million with the banks as well as owing industry 54 million for unpaid deliveries, for total debts of 137 million, we see that the loan is not excessively large. This is especially made clear in relation to the real financial situation of the Federation, if we consider the unfavorable financial condition of the other federal undertakings; for example, in recent months the Housing Administration has indirectly incurred current-account debts through banks, savings and loans, and social insurance institutions. So we see that the amount coming to the Federation by way of the loan is not excessively large. The size of the loan also does not seem particularly large if one assumes that, on the basis of it being granted, it should be possible to domestically raise a loan of 200 million schillings. The amount of the loan, therefore, will play no major role in the financial situation of the Federation.

The federal deficit has been declared to be 450 million by the finance minister, and all the proposals made by the government for tax increases and related measures do not come anywhere near this amount. A sum of 72 million is necessary to cover, alone, the additional requirements for unemployment relief in the current year, and against this amount of 72 million the federal government has set an amount of 54 million that it hopes to obtain by an increase in the value-added tax. Thus even such a radical and debatable increase in the value-added tax is not able to fill this one gap; there still remains a deficit of 18 million in this case. So the federal

total foreign debt, making it one of the most creditworthy countries in Europe in the mid-1930s. — Ed.]

treasury is in an extremely unfavorable position. In fact, it is uncertain how we will be able to manage in the coming months, since we have to deal with a situation in which it may not be possible to pay in full the salaries of government employees and to fully cover the government's expenditures on the various supplies that it uses.

Thus, from the federal treasury's standpoint, the loan offers it only a momentary relief. It is far from actually changing the present situation into a more favorable one. I wish to say up front that this explains the unanimous position taken by the combined [Chamber] sections and the presidency [of the Chamber] in the discussions that were carried out this morning. It is absolutely essential that all those measures of frugality that the economy has required for a long time—but which have always been delayed or sabotaged—be put into effect as quickly as possible. For this loan is nothing more than breathing room for the carrying out of those absolutely necessary reforms and retrenchments. Not for one moment should the government or the political parties assume that the loan should be looked upon as anything removing the necessity for these reforms.

The loan has a quite different importance from the perspective of monetary policy. The National Bank's latest report indicates that at the present time it has about 190 million in gold and foreign exchange, and that this entire amount can be withdrawn if the English advance and the rediscounted credit from the Bank for International Settlements were to be called in. Psychologically, there would be a catastrophic collapse in domestic confidence if these withdrawals were actually to occur. So the loan will certainly improve the National Bank's reserve ratio for covering these amounts and is a necessary precondition for the improvement of the domestic situation.

I do not want to get lost in too many details. I would like immediately to point out that if the loan does not occur—for whatever reason—public confidence would be severely shaken. The shock would be due to the fact that for months our monetary policy has been solely and exclusively based on the assumption that we will receive a loan; all other things have been considered in relation to the loan. A failure in obtaining the loan would inevitably lead to a collapse in confidence, with all the resulting consequences for our financial institutions and, therefore, for the economy as a whole.

It must be stated that just as the loan has to be considered as only offering short-term breathing room for the government to introduce reforms and retrenchment measures, so too it must not be seen as a way to continue our trade and social and budgetary policies of the past. Nor can it be assumed that the same monetary policy that has been followed for months can be continued because we have received the means to do so. Over the last several months the National Bank has used up a considerably larger sum of money than represented by the influx of 100 to 150 million schillings that may come with this loan, through the seizure of foreign exchange and currency on hand under the first Foreign-Exchange Control decree and from the forced transfer of foreign-currency earnings from exporters.

So if the National Bank were simply to continue the present system, Austrian trade would continue to contract, with all the same consequences for foreign exchange and monetary policy that have been seen in recent months. It would be a grave error to believe that the foreign exchange needed to obtain the raw materials, semifinished products, and foodstuffs that we import from abroad can simply be withdrawn from a fund that was once filled up by confiscatory measures and now is supposed to be replenished by the loan. The economy is an ongoing institution, and it can only keep on receiving the needed foreign exchange by constantly replenishing the required funds through exports, foreign trade, business activity, and the like. The idea that we have a certain given amount of capital upon which we can permanently operate would lead to a currency catastrophe.

It cannot be stressed strongly enough that the natural preconditions for an improvement in the currency situation are to be found in the proposals that have been presented several times by the Chambers of Commerce, and in particular by the Viennese Chamber in recent months. In relation to these questions, a few months ago the currency committee that was set up by the Plenum came to a definitive conclusion, which was announced to the public, the government, and the National Bank in an extensive statement; and in the last few weeks, following a direct inquiry from the minister for commerce and trade, the Chamber made the unanimous decision to maintain the policy position of that time.

Seen from this perspective, the loan does not represent salvation; the failure to receive the loan would, however, immediately provoke a severe financial reaction and raise the question of how we would deal with providing essential funding for the next few weeks. Our relationship with the Western financial centers would become extraordinarily tense, with considerable difficulties emerging. In other words, what must be kept in the foreground in considering the pros and cons of the loan is not that it offers salvation from a terrible situation, but that it will prevent a complete collapse from occurring in the coming weeks. If it were impossible to service the interest on the League of Nations' loan, or if the representative of the League or the Control Committee of the League were to cut off a portion of the loan not yet dispersed, this would intensify the financial situation in the extreme and might lead to internal difficulties that certainly cannot be overlooked.

In light of all these considerations, the sections of the Chamber occupied themselves today with the loan treaty. It was the almost unanimous view of all sections that the question of the necessary reforms in Austria cannot be put off any longer. Moreover, the Chamber took the occasion to point out that it has repeatedly made proposals for a change in monetary and trade policy, in social policy and budgetary policy. Up until now they have not been properly taken into consideration, but now they must be put in the foreground. It must be emphatically pointed out that the breathing room provided by the granting of the loan must be used to put the affairs of state in order.

In the morning, the Finance and Trade Section concerned itself first with this question and reached the conclusion that it will recommend the approval of the government's submission for the loan to the full assembly of the Chamber, which is taking place here today in the form of a session of the United Sections. In the afternoon the Industry Section and the Craft Section occupied itself with the issue, and the same decision was unanimously reached in the Industrial as well as in the Craft Section. The Commerce Section came to a similar conclusion.

For all of these reasons the presidency of the Vienna Chamber of Commerce, which considers itself bound by the decisions of the sections in this regard, can only recommend that authority be granted to it to present this position at the presidential conference of all the Austrian Chambers, which will take place tomorrow. The Chamber's position would be not to oppose acceptance of the loan contract. But it must be most urgently pointed out on this occasion that if we wish to avoid a complete collapse, all of the proposals that the Chamber already has made in the past for reforms in trade, monetary, and social policy must be carried out, because, at best, the loan is only a temporary breathing spell. It certainly cannot be considered a deliverance from the present situation.

It is also to be emphasized in this regard that the severe conditions under the loan may open the eyes of the entire population to the fact that the economic policy that has been followed in recent years has brought us to a situation where we really see no other way out than to accept the sort of subjugation which this loan imposes on us. This is a position that is far from viewing the loan agreement as some kind of salvation. It sees this loan contract as nothing other than a starting point for reforms that will have to be carried out in Austria by Austria. In this context, the presidency proposes that the United Sections of the Chamber should grant their acquiescence to the loan agreement. (*Applause*)

CHAPTER 30

On Limiting the Adverse Effects of a Proposed Increase in the Value-Added Tax[1]

The federal finance minister reported to the Presidium of the Chamber of Commerce that the condition of the state budget makes necessary a whole series of radical taxation measures. In the first place, the government intends to propose to the National Assembly putting in place a 100 percent increase in the value-added tax. The yield from this increase is supposed to make it possible for the Federation to defray the additional expenditures imposed by unemployment relief and to cover the budget deficit of the federal railroads. The scope of the increased value-added tax (a luxury tax) is to remain unchanged.

The value-added tax was introduced by a decree of the federal government on March 11, 1923, came into effect on April 1, 1923, at the rate of 1 percent, and was doubled, i.e., raised to 2 percent, starting on January 1, 1924. In the nine months of 1923 during which it was first in place, the value-added tax delivered a yield of around 56 million schillings. With the doubling of the tax rate the revenue from it rose to 202 million schillings in 1924 and continued rising regularly in the following years until the year 1929, when it brought in around 255 million schillings. In 1930 the tax revenue fell to around 250 million schillings and in 1931 to 219 million schillings. For the year 1932, the yield from the tax has been projected at only 198 million schillings; the result for the first half of 1932 shows, however, that one can scarcely count on a higher yield than 170 million schillings. Therefore, if one assumes a further 10-million schilling decrease in the revenues from an unincreased value-added tax, then a 100 percent increase could bring at most an additional revenue of about 160

---

1 [This article was originally delivered as a speech in German before the Vienna Chamber of Commerce on July 25, 1932. It has not been previously published. — Ed.]

million schillings. If the increase becomes effective August 1, then at most $\frac{5}{12}$ of this amount would be collected, i.e., in the best of cases 65 million schillings can be counted on for the remainder of the current year.

The increase in the value-added tax is an extraordinarily radical measure that will affect all of the economic relationships of the country.

In the first place, industry and the import business will be directly affected by the raising of the value-added tax on luxury goods. Due to the nature of the assessment, they have by far the greatest responsibility for collecting, paying, and handing over the tax. This has the effect of imposing the main burden of the tax directly on a relatively small number of firms out of the total number of enterprises in commerce, industry, and trade. Individual categories of enterprises in industry and in wholesale business nowadays already have to pay a considerable tax rate. The overall rate in the cotton industry amounts to 6.5 percent for cotton fabric through the entire production process for cotton goods, including the manufacture of clothing right down to the final consumer stage. The flat tax in the stages of production is levied on the "finisher" of the product (the outfitter, the dyer, the dealers). In the leather industry a 7.5 percent tax is levied on tanned leather and applies to the entire production of leather and leather goods. For imports, many goods are taxed between 6 percent and 10.5 percent. The doubling of these rates would create rates between 13 percent and 21 percent.

The system of a flat tax in the stages of production was created upon the petition of commerce, trade, and industry, and its implementation was the work of representatives appointed for that purpose by the officers of the professional associations and from the leading organizations of commerce, trade, and industry. It proved highly successful in practice. It is because of its success that the Austrian value-added tax is looked upon abroad as a model to be imitated. This system of a flat tax in the stages of production is, however, only possible and workable with a maximum rate of 2 percent for the individual stages. If the value-added tax is raised above 2 percent and, as it is now proposed, even to 4 percent, then the foundations of the system will be shaken, and its future effectiveness may be seriously threatened.

It is also inconceivable that in the present crisis individual enterprises should have an import duty imposed upon them of 15 percent or more of the selling price as a tax, to pass on in the purchase price, and still assume that a certain amount will be guaranteed for the treasury. It will not be possible for many enterprises to pass on such high rates.

It is therefore completely justified on the part of the most severely affected industrial groups, that is, on the part of the leather industry and the textile industry, and especially the cotton industry, that the demand is made to omit the present enforcement of the flat tax in the stages of production, which is the main source of the tax burden on these industries. The difficult situation in which these branches of industry already find themselves would become absolutely catastrophic with the simple doubling of this general tax rate.

Consequently, the introduction of any addition to the value-added tax must not be undertaken until an arrangement is jointly found between the federal government and the most severely affected economic groups (in the first place, the leather industry, the cotton industry, and some other branches of the textile industry) that would make it possible to avoid the disastrous effect this tax increase would have on the existence of these industries.

But with the introduction of the increase in the value-added tax the following principles must still be observed:

1. Restoring the balance in the public budget must not be sought on the side of revenue but on the side of expenditures. The reform of the imperial administration, which was announced years ago, must finally be carried out.[2] The unemployment insurance must be reformed in a way that makes further contributions from public funds unnecessary. The federal railroads and all public enterprises must be reorganized and brought to the point that they no longer require any further subsidies from taxes. The tax increases, and especially the raising of the value-added tax through the introduction of a 100 percent supplement, must be used only to bridge over the temporary difficulties in the state budget and should therefore have a fixed time limit. The 100 percent addition to the value-added tax should go out of effect at the beginning of 1934, since by then the indicated reforms should have gone into effect.

2. The addition to the value-added tax should affect all of the transaction activities, supply operations, and services on an equal basis. All tax rates with the exception of the higher value-added tax at each stage of production (the luxury tax), i.e., the 2 percent tax accruing at each stage of production, the adjusted import tax, and all taxes levied on the basis of subsidy contracts, must be imposed on an equal, nondiscriminatory basis.

2 [This refers to the restructuring of the administrative and jurisdictional divisions between the Austrian federal government and the provincial and municipal authorities. — Ed.]

3. The rates on export subsidies should be raised by the same amount the tax rates are increased.

4. Those subsidy contracts that benefit some enterprises—most especially those subsidy agreements received by agriculture—in relation to other enterprises not receiving such subsidies will be subject to revision.

5. The arrangements for a transition period prescribed in the 40th paragraph of the value-added tax decree that was executed on January 1, 1924, on the basis of which the transition from the 1 percent tax to 2 percent tax was ordered, must also be prescribed for the transition from the currently prevailing tax rate to the tax rate that is raised by 100 percent. Moreover, to avoid any difficulties of interpretation the following provision should be included from paragraph 40, clause 1 of the decree for the implementation of the value-added tax:

"In the case of partial deliveries (or services) by installments that stretch over a relatively long period of time, those partial deliveries (or services) that were provided before the entry into force of the new law are to be taxed according to the previous arrangements."

6. Moreover, to avoid any confusion, it is to be explicitly decreed that the provider of goods and services is authorized to pass on to the customer the value-added tax surcharge, the payment of which is incumbent upon him without regard to any agreements concluded before the new purchase-tax law came into force.

7. In order to facilitate the intended passing on of the value-added tax, it is further proposed that the following provision be included in the law:

"The one who is responsible for the tax is obliged to list the tax separately along with the price of the goods or service in the total bill to the other partner in the transaction. The buyer of a commodity is not authorized to reduce the fee charged to him by the supplier in his bill or the tax listed separately in his bill from the supplier by the amount of the tax payable for the resale of the object."

CHAPTER 31

Foreign-Exchange Policy[1]

The great economic crisis, which has already affected Austria more severely than many other countries, has been made worse by our own economic policy. Among these pernicious measures, the leading one has been
the control of foreign exchange. More than a year has passed since the
foreign-exchange decree came into force.[2] The warnings that were given
by the assembled representatives of commerce, trade, and industry when
the first steps toward foreign-exchange control were being introduced, and
which were repeated again and again, were all in vain. It is now clear that
all the predictions given at the time about the ruinous effects to be expected from foreign-exchange control have been greatly surpassed by the
facts. The consequences of foreign-exchange control have been a catastrophic decline in our foreign trade (especially in our exports), business
cutbacks and business shutdowns, difficulties for many of our most distinguished firms, falling tax revenues, and increasing unemployment.

The defenders of the system of foreign-exchange control willingly concede that the measures imposed by exchange control are extraordinarily se-

1 [This article originally was delivered in German as a conference paper for the 10th meeting of the Austrian Chambers for Commerce, Crafts, and Industry held in Vienna on October 19, 1932. It has not been previously published. A greatly abridged version appeared
in *Österreichs Wirtschaft: Wochenschrift des No. Gewerbevereins* (Oct. 27, 1932). At the
same meeting Mises also delivered another paper on "The Management of Public Expenditures," which except for a few brief passages is taken almost verbatim from the lecture
that he delivered at the Vienna Industrial Club on December 1, 1930, "Adjusting Public
Expenditures to the Economy's Financial Capacity," Chapter 26 of the present volume.
—Ed.]

2 [See Chapter 27, "Foreign-Exchange Control and Some of Its Consequences," footnote 2.
—Ed.]

vere, but they maintain that this severity is necessary to protect the currency. What is all too true is that the very harshness of foreign-exchange control has intensified the economic crisis and increased unemployment. In the first place, it must be understood that foreign-exchange control is not an appropriate means to the desired end of improving the economic situation. And, in the second place, commerce, trade, and industry do not oppose the controls because of an unwillingness to make sacrifices for the good of the country. The controls are opposed because of the desire to prevent the damage that the policy of foreign-exchange control imposes on the entire economy.

It is a disastrous mistake to think that a sound monetary policy can be restored through the use of compulsory methods in the form of foreign-exchange control. Now is not the appropriate time to raise the question of who bears the responsibility for the monetary-policy mistakes of the most recent past. What is required is to point out the appropriate ways to get us out of the difficulties into which we have fallen. The uncertainty of the overall economic situation, especially in regard to monetary policy, makes it seem inappropriate at the present time to propose a comprehensive program for the future currency and banking policy of our country. It is not excluded that the forthcoming World Economic Conference and other agreements between nations will have results that will influence the monetary policy of all countries.[3] The [Austrian] Chambers of Commerce defer focusing on the entire complexity of issues surrounding monetary policy. Instead, they limit themselves to those proposals that must be taken immediately, and above all else in the area of foreign-exchange policy.

It has been officially declared that one of the most important aims of our foreign-exchange policy is to influence the balance of trade by pro-

3 [Mises is referring to the World Economic Conference that was held in London in June 1933, for which the League of Nations had been doing preparatory work for a year. It was meant to reach an agreement among the major industrial powers to restore the gold standard, after several countries including Great Britain had either gone off gold or restricted use and payment in gold in 1931 and 1932. The conference turned out to be a complete disaster when President Franklin Roosevelt, who had taken the United States off the gold standard in March and April 1933, refused to accept any fixing of the international exchange value of the dollar that would restrict the ability for manipulation of the domestic price level through monetary policy. See Benjamin M. Anderson, *Economics and the Public Welfare* (Princeton, N.J.: D. Van Nostrand Co., 1949), pp. 330–32; and Murray N. Rothbard, "The New Deal and the International Monetary System," in Leonard P. Liggio and James J. Martin, eds., *Watershed of Empire: Essays on New Deal Foreign Policy* (Colorado Springs, Co.: Ralph Myles, 1976), pp. 19–64.—Ed.]

moting exports and discouraging imports. From this perspective, the foreign-exchange measures employed appear completely contrary to their stated purpose. This is seen from the fact that the rate of exchange announced by the National Bank differs from the value for the currency that is revealed from comparing the costs of domestically manufactured goods expressed in schillings with the prices at which those goods can be sold abroad on the international market. On the one hand, the exchange controls have fostered imports because the foreign exchange available at the official rate, though the available amount has been constantly decreasing, has reduced the burden of importing goods. On the other hand, the controls have restrained exports because part of the net-export profits earned by exporters in the form of foreign currency must be sold to the National Bank, for which they receive Austrian currency at the official rate of exchange. This operates as a form of export tax. That this tends to foster imports and hamper exports is revealed most clearly in the official clearing agreements that have been concluded with a whole series of foreign countries.[4] On the whole, therefore, it can be said that foreign-exchange control has worked to promote imports and restrict exports. This effect would have been even greater if the business representatives of the economy had not succeeded in preventing the complete catastrophic collapse of our foreign trade by expanding the system of certificates[5] and establishing private clearings.[6]

The most urgent task at the present time clearly is to eliminate all of the remaining elements of this pernicious system. To begin with, it should be demanded that the export fee be eliminated that still exists today in the form of the obligation imposed on exporters to pay over to the National Bank a certain part of their net-export proceeds, the size of which depends upon the discretion of the agencies of the National Bank. A 15 percent so-called "raw-materials rate" means, at the moment, a 3 to 4 percent export tax, and a 25 percent raw-materials rate means a 5 to 7 percent export

4 [Clearing agreements were barter trading arrangements between countries under which goods were imported and exported at nonmarket prices and nonmarket rates of foreign exchange, as determined by the respective governments. In 1931 and 1932, Austria entered into such clearing agreements with Switzerland, Hungary, Italy, and Yugoslavia, and partly with France. See Ludwig von Mises, *Human Action: A Treatise on Economics* (New Haven, Conn.: Yale University Press, 1949), pp. 796–99. This section, "Remarks About the Nazi Barter Agreements," is not included in later editions of *Human Action.*—Ed.]

5 [See Chapter 27, footnote 2.—Ed]

6 [See Chapter 28, "An Agenda for Alleviating the Economic Crisis," footnote 3.—Ed.]

tax. Recently, the president of the National Bank has declared that until further notice a 12 percent maximum raw-materials rate will be considered, but that even this will be gradually reduced. A 12 percent raw-materials rate today still means an export tax of around 2.5 percent of the value. Even this burden is intolerable for Austrian exports and must be eliminated without delay.

If the obligation for exporters to pay over a portion of their export revenues in the original foreign currency to the National Bank at a fictitious rate of exchange is discontinued, then no barrier stands in the way of a general permission for export businesses to take payment in schillings. Even from the standpoint of those who think that the value of the currency is a function of the balance of payments, it must appear as a matter of no consequence whether the payment for Austrian exports is made in foreign currency or in schillings. After all, the foreigner must obtain the means he needs to pay for his purchases from Austria by the delivery of goods or services to Austria. The only reason in favor of hindering exports paid for in schillings is precisely that, without the exchange control, the National Bank could not exercise its claim to have a part of the profits earned from exports.

Thanks to the efforts of the present minister for commerce and trade, it has been possible to arrange private clearings through the Wiener Giro- und Kassenverein.[7] Such private clearing would have been enough to meet the most pressing needs of trade, if the National Bank were not imposing more and more difficulties in the way of making individual clearing deals.

The agents of the National Bank responsible for forming authoritative judgements about various trade-policy problems appear to be totally incompetent, whether due to their educational background or their lack of prior experience. Yet these people, who most certainly cannot be considered qualified experts, have the discretionary power to decide finally whether particular export firms will be "favored" with permission to enter into a private clearing agreement or not. A refusal for this so-called "favoring" is the same thing as a prohibition on export businesses; therefore, in the final analysis, it means an increase in unemployment.

It must be accepted once and for all that the National Bank is not a

7 [The Wiener Giro- und Kassenverein was a Vienna bankers' association that served as a clearing center for bank balances and a depository for securities. On July 17, 1932, it was designated by the Austrian National Bank as the official agency for private clearing.—Ed.]

government agency but a stock corporation that under the foreign-exchange control decrees has had transferred to it certain official bureaucratic functions. But trade policy is exclusively the affair of the federal Ministry for Commerce and Trade and a number of other central agencies. It is completely justifiable, therefore, that all private clearing agreements arranged through the Giro- und Kassenverein should be approved without bureaucratic intervention, except when a strong suspicion exists that such a clearing agreement involves a purely fictitious business, behind which noncommercial transactions of a prohibited type are being hidden.

The supply of foreign currency available in the private clearings of the Giro- und Kassenverein would experience a considerable increase if the circle of the foreign exchange that is authorized on the supply side of the transactions were not so narrowly defined. Only foreign currency and foreign exchange that stems from the delivery of goods is supposed to be included. But, in fact, claims that have nothing to do with delivery of goods are referred to private clearing process. Thus every month the equivalent of about one million schillings must be provided through the private clearings for the payment of pensions to recipients residing abroad. No explanation is given, however, why the circle of the private clearings should be so narrowly drawn on the supply side. It is, for example, completely unjust that the remuneration that Austrians receive from abroad for intellectual work in the form of authors' honoraria of all sorts are not included in the private clearings. It cannot in any way be justified that such extensive expropriation of foreign currency and foreign exchange should take place without full compensation for those who must part with or who do not receive it. It is completely reasonable to demand that all deliveries of foreign currency and foreign exchange received by the National Bank should come through the private clearings at the Giro- und Kassenverein.

On the other hand, the result of this demand would be, of course, that the National Bank should likewise deliver foreign currency and exchange only by way of the private clearings at the Giro- und Kassenverein. One of the most criticized aspects of foreign-exchange control was that the foreign currency and exchange earned by the export industry was largely given to agriculture at the official rate of exchange for the payment of fodder and fertilizer. As the structure of prices shows, this favoring of agriculture is disadvantageous for the consumer though beneficial for the agricultural producers. Foreign-exchange control, therefore, also represents a link in the chain of economically unjustifiable privileges for agricultural producers at the expense of all other strata of the population. In the course of the last few months, the allotments of foreign exchange given out by the National Bank have decreased so much that they hardly play a role any more in the area of commerce. They are supposed to cease completely in the near future, and at that point unjustifiable favors for particular groups and persons will come to an end.

That it was an absolute mistake to arrange clearing agreements with foreign countries, particularly with those countries having a well-ordered currency, is today admitted even in official quarters. And the way these agreements were carried out has disappointed the expectations that many had about the treaties with the Southeast [Hungary and Yugoslavia]. It's unfortunate that this is being realized so late, and that the responsible authorities turned a deaf ear to the warnings that were raised at the time the disastrous idea of these clearing agreements first emerged.

From the very beginning, the representatives of the economy anticipated that the clearing agreements would lead to an uncovered residue of claims, and they raised the question of how liquidation of this residual in the trade balance was to be handled. Those in authority have only answered with evasions. Now these residual amounts are supposed to be paid off through extra payments on the part of importers. In the Austrian-Italian clearing agreement such a regulation has already been stipulated in the contract between the two governments. Many businessmen who were forced to conduct their import business through the clearing agreement months ago sold the goods they had imported. When they obtained these goods they made their calculations on the basis of the rate of exchange according to the legal parity. They had not figured on an obligation for an additional payment. The government's intention in using the procedure provided for through the clearing-agreement treaties was to keep the price level down as expressed in schillings. The obligation to pay additional amounts of money to the government that can no longer be passed on to the consumers would bring many enterprises into extreme difficulties, indeed, even into collapse. The "advantage" from purchasing these imported goods at an exchange rate originally considered to be low has turned out to be to the benefit of the consumer, not the importers. It would be reasonable, therefore, for the whole nation to assume the burden, if the Austrian National Bank, which ought to be called upon first, should not be in a position to assume it. The business world, which proceeded with confidence in the clearing agreements, must not be disappointed in its trust.

Trust in governmental measures is an essential component of any currency policy.

The sums required to pay off this debit item on the government's accounts could be covered by appropriating for the state treasury the fund created from the contributions of the cattle importers.

In summary, the Chamber of Commerce therefore proposes the following guidelines for measures to be taken in the area of foreign-exchange policy:

I   Private clearings

1. No obstacles should be put in the way of arranging clearing agreements in the Giro- und Kassenverein.

2. The National Bank should not be allowed to include questions relating to trade policy in the permitting of clearing contracts. Trade policy is exclusively the affair of the appropriately qualified ministries. A distinction between "supplementary" exports and other exports is not to be made.

3. The National Bank should be entitled to deny authorization in the making of private clearing agreements only if there exists a well-founded suspicion that a fictitious business is hiding behind the law for purposes of undertaking some legally prohibited transaction.

4. The National Bank should not be authorized to demand the payment of a so-called "raw-material quota."

II   Extension of the Sphere of Private Clearing

1. The delivery of foreign currency and exchange, from whatever claim and by whomever, must take place through clearings at the Giro- und Kassenverein. The National Bank must pay the rates of exchange obtained in this clearing.

2. In the same way, the delivery of foreign currency and exchange by the National Bank must occur exclusively through the clearings at the Giro- und Kassenverein, in which the rates of exchange obtained in this clearing are likewise to be paid to the National Bank.

III   *Governmental Clearing Agreements*

1. The official clearing agreements concluded with foreign countries are to be liquidated.

2. This liquidation is to be carried out without the obligation of extra payments on the part of individual enterprises. The debit balance is to be borne by the Federation, for which means, perhaps, the Live Stock Utilization Fund could be drawn upon.

3. Exports in exchange for schillings. No obstacles of any sort whatsoever are to be put in the way of exporting goods for payment in schillings.

[Additional, concluding remarks by Mises, following comments by other participants:]

I am happy that it is now recognized even by the government and the National Bank that the arguments that I had the honor of bringing forward here in the name of the Chamber are completely justified and that the program at hand must be carried out in the interest of the entire Austrian economy. It is to be greatly regretted, however, that this recognition did not come earlier and that bad experiences had to be suffered through before the controlling authorities recognized their mistake. The Chambers are not to blame. From the very beginning they were against the ill-advised foreign-exchange decrees, both in public as well as in the sessions of the foreign-exchange commission that took place without the participation of the public. From the very first day, the Chambers predicted all the evil consequences resulting from the foreign-exchange decrees, and the events that have now occurred have unfortunately confirmed their predictions.

If the Honorable Federal Minister for Finance has said that the carrying out of the proposed measures is a question of time, then I must remark that only the shortest amount of time is suitable for the carrying out of appropriate measures. There is no reason to postpone them even for *one* day, measures like the ones that have been proposed. The abolition of a harmful measure such as the raw-materials quota must not be postponed even for an hour. Unfortunately, when it is a question of introducing appropriate measures, the history of Austrian currency policy in recent years has provided new proof of the correctness of Grillparzer's characterization of Austrian politics: "To strive halfheartedly half the way toward a half deed with half means."[8] Only where something completely wrong is to be undertaken are we accustomed to seizing it quickly and completely.

The federal minister for finance has referred to the fact that the worst defects of the foreign-exchange control policy were given up relatively quickly. It is certain that they were given up too late. The federal minister is wrong, however, if he says that the government and the National Bank were under no illusion about the fact that foreign-exchange control, with its maintenance of a fictitious rate of exchange, promotes imports and hinders exports. I happen to have before me the *Neue Wiener Tagblatt* [New Vienna Daily] for October 11, 1931, with a detailed report about a speech that Section Head Dr. Schiller delivered on the radio the day after the first foreign-exchange decree came into effect. In this speech the section head explained clearly that the exchange control had as its goal the restriction of imports. That is only one of the many official and semiofficial declarations that were delivered with the same message.

I must once again point out that one cannot simply equate Austrian foreign-exchange control with that of Germany or the Western countries. What is characteristic of Austrian exchange control is precisely the continued fiction that the gold parity has not been abandoned. For this policy we can find no models in the West. If we want to find a model, we must turn toward the East. I don't think, however, that anyone will dare to elevate the foreign-exchange policy of Hungary or Yugoslavia as an example worthy of imitation. If the federal finance minister has said that Austria has moderated its foreign-exchange control but Germany has not done so, he has spoken of two things that cannot be compared with each other.

It has been mentioned here today that the balance-of-trade deficit has become smaller. Above all, the volume of export trade has become smaller. The diminution in the balance-of-trade deficit is, however, to be ascribed, in the first place, to the circumstance that we no longer receive any foreign credits. If foreign-exchange control had not artificially restricted exports and promoted imports, the diminution of the foreign-trade deficit would have been still larger.

About the official clearing agreements with the Western nations I do not need to say anything more in my closing remarks. On that matter the books are closed. The government and the National Bank now openly ac-

8 [Franz Grillparzer (1791–1872) was an Austrian dramatist considered to have written some of the greatest works ever performed on the Austrian stage.—Ed.]

knowledge them as a mistake, and we can only regret that this recognition came only after irreparable harm had been done to the country.

Just one last thing still must be said emphatically. There has been talk here about the fact that the schilling could slip downward. I must state explicitly that the schilling cannot slip and cannot sink if inflation is not practiced; and since the government, the National Assembly, and public opinion decidedly abhor any inflation, no danger exists for the schilling. Neither the immediate lifting of the foreign-exchange control decrees, which we have combated most strongly, nor the complete removal of foreign-exchange control can endanger the schilling in any way so long as the absolute condemnation of an inflationary policy persists in Austria. Only inflation and nothing but inflation can harm the currency. If neither open nor concealed inflation is engaged in, then the schilling needs no police for its protection. If, however, inflation were practiced—and I repeat it once more that, at the moment, thanks to the decided loathing of public opinion for inflationist policy, there exists no danger in this regard—then even the most severe police measures could not prevent a currency catastrophe from occurring. Nothing other than wrong actions on the part of the National Bank can endanger the currency. About the past, about the events of 1931, we shall not speak today. But if the National Bank adheres in the future to the law in its discount policy, then no danger can threaten the schilling.

What we demand here is that, in recognition of the requirements of the Austrian economy, a series of deleterious measures be removed as quickly as possible. In the matter of foreign-exchange policy we demand nothing other than what we demand in general in economic policy, namely, that Austrian economic policy conform to the conditions that circumstances impose upon Austria.

CHAPTER 32

The Direction of Austrian Financial Policy:

A *Retrospective and Prospective View*[1]

After last year's stormy political battles and decisions, peace and quiet have returned.[2] Economic and financial policy is now once again in the foreground.

The tasks facing a country's financial policy are determined not only by the current political situation. They are determined to a high degree by the inheritance that has to be taken over from the past.

The Renner System,[3] which came into power through the events of November 1918, was just as destructive in its financial policy as it was in its other policies. It managed things with a free hand and provided the means that it needed for its unrestrained spending by reckless reliance on the printing of bank notes, and by buying on credit from the Entente pow-

1 [This article originally appeared in German in the *Wirtschaftliche Nachrichten* (January 10, 1935).—Ed.]

2 [Mises is referring to the civil war that threatened Austria in 1934. In March 1933, Austrian chancellor Engelbert Dollfuss suspended the parliament and ruled by emergency decree. In February 1934, the Social Democratic party took up arms against the government, and after four days of street fighting in Vienna were defeated by the government and declared illegal. In July 1934 a group of Austrian Nazis, inspired by Hitler's rise to power in Germany the previous year, seized the Chancellery building, captured and killed Dollfuss, and proclaimed a government. They were swiftly forced to surrender to forces loyal to the government. A Nazi uprising in the Austrian region of Styria also was put down. When Mussolini declared his intention to preserve Austrian independence and ordered Italian military forces to the Brenner Pass at the Italian-Austrian border in the Alps, Hitler repudiated his Austrian followers. Kurt von Schuschnigg became Austrian chancellor following the death of Dollfuss, a position he held until March 1938 when Nazi Germany annexed Austria.—Ed.]

3 [See Chapter 9, "Vienna's Political Relationship with the Provinces in Light of Economics," footnote 14.—Ed.]

ers the food supplies that the state then sold to the population. The proceeds received from these sales, however, were not used to pay for these supplies. Instead, they were used to cover current state expenditures.[4] A huge property tax was prepared that was meant to be a decisive and heavy blow against the social order that rests upon the private ownership of the means of production. According to the plans of the leading socialist economic policymakers, it was supposed to lead to complete socialization and to Bolshevism.

If this system, which was rushing toward disaster in giant steps, was to be brought to an end, its destructive fury had to be opposed by a constructive policy that began by calling for a halt to the reckless prodigality in the administration of government expenditures. As a precondition for a return to a balanced budget the subsidies for foodstuffs had to be rescinded as a way to shut down the monetary printing presses. That was the policy that was supported above all by the Vienna Chamber of Commerce, and

---

4 [The printing of paper money was the primary means for the Austrian government to finance a majority of its expenditures during the first four years of the Austrian Republic. Newly created paper money covered the following percentages of government expenditure: January to June 1919—67 percent; July 1919 to June 1920—63 percent; July 1920 to June 1921—58 percent; July 1921 to December 1921—51 percent; January to December 1922—40 percent. See Leo Pasvolsky, *Economic Nationalism of the Danubian States* (New York: Macmillan Co., 1928), pp. 102–3:

> Social burdens undertaken by the state constituted the principal cause of the huge budgetary deficits. There were several such burdens that weighed heavily upon the state budget. These were: unemployment and food relief, low prices of commodities sold by the state, low fares charged by the state railroads and the maintenance of a large number of government officials. Unemployment was especially heavy in Austria during the first half of 1919 [and remained high, though decreasing, until the end of 1921]. Unemployment doles were thus a very heavy burden on the budgets of the first two years. Food relief constituted an even heavier burden.... Foreign relief credits brought food into the country, and these supplies were distributed by the government almost gratuitously. Political conditions prevented even a gradual increase in the price of foodstuffs thus distributed by the state.... The magnitude of the burden thus carried by the state may be seen from the fact that in December 1921, for example, over half of the total expenditures of the government resulted from food subsidies. And it was not until the end of 1921 that the government began seriously to consider the need to abolish this system of almost gratuitous feeding of the population. Food prices immediately began to rise rapidly, and there were riots in Vienna. Nevertheless, the government persisted in its policy of relieving the budget from the burden of food relief, and the system was finally abolished early in 1922.

—Ed.]

it is the everlasting merit of Federal Chancellor Dr. Seipel to have carried it out with strength and determination.[5]

It can hardly be comprehended today the bitter opposition that had to be overcome before these rather self-evident measures could be put into effect. United under the leadership of the Vienna Chamber of Commerce, Trade, and Industry, the leading organizations of the Austrian economy attempted in vain in late autumn of 1921 to make clear to the Social Democratic members of Parliament and the trade-union leaders the urgency of the reforms that these organizations had resolved upon in their "Basic Principles of Economic and Finance Policy" of November 7, 1921. The socialist leaders preferred to fight against the elimination of the food subsidy with wild demagoguery, and they even found support for this outside their party.

Dr. Seipel's reconstructive work was impeded at every step by the policy of the Social Democratic party.[6] The Social Democrats did not, it is true, have a majority in the National Council; but they controlled the populous and economically powerful province of Vienna and were able to exploit this position of power with all the tricks that a false conception of federalism put at their disposal. No less important was the fact that the Social Democrats also controlled the streets. Seipel could perform his work in the Federation, but the financial policy of "Red" Vienna[7]– the Breitner

5 [Ignaz Seipel (1876–1932) was a Roman Catholic prelate and head of the Christian Social party in Austria. He twice served as chancellor of Austria (1922–24 and 1926–29). In general he followed a policy of social welfarism and interventionism, but he opposed the more directly socialist policies advocated by the Austrian Social Democratic party during this time. See Klemens von Klemperer, *Ignaz Seipel: Christian Statesman in a Time of Crisis* (Princeton, N.J.: Princeton University Press, 1972).—Ed.]

6 [On the economic reconstruction of Austria in the early 1920s, see W. T. Layton and Charles Rist, *The Economic Situation of Austria* (Geneva: League of Nations, 1925); *The Financial Reconstruction of Austria: General Survey and Principal Documents* (Geneva: League of Nations, 1926); and *The League of Nations Reconstruction Schemes in the Interwar Period* (Geneva: League of Nations, 1945), pp. 35–74.—Ed.]

7 ["Red" Vienna refers to the period between 1919 and 1934 during which the Austrian Social Democratic party held a large majority in the Vienna city government, enabling them to undertake an extended experiment in what was heralded as "municipal socialism," which was meant to serve as a model for the socialist society of the future. See Helmut Gruber, *Red Vienna: Experiment in Working-Class Culture, 1919–1934* (New York: Oxford University Press, 1991).—Ed.]

System[8]—could have its fling at the same time. That this dualism could not be constitutionally eliminated was the basic problem for the state. Years before it came to the final reckoning, the inevitability of this violent solution weighed on the entire Austrian economy like a nightmare.

Only now, when the destructionist policy of the Social Democratic party no longer stands in the way, can thought be given to following a financial policy of construction and liberation. What Seipel began must now be continued. A design for this has been provided through the collaboration of the economic circles. In 1930 an Economic Commission met in the Federal Chancellery that was composed of the representatives of the professions represented in the Chambers for Commerce, Trade, and Industry, in the Chambers of Agriculture, and in the Chambers of Workers and Employees. In December 1930 the tripartite editorial committee of this Economic Commission, to which the later Federal Chancellor Dr.

---

8 [Hugo Breitner (1873–1946) served as the city councilor of Vienna through most of the 1920s. He introduced vast municipal-housing, health-care, and educational programs for lower-income residents living in the city. The burden for paying for these programs was through heavily progressive taxes imposed on what was labeled bourgeois conspicuous consumption of forms of entertainment, as well as an equally progressive tax on rents earned by landlords and other property owners. See Charles A. Gulick, *Austria: From Habsburg to Hitler*, Vol. I (Berkeley: University of California Press, 1948), pp. 369–70, 374 & 379: "There can be no doubt that Breitner and his associates had largely succeeded in shifting the burden of the exclusively city [Vienna] taxes upon the relatively well-to-do and the rich. At least 60 percent, and probably more, of this revenue came from luxury, broadly defined, property and business." In 1926 and 1927, Leopold Kunschak, the leader of the Christian Socialist opposition in the Vienna city council,

> vigorously attacked the majority's tax policy as "overtaxation"; and described the results as "taxing away of business capital, limitation on production and employment." Proof of over taxation he found in the following way.... Kunschak ... was able to show that strictly municipal taxes [in Vienna] had risen 94.4 percent by comparing proceeds in 1923 with the budget for 1927.... The *Arbeiter Zeitung* [the Workers' Times] replied the next day with figures showing that federal taxes had increased between 1923 and 1927 by 97 percent.... During the following week anti-Breitner speakers charged that the *Arbeiter Zeitung* had "intentionally forgotten" to mention the fact that Vienna received a big slice of the federal taxes, that it had omitted the municipal beer tax in computing city revenues, and that an accurate comparison would show that federal taxes had risen only 68.7 percent, whereas municipal levies had gone up 106 percent.

In January 1927, one of the leading Vienna newspapers warned of "'The Success of the Tax Vampires.' It referred to the 'Breitnerism under which Vienna sighs so much' and to the 'great suffering of entrepreneurs under the city taxes.'"—Ed.]

Dollfuss[9] belonged while he was still director of the North Austrian Chamber of Agriculture, published its report, the financial policy content of which is still valid.

The government and the state can no longer live off the nation's substance.[10] The policy of taxing away capital and consuming the capital accumulated during past years made Austria dependent on foreign countries; she relied on loans from abroad because domestically neither taxation nor borrowing could raise the funds needed by the government. The first aim of our finance policy must be to economically establish our political independence, and in terms of a financial policy enabling the Austrian economy, through careful management, the possibility of strengthening itself again to such a degree that it can provide what the state needs.

This goal can be reached only if in the raising of funds great care is

9 [Engelbert Dollfuss (1892–1934) was a prominent member of the Austrian Christian Social party, who became chancellor of Austria in May 1932. During a failed attempt by Austrian Nazis to seize power in July 1934, Dollfuss was taken prisoner and murdered. —Ed.]

10 [On the growing tax burden on the Austrian economy during the 1920s, see Friedrich Hertz, *The Economic Problem of the Danubian States: A Study in Economic Nationalism* (London: Victor Gollancz, 1947), pp. 145–46:

> When [in 1930] the great economic crisis began to gravely affect Austria's economic life the Government appointed a commission of prominent economists [of whom Mises was one of the leading figures] and other experts charged to inquire into the causes of the difficulties. The Commission published its Report in 1931. It contains a wealth of statistical and other information supplied by the various branches of administration and by industrial and financial experts and covers mainly the period 1925–1929, which was a time of expanding production. In their final conclusions the experts point out that the unfavorable economic development was principally due to the fact that from 1925 to 1929 the cost of production increased much more than prices did. Taxation rose by 32 percent (Federal by 27 percent, provincial and communal by 40 percent), social insurance by 50 percent, industrial wages by 24 percent, agricultural wages by 13 percent, cost of transport by 15 percent. The only decrease was that in the rate of interest, which, however, was still very high. The bank rate declined from 1925 to 1929 from 13 percent to 7.5 percent, and the interest paid by industrial debtors from 16.5 to 13 percent. . . . The decline in the rates of interest, however, was far outweighed by the increase in all other burdens of production. . . . The excessive rise in the cost of production, the experts concluded, had the consequence that the earnings of the industries were inadequate and that new investments were discouraged. Consequently there was a constant rise in unemployment. . . . In the years of depression after the publication of the Report unemployment attained still higher levels.

—Ed.]

taken that productive capital is not taxed away or eaten up and that only the profits and surpluses are drawn upon for taxation. At the same time, spending by the Federation, the provinces, and the local communities must be managed to assure that unproductive expenditures are restricted in favor of productive ones.

That will certainly not be possible without a radical restructuring of the entire system of public administration. Our administrative apparatus is essentially still based on the reforms carried out eighty years ago by Alexander Bach.[11] The radical political, intellectual, and material changes that have taken place since then demand that a new course be followed. When Bach organized the administration, the provinces comprising present-day Austria were parts of a large empire, and these provinces were much more strongly connected to Bohemia and Hungary than with Styria and Tyrol. At that time the Alpine provinces were still hardly penetrated by railways; a single track led over the Alps toward the south and Vorarlberg had no railway connection with Tyrol. Today the Austrian Alpine provinces are traversed by the most modern electrically powered railroads and equipped with the most modern roads, and lie in the center of the flow of European traffic. That presents problems to which any administrative reform must give careful consideration.

The distribution of tax burdens determines the competitive advantage of individual groups and classes. Hence a sound tax system can emerge only from the cooperation of the representatives of all classes. The relationships between commerce, industry, and trade in every individual branch of production will be determined far more by tax-law decrees than by decisions concerning the regulation of trade. It is precisely on questions relating to taxation that there must be close cooperation between the representatives for the credit, financial, and insurance sectors of the economy with those represented by the Chamber of Commerce, Crafts, and Industry. The setting of business taxes in general or the sales tax is far more significant in determining the market relationships between these groups than many of the tax measures considered far more important by the public. Financial and tax policy not only determines the immediate funds available for the public budget; it also reaches deep into the structure of the economy and affects every single company. That emphasizes the role of the tax system in influencing the modern processes of production and

11 [See Chapter 26, "Adjusting Public Expenditures to the Economy's Financial Capacity," footnote 6.—Ed.]

its importance in matters of economic policy when changes in the constitutional order are considered.

Our financial situation today certainly still has room for improvement. Yet there are few countries in the world in which there is a better financial situation. Even with the attention that our financial situation still needs today, it is far better than it was in the fifties and sixties of the past [nineteenth] century. Yet even at that time a period of calm economic growth and an increased strengthening of the public finances followed a situation of deep financial distress. We too will once again find the way to a well-ordered economy and prosperity. Financial policy cannot be separated from the rest of economic policy, and neither of them can be separated from overall policy. In a society in which policy is based on the delusion that an unbridgeable opposition exists between the interests of different classes and that the essence of politics is class warfare, the moral foundation for a successful economic policy does not exist.

What our economic policy urgently needs was clearly expressed at the seventh session of the Chambers for Commerce, Trade, and Industry held on January 28 and 29, 1927; and the eighth session, held on February 11, 1930, fully repeated the remarks from the previous session. Even today not a word needs to be added to this program, and not a word needs to be taken away:[12]

> The structure of our balance of trade makes a reduction in the costs of production appear to be the most important problem for our national economy. Aside from any immediate changes in our international-trade policy, there is no other way effectively to reduce the importation of manufactured products on the domestic market and to increase the sale of Austrian products abroad other than by lowering the costs of production.
>
> But not all the costs of the factors of production in the Austrian economy can be influenced by measures involving changes in domestic economic policy. We have to pay the world-market prices for the raw materials and primary products that we need to import from other countries. As a capital-poor country we must draw upon foreign capital; the state of the foreign money and capital markets, upon which the interest rates we have to pay is dependent, is not subject to the influence of Aus-

12 [This portion of the Austrian Chambers of Commerce policy position was clearly written by Mises, since it is practically verbatim from the text of his 1927 article "The Balance Sheet of Economic Policies Hostile to Property," Chapter 25 of the present volume. — Ed.]

tria. Reductions in the costs of production only can be effected through a lowering of domestic wages or taxes. If we cannot succeed in reducing taxes and the social burdens that the private-production sector has to bear, then wages will inevitably have to go down or unemployment will have to go up.

The reduction of the tax burden on our enterprises is therefore in the interest of all sectors of the population, not only in the interest of businessmen but also and especially in the interest of the labor force.

The reduction of taxes can only occur if the greatest frugality takes place in the public budget. In the national administration a cutting of expenditures must be carried out, and public enterprises must be actively reshaped by appropriate measures. Providing this is done, it will be possible to reduce a number of existing taxes or eliminate them completely, and thereby assist in the improvement of our economy in a very efficient way.

PART IV

The Political Economy of Irrationalism, Autarky, and Collective Security on the Road to War (1935–38)

CHAPTER 33

The Cult of the Irrational[1]

I

Whenever the proponents of statism, socialism, interventionism, and imperialism are pushed very hard in a debate, they always have one last argument to fall back on. They point to the irrational nature of man's ultimate ends. They will admit that liberalism and free trade cannot be proven wrong through straightforward rational argument. If human affairs around the world were determined by reason alone, then free trade would have to prevail everywhere. But there is an irrational element in man, and his nature cannot be understood by the use of reason alone. Man's highest and most profound qualities are immeasurable, incomprehensible, and, indeed, indescribable, and therefore not open to rational reflection. The advocates of the rationalist-utilitarian school of philosophy, it is said, only look at life from the perspective of material profits and losses. The advocates of statism, socialism, and interventionism, on the other hand, claim to have more profound, exalted, and noble ideas in mind.

The advocates of rationalism and utilitarianism have never denied that man has aspirations above and more ennobling than merely wanting to live in a society in which the human needs for health, food, shelter, and security have been provided for in the most optimal manner for his physical well-being. But they do not bring these higher and more sublime callings in man into the discussions about man's worldly affairs. They are so far above daily life and the ordinary concerns of man that there is only one way in which to bring the two together. These higher aspirations are most

1 [This article was originally published in Hungarian in *Cobden*, Vol. II, No. 1 (January 1935), a publication in Budapest devoted to the principles of free trade.—Ed.]

likely to thrive and prosper the more that man's material needs have been fully satisfied. Man's energies are then released from his struggle for mere physical survival. Indeed, politics and especially economic policy can really do very little for these higher callings in man, other than in a negative sense. They should not hamper man's arrangements for the satisfaction of his physical well-being, which are the essential prerequisites for the unrestricted development of his spiritual life. Only the most extreme materialist claims that satisfying man's material welfare can positively, directly, and decisively influence these higher aspects of his existence.

The advocates of rationalism and utilitarianism also have never disputed that man's final or ultimate ends are outside the realm of reason. They do not inquire into the nature and qualities of these ultimate ends. Their concern has been with rationally investigating the secular institutions and societal order that would serve as the best means to attain those higher ends. They believe that the noblest potentials in the free human spirit are unlikely to grow in conditions of poor health, unsanitary surroundings, hunger, violence, murder, and other types of human misery. To the contrary, they argue that creating and advancing the conditions for man's material well-being provides the best soil in which there can bloom the higher potentials in man's mental and spiritual makeup.

Since it has been shown conclusively by economists that an international division of labor and free trade are more effective means than protectionism and autarky for attaining a higher standard of material well-being, it is absurd to offer in refutation to this insight any references to man's irrational desire for the sublime, the exalted, and the profound.[2] Or is the claim really going to be made that in being forced to pay a multiple of the world price for bread, the citizens in Europe's industrial countries are more than compensated for this loss through the noble and exalted feeling they receive in exchange?

The advocates of rationalist and utilitarian philosophy also believe that

---

2 [On Mises's conception of rationality and the role of reason in understanding man, the social and economic order, the functioning of the market, and the impossibilities of both socialism and interventionism, see Richard M. Ebeling, "A Rational Economist in an Irrational Age: Ludwig von Mises," in Richard M. Ebeling, ed., *The Age of Economists: Adam Smith to Milton Friedman* (Hillsdale, Mich.: Hillsdale College Press, 1999), pp. 69–120; and Richard M. Ebeling, "Planning for Freedom: Ludwig von Mises as Political Economist and Policy Analyst," in Richard M. Ebeling, ed., *Competition or Compulsion: The Market Economy versus the New Social Engineering* (Hillsdale, Mich.: Hillsdale College Press, 2001), pp. 1–85. —Ed.]

proper hygiene is necessary for human health, and that this, too, advances the higher ends of man. In this, rationalists and utilitarians are in agreement with the cultists of the irrational, at least those European members of this cult. If the building of bathing facilities were to become an issue, it would be expected that the discussion would proceed on completely rational lines. Given the goal in mind, competing plans would be compared in terms of the available factors of production. It would be considered absurd to challenge the engineer's blueprints on the basis of transcendental or irrational objections.[3]

If, as certain oriental ascetic sects do, some did not view hygiene as a desirable end, and instead uncleanliness was intrinsically considered a good, then opposition to the building of bathing facilities would be understandable in spite of our best moral, aesthetic, and sanitary arguments to the contrary. If, on the other hand, someone does agree with the principle of the benefits from hygiene and the desirability of improving sanitary conditions, then he should not introduce "the irrational" as an element in the discussion over the details for the execution of the blueprint. "The irrational" can only make an appearance in a decision about the choosing of ultimate ends, not in a debate over the selection of the most appropriate means. Do I want to commit suicide? Do I want to live my life in total disregard of worldly matters, in the manner of a Hindu saint? These and similar questions are outside the realm of rational discussion. If, instead, a person has thought about and decided to follow an active life in pursuit of those higher and uplifting ends, it is then inappropriate for him to appeal to "the irrational" when trying to fairly evaluate how best to secure the worldly things needed as the means to those ends.

Society is the great means through which men may peacefully and voluntarily cooperate for the most successful attainment of their material needs. Society, therefore, provides the opportunity for the furtherance of those higher and nobler ends. But to the question of how best to design the structures of the society, what institutions would best advance the achievement of those secular goals, only logical reasoning can provide an answer. The problem must be discussed soberly, calmly, and objectively. Anyone who wants to participate in this discussion must do so without an appeal to "the irrational." He must forthrightly state what it is he really wants. If he actually wants to achieve a lower level of productivity with the use of

---

3 [See Ludwig von Mises, *Liberalism: The Classical Tradition* (Irvington-on-Hudson, N.Y.: Foundation for Economic Education, [1927] 1996), pp. 5–7.—Ed.]

the world's labor and capital, then he should directly say so. If he wants to see fewer goods available at higher prices, he must say so. But he must not hide his purposes behind the artificial façade of "the irrational."

Economics can show to what consequences tariff barriers, quota systems, prohibitions, and autarky must necessarily lead. Anyone wanting to refute these results is welcome to use the tools of logical reasoning to do so. If he can, he is free to try and find the flaw in the economist's chain of reasoning. But if he cannot do so, whether because of incompetence or simply the impossibility of the task, he should keep quiet instead of blathering on about the superiority of "the irrational" in comparison to the supposed inferior results of the "merely" rational arguments of the economist.

II

Proponents of "the irrational" speak a great deal about the "mood of the people" and their nationalist pride in providing support to domestic industry. It is said that the masses, the nation, are not guided by rationality. They are quite willing to endure sacrifices for the attainment of their irrational goals. The people demonstrate a healthy reaction against the arguments of the free trader by rejecting dependency on foreign suppliers of goods and showing their willingness to pay higher prices for the domestic product in place of the less costly import.

If it were really true that consumers were willing to voluntarily pay higher prices for domestic products, then tariff barriers, import quotas, and prohibitions against imports would be totally unnecessary. All that the domestic producer would have to do would be to mark his goods as having been manufactured at home, and the market would then provide him protection from foreign imports. This would be a far more effective device than the intricate methods applied by protectionist policy. It is the very existence of tariff barriers that destroys the pathetic fantasy concerning the "noble mood" and "higher callings" of the people. The governments that construct these tariff barriers to protect domestic producers from foreign competition clearly understand this.

It is, therefore, completely untrue that the masses possess an intuitive propensity for purchasing domestic goods without consideration of the cost. In debating with the free trader, the proponent of protectionism should admit that the transcendental purposes to which he refers are his own, and not that of the consuming public. He should state that what he wants to do is to impose his own views, ideas, and plans on his neighbors by use, if necessary, of government coercion.

III

If the protectionist bases his argument on the desirability of subsidizing a certain fraction of the population at the expense of others in the society because he thinks that those to be subsidized are more deserving or more important, then he should make this case openly and directly. It is absolutely necessary to discuss these matters in the open before the public. It is hypocritical for the advocate of protectionism to make the case for protective tariffs on the claim that they represent the transcendental ends of the masses when in fact they really just represent distributing subsidies to one group of citizens at the expense of others.

There need be no stigma attached to a group that receives public funding through taxes rather than on the basis of voluntary contributions. Policemen, firemen, and doctors in the civil service are examples of people who are paid for their services in this way. No one objects to this because the police and fire departments, public hospitals, etc., are, in everyone's opinion, institutions needing to be maintained at public expense. If in a democratically governed country public opinion concludes, after an open debate of the issues, that agricultural production should be protected through the use of a tariff, even though it is at the expense of consumers, then no one would be able to quarrel with the barriers to trade. If some in the society still continue to disagree with protectionism and subsidies, then it would be their task to try to change the climate of public opinion in an attempt to win over a majority to their point of view. All the questions concerning the case for and against protectionism would be discussed soberly, calmly, and objectively, like any other discussion of the reasonableness of various means in the pursuit of a set of given ends.

There is nothing mystical or mysterious in this. There is nothing not open to reason. There is nothing requiring communion with "the irrational."

CHAPTER 34

Autarky: The Road to Misery

International Division of Labor Is
the Foundation of European Culture[1]

Although public opinion in the whole world seems to be united in its condemnation of an isolationist policy, the struggle against the international division of labor is being carried on with increasing energy, and all nations are marching farther along the road to autarky.[2]

It is generally assumed that the movement towards autarky is caused by policies related to contingencies for war. Yet even from the military point of view, the value of autarky is questionable. It is true that, in our age of international division of labor, the waging of war comes into conflict with the economic foundations for national existence. But autarky cannot remove this difficulty. A country that tries to become autarkic, i.e., economically self-sufficient, so that in a war it can hold out until final victory will have to lower its standard of living in the process. It will also go into a war more poorly armed than its opponents because it will have had to use substitute materials instead of the best resources in preparation for possible conflict. If these substitute materials were not less efficient, then they would not be mere surrogates, and the enemy would willingly use them as well. If a war continues for a long enough time that existing armaments must be supplemented through further production, then the enemy's superior productive abilities will become even more acutely obvious.

1 [This article was originally published in German in *Der Europäer* (March 1937). Mises developed some of the themes discussed in this article in his essay, "The Disintegration of the International Division of Labor" [1938] in Richard M. Ebeling, ed., *Money, Method and the Market Process: Essays by Ludwig von Mises* (Norwell, Mass.: Kluwer Academic Press, 1990), pp. 113–36. — Ed.]

2 [The word "autarky" comes from the Greek word, *autarkeia*, which means "self-sufficiency." For the Greeks, a *polis autarkes* meant a city-state that required no imports. See Allen G. B. Fisher, *Economic Self-Sufficiency* (Oxford: The Clarendon Press, 1939). — Ed.]

These substitute materials are expensive, i.e., they can be produced only with a higher expenditure of capital and labor; their production ties up more of the work force than the production of the better materials used by the enemy, and therefore it takes more men away from the front. The materials for the production of these substitutes will be scarce and will most likely have to be imported or may even be unavailable in wartime. Perhaps synthetic wool can really be made from milk, but one cannot drink milk and use it for cloth production at the same time. How, then, shall a country that is already short of cattle and fodder for alimentary requirements find the needed amounts of milk in wartime for cloth production as well?

One train of thought attempts to justify autarkic policies through reference to the problems of foreign-exchange policy. It is alleged that a shortage of foreign exchange leaves no other way out. But a shortage of foreign exchange can only exist where, under threat of punishment, the government tries to maintain the price of foreign currency below the price that would form on the market if the functioning of the market were not impeded. In a free foreign-exchange market there is no shortage of foreign exchange; at the most there can be foreign-exchange prices that the government does not like. The regulation of foreign-exchange transactions at exchange rates lower than those that would be set by the market is the cause of a shortage of foreign exchange. The more strictly the regulations are enforced the more the shortage of foreign exchange increases.

If foreign-exchange regulation is applied absolutely, then foreign trade completely stops. One cannot export if the obligation to deliver foreign exchange at the official rate represents a significantly high export duty, and one cannot import if the government does not allow foreign exchange. The government then must either offer premiums to promote exports, the burden of which is compensated for by a duty on the delivery of foreign exchange, or it must reach arrangements with foreign countries for balancing its trade, the conditions of which produce the same result in a different way.

It is believed that the need for an appropriate social policy justifies the exclusion of products for whose production lower wages were paid than are in effect at home. This idea also is erroneous.

Since the [First] World War, almost all nations have attempted to protect their respective labor markets through the prohibition of immigration. As a result, the aggregate efficiency of world production is lowered, and consequently the average standard of living in the world is also reduced. But as a consequence of these immigration restrictions, the workers in those nations that are only thinly populated in proportion to their natural wealth will be assured an advantage at the expense of the workers in the relatively overpopulated countries. They will be able to receive wages that are higher than those they could earn if migration were unrestricted. If people were content with this wage advantage, and if government intervened in the labor market only through a prohibition on immigration, then there would be no reason for any further intervention to protect the domestic labor market through restrictions on the importation of goods.

The banning of migration is extremely threatening for the organization of international relations.[3] But such a policy could be practiced and it could exercise its effects in raising wages in those countries where the right conditions exist for this to happen, while at the same time still preserving a full freedom of trade in goods.

But if economic policy pushes wages above the level that would have prevailed on the labor market only on the basis of excluding foreign workers, because this is not considered good enough, then new difficulties will arise in the exporting as well as the importing sectors of the market. Furthermore, pushing wages higher results in the emergence of unemployment as a lasting and massive phenomenon.

It is believed that the competition from those poor countries with lower standards of living and lower wages can be made more difficult through the use of capital-export barriers. But in the long run that, too, proves to be ineffective. After all, the workers of those overpopulated lands of the East want to live and therefore must work. If they are not allowed to migrate into the countries that are richer in capital and better favored by nature for production, and if it is made difficult for capital to seek them out in their own countries, then they will have to be satisfied with wages that are so low that they make up for the disadvantages that arise due to the shortage of capital and unfavorable natural conditions.

Against the price competition from the goods produced in these lower-wage countries, nothing positive can result if recourse is made to the more radical method of prohibiting or rationing imports. For then prices rise and real wages decline in the restricting country. Of course, it is then said that a remedy for the rise in prices has to be found. The answer offered is

3 [See Ludwig von Mises, "The Freedom to Move as an International Problem," [Christmas 1935] in Richard M. Ebeling and Jacob G. Hornberger, eds., *The Case for Free Trade and Open Immigration* (Fairfax, Va.: Future of Freedom Foundation, 1995), pp. 127–30. —Ed]

simply to prohibit price increases and then possibly cover a part of the rising costs of production through government subsidies. Doing this means to engage in a policy of capital consumption.

In the long run a decline in the standard of living cannot be avoided if an exclusionary policy is maintained. If, under the protection of closed borders, goods are produced domestically that can be produced more cheaply abroad, this means that methods of production have been chosen under which a given expenditure of capital and labor generates a smaller output. If less is produced, less also has to be consumed; the fact is, then, that capital is consumed.

Capital consumption is especially harmful for the industrialized nations of Europe and above all for the work force of these nations. The natural conditions of production are more favorable in America and Australia than in Europe. The industrial nations of Europe, whose labor market today can no longer be relieved through emigration, live on their historically acquired industrial superiority. They pay for imported raw materials and foodstuffs by the exportation of industrial products, which, in large part, are produced from imported raw materials. If they consume a part of their capital, that is, their industrial equipment, then they will be able to remain competitive against the industries of America and Australia, which work under more favorable natural conditions, only by further severe reductions in wages.

Long-range economic policy must recognize that a policy of capital consumption gnaws at the roots of the existence of European industries and their workers. To be sure, long-range policy is not popular today. An English economist has made the claim, "In the long run we are all dead."[4]

4 [Mises is referring to John Maynard Keynes (1883–1946), who was the most famous British economist of the twentieth century. He advocated active government intervention in the market to overcome unemployment through deficit spending and monetary expansion. His most influential book was *The General Theory of Employment, Interest and Money* (1936). The phrase, "In the long run we are all dead," was used by Keynes in "A Tract on Monetary Reform," [1923] in D. E. Moggridge, ed., *The Collected Writings of John Maynard Keynes* (London: Macmillan Ltd., 1971), p. 65, in reference to the quantity theory of money and the proposition that, in "the long run," changes in the money supply only influence the general level of prices. In *Omnipotent Government: The Rise of the Total State and Total War* (Spring Mills, Pa., Libertarian Press, [1944] 1985), p. 252, Mises pointed out that, "Lord Keynes did not coin this phrase in order to recommend short-run policies, but in order to criticize some inadequate methods and statements in monetary theory. . . . However, the phrase best characterizes the economic policies recommended by Lord Keynes and his school."—Ed.]

That is nothing other than a modern paraphrase of the frivolous saying that was spoken at the end of the *ancien régime* in France: "Après nous le déluge."[5] Good policy looks ahead and is concerned with the welfare of future generations. There is no method that can eliminate the harmful influence on the standard of living resulting from an exclusionary trade policy. The more that the supply of capital is attacked in the short run in order to avoid these consequences, the more severely the standard of living will finally have to decline in the longer run.

Let us take care that we do not thoughtlessly squander Europe's advantage in the world: The international division of labor is the foundation of the European economy, yea, of all of European culture. Every step away from the international division of labor is a step toward destitution.

---

5 [This is a French expression that means, "After us, the flood."—Ed.]

CHAPTER 35

The League of Nations and the Raw-Materials Problem[1]

On October 9, 1936, the League of Nations resolved to establish a committee to study the question of raw materials.[2] This committee held its first session in Geneva from March 8 to 12, 1937. Members from the following nations participated in it: England, Russia, Switzerland, the Netherlands, Belgium, Poland, Czechoslovakia, Sweden, Portugal, the United States, Mexico, Brazil, Canada, South Africa, and Japan. Germany and Italy stayed away, precisely those two states that complain most vigorously and urgently about the inequality of the distribution of raw materials. Of course, France was likewise not represented, if we leave out of consideration the fact that the general secretary as well as the vice director who represent the International Labor Organization are Frenchmen; the French committee member had, however, apologized for his absence.

The committee first decided on the two questions that the resolution of the League of Nations meeting, to which the committee owed its establishment, had chosen to leave open. For the time being, it decided not to restrict its preparatory statistical work to raw materials in the strict sense of the word but to include, in addition, the most important foodstuffs and fodder. Reserved for a later date is a decision about which materials are to be made the subject of the real negotiations. A further decision was made

---

1 [This article was originally published in German in *The New Commonwealth Quarterly* (June 1937).—Ed.]

2 [The League of Nations was formed in 1919 after the First World War as an international organization to promote peace and security. It was dissolved in 1946 and replaced by the United Nations. President Woodrow Wilson originally sponsored it, but the U. S. Senate rejected American membership.—Ed.]

to deal with raw materials without regard to whether they are produced chiefly in colonial and mandate regions or in the sovereign states.[3]

The Secretariat of the League of Nations was assigned the task of submitting statistical material in preparation for further negotiations. Furthermore, two subcommittees were set up with the responsibility for examining the alleged hardships and the unfavorable conditions about which there are complaints. The first is to occupy itself with questions of market supply. The following issues were assigned to it: export prohibitions and export restrictions, export taxes (including differential levies), trade licensing systems, monopolies, and agreements and cartels for the regulation of production and sale. The second subcommittee is to deal with questions of sales and payments. It is supposed to investigate: the difficulties that arise for importing countries in the matter of payment because of their lack of foreign exchange; customs problems (high or prohibitive duties, preferential tariffs, customs unions, and problems of the "open door"); import limitations (quotas, foreign-exchange controls, clearing contracts); and subsidy systems (production and export premiums, subsidization of the production of substitute materials).

The two subcommittees are supposed to clarify these questions through the objective determination of the real situation and to work out proposals for rectification of whatever unfavorable conditions may be ascertained. They are to meet during the month of June before the full session of the committee. It was determined that it would be advantageous to have recourse to experts from those countries which have to struggle with payment and transfer difficulties in the purchase of raw materials.

This is the sum total of all that the League of Nations has accomplished in this area up to now. A program has been set up for further discussion of the problem of raw materials. It has still not gotten beyond the preliminary steps.

For the sake of completeness it must be mentioned that a second authority of the League of Nations is presently dealing with the problem of raw materials. The International Institute for Intellectual Cooperation,[4]

3 [At the end of the First World War, the overseas colonies of imperial Germany in Africa and portions of the former Turkish Empire in the Middle East were transferred to British and French administration as "mandates" under League of Nations supervision. Their final status was to be determined in the future.—Ed.]

4 [The International Institute of Intellectual Cooperation was founded in 1928, with its headquarters in Paris. Its stated purpose was to offer solutions for peaceful change in response to international political and economic conflicts. It suspended operations shortly after the start of the Second World War in 1939.—Ed.]

which is associated with the League of Nations, has chosen the problem of "Peaceful Change" for the session of the International Studies Conference meeting in Paris in June of this year.[5] In this framework, not only the problems of population, colonies, and migrations will be discussed but the problem of raw materials, as well. The national groups existing in the individual countries of the International Studies Conference have worked out detailed memoranda concerning all of these questions. Professor Etienne Dennery, General Secretary of the Centre d'Études de Politique Etrangère [Center for the Study of Foreign Policy] in Paris, has been designated as presenter of the report on raw materials. The office of chief report-presenter lies in the worthy hands of Professor Maurice Bourquin.

What hopes and expectations can be attached to the activities of the League of Nations in the area of raw-material problems?

In the political area the League of Nations has completely failed in its present form of organization. There is no point in deceiving oneself about the matter or in refusing to speak the truth out of inappropriate courtesy toward the persons responsible. Its failure in the Italian-Abyssinian conflict has given the deathblow to the political value of the League of Nations in its present form.[6] Whether the League of Nations Secretariat continues to work away, whether the statesmen keep on coming to Geneva for plenary assemblies, for counsel and commission sessions, the great political negotiations will be carried on far away. Even the preliminary studies and preparations for a possible new economic conference were not entrusted to the League of Nations. The League concerns itself with things that, no matter how important they may be in themselves, have only ancillary importance in regard to the main task that was intended for it. The Secretariat publishes interesting statistical surveys, which could, however, be just as well taken care of by an international organization of statistical agencies.

5 [See *Peaceful Change: Procedure, Population Pressure, the Colonial Question, Raw Materials and Markets. Proceedings of the Tenth International Studies Conference, Paris, June 28th–July 3rd, 1937* (Paris: International Institute of Intellectual Cooperation, 1937). —Ed.]

6 Cf., in this regard, Lord Davies' book *Nearing the Abyss: The Lesson of Ethiopia* (London: Constable & Co., 1936), which comes to terms with this problem. [Fascist Italy invaded Ethiopia (Abyssinia) on October 3, 1935. The League of Nations condemned the invasion and economic sanctions were imposed on Italy. The sanctions, however, were ineffective because of a failure to fully adhere to them by many League members. The Italian military forces entered the Ethiopian capital of Addis Ababa on May 5, 1936, and shortly afterwards the Italians declared victory.—Ed.]

Now, however, a task again has confronted the League that is in its line of business: to ensure world peace. Leading statesmen of the countries that have reasons to fear the interruption of peace have publicly stated their grievances, which they argue show the unsatisfactory nature of the present political order of the world. They have labeled the "unequal distribution" of raw materials a severe disadvantage for their nations;[7] and, even though they have not said it explicitly, they have announced clearly enough that they look upon this disadvantage as such a severe evil that under the circumstances even a war would seem justified for their relief. These declarations have made a deep impression on the public opinion of the whole world. The League of Nations must not be silent about such a state of affairs. If it should be silent, then it really would be more reasonable to dispense with the League entirely.

It was therefore by all means imperative for the League to take hold of the problem of raw materials. It is, of course, another question whether the way chosen to deal with it is the most appropriate one.

The League of Nations is not supposed to be a debating club or a statistics seminar. It must not consider its duty to be to assemble data relative to raw materials from the available statistical material, to present them in neatly printed form, and then discuss them. It goes without saying that the Secretariat has to prepare the deliberations of the committee by the collection of all useful data. But that has nothing to do with the real work that is to be performed.

What is needed is a *hearing of opposing views* concerning the declared grievances. This discussion should take place in full view of the public. No word that is spoken about these things in the League must remain hidden from the world. An appropriately organized press service should see to it that the discussions are known everywhere through the press and through the radio, and that, above all, they reach those countries whose governments may only inadequately inform their subjects about the course of the negotiations. It is absolutely incomprehensible why the representatives of the press have been kept away from the sessions of the committee. What

7 [It was argued by fascists and Nazis that the control of colonial territories with large deposits of raw materials by countries such as Great Britain and France put Italy and Germany at a disadvantage for their economic development and for military security in case of war. They called for the redistribution of Asian and African colonies to even the political and economic playing field. For a critical evaluation of the idea, see Norman Angell, *This Have and Have-Not Business: Political Fantasy and Economic Fact* (London: Hamish Hamilton, 1936).—Ed]

secrets are there, after all, in this area that ought to remain hidden from the public?

Everything should be gambled on the idea of inducing the states that claim these grievances to formulate their complaints precisely, to support them as thoroughly as possible and present them before the committee. If, as unfortunately is to be expected on the basis of their previous behavior, they should decline to accept this invitation, then the League itself would have to appoint representatives of this viewpoint. Experts can be found outside Germany and Italy who consider these complaints about the unequal distribution of raw materials to be justified. Representatives of the opposite point of view should confront these champions of those who are supposedly discriminated against. In these proceedings of opposing views all sides of the problem would be discussed exhaustively. The result would then be set down in a final report, which would make the standpoints of both sides known as clearly and plainly as is possible.

No political economist who really deserves this name can doubt what impression such a final report will awaken in the impartial reader. The report will cause the specter of the raw-materials question, which so agitates the world today, to disappear. It will show that the source of the difficulties of the provision of raw materials is to be found in the trade and foreign-exchange policy of the states that consider themselves discriminated against and not in the "unequal distribution" of raw materials. It will also show that no war and no territorial alterations could put the aggrieved countries in a better position in regard to the provision of raw materials.

By no means must only representatives of the government be allowed to speak before the committee and in the committee. More important than the representatives of the governments, who are hampered in their freedom of argument by their diplomatic duty, are independent experts, who would be appointed by the League without regard to their citizenship. Of course the importance of the personal question must not be underestimated. The prestige which the utterances of men like Mussolini,[8] Hitler,[9]

8 [Benito Mussolini (1883–1945) formed the Italian fascist movement after the First World War. He was prime minister of Italy from 1922 to 1943. He was shot and killed by Italian antifascist partisans in Milan near the close of the war on April 28, 1945.—Ed.]

9 [Adolf Hitler (1889–1945) was the leader of the German National Socialist (Nazi) Workers party from 1920/1921, and chancellor and führer of Germany from 1933 to 1945. Near the end of the Second World War in Europe, on April 30, 1945, Hitler committed suicide in his Berlin bunker as the city was falling to the advancing Soviet army.—Ed.]

Göring,[10] and Goebbels[11] enjoy today can only be countered if men of the first rank who are not limited in their freedom by any diplomatic office are allowed to speak.

The outcome of the League's work must not be merely the production of another new League of Nations document that will be entombed in archives and libraries. It must arouse the world, and it must be effective. But it can do that only through the power of the personalities who find expression in its pages. It is undeniable that this procedure would mean a break with the previous diplomatic-bureaucratic tradition of the League of Nations. But from its creation the League was intended to be neither a bureaucratic organization nor a stronghold for diplomatic pussyfooting and awkward business dealings. It was precisely intended to replace the inherited methods of secret diplomacy by a procedure better fitting democratic requirements. That these expectations were disappointed is one of the reasons for the League's failure. It is an unbearable situation that people in the world today are more interested in everything other than what takes place in the broad halls of the Palais des Nations[12] and that they pay hardly any attention to the declarations that are made in the sessions of the League. All countries are arming themselves feverishly, and all statesmen are actively trying to assure their respective countries the most favorable position possible in the new war that is threatening the world. The League of Nations only can do *one thing* about it: It must bring the issues creating conflict to the discussion table. It must show them to the world in their true form, it must raise the question: How can a war, and how is a war supposed to, produce anything good?

The League of Nations must not be satisfied being an organization that regards as its most important task to be to cause as little annoyance as

10 [Hermann Göring (1893–1946) was a leading figure of the Nazi party in Germany, serving as minister of the interior, Reich commissioner for aviation, minister of economic affairs, commissioner for the Nazi four-year economic plan, and Reich marshal for the Greater German Reich. He committed suicide on October 15, 1946, shortly before he was to be executed as a war criminal.—Ed.]

11 [Joseph Goebbels (1897–1945) was the minister for public enlightenment and propaganda and the president of the Chamber of Culture in Nazi Germany. Having remained in Hitler's Berlin bunker at the end of the Second World War in Europe, Goebbels committed suicide with his wife on May 1, 1945, after they killed their six children.—Ed.]

12 [The Palace of Nations, the building complex in Geneva, Switzerland that served as the headquarters for the League of Nations, is now a part of the United Nations organization. —Ed.]

possible for the governments of the more than fifty member nations. It must strive to become a moral authority that is taken seriously by the world. Its commissions, which have more freedom of activity than the full council sessions of official government representatives, must become a sort of world parliament. Here conflicts should not be hushed up by finely tuned speeches; here the nations must have it out with each other, spiritedly, in public, with the greatest passion and with full use of all available arguments. It must not be viewed as the job of the Committee on Raw Materials to ponder projects for international arrangements that either are so trivial that their ratification is meaningless or that never reach ratification. Under the present conditions the League only has a possibility of having a moral influence by working for enlightened understanding. Only small-minded bureaucrats will regard the moral successes that might be achieved as less important than the authentically correct execution of professional documents, of which nobody takes any notice except other bureaucrats and diplomats.

The proposed procedure recommends itself not just for dealing with questions that—like the raw-materials problem, the colonial problem, and the problem of barriers to trade—appear to be due merely to the opposing interests of individual nations. The direction of recent discussions of these problems demonstrate that people are starting to understand that any justifiable distinction between privileged and disadvantaged nations has nothing to do with either an unequal distribution of raw materials or an unequal distribution of colonial and mandate regions. Rather, the cause is to be found in immigration restrictions.

The fact that the United States, the British Dominions, and a number of other states allow immigration only within narrow limits discriminates against all nations whose people could better their living standard by immigration to those countries. In this sense the slogan, a "nation without room" has a justifiable content. A completely public discussion of the migration problem would show conflicts of interest existing between the workers of Europe and Asia and those of the other parts of the world. But it would also show that it would be hopeless to try to remedy the disadvantages that these migration restrictions inflict on the peoples of large and "small" European and Asiatic nations by means of war and colonial conquests.

The importance of what occurs in the Raw Materials Committee of the League of Nations must not be underrated. The League is offered once more the opportunity—perhaps for the last time—to play a decisive role in world politics. The League can show whether it is capable of cooperating in pacifying the world. The reform of the League of Nations cannot come from a change in the regulations of the pact. Deeds, not paragraphs, decide. The League of Nations must be made into what it was originally supposed to become: the highest *moral* authority in all matters of international politics. Nationalist statesmen and politicians repeat over and over again that nothing is more urgent than armament, that every day one must be ready to draw the sword from the sheath, and that there is no better cure for economic distress than a victorious war. A powerful propaganda machine tries to steel people spiritually for the coming war. In many nations the educational system is given only one assignment: to educate youth, including the female half, for the requirements of war. A peacetime economy is regarded only as a preparation for the war economy. It can be said without exaggeration that—at least in the totalitarian states—everything else is considered secondary to the material and spiritual preparation for the coming war.

The League of Nations has to turn against this unrestrained war propaganda. It should compare the emptiness of discussions about economic policy with the fantasies of the militarists, who bring into the modern world of the international division of labor and an interdependency of national economies the mentality of the plundering nomads of primeval times. If others preach the necessity and inevitability of war, then the League has the duty to show that war must be avoided if we do not want to destroy our entire civilization and bring on unspeakable misery. It has the duty to expose mercilessly the absurdity of the economic arguments for war, and it must begin with the raw-materials problem because this is the issue put on the front line today by the advocates of war.

Only in this way could the League act in a useful way and do justice to its duties in the face of the immediate world situation. As an organization among a thousand other organizations, as a forum for debate among a thousand other places of debate, as a publisher among a thousand other publishing establishments, it is superfluous.

CHAPTER 36

Guidelines for a
New Order of Relationships
in the Danube Region[1]

I

All plans for a new order of the political and economic relationships in
the Danube region are based on the erroneous notion that neighboring
areas "economically" complement each other and that therefore a special
incentive exists for them to enter into a closer association. This concept is
upside down. Neighboring countries generally have similar climatic and
geological conditions, they have similar production possibilities, they make
approximately the same products, and they are therefore competitors both
in the sale of their own products and in the purchase of various goods that
are imported from abroad.

　　If we consider the Danube countries as they were organized as nations
on the basis of the Treaties of Versailles, Saint-Germain, and Trianon,[2] we

---

1 [This article was originally written in German in 1938 and has not been published before. It presents the case for and an outline of a unified political state in the Danube region
of Eastern Europe. Mises developed this idea more fully in a monograph that he wrote in
October 1941, "The Eastern Democratic Union: A Proposal for the Establishment of a
Durable Peace in Eastern Europe," which has been published in Richard M. Ebeling, ed.,
*Selected Writings of Ludwig von Mises, Vol. 3: The Political Economy of International Re-
form and Reconstruction* (Indianapolis: Liberty Fund, 2000), pp. 169–201. A short presen-
tation of the same idea was published by Mises in *Omnipotent Government: The Rise of the
Total State and Total War* (Spring Mills, Pa.: Libertarian Press, [1944] 1985), pp. 271–78.
—Ed.]

2 [The Treaties of Versailles, Saint-Germain and Trianon (1919–20) ended the state of
war between the Allied powers and Germany, Austria, and Hungary, respectively. They
also resulted in the transfer of territories and construction of new nation-states in Central
and Eastern Europe.—Ed.]

can distinguish among them a predominantly industrial group (Austria and Czechoslovakia) and a predominantly agrarian group (Hungary, Romania, Yugoslavia, Bulgaria, and Poland). If the industrial states had not carried out a policy of agricultural protectionism and if the agrarian states had not carried out a policy of industrial protection, then the exchange of goods between these two groups of nations could have been more intense.[3] But all the attempts that were undertaken between 1919 and 1938 to establish a closer economic association among the Danubian nations failed because no state was ready to make even the slightest concession in this regard.

The old Austro-Hungarian monarchy seemed to be injurious to the national interests of the various peoples included in the empire because it prevented them from engaging in policies of self-sufficiency. The Hungarians, especially, raged passionately against the common customs and currency system.[4] Today many Hungarians of course admit that that was a mistake. Nonetheless, no Hungarian politician is inclined to moderate or indeed discard the system that hinders the importation of all industrial articles that are produced by one of the artificially created industries in his country. And no Hungarian statesman would be willing to forgo building up the Hungarian industrial structure by the establishment of new enterprises that can only be made somewhat profitable through the severest restriction of all competing imports. In the other nations it is not much different.[5]

So long as this mentality is not completely done away with, it is use-

3 [For a critical analysis of "the agrarianization of industrial countries" and "the industrialization of agrarian countries" during this period between the two world wars, see Wilhelm Röpke, *International Economic Disintegration* (Philadelphia: Porcupine Press, [1942] 1978), pp. 111–87.—Ed.]

4 [On the economic nationalistic conflicts and tensions in the Austro-Hungarian empire that hampered the success of any fully free-trade regime, see Oscar Jaszi, *The Dissolution of the Habsburg Monarchy* (Chicago: University of Chicago Press, [1929] 1961), pp. 185–212; and Gustav Gratz and Richard Schüller, *The Economic Policy of Austria-Hungary During the War in its External Relations* (New Haven, Conn.: Yale University Press, 1928), pp. 13–35. On the degree to which the empire was an integrated economic area on the basis of trade and investment before the First World War, see David F. Good, *The Economic Rise of the Habsburg Empire, 1750–1914* (Berkeley: University of California Press, 1984), pp. 96–124.—Ed.]

5 [On Hungarian economic policy in the period after the First World War, see Leo Pasvolsky, *Economic Nationalism of the Danubian States* (New York: Macmillan Co., 1928), pp. 291–380.—Ed.]

less to talk about an economic confederation of the Danubian nations. So long as these nations regard every importation of goods as unhealthy and consider every method that can impede imports as admissible, it is a waste of time to occupy oneself with projects for the creation of a Danubian economic association.

But if an economic consolidation of the Danube countries is to come about, then it cannot be limited to the establishment of a customs union. In our age of state interventionist policies, governments have an endless number of other measures at their disposal besides customs duties and importation prohibitions that can be used for the protection of domestic production against foreign competition. Currency and credit policies, tax laws, occupational, health, and construction police, policies regarding the distribution of public contracts, the tariff structure of the railroads, and most of the other areas of public administration can serve protectionist purposes. It would, therefore, not be sufficient to restrict the sovereignty of the individual Danubian states only with regard to the customs system. All administrative matters would have to be put under the sovereignty of the union.

II

The political relationships in the Danube region are intolerable. Every nation sees its neighbors as mortal enemies and strives to enlarge its national area by the incorporation of pieces of territory in which the members of its own people are in the minority. Since 1918, not peace but a truce has reigned in the Danube region. Every country has been preparing for war against all of its neighbors.

This situation cannot be remedied by letting the individual nations keep their full sovereignty and simply bringing them together in a union of sovereign states. The conflicts between them cannot be cleared away in this manner. The root of these conflicts lies in the minority question. One cannot evade this problem; the fact that not much less than half of the Danube region is of mixed languages must be a starting point for any attempt at a solution. In the Danube region, and in Eastern Europe in general, no drawing of boundaries is conceivable that can put an end to the minority problem. Ask the representatives of the individual nationalities how they imagine the borders of their countries should be drawn on the map, it will be seen that the greater part of the region is claimed by two or even by several countries.

Every protection of minorities will be ineffective that does not essentially restrict the sovereignty of the countries, otherwise it will leave a source of permanent frictions that must in the end break up any association of these nations. If the member of a minority believes that the laws or administrative measures of the state in which he lives violate his right to equal treatment, he must be offered the possibility of demanding and receiving relief from a central government and a central tribunal. Federal law must therefore take precedence over the law of the individual member states, decisions of the federal court of justice must be executable in the entire federal territory (including against the individual states), and the governments of the individual states must obey the commands of the federal government. That means, therefore, not an association of states (not a Danubian League of Nations) but a federal state in the American sense.

In the entire federal region all members of each individual state must be treated absolutely equally. They must enjoy full freedom of movement, they must have the right to practice any vocation, to use their own language in their private and social life, and to bring up their children in this language. In all mixed-language regions the courts and public authorities in dealings with the public must use every language that is designated as their own language by more than 155 of the inhabitants in their district. Economic legislation must be uniform in the entire federal territory. The money and note-issuing central bank system must be uniformly regulated and administrated. No impediments should be put in the way of the free movement of capital and goods.

All this requires a central parliament, a central government, and a federal jurisdiction. For the proceedings of these agencies an official language must be chosen. The choice should be either French or English.

For the seat of the central offices only Vienna could be considered. The region of Vienna and its environs would then have to be separated from the territory of the Austrian state and would have to be administered after the fashion of the American District of Columbia.

To spare national sensitivities it is recommended that part of the positions in the central offices be filled not by members of the Danube countries but by Englishmen and Frenchmen.

Only an arrangement of this sort could guarantee the peaceful coexistence and cooperation of the nations of the Danube region. It would not give hegemony to any single one of these nations, and it would allow none of them to rule over minorities.

III

There is no doubt that this proposal will be indignantly labeled unacceptable by all the governments of the Danube states. It is perfectly natural that the beneficiaries of the prevailing chaos do not want to give it up.

If the question is looked at not from the standpoint of the special interests of the current power-holders but from that of the interests of the peoples as a whole, then one reaches a different opinion concerning these proposals.

The nations of Eastern Europe have a choice between uniting to form a structure that makes it possible for them to hold their own in the world or the loss of their freedom. Either they will become provinces of Germany, Russia, and Italy and be treated as pariahs, or they must become parts of a superstate in which they govern themselves. If the Poles, Czechs, Estonians, Latvians, Lithuanians, and Albanians have learned anything at all from their history, they will not be able to dispute this. The Hungarians, Romanians, and Yugoslavians may soon undergo experiences that will show them clearly the precariousness of their present sovereignty.

The politicians who support the maintenance of the absolute sovereignty of the individual Danubian states rest their case on the assumption that England and France will protect their freedom. They believe that they can raise a claim that this protection is granted to them, and they are unwilling to make any sacrifice themselves in order to set up a system that could be maintained by its own strength without any outside help. But England and France will eventually become tired of fulfilling the task assigned to them. They will demand that the Eastern states create a political system that is capable of defending itself. For a European balance of power the existence of a great power that can hold its own against Russia, Germany, and Italy is indispensable. But the amalgamation of the Eastern states is above all a question of life and death for the Eastern nations themselves.

IV

Consequently, the Danube question should be looked upon and dealt with not as an economic problem but as a purely political one. The political inevitability of the unification of the Danube states is clearer and easier to understand than the economic chain of reasoning that shows the absurdity of protectionist and autarkic policies.

Two questions must be presented to the statesmen and politicians of the individual Danubian countries. First, how do you imagine a drawing of boundaries that makes it possible for your nation to coexist peacefully with its immediate neighbors? Second, how do you expect to ensure the independence of your nation against the possible protectorate intentions of Germany, Russia, or Italy?

The statesmen and politicians of England and France, on the other hand, must be asked, how often are you willing to have your soldiers fight again for Sarajevo[6] or for Danzig?[7] Do you not prefer a system that provides peace in the Danube region for the foreseeable future?

The Danube or East Federation should give Eastern Europe that which the League of Nations was not able to give it: freedom based on collective security.

6 [Sarajevo is the capital of Bosnia, which in 1914 was a part of the Austro-Hungarian empire. The assassination of Austrian Archduke Francis Ferdinand and his wife Sophie on June 28, 1914, by a Bosnian-Serb nationalist in Sarajevo is usually said to have been the "spark" that resulted in the start of the First World War in August of 1914. Imperial Russia came to the support of the Serbian government (suspected of being involved in the assassination plot) when Austria made demands on the Serbs; imperial Germany declared its support for Austria-Hungary under the Russian threat; and France and then Great Britain were drawn into the emerging conflict through France's respective alliances with Russia and Britain. — Ed.]

7 [Danzig (Gdansk) was an old German city on the Baltic coast that was separated from Germany and made into a "free city" as part of the Treaty of Versailles under League of Nations auspices, but with administrative oversight by the government of Poland. Throughout the 1920s and 1930s, between the two World Wars, it was a growing point of political tension between Germany and Poland as part of the dispute over what was known as the "Corridor" of territory leading to the Baltic Sea that had been ceded to Poland at the end of the First World War, but which then separated the German state of East Prussia from the rest of Germany. — Ed.]

PART V

Austrian Economics

CHAPTER 37

The Austrian Economists[1]

Almost all of those who were appointed in recent decades as Austria's representatives to deal with Hungary concerning economic problems came from the school of Carl Menger[2] and his successors, that school that is known as the Austrian School of economics. Two of its masters, Eugen von Böhm-Bawerk[3] and Friedrich von Wieser,[4] served under the old

1 [This article originally appeared in German in *Der Wirtschafter* (April 27, 1934). — Ed.]

2 [Carl Menger (1840–1921) was the founder of the Austrian School of economics. After working as a journalist and civil servant in the Austrian Ministry of Prices, he was appointed as a professor of political economy at the University of Vienna in 1873, a position he held until his retirement in 1903. In 1876 he was tutor for Crown Prince Rudolph of Austria. He also served on the Imperial Commission on Currency Reform in 1892, which resulted in Austria-Hungary formally going on the gold standard. — Ed.]

3 [Eugen von Böhm-Bawerk (1851–1914) was one of the leading members of the Austrian School of economics in the years before the First World War. His major contributions were to the theory of capital and interest, as well as to the general theory of value and price. He was professor of political economy at the University of Innsbruck from 1880 to 1889. Böhm-Bawerk worked in the Austrian Ministry of Finance throughout the 1890s and served three times as minister of finance, the longest and last time from 1900 to 1904. He returned to teaching as a full-time professor of political economy at the University of Vienna in 1905, a position he held until his death. — Ed.]

4 [Friedrich von Wieser (1851–1926) was one of the leading members of the Austrian School of economics in the period before and immediately after the First World War. His major contributions were to the theory of marginal utility, the concept of opportunity cost, and the theory of the determination of the value of the factors of production. After serving in the Austrian civil service from 1872 to 1883, he was appointed professor of political economy at the University of Prague in the Austrian province of Bohemia. He was appointed professor of political economy at the University of Vienna in 1903, following Carl Menger's retirement. He served as minister of commerce from 1917 to 1918, in the last government of the Austro-Hungarian empire. — Ed.]

Austro-Hungarian empire, the former as minister of finance, the latter as minister of commerce. But on the other side of the conference table, among the distinguished men whom Hungary is accustomed to sending to such negotiations there also sat and still sit economists whose development was influenced by the writings of the Austrian School. It may therefore seem reasonable also to speak of the Austrian economists when the economic relations of Austria and Hungary are discussed.

I

The historical starting point for the development of scientific economics began with the eighteenth-century achievements of the Physiocrats in France[5] and by the Scotsmen David Hume[6] and Adam Smith,[7] who realized that prices, wages, and interest rates are determined precisely, or at least within narrow limits, by the condition of the market and that market prices function as the regulator of production. Before their contributions, it was customary to see only chance and arbitrariness in market activities; now it was recognized that regularities were at work in the market. The Classical School of economics, whose achievements reached their zenith in the work of David Ricardo,[8] assigned itself the task of elaborating a unified system of *catallactics*, the theory of exchange and of income.

5 [The Physiocrats were a group of eighteenth-century French Enlightenment thinkers, who often referred to themselves as "the Economists." Opponents of mercantilism, they developed a theory of society's "natural order" that emphasized the self-regulating patterns of the market. — Ed.]

6 [David Hume (1711–76) is considered one of the leading Scottish moral philosophers of the eighteenth century. In 1754, Hume published a collection of essays in which he explained the self-correcting and self-ordering processes of market interactions, which later became known as the specie-flow mechanism in the theory of international trade. — Ed.]

7 [Adam Smith (1723–90) is considered the father of modern economics due to his development of the concept of the "invisible hand" in his 1776 volume, *The Wealth of Nations*, which demonstrated the self-coordinating processes of the market. — Ed.]

8 [David Ricardo (1772–1823) spent his formative years in his family's stockbrokerage business, until his retirement at the age of 42 following the accumulation of a large fortune. He devoted his time to the study of political economy, writing several influential essays on inflation, gold, and monetary reform in the early nineteenth century during Britain's war with France. In 1817, he published his most famous work, *The Principles of Political Economy and Taxation*, which became a cornerstone of the Classical system. Among his contributions was the development of the theory of comparative advantage. He served as a member of Parliament in the House of Commons from 1819 until his death. — Ed.]

Classical economics was never able to satisfactorily solve the problem of price formation. There did arise the idea that in the evaluation of goods their utility (their usefulness for the satisfaction of human wants) formed the foundation of the structure of prices. But there arose a special difficulty that the Classical economists, with all their acumen, did not solve. Many of the most useful commodities, like iron, coal, or bread, possessed a low exchange value on the market, or, like water or air, were assigned no exchange value at all; whereas other things of undoubtedly much lower usefulness, e.g., precious stones, had a very high exchange value on the market. The failure of all attempts to explain this antinomy resulted in other explanations of the phenomenon of value; however, without various artificial assumptions they could not be thought through without contradiction. Obviously something was not right.

Then Carl Menger, in his brilliant first work,[9] succeeded in overcoming the apparent antinomy. It is not the importance of the entire class of commodities but the importance of the part that is available for use that determines their value. Not the value of the class of goods, but only the value of the concrete partial quantities at our disposal, influences the formation of prices. We assign to each individual portion of a given supply of a good the importance that that portion has for the satisfaction of our wants. And since in the case of each of our individual wants each additional concrete want satisfied has a decreasing intensity, we evaluate each individual unit of the available supply by the standard of the last, or least important, of the uses that can be satisfied by that good; i.e., the marginal utility of that good. The formation of the prices for goods of the first order, i.e., goods which serve immediate use and consumption, are thus attributed to the subjective evaluation of the consumers. The formation of the prices of higher-order goods, i.e., the means of production (capital goods as well as wages, the cost of labor), which are used for the production of both necessities and luxury goods, is derived from the prices of first-order goods; in the final analysis it is really the consumers who determine and pay both the wages and the prices of the means of production. To develop this analysis in detail is the task of the theory of imputation; it deals with the prices of land and resources, with wages and the prices for capital, as well as with entrepreneurial profit.

Building on the accomplishments of the Classical economists, Menger

9 [Carl Menger, *Principles of Economics* (New York: New York University Press, [1871] 1981).—Ed.]

and his successors erected a unified system for the explanation of all economic phenomena on the new foundation of subjective value (or marginal utility).[10]

II

More or less contemporaneously and independently of Menger, the Englishman William Stanley Jevons[11] and the Frenchman Léon Walras[12] (who worked in Lausanne) heralded a similar doctrine. After the usual amount of time that must pass before every new idea establishes itself, the subjective value, or marginal-utility, theory made its triumphant advancement around the world. Menger was more fortunate than his most important predecessor, the Prussian governmental assessor, Hermann Gossen,[13] in

10 [On the ideas and historical context of the Austrian economists, see Ludwig von Mises, "The Historical Setting of the Austrian School of Economics," [1969] reprinted in Bettina Bien Greaves, ed., *Austrian Economics: An Anthology* (Irvington-on-Hudson, N.Y.: Foundation for Economic Education, 1996), pp. 53–76; Ludwig M. Lachmann, "The Significance of the Austrian School of Economics in the History of Ideas," [1966] in Richard M. Ebeling, ed., *Austrian Economics: A Reader* (Hillsdale, Mich.: Hillsdale College Press, 1991), pp. 17–39; and Richard M. Ebeling, "The Significance of Austrian Economics in Twentieth-Century Economic Thought," in Richard M. Ebeling, ed., *Austrian Economics: Perspectives on the Past and Prospects for the Future*, Champions of Freedom Series, Vol. 17 (Hillsdale, Mich.: Hillsdale College Press, 1991), pp. 1–40.—Ed.]

11 [William Stanley Jevons (1835–83) was one of the first developers of the theory of marginal utility, which he formulated in his 1871 volume, *The Theory of Political Economy*. He also wrote extensively on monetary theory and reform and a sunspot theory of business cycles. He was appointed to a chair in political economy at University College, London in 1876. He died in a drowning accident.—Ed.]

12 [Léon Walras (1834–1910) formulated a version of the theory of marginal utility in his 1874 book, *Elements of Pure Economics*. Walras is also recognized as one of the early developers of mathematical general equilibrium theory. He was appointed to a chair in political economy at the University of Lausanne, Switzerland in 1870 and stepped down from his position in 1892 following a nervous breakdown.—Ed.]

13 [Hermann Heinrich Gossen (1810–58) developed a systemic theory of economic relationships based on the concept of marginal utility in his 1854 book, *The Law of Economic Relations, and the Rules of Human Action Derived Therefrom*. The book was totally ignored following its publication. William Stanley Jevons rediscovered it in the 1870s after the publication of his own version of the marginalist concept. Gossen worked in the Prussian civil service, but was constantly criticized by his superiors for living a life of drinking, gambling, and "bad company."—Ed.]

that he was able to experience the acknowledgment of his doctrine by the economists of the whole world.

In the United States, especially John Bates Clark,[14] the founder of the great American school, has utilized and elaborated the ideas of the Austrian School. In the Netherlands and in the Scandinavian countries the doctrine was accepted early on. But especially in Italy, successful scientific work flourished on its foundations. Menger never established a school in the usual sense of the word. He stood too high and thought too much of the dignity of science to use petty means to try to advance himself through others. He researched, wrote, and taught; and the best that was accomplished in the Austrian government and the market economy in the last decades resulted from his school. Moreover, full of the optimism of all liberals, he expected that rationality would finally prevail in the end.

And one day two colleagues stood beside him, two developers of his work, who—a decade younger than Menger—as mature men, and with knowledge of Menger's writings, elaborated his ideas for the solution of various theoretical problems. Böhm-Bawerk and Wieser—the same age, friends since youth, related by marriage, closely allied in convictions, character, and intellectual background, and yet as different as two like-minded scholarly, contemporary personalities could ever be—each in his own way undertook to continue Menger's work where he had left it off. In the history of our science their names are inseparably linked with Menger's.

These two have finished their work and their lives. But a new generation has followed, and the excellent economic studies that have been published in recent years show that the intellectual fertility of the doctrine of subjective value is proving itself over and over again.[15]

14 [John Bates Clark (1847–1938) was a leading proponent of the marginalist approach in the United States. His 1899 volume, *The Distribution of Wealth*, developed the theory of marginal productivity to explain the allocation of income among the factors of production. He was professor of economics at Columbia University from 1895 to 1923.—Ed.]

15 [For summaries and expositions of Mises's own contributions to the Austrian School of economics, see Richard M. Ebeling, "A Rational Economist in an Irrational Age: Ludwig von Mises," in Richard M. Ebeling, ed., *The Age of Economists: From Adam Smith to Milton Friedman* (Hillsdale, Mich.: Hillsdale College Press, 1999), pp. 69–120; and Israel M. Kirzner, *Ludwig von Mises: The Man and His Economics* (Wilmington, Del.: ISI Books, 2001).—Ed.]

III

Political difficulties still stand in the way of fully applying the doctrines of modern economic theory in the economic life of nations. Perhaps many years will pass before the practice of economic policy will have made use of all that could already have been learned from modern economics.

Economic theory in Austria and Hungary is intellectually the same due to the fact that they are based on the same foundation. This is shown most clearly in the fact that those who prepared the Hungarian encyclopedia of economics used Austrian collaborators, and that Hungarian economists heavily use the works of the Austrian economists in their own works. On the other hand, the writings of Hungarian economists are paid attention to with the greatest interest in Austria, since the important contributions to science by Hungarians also receive their much deserved recognition outside of their own country in this area of knowledge as well. In the work of the Austrian and Hungarian institutes for the study of business cycles there has also developed a gratifying cooperation. The reports on economic activity and the continuous economic bulletins in the Hungarian press offer excellent sources of information, which are studied very profitably in Austria.

The right men to lead the negotiations over economic policy are available in both countries, and the economic statistical materials are adequately prepared in both nations. From the point of view of economics, everything is ready to begin and successfully conclude the negotiations that promise the greatest profit for both of the contracting parties.

CHAPTER 38

Eugen von Böhm-Bawerk:
In Memory of the Tenth Anniversary of His Death[1]

Eugen von Böhm-Bawerk will remain unforgettable to all those who have known him.[2] The students who were fortunate enough to be members of his seminar [at the University of Vienna] will never lose what they have gained from their contact with this great mind. To the politicians who came into contact with the statesman, his extreme honesty, selflessness, and dedication to duty will forever remain a shining example. And no citizen of this country should ever forget the last Austrian Minister of Finance who, in spite of all obstacles, was seriously trying to maintain order in the public finances and to prevent the approaching financial catastrophe. Even when all those who have been personally close to Böhm-Bawerk will have left this life, his scientific work will continue to live and bear fruit.

From the beginning, Böhm-Bawerk concentrated his scientific work

1 [This article first appeared in German in the *Neue Freie Presse*, No. 21539 (August 27, 1924). — Ed.]

2 [Eugen von Böhm-Bawerk, born on February 12, 1851, is considered one of the most prominent members of the Austrian School of economics in the period before the First World War. Besides his writings in economics, he served as finance minister of the Austro-Hungarian empire in 1895, 1896 through 1897, and 1900 through 1904. He also taught at the Universities of Innsbruck (1880 to 1889), and while serving in the Austrian Ministry of Finance in the 1890s he led an internationally famous seminar at the University of Vienna, and then again beginning in 1905 until his death on August 27, 1914. For descriptions of Böhm-Bawerk's seminar at the University of Vienna, see Henry Seager, "Economics at Berlin and Vienna," [1892] in Bettina Bien Greaves, ed., *Austrian Economics: An Anthology* (Irvington-on-Hudson, N.Y.: Foundation for Economic Education, 1996), pp. 44–46; and Ludwig von Mises, *Notes and Recollections* (South Holland, Ill.: Libertarian Press, 1978), pp. 39–41. For a short account of Böhm-Bawerk's scholarly and political activities, see Richard M. Ebeling, "Eugen von Böhm-Bawerk: A Sesquicentennial Appreciation," *Ideas on Liberty* (February 2001), pp. 36–41. — Ed.]

on a central problem of theoretical economics, namely, the problem of interest. In the spring of 1876, at the age of twenty-five, he presented in Karl Knies's seminar in Heidelberg[3] a paper on interest that already contained the basic ideas of the soon-to-be-famous agio theory.[4] Before he could present his work to the public, some difficult preliminary problems had to be solved. And he first turned his attention to them. Always with his final goal in mind, he published in 1881 the essay "Whether Legal Rights and Relationships are Economic Goods,"[5] in 1884 *The History and Critique of Interest Theories*,[6] in 1886 "The Essential Theory of the Value of Economic Goods,"[7] which was finally followed by the publication of *The Positive Theory of Capital* in 1889.[8] With the publication of the latter work, his writing temporarily ceased. As cabinet adviser and secretary of a department in the Ministry of Finance, as imperial finance minister and senate president in the administrative court, he had little time for scientific work in the following years. It was not until 1904, when he left the cabinet for the third and last time, that he could resume his studies without interference. A series of outstanding writings is the fruit of the tireless work of the last decade of his life.[9] He died on August 27, 1914, when the armies

3 [Karl Knies (1821–98) was one of the leading figures of the German Historical School. He wrote extensively on the impact of railroads and the telegraph system on the world in general and the German states in particular. He was a strong advocate of German nationalism against liberal cosmopolitanism, and a critic of the "individualism" of the British Classical economists in comparison to the idea of an "organic" community and social order. From 1865 to 1896, Knies taught at the University of Heidelberg, with his seminar considered one of the principal centers for the study of political science in Germany.—Ed.]

4 [The "agio theory" refers to Böhm-Bawerk's development of a time-preference theory of the rate of interest, in which interest is the "premium" received on a loan due to the general preferring of present goods over goods only available later in the future.—Ed.]

5 [Eugen von Böhm-Bawerk, "Whether Legal Rights and Relationships are Economic Goods," [1881] in *Shorter Classics of Böhm-Bawerk* (South Holland, Ill.: Libertarian Press, 1962), pp. 25–138.—Ed.]

6 [Eugen von Böhm-Bawerk, *Capital and Interest, Vol. I: History and Critique of Interest Theories* (South Holland, Ill.: Libertarian Press, 1959).—Ed.]

7 [Eugen von Böhm-Bawerk, "Grundzüge der Theorie des wirtschaftlichen Güterwertes," *Jahrbucher für Nationalökonomie und Statistik*, Vol. 13 (1886), pp. 1–88.—Ed.]

8 [Eugen von Böhm-Bawerk, *Capital and Interest, Vol. II: The Positive Theory of Capital* (South Holland, Ill.: Libertarian Press, 1959).—Ed.]

9 [Eugen von Böhm-Bawerk, *Capital and Interest, Vol. III: Further Essays on Capital and Interest* (South Holland, Ill.: Libertarian Press, 1959).—Ed.]

of Austria were fighting the first heavy battles of the World War in Poland and Eastern Galicia.

Böhm-Bawerk's scientific work soon found the recognition that it deserved. As early as 1890, William Smart had translated his main work into English.[10] Not long after that there appeared a French edition. In England, the United States, France, Italy, the Netherlands, Sweden, and Denmark, his teachings became the starting point for intensive studies and research. In Germany, however, an appreciation for the greatness of Böhm-Bawerk's accomplishments was long in coming. The establishment at the universities ignored him. Decades had to pass until the Germans recognized the important accomplishments of the Austrian School. It was indefensible that only his main work, which had gone through four editions in German, was readily available. However, his shorter works, which are indispensable for all friends of economic analysis, were very hard to find. To republish them in book form was a valuable enterprise. A well-known student of Böhm-Bawerk's, who had distinguished himself with a number of scientific studies, undertook the project.[11] This nicely done volume, which includes an attractive picture of Böhm-Bawerk, contains the already mentioned essay, "Legal Rights and Relationships," the treatises on general theory and methodology, the writings on value theory, and finally a piece entitled "Our Passive Balance of Trade," which had appeared in the *Neue Freie Presse* on January 6, 8, & 9, 1914. The volume begins with a short biographical introduction by the editor, Dr. Franz X. Weiss. The essays on capital and interest, which are not contained in this collection, will follow in a separate volume.

It would mean carrying coals to Newcastle to praise the high value of Böhm-Bawerk's theoretical writings that are brought together in this collection. Such praise would contain nothing new for the expert and the numerous educated people who deal with economic questions. Just to show with what sharpness Böhm-Bawerk recognized early on the basic evil of our public finances, I want to quote from the previously mentioned essay on the passive balance of trade. It says there, "thrift is never popular.... If

---

10 [Eugen von Böhm-Bawerk, *Capital and Interest: A Critical History of Economical Theory,* translated and with a preface and analysis by William Smart (New York: Augustus M. Kelley, [1890] 1965); and *The Positive Theory of Capital,* translated and with a preface and analysis by William Smart (Freeport, N.Y.: Books for Libraries Press, [1891] 1971).—Ed.]

11 [Franz X. Weiss, ed., *Gesammelte Schriften von Eugen v. Böhm-Bawerk* [The Complete Works of Eugen von Böhm-Bawerk] (Wien: Hölder-Pichler-Tempsky, 1924).—Ed.]

formerly the Parliaments were the guardians of thrift, they are today far more like its sworn enemies. Nowadays, political and nationalist parties are in the habit of cultivating a greed for all kinds of benefits for their co-nationals or constituencies that they regard as a veritable duty, and should the political situation be correspondingly favorable, that is to say correspondingly unfavorable for the government, then political pressure will produce what is wanted." Our people suffer from economic delusions of grandeur. It is seen also in the so-called "investment with public funds." One is easily misled in this connection by the popular and dangerous slogan of the "indirect productivity of public expenditures," according to which basically unprofitable state enterprises provide the economy with indirect advantages that exceed the deficit covered by the public treasury. The "blind praisers of a lighthearted investment policy" do not realize the failure of their policies until "as today, our ability to raise capital has been exhausted by the excessive demands on the public budget. There is not enough capital left for the most useful and vital private enterprises, with a lot of economic activity slowing down and sometimes even coming to a standstill; and everything suffers from the effects of the exceedingly high rate of interest."

These were the last words that Böhm-Bawerk dedicated to Austria's financial policy. Today they will be met with more respect than at the time they first appeared in these pages.

PART VI

Methodology of the Social Sciences

CHAPTER 39

The Logical Problem
of Economics[1]

The history of empirical science is a chain the links of which are ingenious ideas and fortunate discoveries. Some of these discoveries are owed to chance, though most derive from purposeful research on the basis of theoretical thought. But the result of methodical research, too, depends on chance. We have at least to admit that the magnitude and importance of a discovery are not always proportionate to the intellectual labor that has been invested. Discoveries may be accidental, and a romantic glow emanating from them may brighten sober laboratory work.

The progress of theoretical science, however, is of a different nature. Theory is at first the self-reflection of a thinker and his subsequent partic-

1 [This article was written in German in 1933 for a festschrift in honor of the sixtieth birthday of Christian Eckert (1874–1952), a leading German social scientist. Eckert taught economics and political science at the Business School in Cologne, Germany, beginning in 1901. He was the first rector of the University of Cologne (1919–20) and president of the university's board of trustees until 1930. The Nazis dismissed him from his teaching position in 1933. After 1945 he was professor emeritus at Cologne. In June 1933, Leopold von Wiese, professor at the Institute for Social Science Research in Cologne, invited Mises to contribute an essay to the planned volume for Eckert's sixtieth birthday, which was to be celebrated on March 16, 1934. Mises submitted the essay in September. However, on December 21, 1933, Wiese wrote to the contributors, including Mises, that due to the new circumstances under the National Socialist regime the time did not seem opportune to bring out the volume, since it might create a wrong impression. Wiese hoped that he still would be able to bring out the volume at some future date. He returned the manuscript to Mises and said that he was at liberty to try to find some other publishing outlet for it. A *Festschrift* in honor of Eckert was finally published after the Second World War—Anton Felix Napp-Zinn and Michael Openheim, ed., *Kultur und Wirtschaft im rheinschen Raum* [Culture and Economics in the Rhineland Area] (Mainz: Selbstverlag der Stadt Mainz, 1949)—but without Mises's essay. It is published here for the first time.—Ed.]

ipation in a dialogue that is carried on over millennia. The theoretician responds to questions posed by the intellectual work of the past and addresses his words to contemporaries who are able to listen, and even more so to future generations. Scientific thinking frequently picks up problems and solutions overlooked in the past and proceeds along avenues that long have been considered to be barren. If Greek philosophy and mathematics still appear relevant today it is because they were the introduction to a dialogue that, though it may have been muted for centuries, has continued until the present day. Contemporary thinking is but its preliminary end. Being rooted in Greek thought, all philosophical and mathematical problems of concern to us are but the results of this dialogue. (The questions of whether and to what extent Greek thinkers were in turn dependent on precursors unknown to us or underestimated by us is likely to remain unanswered.)

Philosophy and mathematics thus constitute a permanent and continuous stream of thought. The transformation and expansion of problems and the introduction of new perspectives to the treatment of these problems have advanced intellectual work beyond its starting point without severing the tie with its roots. In many respects, philosophy and mathematics today are fundamentally different from those of the Greeks or those of the sixteenth to eighteenth centuries. Already the pre-Socratics,[2] of course, have demonstrated what it means to engage in philosophy or mathematics. The eighteenth-century thinkers, however, introduced an innovation.[3] By substituting the doctrine of the "natural" in the economy for the mercantilist contrivance of a wise ruler and a benign police, it opened up a field of thought that had hitherto been unknown.

In spite of its undoubted fecundity and overwhelming practical success, science did not appreciate the new stream of thought. Even those

2 [Pre-Socratic philosophy originated in the Greek cities of Ionia at the end of the seventh century B.C. They combined Greek mythology with rational thinking, and were concerned with unearthing the forces that comprise nature. The concepts of "substance," "infinity," "power," "motion," "atom," and space-time started with them. — Ed.]

3 [Mises is referring to the French Physiocrats, who formulated a theory of "natural order" in society that is self-generating and self-ordering. They developed the idea that men's natural self-interests are compatible and harmonious with each other in an institutional setting of individual liberty, private property rights, and market competition. They used these arguments against the prevailing mercantilist ideas of government control and direction of economic affairs. — Ed.]

philosophers like David Hume[4] and William Stanley Jevons[5] who made pi-
oneering [contributions], or like Richard Whately,[6] John Stuart Mill,[7] and
John E. Cairnes,[8] who certainly made extraordinary contributions to economics, did not appreciate what was important about the new procedure
for logic. Their logical thinking, like that of all logicians and epistemolo-
gists, focused on problems and solutions developed in physics. The
method of experimental physical science was regarded as the only one legitimate for all science. Just as mathematics was presumed to be an empirical science, so, too, economics was to be seen that way as well.

4 [David Hume (1711–76) is considered one of the leading thinkers among the eighteenth
century Scottish moral philosophers. Taking the scientific method of Sir Isaac Newton as
his model, he viewed philosophy as an inductive and experimental science of human nature. He argued that human knowledge was limited to the experiential. His major works
in political economy are contained in Eugene F. Miller, ed., *Essays: Moral, Political and
Literary* (Indianapolis: Liberty Fund, 1987).—Ed.]

5 [William Stanley Jevons (1835–82) was a leading English logician and economist. He
was one of the early formulators of the theory of marginal utility, in *The Theory of Political
Economy*. He also wrote *Pure Logic* (1864) and *Principles of Science* (1874), in which he
argued for a mathematical and symbolic formulation of logic. In addition, he advocated and
applied the inductive method for trying to derive empirical relationships in political economy.—Ed.]

6 [Archbishop Richard Whately (1787–1863) authored widely used books on logic and
rhetoric. He was appointed archbishop of Dublin, Ireland, in 1831, and held a seat in the
British House of Commons. His book, *Introductory Lectures on Political Economy* (1832),
attempted to show that political economy was not inconsistent with Christian theology,
and offered a logical and useful understanding of the sources of poverty and the methods
for improving the material wealth of all the members of society. He popularized the term
"catallactics"—exchange—as a legitimate name for the subject matter of political economy.—Ed.]

7 [John Stuart Mill (1806–73) was one of the leading members among the British Classical economists, with his most important work on this subject being *Principles of Political
Economy, with Applications to Social Philosophy* (1848). He also wrote *A System of Logic*
(1843) and *Auguste Comte and Positivism* (1865), and is known for his works on *Utilitarianism* (1863) and *On Liberty* (1859). Mill argued that even the axioms in *a priori* deductive reasoning are "a class, the most important class, of inductions from experience."—Ed.]

8 [John E. Cairnes (1823–75) was one of the last of the important British Classical economists, as represented in his work, *Some Leading Principles of Political Economy Newly
Expounded* (1874). He also wrote *The Character and Logical Method of Political Economy*
(1875), in which he explained that the essential concepts of economic logic and reasoning are derived from introspective reflection on the working of the human mind.—Ed.]

Whoever takes this viewpoint must expect that one day the rationale for this new science will be radically criticized. The various schools and sects that rebelled against the "inadmissible and premature generalizations" of theory and its "unworldly deductions" found, in the epistemology of their time, arguments on which to base their views. Economic propositions built on abstractions derived from historical experience led some to ask whether these generalizations had not been reached too soon and others to raise the more general question of whether general propositions could be derived from historical experience at all. Against the background of modern epistemology, both of these critical questions are surely justified.

Historical experience indeed does not lead to any theory because it only offers observation of complex phenomena without our being able to isolate the elements of change through experimentation. Wherever empirical science investigates the regularity of events it is, after all, based on experimentation. The social sphere, also, allows for the formulation of general propositions as hypotheses though, unlike in experimental physics, we lack methods for empirically verifying them. Even the most abundant historical evidence can never enable us to derive a theory. If there is any theoretical science of human action at all, it cannot be drawn from experience.[9]

This implies that all attempts at understanding economics and sociology as historical disciplines or as following historical methods are illogical. Historical theory is just as much a contradiction in terms as theoretical history. Historians and economists alike are justified in their aversion to this hybrid entity. It is not very surprising that logically thinking students and educated people who are interested in the progress of science do not appreciate doctrines within which the negation of propositions can be upheld as being just as "correct" or "true" as the propositions themselves.

It is amazing that the champions of the historical method in economics should not have realized that they are based on the same logical foundation as the champions of positivism, which they consider to be a methodology antagonistic to their own. Positivism, too, embraces the illusion that the evidence of historical experience permits the derivation of

---

9 [The year Mises wrote this essay, he had published a collection of writings on the methodology of the social sciences, in which he had argued that the laws of economics were based on an axiomatic-deductive method derived from the logic of thought. See Ludwig von Mises, *Epistemological Problems of Economics* (New York: New York University Press, [1933] 1983). — Ed.]

general propositions in the same way the propositions of experimental physics are related to observational data. The historical method and positivism coincide. As methods of social and economic science (i.e., of the science of human action) they are logically identical, even though historicism and positivism may oppose each other on ideological and political grounds.

The historical method of sociology and economics, on the other hand, has nothing to do with the historical method in the humanities and in jurisprudence. All cultural phenomena can be studied historically in terms of their growth and decay. Nobody doubts that the history of law and the history of art are worthwhile disciplines. But if one imputes a normative character to historically evolved law and rejects the admissibility of present-day legislation, this has nothing to do with the value or lack thereof of history as a science or of the historical method as a scientific procedure. The issue at stake here is one of *ought* and not of *is*, a question of social valuation and not one of the cognition of social phenomena. Accepting only historically evolved law may be rooted in the same political considerations that have led the "historical school of political science" to dismiss economics.[10] The Historical School of jurisprudence[11] opposed Bentham's

10 [The German Historical School of political science and economics argued that the British Classical economists had been wrong when they argued that there were universally valid and applicable laws of economics. The proponents of the Historical School said that any economic "laws" were necessarily relative to the changing circumstances of historical time and place. Thus, to determine what economic relationships might be present and applicable at different times in history, including one's own, it was necessary to undertake inductive studies of the institutional, legal, cultural, and ideological currents and ideas of particular periods of time. They also argued that economics could not be separated from ethical matters, leading most members of the school to argue for various forms of interventionist and welfare-redistributive programs in imperial Germany to ameliorate the "abuses" and disregard for the national interest and welfare that, supposedly, prevailed in the free market. For a summary of their views, see Émile de Laveleye, *The Socialism of Today* (London: Field and Tuer, 1890), pp. 265–83.—Ed.]

11 [The Historical School of jurisprudence developed in the nineteenth century, arguing that the legal order is based neither on "natural law" representing a universal code of rights and justice nor on pure reasoning from, for example, utilitarian premises. Rather, law evolves out of the *Volksgeist* (the spirit of the nation) based on the innate consciousness of a people and takes form through historical development as reflected in custom and tradition. It was claimed, therefore, that law, justice, and rights are specific and distinct for each national group and changes through time. See Eugen von Philippovich, "The Infusion of Socio-Political Ideas into the Literature of German Economics," *American Journal of Sociology* (September 1912), p. 160: "The historical school of jurisprudence had taught

utilitarian position in order to defend the "eternal disease" and "plague" of old law against the "benefit" of modern rational law.[12] The political rationale of this defense was not very different from the objectives of the Historical School in economics, which could justify its support for mercantilism only by referring to the necessity of a "historical" underpinning for economic knowledge.

What matters for us, however, is only that the epistemological and logical problems that were raised in the debate over the logical status of economics should not reemerge in the debate over the Historical School of jurisprudence.[13]

Educated persons have a sense for and understanding of historical studies. This can be easily turned into a prejudice against a general science of human action, against economics and sociology, if these disciplines are presented as opponents of history and of the method of the humanities. This warrants repeating the statement that history and sociology, economic history and economic theory are only opposed to each other in a logical sense. Opposition, however, is not antagonism, and logical difference does not mean enmity.

---

scholars to regard the law as a product of the whole life of the *Volk*. Like language and morality, it arises not through volition and reflection merely. It is not a conscious creation of men, but an organ that has come into existence historically, a member of the total life of the *Volk* which can be understood only in close correlation with the whole national life." —Ed.]

12 [Jeremy Bentham (1748–1832) is considered the founder of modern utilitarianism, a concept presented first in his work, *An Introduction to the Principles of Morals and Legislation* (1789). He argued that all institutions and legal arrangements should be judged by their "utility" for bettering the interests of men in society. He therefore was highly critical of accepting social, legal, and political rules and institutions simply on the fact that they exist as the outgrowth of custom and tradition. —Ed.]

13 Carl Menger, *Investigations into the Method of the Social Sciences with Special Reference to Economics* (New York: New York University Press, [1883] 1985), pp. 223–34.

CHAPTER 40

The Logical Character of the Science of Human Action[1]

I

Positivism emphasizes the fact that in the natural sciences all our insight is founded on experience alone. This statement is by no means an achievement of positivism; scientists have not disputed it for many hundreds of years. If positivism limited its teaching to this principle, nobody would contest its theories.

But the positivists go beyond this. They assert that history and all historical and moral disciplines are not to be included in the term science. Their unsatisfactory methods would have to be replaced by a new science of social relations modeled according to the standards of experimental science as developed by physics, especially by the so-called Classical physics of the Newtonian type. For this new science Auguste Comte suggested the name of Sociology.[2]

---

1 [This article was first delivered as a lecture at a conference in Paris in August 1937 and then published in Raymond Bayer, ed., *Travaux du IXe Congrès International de Philosophie: Congrès Descarte*, Vol. V: "L'Unité de la Science; la Méthod et les méthodes" (Paris: Hermann et Cie, 1937).—Ed.]

2 [Auguste Comte (1798–1857) was a leading French philosopher and the founder of positivism. He said that the methods of observation and experimentation being widely used in the natural sciences had to be applied to the study of human relationships. Out of this would come a "science of society"—sociology—from which would be derived objective and exact "laws" concerning the workings of the social order for purposes of social engineering. He developed these ideas in his four-volume work, *A System of Positive Politics* (1851–54). In his essay *On Liberty*, John Stuart Mill commented that, "M. Comte... aims at establishing...a despotism of society over the individual, surpassing anything contemplated in the political ideal of the most rigid disciplinarian among the ancient philosophers."—Ed]

What Comte ignored was that the science of social relations that he wished to see developed in the future already existed in the form of Political Economy as elaborated by the Classical economists. Still more fatal was that he and all other positivists and empiricists overlooked the fact that conditions for research in social life differ radically from those in the field of nature. The experience of complex phenomena does not enable the elaboration of a scientific system. Empirical science is based on experiments that isolate the conditions of a change. The social sciences, however, do not have the ability to make experiments. They therefore can never use the same experimental methods that are the glory of the natural sciences and to which the natural sciences owe their success. Every social experience is a historical fact that can be and is explained in different ways. Social experience can neither prove nor refute any doctrine in the way in which a laboratory experiment achieves verification or falsification in the natural sciences.

History is a branch of knowledge based entirely on experience. But there is no way to get from this historical experience to a science of general rules of human conduct. The unfeasibility of experiments makes it impossible to build up, *a posteriori*, a system of insights about human conduct.

The foundations of our knowledge concerning the principles governing the phenomena of human action are essentially different from the sources about our knowledge of the principles governing the phenomena of the outer world. Being an acting being, himself, man has in his mind and consciousness a knowledge of the essence and logic of action. To develop this insight into a system does not require him to observe external facts. On the contrary, he succeeds in conceiving the historical facts solely by means of the direct—let us say *a priori*—knowledge that is present in the mind of an acting human being.

The whole system of economics is deduced from an ultimate principle that itself is not the outcome of an experience but of insight into the meaning of action. This principle is known as the economic principle, or as the principle of choice, or as the principle of scarcity, or as the principle of alternative uses.

II

Behaviorism, an outgrowth of positivist thought, approaches the study of human conduct like the study of physical and physiological facts. It believes that it can study man's conduct from the outside by observing movements and external changes. But behaviorism deludes itself. Thinking that it studies human activities like studying the behavior of animals, it overlooks the fact that the cognition of the behavior of animals, of infant children, and of morons is already shaped by our insight into human action. And in the study of human conduct we cannot do without reference to the meaning that the acting man then attaches to his action. To comprehend the meaning of action is the essence of all disciplines dealing with man's activities, with social relations, and with civilization, in short, of all branches of economics and sociology as well as historical and moral sciences. But the meaning of actions cannot be grasped by external observation of the kind applied in physics and biology.

Sounds that are alike and therefore identical for physical observation can be employed with different meanings. Their effect in social life differs. One cannot realize these differences without reverting to the meaning of the speaker. It is the meaning attached to a sound that makes it a word. Physics does not know words, it only knows sounds. Behaviorism says that it wishes to study situations and reactions to these situations. But neither the situation nor the reaction can be grasped except by reference to the meaning. Try to grasp the situation arising from an offer to sell and the reaction resulting from it without reference to human meanings!

The specific task of all cognition of human action is to comprehend or to grasp the meaning attached by the doers to their actions and the effects of these actions as far as they depend on other people's actions.

The comprehension of the meaning of human actions is twofold. We conceive and we understand.

We conceive the logic of action because we ourselves act. We conceive all categories of action because we know *a priori* the general meaning of human action. If we did not possess this *a priori* insight nobody could teach it to us. From the very concept of action we are able to develop all of the logic of action, the system of praxeology. This is the exact science of human conduct or action. That such a science is possible and exists was unknown to Comte and is ignored by all positivists. They cannot grasp the idea that there is an *a priori* science of human action and that all empirical insight in this field has the scientific and logical character of history.

III

Those principles, theorems, and laws that are the content of the teaching of economics are neither the result of an observation of historical facts nor abstractions from reality. They have not been discovered by the study of facts. On the contrary, what enables us to comprehend historical facts is only the circumstance that we possess at the outset of our study, an amount of insight into the nature and essence of human action. Without the logical apparatus of this knowledge we could not grasp the meaning and significance of any action. There is no such thing as pure social facts, which the student's mind may comprehend without the aid of a framework of theories based on the logic of action.

Economics as it has been developed since the eighteenth century is a part—maybe the most important part, in any case the most highly developed part up to now—of a more general science of human action. This science endeavors to expound the categories of action, building them up into a system that logically belongs to the same class of knowledge as logic and mathematics. It may be styled the logic of human action. It is immaterial whether one is ready to call logic, mathematics, and praxeology (which may be the most apt expression to signify the whole of this theoretical discipline of human action) *a priori* knowledge and to discriminate them by this term from the knowledge founded on experience.[3] Even if one accepts empiricism's view according to which these branches too are to be considered as growing out of our experience, one cannot bridge the gulf that separates them from the rest of human science. What we have to recognize is that the logical character of economic theory is not to be compared with that of experimental science, e.g., physics, but with that of the "pure" sciences, logic and mathematics.[4]

We define the logical character of economics as an *a priori* science

3 [Mises developed his theory of praxeology, the science of human action, in a series of articles that he published under the title, *Epistemological Problems of Economics* (New York: New York University Press, [1933] 1983), and then more fully in his treatises, *Nationalökonomie: Theorie des Handelns und Wirtschaftens* (Munich: Philosophia Verlag, [1940] 1980) and *Human Action: A Treatise on Economics* (Irvington-on-Hudson, N.Y.: Foundation for Economic Education, 4th rev. ed., 1996), as well as in *Theory and History: An Interpretation of Social and Economic Evolution* (New Haven, Conn.: Yale University Press, 1957) and *The Ultimate Foundations of Economic Science: An Essay on Method* (Princeton, N.J.: D. Van Nostrand, 1962). Shorter expositions of some of these methodological themes were also developed by Mises in his essays, "Social Science and Natural Science," (1942) "The Treatment of 'Irrationality' in the Social Sciences," (1944) and "Epistemological Relativism in the Sciences of Human Action," (1962) all in Richard M. Ebeling, ed., *Money, Method and the Market Process: Essays by Ludwig von Mises* (Norwell, Mass.: Klewer Academic Press, 1990), pp. 3–51.—Ed.]

4 This statement does not at all interfere with the problem whether mathematics is a useful tool in treating economic problems. But within the limits of this paper it is impossible to touch upon this question.

that is not deduced from external experience but that, on the contrary, is the condition of all our experience of human action. This definition does not signify the agenda of a science that does not yet exist and that is still to come. It does not mean to say that a change in the methods of the existing science is wanted. It merely defines the logical character of all economic science, both of the past and of our own time.

It is true that some economists have misunderstood the logical character of their own method. They believed that the theories they taught had been discovered in the same way that physicists have discovered natural laws. In fact, these economists too, notwithstanding their opinion on method, proceed and argue in their economic reasoning in the same way as all other economists. They deduce from ultimate principles that are not founded on experience, but are from our insight in the essence of human action.

IV

In examining the positivist postulate that history has to be replaced by a discipline according to the standards of natural science, some German philosophers have declared that there is an unbridgeable gulf between history on the one hand and the natural sciences on the other hand. Whereas the natural sciences aim at the cognition of generalities, history aims at the cognition of the individually unique and of individual coincidences. It seeks to expound that which happened once and will never occur again. In doing so it employs all the logical tools of the other branches of knowledge. But over and above this it employs a special mental faculty that is of no use for the naturalist. It is the historian's duty to try to understand the meaning of the historical facts and the qualities of the individual agents.

Understanding in this technical meaning of the word is not ratiocination. It differs in principle from the way in which the naturalist describes and explains facts. In the understanding there is always contained an irrational element, something that cannot be totally imparted to another. We are sure that in explaining some mathematical or physical formula or stating a fact about the outer world we shall be rightly understood by everybody who has the requisite mental capacity. In dealing with the qualities and individualities that the understanding grasps, we lack this certainty. We never know whether we have been understood in the way in which we wish to be understood. There is receptiveness and there is nonreceptiveness in reference to these matters. And there are different points of view, and it depends on which of them we have chosen.

The consequence is that there are differences among the historians in the understanding of unquestionable facts. They may agree on the statement of the bare fact, but they differ as to its meaning and importance. In the historian's work there is always an element of subjectivity, which is an emanation of the historian's personality. Not only with respect to the men, conditions, and facts that form the subject of history, but to the historian's personality as well, does *individuum est inetfabile* hold good.

The philosophers and historians who have expounded these teachings —Dahlmann,[5] Dilthey,[6] Windelband,[7] Wundt,[8] Max Weber[9]—ignored the fact that since the middle of the eighteenth century a generalizing science of human conduct has been developed. Living in the Germany of the Historical School, they ignored both economics and social philosophy. They, therefore, overlooked the existence of the science that aims at an insight into human conduct that is applicable to all human action, irrespective of age, racial and social conditions, country and opinions. In their eyes, the study of human action was only history.

5 [Friedrich Christoph Dahlmann (1785–1860) was a German historian most famous for *Official Sources in German History* (1830). In 1837, King Ernest Augustus of Hanover dismissed him from his professorship at the University of Göttingen for protesting the abrogation of the constitution. He also taught in Bonn and was a member of the Frankfurt Parliament (1848–49).—Ed.]

6 [Wilhelm Dilthey (1833–1911) was an influential German philosopher of history and culture who was critical of the attempt to introduce the methods of the natural sciences into the study of history. He argued that there is a subjective element in human events relating to the interpretive meaning given to objects, events, and actions by the human agents. He said that historical analysis, therefore, was hermeneutical in quality in that it required the historian to discern the meanings in the doings of men.—Ed.]

7 [Wilhelm Windelband (1848–1915) argued against the introduction of the positivist approach to the human sciences. He argued that the study of men is inseparable from an understanding of the values and meanings that men assign to their activities in the distinctive historical process.—Ed.]

8 [Wilhelm Wundt (1832–1920) was an early developer of experimental psychology. However, he strongly opposed the attempt to reduce this field to behavioral observation and measurement, arguing that what matters for the human subject and influences his conduct is his lived experiences with their specific meanings for the individual.—Ed.]

9 [Max Weber (1864–1920) is considered one of the greatest contributors to sociological theory in the last hundred years. He developed the concept of the "ideal type" for sociological and historical analysis, and emphasized the importance of subjective meaning—the meaning in an action from the individual human actor's point of view—in social theory. —Ed.]

V

The German economists of the Historical School have grossly misunderstood both the significance of the specific understanding of the historical disciplines and the essence of praxeology. They believe that they are fundamentally opposed to the positivist mentality and to its judgment of history. They, in fact, accept the main principle of positivism when they declare that economics and sociology have to be pursued as experimental sciences based on historical experience.

The youngest branch of German economic methodology has been in some respect both more and less consistent in proclaiming the specific understanding of the historical disciplines to be the be-all and end-all of economic method. According to them, economic "theory," as distinguished from economic history, has the task of describing the economic styles of the different epochs of economic history and of finding out their interactions and their interconnections. In their eyes economic theory is logically something like the history of art and literature. These too, of course, describe styles and their interactions. But has anybody, on that account, called the history of art a theoretical science?

A theory of human action, distinct from history, only can be based on *a priori* insight, since it's impossible to build up such a theory on the basis of experience without experiments.

VI

Positivism's failure in its endeavors to reform the moral and social sciences lies in its logical prejudice that the method of physics is the only scientific method. Positivism emphasizes its independence from any kind of metaphysics. In fact, it is in itself a rather poor and naive school of metaphysics, as it proposes to solve all problems of scientific method by preconceived ideas, without paying due consideration to the peculiarities of their subject.[10]

10 See John E. Cairnes, *The Character and Logical Method of Political Economy* (New York: Augustus M. Kelley, [1888] 1965); Ludwig von Mises, *Epistemological Problems of Economics*; and Lionel Robbins, *An Essay on the Nature and Significance of Economic Science* (London: Macmillan, 2nd rev. ed., 1935).

PART VII

Economic Calculation under Socialism

CHAPTER 41

New Contributions to the Problem of Socialist Economic Calculation[1]

The problem of economic calculation is the central and fundamental problem of socialism. That this was not seen until very recently is attributable to two circumstances. The problem did not exist at all for the adherents of an objective theory of value. If value is objectively discernable and calculable, then no difficulty need arise for purposes of economic calculation. Of course, if the attempt had been made to think carefully about the structure of a collectivist social system, then the contradictions in the objective theory of value would soon have been obvious. Seen from this perspective, it would have been realized that the problem of value couldn't be satisfactorily resolved with the Classical economists' theory of value. But Marxism had placed a strict prohibition on any preoccupation with the problems of the socialist social and economic system. Everyone had to obey this stricture or be exposed to the suspicion of being unscientific. Socialism had to be praised, but not thought about.

Now, however, the problem has finally been posed, and it can no longer be cautiously evaded. I believe that I have proven that economic calculation in a socialist society would be impossible.[2] Three works have now come out that attempt to reach a different conclusion.[3]

1 [This article originally appeared in German in *Archiv für Sozialwissenschaft und Sozialpolitik*, Vol. 51 (December 1923). In correspondence at the time when this article was in galleys, Mises accused Joseph A. Schumpeter, who was one of the editors of the *Archiv*, of attempting to change a part of the text without Mises's permission.—Ed.]

2 [Ludwig von Mises, "Economic Calculation in the Socialist Commonwealth," [1920] in F. A. Hayek, ed., *Collectivist Economic Planning* (London: George Routledge & Sons, 1935), pp. 87–130, and in Israel M. Kirzner, ed., *Classics in Austrian Economics: A Sampling in the History of a Tradition* (London: William Pickering, 1994), pp. 3–30; and Mises, *Socialism* [1922] (Indianapolis: Liberty Fund, [1951] 1981), pp. 95–130; 186–94.—Ed.]

3 The short essay by Franz Meyer, "Die Krisis in der Theorie der Sozialisierung" [The Crisis in the Theory of Socialization], *Sozialistische Monatshefte*, Vol. 60, pp. 150–54, is

The book by Arthur Wolfgang Cohn is the doctoral thesis of a highly talented and very promising young scholar, whom a lamentable accident has snatched away prematurely.[4] Cohn first reviews the literature dealing with the problem, citing word for word those passages of my above-mentioned essay that seem most important to him. At first he seems to be in general agreement with my arguments. Then, however, he abruptly comes to the conclusion that the problem, the solution of which I have said to be impossible, was solved long ago by Schäffle's "social tax" and that it was a mistake for me not to have taken into consideration the idea of the social tax.[5] Unfortunately, Schäffle's proposal is completely and absolutely useless. It rests upon a misunderstanding of the nature of our problem.

Schäffle wants his tax established by official decree. "Representatives of industrial trade associations and representatives of the consumers (for example, warehouse administrators, who reflect the demands for consumption), would have to come together. . . . The central accounting office for production would make known to them the costs of various amounts of different types of goods delivered to certain locations at a certain time as a fraction of the total social labor incurred in production. It would be known to them, through the central office of production accounting, what fraction of the social-labor time a certain amount of a certain kind of good (delivered to a certain place at a certain time) costs. In a situation where demand exceeds supply the tax would be set higher than the average labor-cost of manufacturing that good; in the reverse case the tax would be set lower. Instead of this method, perhaps a scale could be established on the basis of past experience that would assure an almost mechanical, certain, and non-arbitrary tax regulation."[6]

satisfied with defining the problem of socialist economic calculation, but abstains from attempting to offer any solution.

4 A. W. Cohn, *Kann das Geld abgeschafft werden?* [Can Money Be Eliminated?] (Jena: Gustav Fischer, 1920).

5 Ibid., p. 128.

6 Cf., Albert Schäffle, *Bau und Leben des sozialen Körpers* [The Structure and Life of the Social Body] (Tübingen, 1878) p. 354f. [See Schäffle, *The Quintessence of Socialism* (London: Swan Sonnenschein, 1892), pp. 90–96. Albert Schäffle (1831–1903) was a prominent advocate of social reform in imperial Germany, and affiliated with the German Historical School. While expressing concern that a collectivist economy could endanger freedom of choice, he believed that the planned society was inevitable. He briefly served as Austrian minister of commerce and agriculture, and designed a plan for redefining the

That is the procedure Schäffle recommends for "the determination of the liquidation tax between labor credits [assigned to workers for purchasing goods] and social supplies in the socialist state." For this purpose and for this purpose only, it is no doubt just as useful as any other procedure that could be proposed. Whether one wishes to consider it "fair" is another question, and is one that need not concern us any further. It only remains to ask whether this method can be applied, and this question can be answered in the affirmative. For the socialist society can deal with the distribution of goods according to any principles it wishes. Only if it is desired to make the allocation of the shares to different goods mutually compatible is it constrained in establishing the conditions under which consumer goods are to be exchanged for labor credits. This method would only be applicable for the terms under which consumer goods are to be exchanged one for the other.[7] It is a different matter when it comes to using this social tax for purposes of economic calculation, and for this purpose it completely fails. Everything that I have presented in my previously mentioned work applies to this case.

Schäffle's basic error is that he believes that there is a socialist procedure, that is to say, a "direct social measure of value," consisting "of a definite fraction of the yield actually created by the total mass of social (socialized) labor-time."[8] "Labor exploited under capitalism," of course, "cannot be used as a social measure of value. It cannot really be embodied as a unit, and therefore cannot be converted into a definite fraction of the measure of value. Under collectivist production, on the other hand, social labor would be a tangible reality and useable as a measure of natural value."[9] Schäffle's ideas on the theory of value were far too inadequately thought through for him to notice the elementary defects in his proposal. Certain thoughts, of course, later occurred to him.[10] But in spite of this

status of Bohemia within the Austro-Hungarian empire; the plan was never implemented because of opposition by the Hungarians.—Ed.]

7 Cf. my *Socialism*, pp. 137–38.

8 Schäffle, op. cit., 474 (also pp. 332ff.). [Schäffle, *The Quintessence of Socialism*, pp. 77–89.—Ed.]

9 Ibid., p. 476 (in the 2nd ed., 1896, Vol. II, p. 306). ["Natural value," or value *in natura*, refers to the idea that goods could be valued and allocated and resources could be distributed among alternative production uses without the intermediation of money, and without money serving as the general unit of account for purposes of economic calculation.—Ed.]

10 Albert Schäffle, *Die Quintesenz des Sozialismus* (Gotha, 18th ed., 1919), pp. 47ff.; and *The Impossibility of Social Democracy* (London: Swan Sonnenschein, 1890), pp. 27ff.

he basically maintained his ideas.[11] Schäffle was far from even correctly grasping the nature of the problem. The assertion that he had solved it, in the sense of a feasible method of calculating values under socialism, is absolutely wrong.[12]

In an article entitled "Socialist Accounting," Karl Polanyi attempts to solve what he believes "to be generally recognized as the key problem of the socialist economy."[13] Polanyi, at first, frankly admits that he considers the solution of the problem to be impossible "in a centrally administered economy."[14] His attempted solution is tailored only to the conditions of "a transformed, functionally reorganized socialist economy." He designates by this name a type of society that approximately corresponds to the ideal of the English Guild Socialists.[15] And his conception of the critical points concerning the nature and effective possibilities of his system are unfortunately no less nebulous and vague than that of the Guild Socialists.

The political community "is considered" to be the owner of the means of production. However, no direct right of disposal is connected with this "ownership." This belongs to the producers' associations that are set up by

11 Schäffle, *Die Quintesenz der Sozialismus*, p. 47: "As has already been noted, socialism must figure out how to correct radically its fundamental social-labor-cost theory of the value of goods. This does not seem impossible to us; we will leave it at that."

12 [For a critical analysis of Schäffle's work on socialism in contrast to Mises's views on the problems of economic calculation, see Richard M. Ebeling, "Economic Calculation Under Socialism: Ludwig von Mises and His Predecessors," in Jeffrey M. Herbener, ed., *The Meaning of Ludwig von Mises* (Norwell, Mass.: Kluwer Academic Press, 1993), pp. 56–101.—Ed.]

13 Karl Polanyi, "Sozialistische Rechnungslegung," *Archiv für Sozialwissenschaft und Sozialpolitik*, Vol. 49, pp. 377–420. [Karl Polanyi (1886–1964) was a famous economic anthropologist, best known for his 1944 book, *The Great Transformation*, about the industrialization of Europe. A Hungarian by birth, after the First World War Polanyi founded the Radical Citizens of Hungary. He worked as a journalist in Vienna from 1924 to 1933. After living in England for several years he moved to the United States in 1940, and was a professor of economics at Columbia University (1947–53). He was a leading advocate of a collectivist society freed from self-interest and monetary concerns.—Ed.]

14 Ibid., pp. 378 & 419.

15 [Under Guild Socialism each industry would be managed and controlled by the workers in that sector of the economy. The coordination of production and distribution for the economy as a whole would be arranged through central agreement among the respective industrial groups. One of the most detailed outlines for such an economic order was developed in the period immediately after World War I by Sidney and Beatrice Webb, *A Constitution for the Socialist Commonwealth* (London: Longmans, Green, 1920).—Ed.]

the workers through elections in each of the individual branches of production. The individual producer associations are brought together to form the Congress of the Producers' Associations that "represent production as a whole." Standing opposite them is the "Commune," which serves as a second "main functioning association of the community." The "Commune" serves not only as a political organization but also "as the real representative of the higher goals of the society." Both of the two functional associations exercise legislative and executive functions in their respective spheres. The arrangements between these chief functional associations embody the highest power of the society.[16]

The defect in this construction lies in the obscurity by which it seeks to avoid the core question: socialism or syndicalism? Similarly to the Guild Socialists, Polanyi expressly awards the ownership of the means of production to society, to the Commune. He thinks he has said enough to save his construction from the accusation of syndicalism. Yet in the very next sentence he takes back what he has just said. Ownership is the right of disposal. If the right of disposal does not belong to the Commune but to the producers' associations, then the latter are the owners and what we have is a syndicalist society. It can only be one or the other; between syndicalism and socialism there is no middle ground and no reconciliation. Polanyi does not see this. He says, "Functional representatives for one and the same people can never come into irreconcilable conflict with each other —that is the basic idea behind every functional constitutional design. For the arbitration of occasional disagreements either joint committees of the Commune and the producers' associations, or some sort of supreme constitutional tribunal, will be provided as coordinating organizations, which, however, will have no legislative and only very limited executive power (the administration of justice, security services, etc.)."[17]

The basic idea, however, of a designed functional constitution is mistaken. If—and this is the unstated presupposition in Polanyi's and similar constructions—the political parliament is to be set up by the ballot of all the citizens, each having an equal right to vote, while the parliament of the producers' associations are based on a quite different electoral arrangement, then a conflict between them can very well emerge. The committees could then successfully arbitrate a conflict between them only if one or the other main association is dominant in them; if both are equally rep-

16 Ibid., p. 404f.
17 Ibid., p. 404, footnote 20.

resented, then no decision could be reached in the committee. But if one of the two associations has preponderance in either the structure or the procedures of the committee, then the final decision rests with it. A tribunal cannot settle questions of political or economic practice. Courts can only render their judgments on the basis of already existing norms, which they can apply to the individual case. If they are to deal with questions of expediency, then in reality they are no longer courts of law but the supreme political authority; and all we have said about the committees applies to them too.

If neither the Commune nor the Congress of the Producer Associations has the final decision, then the system is simply not viable. If the Commune has the final decision, then we are talking about a "centrally administered economy," under which even Polanyi concedes the impossibility of economic calculation. If, however, the final decision is with the producer associations, then we are looking at a syndicalist society.

Polanyi's confusion about this fundamental point makes him view a phantom solution as a practicable solution of the problem. His associations and subassociations stand in a relationship of reciprocal exchange, they receive and give as if they were owners; this is the way in which a market and market prices are formed. Polanyi does not notice that this is irreconcilable with the essence of socialism, since he has ignored the unbridgeable conflict between socialism and syndicalism.

Considerably more could be said about the particular defects that are inherent in Polanyi's construction. They are, however, insignificant in comparison with this fundamental defect and can only claim minor attention since they are characteristic of Polanyi's chain of reasoning. That principal defect is, however, not peculiar to Polanyi; it is shared by all constructions of a guild-socialist system. Polanyi has the unquestionable merit of having worked out this construction much more precisely than the majority of other writers; thus, he has presented its weaknesses more clearly. Also, he must be highly credited for perceiving the impossibility of economic calculation in a centrally administered economy in which exchange does not occur.

The third contribution to the treatment of our problem comes from Eduard Heimann.[18] Heimann is a devotee of an ethically and religiously

18 Eduard Heimann, *Mehrwert und Gemeinwirtschaft, Kritische und positive Beiträge zur Theorie des Sozialismus* [Surplus Value and the Collective Economy, Critical and Positive Contributions to the Theory of Socialism] (Berlin: Hans Robert Engelmann, 1922). [Eduard Heimann (1889–1967) was a prominent German economist and a member of the Christian Socialist party. He came to the United States in 1934 and taught at the New

motivated socialism. His political convictions, however, do not in the least blind him to the problem of economic calculation. In his treatment of the problem he follows the arguments of Max Weber.[19] Max Weber had understood that the problem is "absolutely central" for socialism. In an exhaustive discussion, in which Weber dismissed the "natural-accounting" visions of Otto Neurath,[20] he had shown that without the use of money and monetary calculation any rational economic action is impossible.[21] Heimann now wishes to demonstrate that even in a socialist economic system calculation would be possible.

If Polanyi starts from a conception that is close to English Guild Socialism, Heimann develops his proposals in connection with German ideas of the planned economy. Characteristically, his arguments nevertheless resemble those of Polanyi on the only point that matters. They are regrettably vague at exactly the point where a specific answer is needed: on the relationship between the individual production groups, into which the society is divided according to the organization of the planned economy, and the society as a whole. Thus he comes to the point at which he speaks about trade in a functioning market[22] without noticing that in a fully and consistently practiced planned economy, there is no trade, and that what one might perhaps want to call buying and selling must, by its very nature, be something of a quite different character. Heimann falls into this error because he sees the monopolistic consolidation of the individual branches of production as the characteristic feature of a planned economy, rather than the dependence of production on the single will of a central social agency. This misconception is all the more surprising considering that the very name "planned economy," and all the arguments brought forth in

---

School for Social Research in New York. He authored *History of Economic Doctrines: An Introduction to Economic Theory* in 1945.—Ed.]

19 [See Chapter 40, "The Logical Character of the Science of Human Action," footnote 9. —Ed.]

20 [Otto Neurath (1882–1945) was most famous for his attempt to develop a theory of a natural, or moneyless, economy. In 1919 he played the role of "social engineer" by serving in the Central Economic Office in Bavaria for the planning of the socialization of industry. He also was a prominent member of the Vienna circle of Logical Positivists.—Ed.]

21 Max Weber, *Economy and Society: An Outline of Interpretative Sociology*, Vol. I (Berkeley: University of California Press, 1978), pp. 104–7. As Weber remarks on p. 107, his book was already in press when my previously mentioned article, "Economic Calculation in the Socialist Commonwealth," appeared in the *Archiv für Sozialwissenschaft* (Vol. 47).

22 Heimann, op. cit., pp. 184ff.

favor of the idea, strongly emphasize the centralized direction of the economy. Of course, Heimann recognizes the hollowness of the argument that uses the slogan, "anarchy of production."[23] But he never should have forgotten that it is precisely here and nowhere else that the distinction separating socialism from capitalism is most sharply made.

Like the majority of all writers who have concerned themselves with the planned economy, Heimann does not perceive that a strictly implemented planned economy is nothing other than pure socialism and that it differs only in outward appearances from the rigid, centrally organized socialist society. The fact that under the unified direction of a central authority a series of apparently independent departments is entrusted with the administration of individual branches of production does not change anything about the fact that the central authority alone holds the reins. The relationships between the individual departments are not regulated on a market through the competition of buyers and sellers, but by government command. The problem is that these commands have no yardstick available for purposes of economic calculation and computation because there are no exchange relationships formed on the market to guide the government. The government can, no doubt, set up substitution ratios determined by itself for accounting purposes. But the determination of these ratios is arbitrary. They are not based on the subjective valuations of individuals and imputed to the means of production in the form of market prices through the collaboration of all those who are active in producing and exchanging. It therefore cannot serve as the foundation for rational economic calculation.

Heimann reaches his illusory solution of the problem by utilizing the theory of costs. Economic calculation is to be guided by costs. Prices are to be calculated on the basis of the "costs of production that the enterprises that are connected to the clearing house will have expended on average, including on workers' wages."[24] This is a solution with which economic theory would have been satisfied two or three generations ago. It is not sufficient for us today. If costs are understood as opportunity cost, i.e., that which would have been avoided by an alternative application of the expenditures, it is easily seen that Heimann's arguments move around in circles. In the socialist society any alternative application is possible only by order of the government. The problem we are faced with is precisely whether the government could have the means to calculate in order to

23 Ibid., p. 174.
24 Ibid., p. 185.

reach its decisions. The competition of the entrepreneurs who, in the social system based on private ownership, strive to supply goods and services to their most profitable uses is replaced in every conceivable type of socialist system by the planned economy, which is directed by the government. It is the competition among the entrepreneurs that forms the prices for the factors of production, as they mutually try to wrest the labor force and the material means of production away from each other.

Where the economy is "planned," i.e., managed by a central authority to which everything is subordinated, the basis for calculating profitability disappears; only the natural calculation of productivity is left. Heimann says, "As soon as real competition reigns on the market for consumer goods, the resulting structure of prices immediately spreads throughout all stages of production, provided the price relationships emerge in the same competitive way on each market and are independent of the influence of the parties on the producers' side of the market."[25] That would only be the case, however, if real competition existed. Heimann imagines society being comprised of an association of a number of "monopolists." Each one is a department in the overall socialist economy, with respectively assigned exclusive management over a part of the production process. If *they* purchase producers' goods on the "market" this does not represent real competition because the government assigns to them in advance the particular areas over which they are actively to busy themselves and from which they are not allowed to deviate. Competition only exists when everyone produces what seems to him to offer the prospect for the greatest profit. I have attempted to show that only private ownership of the means of production corresponds to such situations.[26]

Heimann's image of the socialist society only considers the repetitive manufacturing of consumer goods from raw materials into consumer goods. Thus it gives the impression that the individual divisions of the collectivist economy would be in a position to operate independently. Far more important than this aspect of the production process, however, is the reinvestment of existing capital and the investment of newly formed capital. The essence of economic decision-making concerns these matters, and not in the use of circulating capital, which is determined as part of the investment and reinvestment decisions. But these decisions, which are binding for years and decades, cannot be made on the basis of the momentary state of the demand for consumer goods. They must always be oriented toward the future; that is, they must be "speculative." Here Heimann's sys-

25 Ibid., pp. 188ff.

26 Cf., my *Socialism*, pp. 192–94.

tem, which makes the expansion or contraction of production proceed more or less mechanically and automatically on the basis of the current demand for consumer goods, fails completely. Solving the problem of value by reducing it to costs would be sufficient only for the theoretically conceivable situation of a state of equilibrium, which never and nowhere is in existence. Only in the imagined state of equilibrium do price and costs coincide. This is not the case in a dynamic economy.

Heimann's attempt to solve the problem of economic calculation, which I believe I have shown to be insoluble, is a failure in my opinion. Nevertheless, his book is still a fine performance, above all because it recognizes the fundamental importance of the problem of economic calculation for socialism and consequently contributes to putting the discussion about the question of social organization back on a scientific basis. In addition to our problem, it deals with a whole series of other important issues in economic theory through a critical discussion of Karl Marx, Franz Oppenheimer, Gustav Cassel, and Joseph A. Schumpeter. Moreover, it is a thoroughly honest book, in that it is not satisfied with superficial observations but attempts to deal with the difficulties at hand. It will have to be dealt with more thoroughly on several points.

The literati of the Marxist party also no longer can refuse to deal with the problem of economic calculation in the socialist society. Only half a year after the appearance of my essay "Economic Calculation in the Socialist Commonwealth," the Bolsheviks Alexander V. Chayanov,[27] Stanislav G. Strumilin,[28] Nikolai I. Bukharin,[29] Yevgeny Varga,[30] and oth-

27 [Alexander V. Chayanov (1888–193?) was a Russian economist who constructed an agricultural planning model for rural development in his 1918 book, *The Theory of the Peasant Economy.* He emphasized the role of the family farm as a basic unit for agricultural development and disagreed with the forced collectivization of the land that began in 1929. In 1930 he was indicted in one of Stalin's early show trials in Moscow and sentenced to prison, where he died at some unknown time.—Ed.]

28 [Stanislav G. Strumilin (1877–1974) participated in the development of planning models in the Soviet Union and wrote *Economic Significance of National Education* (1924).—Ed.]

29 [Nikolai Bukharin (1888–1938) was a leading Marxist economist, who was close to Lenin before and after the Bolshevik revolution in 1917. He served on the ruling Politburo after Lenin's death in 1924 but was removed in 1929 by Stalin, who then ordered his arrest and execution after a show trial in Moscow in 1938.—Ed.]

30 [Yevgeny Varga (1879–1964) was one of Stalin's leading economic advisors on planning and international capitalism throughout the 1930s until Stalin criticized him in 1947. Born in Hungary, he served as a people's commissar of the Hungarian Soviet Republic during the short-lived communist government in 1919 under Béla Kun. After moving to

ers dealt with the problem in a series of articles in the *Economicheskaya Shishni*, an official publication of the Soviet government.[31] The outcome of this discussion was deplorable. Chayanov did not get beyond a failed attempt to construct arbitrary numerical ratios for purposes of calculation in the individual branches of production in a natural [nonmonetary] economy. Strumilin rejected Chayanov's proposed solution and tried to replace it with a system for determining the value of labor. His remarks about the relationships of the value of labor to utility are mentioned only briefly in the summaries we have before us. Varga concerns himself only with the calculation of labor time without going deeply into the difficulties that stand in the way of its application.

Karl Kautsky[32] makes the solution of the problem especially easy for himself. He finally now sees that a calculation of labor-time cannot work. "Instead of attempting the hopeless task of measuring running water with a sieve—and this is what the establishment of value would be—for the circulation of goods, the proletarian regime will have recourse to what it finds ready at hand. These are the prices that have developed historically, which today are measured in gold and which even the greatest inflation can only mask or distort, but not abolish. What even the largest and most complete statistical apparatus could not accomplish—the appraisal of goods according to the labor contained in them—we find given to us in the traditional prices resulting from a long historical process. However incomplete and imprecise they may be, they are the only possible foundation for the smoothest and easiest possible continued functioning of the economic process."[33]

Moscow he was director of the Institute of World Economy (1927–47) and worked for the Secretariat of the Communist International in Moscow.—Ed.]

31 These articles were not accessible to me since I do not speak Russian. Only the summaries were available that are given by Leichter on pp. 85–92 in his article that is discussed below. They are of Chayanov's and Strumilin's articles and a short comment about Chayanov's paper by Varga. Varga's article also appeared in German in the second volume of the Viennese periodical, *Kommunismus*, No. 9/10 (1921), pp. 290–298, under the title, "Die Kostenberechnung in einem geldlosen Staat" [The Calculation of Costs in a Non-Monetary State].

32 [Karl Kautsky (1854–1938) was a leading Marxist theoretician and a leader of the German Social Democratic movement. Lenin once said that Kautsky knew by heart every word written by Marx. He advocated a peaceful transition to socialism and strongly opposed Lenin's revolutionary, violent, and dictatorial methods in Russia.—Ed.]

33 Karl Kautsky, *Die Proletarische Revolution und ihr Programm* [The Proletarian Revolution and Its Program] (Berlin/Stuttgart, 2nd ed., 1922) p. 321.

Nothing reflected in these traditional prices will be changed all at once. But "if the social interest requires it, the quantities of production and of the prices of individual goods" can also "be established as a variance with those handed down from capitalist times." This, Kautsky opines, "taken case by case, provides a much simpler operation than the calculation of the value of labor in all goods for the introduction of a labor-money. Of course, one will not be able to proceed with this in an arbitrary manner."[34] Unfortunately, however, Kautsky neglects to indicate how that can be done other than in an arbitrary way. And when he recommends the retention of the capitalist monetary system, he declares that he must limit himself only to suggestions and does not want to offer any theory of money.[35]

No injustice is done to Kautsky by declaring that the solution proposed by him is not worthy of any further discussion. He himself admits that in the long run the prices handed down from the past will not suffice. Yet he does not indicate how the necessary corrections would be dealt with.

In contrast to Kautsky, Otto Leichter[36] holds strictly to the idea of calculation through the use of labor-time.[37] He easily succeeds in demonstrating that Marx too "sees in this measure of value the only possibility for a socialist economy." Hence his task is really fulfilled in the sense of Marxist science; he declares with satisfaction that he can refer "directly to the intellectual tendency of capitalism."[38] Leichter, however, wishes still to do one other thing, and that is to refute the criticisms that have been raised against the idea of calculation through labor-time. He fails completely in this attempt.

Labor-time calculation is unsuitable for purposes of economic calculation. Firstly, it is impossible to reduce labor of different qualities to a single common unit, and then, secondly, in the calculation it only includes the production factor of labor, not also the material factors of production.[39]

34 Ibid., p. 322f.

35 Ibid., p. 324.

36 [Otto Leichter (1898–1973) was a prominent Austrian socialist who was editor of the Vienna newspaper, *Arbeiterzeitung* from 1924 to 1934. He moved to the United States in 1938, and after 1945 worked as a correspondent affiliated with the United Nations.—Ed.]

37 Otto Leichter, "Die Wirtschaftsrechnung in der sozialistschen Gesellschaft" [Economic Calculation in the Socialist Society] *Marxstudien*, Vol. 5, No. 1 (1923).

38 Ibid., p. 50.

39 Cf., my *Socialism*, pp. 114–16.

Leichter does not wish to let that pass. One can, he says, "compare the importance of different labor functions with each other; one can very well compare the importance of a forge operator in a large steel firm with the qualification of a stoker's boy more or less in the sense of how much more important it is that the forge operator is at his job or how much better he works than the stoker boy or how much more difficult or demanding is the work of the forge operator."[40] One can make such comparisons, certainly, but they will always lead to different results, according to the subjective viewpoints of those who are making them. And what does "importance" mean here? If it is supposed to be importance in regard to the achievement of the product of labor, then one must have recourse to sophistic discussions about the question of whether the hammer or the nail, the paper or pencil is more important. Leichter, who shows himself to be a dyed-in-the-wool adherent of the Marxist labor theory of value, cannot, of course, have meant importance in regard to the satisfaction of human needs, i.e., subjective value. But quite aside from that, which of the four questions that arise from Leichter's arguments should be presented to these judges? Should the importance of "being at the job" or the importance of "working better" or the difficulty of the work or the strain which it causes be compared? Or should the two jobs be compared in a hundred other conceivable ways, perhaps in regard to whether they are injurious to health or in regard to the difficulty of learning them? Each one of these comparisons yields a different result, and only one can be taken as the basis for the ratio of comparison. Or should the results of several comparisons be combined for the computation of a scale of comparison?

Leichter's assertion that ordinary routine solves all of these problems, since it forms the basis for the wages of all kinds of work, is completely mistaken. Wage rates are formed through the commercial exchanges of the marketplace on the basis of subjective valuations. The problem is precisely to examine whether even in a society without exchange the reduction of different qualities of labor to a single uniform standard is possible. Leichter sees nothing in this objection but "market fetishism" (he is especially proud of having coined this expression).[41] He thinks that in the negotiations that are carried on between the individual entrepreneurs, the workshop managers, and the individual workers about the wage rates for different skilled labor jobs, it is not a question of "market bargaining in the

40 Leichter, op. cit., p. 62.
41 Ibid., pp. 26ff.

ordinary sense. The remuneration of the skilled and less skilled workforce, especially the relationship between the remuneration of different professional categories or the payment for different machine work in the same professions has almost nothing to do with the condition of the labor market or with the momentary amount of unemployment. Hence, supply and demand also play almost no role at all in the sense of the transactions of the market."[42] Unfortunately Leichter neglects to provide any evidence for this claim. It should also be noted how he takes all fundamental meaning away from his thesis by twice inserting the little word "almost."

The source of Leichter's errors is to be found in the inadequacy and lack of clarity in his conception of the nature of the market and of price formation on the market. The essence of the market seems to him to lie in "bargaining" and in the appeal of the parties to supply and demand. But bargaining can be completely absent; even where "rigid prices" exist, in regard to which "nothing can be negotiated," the mechanism of the market is always at work, except that the state of the market influences the price not directly through the negotiations of the parties but indirectly through their behavior (i.e., their failure to come forward or the overabundance of buyers and the corresponding behavior of sellers). Moreover, Leichter also must admit that there is bargaining in the wage negotiations that he cites. He only says that there is no "market bargaining in the usual sense"—obviously, because here the parties do not refer to supply and demand. But such reference never comes up; the parties busy themselves with referring to the righteousness of their demands, the size of the "primary costs," and "the necessity of the achievement of a certain income." But what the parties say during the act of exchange is meaningless for understanding the nature of the process; it is their conduct and not their speech that matters.

If Leichter had kept that in mind, he could not, in the zeal of his Marxist bias, have hit upon the idea of questioning the influence of the state of the labor market on the formation of wages. If a certain group of workers is paid less than is appropriate to their marginal productivity, then the outflow of the work force to other, comparatively better paid work will quickly lead to an adjustment; and in the case of relatively too high remuneration, the influx of workers brings the situation back into order. One can readily admit that the labor-union bureaucrat and the shop steward do not recognize these relationships; but he who occupies himself with the economic

42 Ibid., p. 63.

problems of wage formation should at least try to consider matters less superficially.

Leichter is equally unsuccessful in his attempt to refute the other objection made against the usefulness of labor-time calculation. His polemic is built on a misunderstanding of my remarks. This misunderstanding reveals an astonishing lack of familiarity with the elementary concepts of economic theory and is so flagrant that one is inclined to assume that Leichter has intentionally misconstrued my words only to be able to bring up something against them. I had said that economic calculation had to include not only labor but also the material factors of production; and that it was true that these, as Marx says, "are available from nature without the aid of men." But if they are only available in such a quantity that they need to be economized, then they also must be included in the economic calculations.[43]

Leichter replies, "In the first place Mises... approaches the problem ... as if it were a question of all spheres of production in which material means of production are involved along with human labor. In this general formulation his objection is absolutely unjustified, for most goods are fully comprehended by the normal tabulation of costs in terms of labor hours. Only at the conclusion of his argument does he add the decisive restriction that his assertion has meaning only for the case in which it is a question of scarce goods, for which economizing is necessary."[44] The "decisive restriction" of which Leichter speaks is that free goods—like air, water, and sunlight—precisely do not enter into any economic calculation, since it only includes economic goods, i.e., those goods that are not available in a practically unlimited quantity so that one must economize them. Leichter's expression "scarce goods, for which economizing is necessary" and the expression "economic goods" mean the same thing. But Leichter presents the matter as if only a few goods had to be economized. The inexact expressions "scarce goods" and "most goods" only obscure the clear and transparent state of affairs. Let Leichter name one economic good that does not have to be economized!

But even in the context of his own confused remarks, Leichter would have been obliged to indicate how the problem of socialist economic cal-

---

43 See my *Socialism*, p. 114–15; also, "Economic Calculation in the Socialist Commonwealth," [in Hayek, ed., *Collectivist Economic Planning*, pp. 113–14; and in Kirzner, ed., *Classics in Austrian Economics*, pp. 18–19. — Ed.]

44 Leichter, op. cit., pp. 69ff.

culation is to be solved in connection with his "scarce goods." He prudently avoids the matter. He is content to say that society "in its plan for economic activity, e.g., in mining, will determine the exact amount of work to be done. And if higher prices for these scarce goods should be required, they will come about by assigning a higher productivity to the labor hours used in the production of these goods in the setting of their prices rather than in the compensation paid."[45] Now our problem does not concern the question of whether the society can determine the limits of mining or not and whether it can demand higher or lower prices, but whether it will be in a position to make decisions on the basis of economic calculation. It has never been doubted that society can decree. I stated, however, that it couldn't proceed rationally, i.e., on the basis of economic calculation. Therefore the matter is settled in terms of the essence of Leichter's comments. Everything else that his book contains is superfluous padding, which is intended to conceal the weaknesses in the crucial passages.

Orthodox Marxists have succeeded no better than others in finding a workable system of economic calculation for the socialistic society.

---

45 Ibid., p. 70.

CHAPTER 42

Recent Writings Concerning the Problem of Economic Calculation under Socialism[1]

The question of whether economic calculation is possible within a socialist system of society has once again occupied a group of writers.

Jacob Marschak attempts to get at the problem by criticizing economic calculation under the social system that is based on private ownership.[2] He says that economic calculation under capitalism does not provide an accurate calculus of value. Marschak reaches this extraordinary conclusion by referring to a few theorems from monopoly theory. The idea never seems to have occurred to Marschak that someone might not agree with his remarks about the workings of monetary calculation. And he seems just as little to have asked himself whether anything could be gained in the way of evidence about the possibility of economic calculation in a socialist society by criticizing economic calculation in a capitalist society. He simply follows the example given by all socialist authors and speaks as little as possible about socialism and as much as possible about the shortcomings of the capitalist social order. Marschak then seeks to demonstrate that economic calculation is also possible under syndicalism. That has never been contested, at least not by me. But the economic problem that

---

1 [This article originally appeared in German in the *Archiv für Sozialwissenschaft und Sozialpolitik*, Vol. 60 (1928).—Ed.]

2 Jacob Marschak, "Wirtschaftsrechnung und Gemeinwirtschaft. Zur Misesschen These von der Unmöglichkeit sozialistischer Wirtschaftsrechnung" [Economic Calculation and the Socialist Economy. Concerning the Misesian Thesis on the Impossibility of Socialist Economic Calculation] in the *Archiv für Sozialwissenschaft und Sozialpolitik*, Vol. 51, pp. 501–520. [Jacob Marschak (1898–1977) was a leading proponent of general equilibrium theory in economics and an early developer of econometric analysis. Born in Russia, he moved to Germany in 1919 and to the United States in 1940. His major work was on the problems of uncertainty and information in economic theory.—Ed.]

is under discussion is whether or not economic calculation is possible in the socialist society, and not whether economic calculation is possible in the syndicalist system. Marschak makes a wide detour around this problem, which is the only one under discussion, and squanders his dialectics on things that have nothing to do with it.

Otto Neurath has published a work that is again concerned with natural calculation.[3] Neurath expresses his often-repeated belief in natural calculation, a belief in which, as one can easily establish, he stands alone.[4] Neurath also prefers, of course, to speak about many other things than natural calculation, since he has nothing new to offer as a solution to the problem of how apples and pears can be added together. It is true, of course, as Neurath declares, that one can compare two concrete subgroups of different kinds of goods with each other without having the need for money and can designate that one is more valuable and the other is less valuable. That has never been denied, but it doesn't have the least bit to do with the question how a general calculation and comparison of quantities of different kinds of goods and services can be made.

In contrast to Neurath, Erich Horn is concerned with the economic limits of a collectivist economy.[5] He comes to the conclusion that "[t]he capitalist method of calculation—which determines the profitability of an enterprise by estimating its financial situation in money terms—will also have to be utilized in a more collectivist-oriented economic system if such a system places any value on economizing behavior. Capitalism is, therefore, unalterably and permanently resistant to all radical change and socialization because it is the fundamental form of economic order."

The short and exceptionally instructive work by the Russian Boris

3 Otto Neurath, *Wirtschaftsplan und Naturalrechnung. Von der sozialistischen Lebensordnung und vom kommenden Menschen* [Economic Planning and Natural Calculation. Concerning the Socialist Way of Life and the Man of the Future] (Berlin: E. Laubsche, 1925). [See Chapter 41, "New Contributions to the Problem of Socialist Economic Calculation," footnote 20.—Ed.]

4 ["Natural calculation," or calculation *in natura*, referred to the idea that goods could be valued and allocated and resources could be distributed among alternative production uses without the intermediation of money, and without money serving as the general unit of account for purposes of economic calculation.—Ed.]

5 Erich Horn, *Die ökonomischen Grenen der Gemeinwirtschaft. Eine wirtschafts theoretische Untersuchung über die Durchfürhrbarkeit des Sozialismus* [The Economic Limits of a Collectivist Economy. A Theoretical Inquiry into the Feasibility of Socialism] (Halberstadt: H. Meyers, 1928) pp. 60ff.

Brutzkus, *The Doctrines of Marxism in Light of the Russian Revolution*, deserves special attention. Brutzkus's work was already published in the Russian language in 1922 and led to the author's imprisonment by the Cheka[6] and finally his expulsion from Russia.[7] Now the work has appeared in German translation. Within its ninety pages he deals with all questions concerning the socialist system. In particular he provides a thorough analysis of the central problem of economic calculation under socialism. Brutzkus's writing stands out in comparison to the failed attempts by Chayanov, Strumilin, and Varga. Immediately after the publication of my essay on "Economic Calculation in the Socialist Commonwealth" they attempted to come up with a socialist system of calculation.[8] Brutzkus affirms that this discussion has led to the recognition that without economic calculation rational conduct is entirely impossible, no matter under what kind of economic system.

In light of Varga and Strumilin's recent declaration that labor is the measure of value, Brutzkus also analyzes the fundamental problem of economic calculation on the basis of the value of labor. He concludes that even the socialist economic system cannot ignore that production always represents the combined effort of three factors: labor, capital, and material resources. Calculation on the basis of labor costs alone is not a usable indicator of the greater or lesser efficiency of enterprises. As a result, the fundamental Marxian idea of constructing a plan on the basis of a single labor standard of value is impossible. "So the socialist society, in spite of the

6 [The "Cheka" was the acronym for the first Soviet secret police—the All-Russian Extraordinary Commission to Combat Counterrevolution and Sabotage—established on December 20, 1917, six weeks after the Bolsheviks under Lenin came to power. The organization was later reorganized and renamed several times under the acronyms OGPU, NKVD, and KGB.—Ed.]

7 Boris Brutzkus, *Die Lehren des Marxismus im Lichte der russischen Revolution* (Berlin: Hermann Sack, 1928). [This work is included as the first part of Brutzkus's volume, *Economic Planning in Soviet Russia* (London: George Routledge, 1935), pp. 1–94. It has been reprinted in Peter J. Boettke, ed., *Socialism and the Market: The Socialist Calculation Debate Revisited*, Vol. III (London/New York: Routledge, 2000). Boris Brutzkus (1874–1938) served briefly as the chairman of the agricultural planning commission for the Petrograd district in the people's commissariat for agriculture in 1922, but he was arrested and forced to leave Russia at the end of that year. From 1923 to 1933 he was a professor at the Russian Scientific Institute in Berlin, Germany, a position from which he was removed following Hitler's coming to power in January of 1933.—Ed.]

8 [See Chapter 41, "New Contributions to the Problem of Socialist Economic Calculation."—Ed.]

whole panoply of its scientific theory and a gigantic statistical apparatus, is incapable of determining the needs of its citizens and therefore is not in a position to provide the required direction to production." Hence the socialist economy lacks "a mechanism for the coordination of the individual branches of production in the economy as a whole."

Brutzkus's work is the first and up to now the only scholarly publication dealing in a fundamental way with the problems of the Soviet state in Russia. All other works are of a descriptive nature, in which the presentation of the facts generally suffers from being marred by either an uncritical hatred of the Soviet idea or, as is more often the case, an uncritical extravagant praise for the system. Here for the first time we find a work that examines the problems of socialism in a scholarly fashion rather than presenting piquant and sensational details about the Russian conditions in more or less clever and propagandistic style. In the flood of worthless publications about Russia, which the book trade brings us day after day, Brutzkus's book stands out as a work of unbiased scholarly thought.

Today a conclusive judgment can be passed on the socialist literature of the decade that followed the unrivaled political success of uncompromising socialism that started with the Russian Revolution. One author who is very favorably inclined toward socialism, Theodor Cassau, has said (in the *Festschrift* published for Lujo Brentano's eightieth birthday) that all the experiences of the last decade have passed over and left no mark on the ideology of proletarian socialism. He said that this ideology has scarcely ever had as much possibility for growth and has scarcely ever been so sterile as in the heyday of the debates about socialization.[9] This may sound like a very harsh judgment, but it is valid without any reservation for the entire literature about socialism, and not only for Marxist or—as it is customarily called today—proletarian socialism.

In his recently published work, *General Economic Theory*, Adolf Weber summarizes the results of the discussions devoted to our problem in the following way: "If, however, we now further ask how the goal of establishing a socialist economy must look on the basis of the most recent and serious scholarship, and if we want to maintain the principle of ratio-

9 [Theodor Cassau, "Die sozialistische Ideenwelt vor und nach dem Kriege," [The World of Socialist Ideas Before and After the War] in *Die Wirtschaftswissenschaft nach dem Kriege. Festschrift für Lujo Brentano zum 80.* Vol. I. [The Science of Economics after the War. A Tribute to Lujo Brentano on His Eightieth Birthday] (Munich: 1925).—Ed.]

nality, then there are three important and generally recognized postulates that have emerged today:

"1. The competition of the consumers cannot be gotten around. Quite apart from the psychological impossibility of establishing by force any pattern of consumption in the place of free consumption, there speaks against it the fact that only with the free competition of buyers can there be a basis for the formation of market prices, which serve as an indicator of how to broaden or narrow production to meet the demand for goods.

"2. Without monetary calculation there can be no calculation of profitability in the economy, no interconnection of individual enterprises in order to form a rationally operating community of men within the complicated system of division of labor. For this purpose, it is necessary that prices be formed not only for finished goods but also in all earlier stages of the process, especially for scarce material factors of production, and for labor and capital. 3...."[10]

One can hardly raise any objection to Weber's remarks.

10 Adolf Weber, *Allgemeine Volkswirtschaftslehre. Eine Einführung* [General Economic Theory. An Introduction] (Munich/Leipzig: Duncker & Humblot, 1928) pp. 485ff.

CHAPTER 43

Economic Calculation under Commercial Management and Bureaucratic Administration[1]

1   *The Limits of Capitalist Economic Calculation*

Human action is economizing, i.e., preferring what is deemed to be more important in relation to what is regarded as less important. Economizing distinguishes means and ends, expenditure (costs) and outcome. Costs are the meaning attached to the achievement of the most important among those goals that can no longer be achieved because another goal has been preferred.

In a society based on the division of labor in which there is private ownership of the means of production (i.e., goods of higher order) and a good is used as a general medium of exchange (i.e., money), economizing permits calculation. Since markets form monetary prices for all economic goods—for the means of production just as much as for more or less durable goods of consumption (first-order goods)—expenditure and outcome can be set against each other and compared in a *computational* (more exactly: in an arithmetic) way. It is the calculation of profitability that guides the behavior of businesses.

Where elements enter economic considerations for which no monetary prices are formed in markets, monetary calculation and consequently

1 [This article was originally handwritten in German and is previously unpublished. It was written on the back of copies of the Vienna Chamber of Commerce report that Mises delivered on July 25, 1932, and which is included in the present volume as Chapter 30, "On Limiting the Adverse Effects of a Proposed Increase in the Value-Added Tax." It was most likely the basis for a lecture that he delivered sometime in the summer or autumn of 1932. The theme of government versus private management of enterprises was developed by Mises after he came to the United States during the Second World War; see Ludwig von Mises, *Bureaucracy* (Spring Mills, Pa.: Libertarian Press, [1944] 1983).—Ed.]

the numerical comparability of means and outcome reach their limits. *Res extra commercium* and things that cannot be obtained for money are excluded from monetary calculation. To be sure, I may be able to determine my actions according to the amount of money I am willing to spend on obtaining or not forgoing such a good. But if I have to balance such goods one against the other, I lack even this mode of thought and expression.

In a society that does not recognize private property in the means of production, economic calculation is impossible.[2] This is no longer contested today. It is less noticed that economic calculation, as a mental tool for economic evaluation, cannot be applied where there is no inclination to accept profitability as a gauge of economic behavior. If we do not want to be guided by the decisions of the consumers on the market or produce what they regard as most important, then monetary calculation cannot be applied and neither what follows from it, the calculation of profitability. Whoever takes productivity as his gauge and places his own subjective judgment above that of the decision-makers on the market must proceed in a different manner than the entrepreneur, who is guided by no other goal than that of profit and who therefore must be intent on satisfying the wants of consumers in the best and cheapest way. It matters very little that whoever strives for productivity may believe he is pursuing "true needs," and that the general manager of a socialist economy would act no differently than he.[3]

2   Commercial Management

Businesses striving for profitability and "profits" are managed on a "commercial" basis. Every division, department, and individual transaction is based on economic calculation. Calculation precedes action, and accountancy controls the outcome of action. Whatever is not profitable shall not be undertaken. Unprofitable divisions and departments will be reor-

---

2 See my book, *Socialism: An Economic and Sociological Analysis* (Indianapolis: Liberty Fund, [1951] 1981), pp. 97–105; 112–23; 473–78.

3 [Mises, *Socialism*, p. 125: "The contrasting of production for profit and production for needs is closely connected with the common practice of contrasting productivity and profitability or the 'social' and 'private' economic point of view. An economic action is said to be profitable if in the capitalist system it yields an excess of receipts over costs. An economic action is said to be productive when, seen from the point of view of a hypothetical socialist community, the yield exceeds the costs involved." — Ed.]

ganized or abandoned. Workers whose costs of employment are more than they contribute will be laid off. Managers who have no success in carrying out their business will be dismissed. All affairs of a business are placed under the sober guidance of accountancy, which controls all transactions in dollars and cents. Monetary calculation alone determines profitability. Profits reign supreme. The sole order an entrepreneur gives his employees of whatever rank is to produce profit margins.

This order is clear and unequivocal, and whoever wants to follow it must work in a computational and sober manner. Personal discretion finds no place in such an enterprise. If an employee buys at a higher or sells at a lower price for personal reasons, or remunerates employees at a higher or lower rate than the wages they can earn on the labor market, or fails to dismiss lazy and incompetent workers or dismisses diligent and competent ones, then he impairs the success of the business entrusted to him, and in doing so imperils his own income. Where ledgers speak their numerical language, all further controls, regulations, and orders become redundant. An entrepreneur *must not* incur losses for any length of time. Whoever does so will soon cease to be an entrepreneur.

To whatever size a business may grow that is striving for profit and only for profit, consistent management by its head remains a technically rather simple matter. If cost accounting, bookkeeping, and their ancillary services are in order, it is easy to assess and manage even the largest institution. Monetary calculation sheds light on even the most distant subsidiary and the most hidden corner of a workshop. In every case, there is always an optimal size of a firm and of individual businesses with regard to location, transport conditions, market situation, the proportion of fixed to variable costs, etc. In a technical sense, however, the dimension of any firm and business is neutral. The mental tool of monetary calculation permits the mastery of the arduous task of relating the dimension of a firm to what occurs in it.

3   Bureaucratic Administration

Agencies and courts exercising the administration of the state operate according to a fundamentally different pattern. Expenditure and outcome cannot be computed and compared. Superior agencies can never define the tasks to be accomplished by judges and public officials in the same simple and unequivocal manner as a corporation defines the tasks of its subsidiaries. If the integrity of the administration is to be maintained and not all discretionary power is to devolve to management from the executive levels, detailed regulations must be established for the actions of these officials in every conceivable case. Unexpected cases must be reported to the superior levels for a special order to be issued. The duty of inferiors is solely to obey orders. They consequently cannot be blamed for failure if they have not acted against their orders. Even success may attract blame if it was the result of not following regulations. It is not the success or failure of an official's actions that counts, but whether these actions were formally covered by existing regulations.

This means that the question of whether an action was a success or a failure cannot be answered as clearly and simply as in profit-oriented businesses. What are the criteria for judging the successful performance of a minister of government, of an ambassador, of a provincial governor, or of a judge? And what is the relationship between this "success" and the expenditure incurred? The regulations that define the course of action of administrative officials (in the broadest sense of this term) have their origin in the activity of administration, which by its very nature is not carried out according to any calculation of profitability. It cannot be left to individual officials to decide on the ways and means of administration, for if this were so it would be they who govern and not the elected heads. It cannot be left to individual heads of departments to decide on hiring, promoting, remunerating, and firing his inferiors if these are not to be subject to indiscriminate discretion. It cannot be left to individual heads to decide how much to spend on the exigencies of their service. In their endeavor to achieve their tasks as well as possible, they would likely take the position that the amount of expenditure does not matter. For the outcome to be reached is not commensurable with the monetary cost. All acceptable expenditure must therefore be well defined.

What is generally castigated as bureaucratic regimentation, pettiness, fearfulness, formalism, and ponderousness is indispensable in an administration that does not seek profit. Administration must be bureaucratic if it is not to degenerate into one of despotism and subservience. It requires regulations imposed from above, which determine the management both of major and minor issues. It must be laid down how often the windows of a public building are to be cleaned, how much ink may be used in a year, when offices are to be heated, which officials shall have padded chairs and which a special towel. If this were neglected the costs of administration would multiply. There is no need to make fun of this, for pettiness also exists elsewhere. Since judges and night guards are indispensable, everything their service requires must be undertaken. Bureaucracy and public agencies have a necessary function in a society based on the division of labor.

The functioning of courts and government agencies must be defined in minute detail if the integrity of jurisdiction and administration is to be upheld. An absolute dictator cannot dispense with regulations, unless he wants to abdicate in favor of the lowest level. A liberal state under the rule of law can much less renounce bureaucratic regulations if it wants to recognize the individual political rights of its citizens and to protect these from the arbitrariness of officials. By their very nature, however, regulations imply formalism, which is the essence of bureaucracy.

4   Administration of Public Enterprises

Though full socialism is not feasible, since a socialist society must dispense with economic calculation, it is conceivable that there are individual public enterprises within a society based on the private ownership of the means of production. These enterprises are typical of state and municipal socialism and of some communist countries that still practice exchange on markets and therefore can use market prices to perform economic calculations. In a purely technical sense, a public enterprise could be managed in the same commercial spirit as a private enterprise.

The fact that this does not happen is due to the unwillingness of government to regard its enterprises purely under the heading of profitability. It always imposes on management other concerns as well, such as "general economic," political, or military considerations. Because government thinks that private business tends to neglect these concerns, it has assumed and maintained the management of such businesses. Though the realization of net profits is not explicitly excluded, it is nonetheless clear that other objectives are primarily being pursued other than that of profit. But as soon as net profit no longer is the sole guide, calculation of profitability loses its meaning. If other nonmonetary objectives are placed next to or before monetary gain, monetary calculation has lost its function. Suppose the head of an enterprise or of a division within such an enterprise is confronted with the insufficient profitability of a business entrusted to him. If he is able to claim that he has been successful on the basis of things that cannot be expressed in the balance sheet and that are of a nonmonetary nature, then profit and loss calculations no longer play a decisive role for assessing the success of the management. In this case, however, the discretion exercised by heads of public enterprises must be limited by instituting all those regulatory measures that are practiced in government administration. These enterprises, then, become bureaucratic.

No reform would make public enterprises less bureaucratic without, as in private business, making profitability the sole arbiter. We may reasonably disregard whether a public enterprise that focused solely on maximum profitability is psychologically even possible at all, or whether the bureaucratic mentality of government administration and nonprofit public enterprises would not end up infecting it. According to the intention of those governing on the state and municipal levels, profitability should not be the only criterion for the management of a public enterprise. But then it must be managed bureaucratically, i.e., in accordance with particular regulations imposed on its administration.

The management of every public enterprise will, of course, endeavor to achieve as much excess cash flow or to incur as little loss as may be possible given its defined objectives and the corresponding regulations. However, thriftiness is by far not the same thing as management according to profitability. Only if nothing but profitability is the guiding principle behind every single decision can an enterprise be managed along commercial lines. As soon as other considerations enter the picture, an enterprise will necessarily become bureaucratic.

All attempts at changing the regulations so as to reverse the indisputable inferiority of bureaucratically administered public enterprises in comparison to commercially managed private businesses neglect this fact. Every set of regulations is of necessity bureaucratic. It matters very little whether a single person or a committee heads a public enterprise, whether these heads share in the profit or not, whether the minister of finance and Parliament, who have to stand the loss, may influence its administration or not, whether politicians or trade unions may legally or illegally impinge on its management, whether leading positions are filled by "experts" or by just anyone, or whether such experts have a legal, technical, commercial, or other background. The enterprise becomes bureaucratic by the very fact that management is expected to aim not exclusively at profitability but at other objectives as well.

It is a task for applied economics to assess these other objectives for the attainment of which management is expected to comply. Suffice it to say here that the "general economic" objectives of public enterprises amount to the subsidization of one group of citizens at the expense of the rest. The examples of a railroad that is not and cannot be profitable and of transport fees which are lower than those which would have to be charged in order to attain profitability make it clear who is being favored and at whose expense.

5 Bureaucratization of Private Enterprise in the Interventionist State

In a liberal capitalist state all—and even the largest—enterprises can steer clear of bureaucratization. An enterprise never becomes bureaucratic just because of its size. If it abides by the profitability principle, even the largest business can determine the precise contribution of every single transaction and every division in relation to the total result. Only the ineptness of their proprietors can result in the enterprises being managed bureaucratically. Such enterprises cannot maintain themselves in the competition of the market and will disappear in a short time.

However, we do not live in a liberal and capitalist society but in an interventionist state, in which every enterprise—and particularly large enterprises that are despised by demagogues and aristocrats alike—must be intent on currying and maintaining the favor of those in power so the government interventions can be in its benefit and not to its detriment. A business that wants to guard itself from destruction by interventionist policy must ingratiate itself both "above" and "below" and must take a myriad of issues into consideration that it would neglect under purely commercial conditions. This influences not only industrial relations but also all other aspects of management. One has to make an accommodation with government and local authorities, one has to allow for all prejudices and wishes of public opinion, one has to trim one's sails to the wind. One has to do obviously unprofitable business, contribute money to election funds and newspapers, employ friends of government and of politicians, and dismiss those who have fallen out of favor. One has to get on good terms with trade unions and churches, support the arts and sciences, and be "charitable." In a word, one has to incur all sorts of expenditure for matters not related to one's business.

Since the impact of these individual expenditures on business success cannot be measured in monetary terms, they throw the calculation of profitability severely into disarray. *How* is one to account for the benefits derived from governmental favors and other noneconomic factors and balance them against the losses caused by an incompetent director who is well liked "above," or by the employment of engineers who are agreeable to political parties instead of engineers who are capable? If former ministers of government and relatives and friends of active statesmen and politicians are appointed to the boards of companies, if public officials and members of respected clubs and organizations occupy positions of middle management, and if all workers are union members, the enterprise will necessarily perish. If it can keep its competitive position in spite of its bureaucratic nature, this can only be due to government intervention. But since it could not survive without intervention in its favor it is forced to become ever more bureaucratic.

6   Sociopsychological Effects
of Bureaucratization

My preceding remarks concerned only what can be said about bureaucratization from a sociological standpoint. Whoever confuses sociology with social psychology or with philosophy of history will certainly say that these remarks are "simplistic" and not "profound" enough. I would not regard this as a criticism.

The effects of a bureaucratic business from the perspective of social psychology have been well described by *belles-lettres* and newspapers alike. Some particularly pertinent remarks are found in the periodical *Simplicissimus*. Much to their exhilaration or chagrin, every circle of friends tells stories about Gothamite pranks of bureaucrats. Bureaucratic management is generally disparaged, while at the same time many demand that the interventionist and socialist economic policy be continued that necessarily leads to bureaucratization. Bureaucrats are scorned while many want to become bureaucrats, if they are not already.

Bureaucratization is no more an inescapable destiny than interventionism and socialism are necessarily "destinies." Our contemporaries *want* intervention, state and municipal enterprises, socialization, and with these necessarily comes the expansion of the bureaucratic at the expense of the commercial. Of course they pretend to want an "unbureaucratic" socialism and an "unbureaucratic" interventionism, just as revolutionaries once demanded a "republic led by a grand duke."

Appendix: A Soviet Response to Mises

CHAPTER 44

"Anti-Marxism": Professor Mises as a Theorist of Fascism[1]

BY F. KAPELUSH

Viennese professor Ludwig Mises is a very angry guy and he very strongly dislikes Marx and Marxism. Just speaking between us, he shouldn't dislike it one bit. If not for Marxism, our professor would have to beg for handouts, since he has never managed to prove himself in science. Crushing Marxism, however, is a very profitable business.

1 [This article originally appeared in Russian in the Soviet journal, *Bolshevik,* a leading publication of the Communist party in the Soviet Union, on August 15, 1925. On September 17, 1925, Karl Mudeczek, a senior staff member of the Austrian embassy in Moscow, sent Mises a letter informing him that this article had appeared and that he had taken the liberty of having it translated into German. As a "polemic" against Mises's article, "Anti-Marxism," which had appeared in the *Weltwirtschaftliches Archiv* (April 1925), Mudeczek thought Mises would find it of interest. Mises replied on September 24, 1925, offering his "many thanks" for the copy of the article and the translation. In "Anti-Marxism," reprinted in *Critique of Interventionism* (Irvington-on-Hudson, N.Y.: Foundation for Economic Education, [1929] 1996), pp. 71–95, Mises explained the process by which Marxian thought came to have such a strong hold on German intellectuals and the division of these intellectuals into different anticapitalist camps. Looking over the ideological and political landscape of Germany in the middle of the 1920s, Mises argued that the rising force in opposition to Marxian socialism was "national socialism." The national socialists insisted that "proletarian interests" had to be submerged in the wider interests of the "fatherland." The strong state would also control and repress the profit motive of the private sector and pursue an aggressive foreign policy. As Mises put it in an accompanying article, "Social Liberalism," the following year in 1926 (reprinted in *Critique of Interventionism*, pp. 43–70), a growing number of people in Germany were "setting their hopes on the coming of the 'strong man'—the tyrant who will think for them and care for them" (p. 67). What Mises clearly saw and explained in the mid–1920s were the political, cultural and ideological forces at work in Germany that were creating the conditions for the victory of Adolf Hitler and the Nazi movement in 1933. In 1925, in "Anti-Marxism," Mises also anticipated the Nazi-Soviet Pact of August 1939 that would divide up Eastern Europe between Nazi Germany and the Soviet Union, and which set the stage for the Second World War. Mises

"The science of the so-called Marxists," states Mises, "can be no more than 'scholasticism.'" Mises talks about "men and women who are in this business" with total disregard. They beat the air, live by canonized Marxian dogmas, with their writings mattering only because it helps their political careers; their "science" only pursues party goals; and the whole argument about revisionism and dictatorship is not scholarly, but is purely political.[2]

That's how angrily Mises talks about Marxists. But further on Mises puts himself in a very unpleasant position. It happens to be that the leading figures of German bourgeois [social] science, the representatives of the Historical School in political economy and the so-called Socialists of the Chair, borrowed a lot from Marx.[3] Mises doesn't dare to criticize them.

---

stated that if Germany were to follow a policy of aggression, it would find only one ally in this endeavor, Soviet Russia: "If Germany, a nation surrounded by other nations in the heart of Europe, were to assault in accordance with this principle, it would invite a coalition of all its neighbors into a world-political constellation: enemies all around. In such a situation Germany could find only one ally: Russia, which is facing hostility by Poles, Lithuanians, Hungarians, and possibly Czechs, but nowhere stands in direct conflict with German interests. Since Bolshevist Russia, like Czarist Russia, only knows force in dealing with other nations, it is already seeking the friendship of German nationalism. German Anti-Marxism and Russian Super-Marxism are not too far apart" (pp. 81–82). F. Kapelush's article from *Bolshevik* was clearly meant to debunk and ridicule Mises's arguments. No information was obtainable about the article's author. An attempt has been made to retain the rather crude style and tone of the original Russian, from which this translation has been done. The stilted grammar in places is the author's and has been kept, for the most part, in the translation for the original intended effect.—Ed.]

2 [In the 1890s a number of German socialists challenged and "revised" some of the assumptions of Marx's "scientific socialism," and argued, among other things, that a socialist transformation of society could be introduced not through violent revolution but through incremental change using the democratic political process. These differences were reinforced following the Bolshevik revolution in Russia in November 1917, when Lenin established a "dictatorship of the proletariat" under the leadership of a "revolutionary vanguard" meant to represent, lead, and educate the masses for the bright socialist future to come. A sizable number of German Social Democrats strongly disagreed with the use of nonparliamentary methods, violence, and terror as the means to achieving socialism. This dispute became the basis for the official Soviet line in the 1920s and 1930s that the Social Democrats were "social renegades," "social fascists," and "enemies of the people."—Ed.]

3 [Members of the German Historical School of political science and economics were sometimes referred to as the "Socialists of the Chair," since some of them, as occupants of chairs at prominent German universities, viewed themselves as defenders of the Prussian and imperial German paternalistic state, with its welfare state, regulation of industry, and political and economic nationalism in the international arena. See Chapter 39, "The Logical Problem of Economics," footnote 10; and Richard M. Ebeling, "Political Myths and Economic Realities of the Welfare State," in Richard M. Ebeling, ed., *American Perestroika:*

With great sadness he quotes Professor Schmoller[4] that Adam Smith's school became "a doctrine of narrow class interests" and that "socialism can be denied neither its justification for existence nor that it has had some good effects." With the same degree of sorrow Mises quotes Friedrich Engels, that Professor Wilhelm Lexis's theory of interest merely presents the Marxist theory in different words.[5]

But then Mises's great anger falls on Schmoller's students, the entire generation of the German bourgeois [social] science. He doesn't mention names. "This generation had never been exposed to university lectures on theoretical economics. They knew the Classical economists by name only and were convinced that they had been vanquished by Schmoller. Very few had ever read or even seen the works of David Ricardo or John Stuart Mill. But they had to read Marx and Engels. Which became all the more necessary, as they had to cope with the growing social democracy. They were writing books in order to refute Marx.... They rejected the harshest political demands of Marx and Engels, but adopted the theories in milder form.... For this generation... Marx was the economic theorist par excellence."[6]

The angry professor continues to snort for a long while. But finally he finds satisfaction in the fact that the current generation, "some pupils of these pupils" [the students of Schmoller's students], rejected Marx. Of course we are talking about bourgeois science. A new trend now appeared, anti-Marxism, which Mises talks about with such admiration. The Austrian school, Böhm-Bawerk[7] and others, demonstrated "how petty and insignificant the role of Marx is in the history of political economy." On his own behalf Mises also states that "those few possibly defensible thoughts" in Marx's study of society have been analyzed much more deeply by Taine[8]

The Demise of the Welfare State (Hillsdale, Mich.: Hillsdale College Press, 1995), pp.3–38, especially 3–13.—Ed.]

4 [See Chapter 20, "The Myth of the Failure of Capitalism," footnote 14. For almost a generation, Schmoller influenced the direction of economic and historical teaching and research at the universities in Germany, especially in emphasizing the role of the government in instituting welfare statist policies for purposes of assuring "social justice."—Ed.]

5 [Mises, "Anti-Marxism," p. 73. Wilhelm Lexis (1837–1914) was a prominent member of the German Historical school.—Ed.]

6 [Ibid., pp. 72–73.—Ed.]

7 [See Chapter 37, "The Austrian Economists," and Chapter 38, "Eugen von Böhm-Bawerk."—Ed.]

8 [Hippolyte Adolphe Taine (1828–93) was a French historian, social critic, philosopher,

and Buckle;[9] and his theory of the withering away of the state is "utterly insignificant for science."(!)[10] A poodle is barking at the elephant. Mises has not yet named the representatives of this school of "anti-Marxism." But one should read between the lines: The professor is too modest to name himself.

What is the contribution of this school to science? What is Mises offering us? He is advocating "utilitarian sociology" and states that "the success that Marx's study of society had in Germany is explained by the fact that utilitarian sociology of the eighteenth century was rejected by German [social] science." That isn't bad, is it? On the other hand, Mises—let's do him justice—puts his own meaning (or meaninglessness) in this Stone Age "utilitarian sociology." This meaning is—the harmony of interests. Society is founded on the division of labor, and because of this does not contain any conflicts of interest. This is a commonplace, and it is also an incorrect one. Mises, to push himself up, puts it into a Gelerterian abracadabra:[11] "The utilitarian social doctrine does not engage in metaphysics, but takes as its point of departure the established fact that all living beings affirm their will to live and grow."[12] Isn't that metaphysics? Here is a reference to Adam Smith, "even the weakness of men was not 'without its utility,'"[13] and all of it for the sake of the revelation that private property is in the interests of all the members of the society. Along the way there is such childish ignorance as the statement that "wars, foreign and domestic, (revolutions, civil wars), are more likely to be avoided the closer the divi-

---

and advocate of positivism, who argued that the study of history, art, and literature must be conducted with the same methods used in the natural sciences. He also argued that the liberal ideas of the eighteenth century had undermined the social and religious institutions upon which a stable society was based; he became a leading figure in defense of political and social conservatism in France.—Ed.]

9 [Henry Thomas Buckle (1821–62) was an English historian well known for his two-volume *History of Civilization in England* (1857–61). He argued that the history of society should be an investigation of "mass behavior" in the form of statistical aggregates, which would transform historical understanding by applying to human activities the methods of the natural sciences, making history as much of a science as physics.—Ed.]

10 [Ibid., p. 74.—Ed.]

11 ["Gelerterian" refers to a nineteenth-century Russian magician, Gelerter, who was well known for his sleight of hand.—Ed.]

12 [Mises, "Anti-Marxism," p. 75.—Ed.]

13 [Adam Smith, *The Theory of Moral Sentiments* (Indianapolis: Liberty Fund, [1759] 1976), p. 195.—Ed.]

sion of labor binds men."[14] But what about trade wars of capitalism? What about the whole history of capitalism?

Here is another pearl. "Why does the conflict occur between classes, and why not within the classes?" Mises is persuaded that here he has a trump card against Marx. If there is no conflict within a class, then there can be no conflicts outside of a class, i.e., between classes. "It is impossible to demonstrate a principle of association that exists within a collective group only, and that is inoperative beyond it." Of course this is an absolute absurdity. Quite definite, specific interests connect the working class, and not by some cloudy principle of association. "Taken to its logical conclusion, class conflict is not a theory of society but a theory of unsociability, i.e., a conflict of each against all."[15] This masterpiece Mises borrows from Paul Barth.[16] Now it is clear who are Mises's spiritual associates in this "anti-Marxism"! One is worth as much as another. This Paul Barth has a quite deserved reputation as a desperately boring mediocrity.

And there is one more "scholar" of the same caliber and manner that our angry professor is quoting: Othmar Spann.[17] This Spann is an absolutely open "scholar" of fascism, spiritual leader of "national socialism." He is a branch on the same tree as the ignoramus Hitler and philologist-historian Oswald Spengler.[18] Spann, whose very being is a telltale proof of

14 [Ibid., p. 77.—Ed.]

15 [Ibid., p. 77.—Ed.]

16 Paul Barth [1858–1922], *Die Philosophie der Geschichte als Soziologie* [The Philosophy of History as Sociology] (Leipzig: 3rd ed., 1922), p. 260.

17 [Othmar Spann (1878–1950) was a prominent and highly popular professor at the University of Vienna during the period between the two world wars. He was an opponent of individualism, political and economic liberalism, Marxism, and materialism. He referred to individualism in all its forms as "the dragon-seed of evil." Instead, he advocated what he called "universalism," a conception of society as an organic whole or totality, greater than the individuals of which it was comprised. He proposed a corporativist structure to society, in which the sectors of the economy would be organized in a hierarchy of guilds. He was greatly admired by many Austrian fascists, but was prevented from teaching by the new Nazi regime after the German occupation of Austria in 1938.—Ed.]

18 The author of the book *The Decline of the West*, 2 Vols. (New York: Alfred Knopf, 1926–28), who is in the political sense an inveterate Black-Hundreder and a committed fascist. [Osward Spengler (1880–1936) is best known for his *Decline of the West*, in which he argued that each culture and civilization passes through youth, maturity, and decline. He claimed that the West had all the symptoms of entering the age of decline as represented by such things as the "atomizing" of human life in modern cities and the reduction of human relationships to money exchange. He rejected liberalism, democracy, and the

the class character not just of the society as it is, but of the whole of [bourgeois] science as well, states that Marx gave no definition and delineation of the notion of a class, and that terms "class interest," "class status," "class conflict," "class ideology" are imprecise and indeterminate.

Mises adds that the third volume of [Marx's] *Das Kapital* abruptly breaks off at the very place where there was to be an interpretation of the meaning of "classes."[19] Nevertheless, as Mises sadly remarks, " the concept of a class became the cornerstone of modern German sociology." "Dependence on Marx is the special characteristic of German social sciences. Surely Marxism has left its traces as well on the social thinking of France, Great Britain, the United States, the Scandinavian countries, and the Netherlands."[20] That is how Mises complains. Obviously the state of affairs of "anti-Marxism" does not look too bright. Mises, the spiritual gendarme of the bourgeoisie, having no arguments whatsoever, is simply appealing to the interests of the bourgeoisie. Sure! This is another obvious "refutation" of Marx's analyses of classes.

But what "anti-Marxism" is challenging is "not socialism but only Marxism." And after his "crushing" criticism Mises gives his positive analyses. He titles it "National (Anti-Marxian) Socialism."[21] So here are old ac-

---

"decadent" values of the West. He called upon the Germans to be "the last race" of strong and heroic Prussians. While greatly admired by many German National Socialists, he ended up repudiating the Nazi movement and they, in turn, rejected him. The use of the term "Black Hundred" refers to a Russian political movement between 1900 and 1917 made up of a variety of groups, all of whom accepted the common idea of a national uniqueness to the Russian culture and people and suspiciousness of the introduction of Western liberal thought into Russia; they were extremely anti-Semitic (and helped organize the anti-Jewish pogroms of 1905–6); and they supported acts of terror and murder against those they considered a threat to the purity of Russia; see Walter Laqueur, *Black Hundred: The Rise of the Extreme Right in Russia* (New York: Harper Collins, 1993), pp. 3–57.—Ed.]

19 [Karl Marx, *Capital, Vol. 3: The Process of Capitalist Production as a Whole* (New York: International Publishers, [1894] 1967), was published posthumously (Marx having died in 1883) by his lifelong friend and collaborator, Friedrich Engels. In the two pages of chapter 53 (pp. 885–86), devoted to the discussion of "Classes," Marx says that, "The first question to be answered is this: What constitutes a class?— and the reply to this follows naturally from the reply to another question, namely: What makes wage-laborers, capitalists and landlords constitute the three great social classes?" He then admits in two short paragraphs the difficulty of determining class distinctions on the basis of sources of income and revenue—at which point, Engels adds in brackets, "Here the manuscript breaks off."—Ed.]

20 [Mises, "Anti-Marxism," p. 80.—Ed.]

21 [Ibid.—Ed.]

quaintances: "National Socialism," and the "national-socialistic" trend of Hitler-types. Mises unifies all of this under the umbrella of the fascist movement.

Here we have right in front of us the so-called first theoretical attempt to provide a foundation for German fascism. As for right now, this attempt by Mises looks more like a mixture of tangled amusements and contradictions; but let's see where this beginning takes him. Now we will see that the contradictions in which Mises is entangled are not just amusing, but in a certain sense also symptomatic and characteristic.

German "étatists"[22] (that is how for some reason Mises chooses to label the representatives of German social sciences who were taken prisoner by Marx) "see in modern imperialism of the countries of *Entente* the same thing as do Marxists: the development of capitalist aspiration for expansion." Mises obviously doesn't like this. But only in the sense that he considers the primary factor to be national hatred. Mises, the theorist of fascism, elevates national hatred to the pearl of creation. Here is his "theory": "The Marxian socialist proclaims: The conflict of classes but not the conflict of peoples, away with imperialistic war! But having proclaimed this he adds: but always (!) civil war, revolution. National Socialism proclaims: Unification of the people, class peace; but he adds to it, a war against the foreign enemy." So the thunder of victory can be heard....

But the World War made a breach in this Gelerterian symmetrical construction. Mises advocates the sergeant-major, Hindenburg psychology of no defeat,[23] but at the same time he would like to use the lessons of defeat. "German theory and practice could only proclaim the principle of force and struggle. Its application isolated the German nation from the world, and led to its defeat in the Great War." Mises wants to have his cake and eat it, too. And now Mises admits, "for the German nation a violent solution to the problem is least satisfactory."[24] Mises thinks, though, that

22 [See Chapter 5, "On the Actions to Be Taken in the Face of Progressive Currency Depreciation," footnote 10. — Ed.]

23 [Paul von Hindenburg (1847–1934) became viewed as one of the legendary military leaders of the German army in the First World War, and took on the status of a national icon in the period after the war. He ran for the presidency of the German Republic in 1925, a position that he retained until his death. In 1916, when German victory on the Western front was stalemated by French and British resistance, he proposed the "Hindenburg Program," which called for the full and total mobilization of the German economy for the war effort to assure against defeat. — Ed.]

24 [Mises, "Anti-Marxism," p. 81. — Ed.]

the same principle of self-determination of people cannot help in those areas where Germans live together with other people and represent the minority (among Danish, Lithuanians, Poles, Czechs, Hungarians, Croats, Slovenians, and French).

Obviously, one has to seek allies and coalitions. So Mises comes to what for a fascist is an absolutely unexpected conclusion: "German anti-Marxism and Russian super-Marxism are not too far from the politics of mutual agreement and alliance." "In such a situation Germany could find only one ally: Russia, which is facing the same hostility as Germany from Poles, Lithuanians, Hungarians, and in some sense even Czechs, but nowhere stands in direct conflict with German interests." Mises assures that "Bolshevist Russia, like czarist Russia, only knows force in dealing with other nations."[25]

This absurdity and slander is not Mises's original concoction; the tales about our "Red imperialism" are blossoming in bourgeois Europe. But how he plans to combine, in this case, an alliance with Russia after he has just proclaimed the rejection of the politics of force, well, this remains Mises's secret. The following is also amusing: The reconciliation of German "anti-Marxian nationalism" (which is fascism) with the anti-Marxian nationalism of so-called Fascist Italy, as well as with the awakening of Hungarian chauvinism, is not possible, according to Mises, because German national interests come into conflict with Italian interests in South Tyrol and Hungarian interests in western Hungary.

Even here in the arena of national politics Mises has his "theoretical" trump card against Marx. This is the problem of immigration. According to Mises, it is an essential question for the Germans, and he is indignant at the fact that in the entire prewar German literature there is no published research analyzing the limitations and restrictions on immigration. "This silence, better than anything else, reveals the Marxian bias in social literature." Mises also refers to the Congress of the Second International in Stuttgart in 1907, where there was passed the compromising resolution in reference to the immigration of colored workers. The Austrian representative stated that the majority of the Austrian Labor party is against such immigration. Mises keeps discussing the fact that the U. S. trade unions are undertaking "class conflict" not against their own employers but against European workers and Negroes.[26] He conscientiously closes his eyes to the

25 [Ibid., p. 82.—Ed.]
26 [Ibid., pp. 82–83.—Ed.]

fact that those trade unions are yellow Gomperists,[27] anti-Marxian, and that the Communist International makes as its cornerstone exactly the international solidarity of all workers and of all races, and gives special significance to the people of the Orient.[28]

Mises presents the issue as if the whole social problem has its modern roots in the impossibility of free immigration, while in his own German fatherland everything is fine concerning this matter. In fact, immigration for Mises serves as a channel to fulfill the economic interests of the German bourgeoisie, though it wraps it in the cloths of "national socialism." Marx irrefutably proved that the laws of the growth in population are dependent upon the economic system; the overpopulation of Germany, which makes the country seek colonies, is a pure capitalist population problem, the result of capitalist exploitation.

In this context, Mises's argument has the purpose of hiding the real reasons: the wounding of the imperialist interests of the German bourgeoisie as a result of the World War. So, Mises's "national socialism" is socialism without Marxism, and is nothing but a mask to cover the class interests of the bourgeoisie. Here, as before, "anti-Marxism" is one more

27 [Samuel Gompers (1850–1924) founded the American Federation of Labor (AFL) in 1886. He emphasized practical concerns in the use of union pressure and negotiation with employers, especially relating to wages and work conditions. He was highly critical of the more ideological motives and actions of the socialist unions in Europe and in the United States. "Yellow Gomperists" was one of the slur terms the Communists in the United States used against Gompers and the AFL in attempting to tag them as traitors to the "real" class interests of the workers. — Ed.]

28 [See "The Theses and Statutes of the Communist International," as adopted at the Second World Congress, July 17 to August 7, 1920, Moscow, in William Henry Chamberlin, ed., *Blueprint for World Conquest, as Outlined by the Communist International* (Washington/Chicago: Human Events, 1946), p. 35:

> The Communist International considers the dictatorship of the proletariat as the only means for the liberation of humanity from the horrors of capitalism. The Communist International considers the Soviet form of government as the historically evolved form of this dictatorship of the proletariat....The imperialist war [the First World War] emphasizes once more what is pointed out in the statute of the First International: that the emancipation of labor is neither local, nor a national task, but one of an international character. The Communist International once and forever breaks with the traditions of the Second International, which in reality only recognized the white race. The Communist International makes it its task to emancipate the workers of the world. The ranks of the Communist International fraternally unite men of all colors: white, yellow and black — the toilers of the entire world.

—Ed.]

confirmation of Marxism. By the way, to where did Mises's much-praised "utilitarian sociology" disappear, his theoretical heavy artillery? It happens to be that his "harmony of interests" exists only in the national arena among the employers and workers of the same nation, but in the international arena even workers go against workers—that's what Mises states based on the practice of the yellow unionism of Gompers (his "workers aristocracy"); this is the fruit of imperialism.

In one way or another, Mises assures that "a violent solution (of the national problem) is even less applicable today than it was in prewar Germany."[29] The fascist in the role of peacemaker, isn't that a spectacle for the gods? But the solution is quite simple, and Mises shows his own cards. In Czechoslovakia the German minority has to fight for its democracy and freedom from state interference in economic life; the same as in other countries where Germans are in a minority. How can we, he openly admits, combine it with the politics of intervention in Germany itself!

Mises also finds shortcomings in the newest, but very anemic and weak, "anti-Marxism." The representatives of anti-Marxism, Mises says, are satisfied with criticizing the political conclusions of Marxism, but they don't challenge the sociological doctrine behind Marxism. Who are those representatives? Mises actually only mentions Spann. Forgive us this vulgar joke: The whole "Spanna"[30] of the German fascists found their "theorist" in this one and only Spann. This Spann, believe it or not, attacks Marxism because Marxism is "a product of Western individualism, which is foreign to the German spirit." (By the way, when did Germany become the East?) Mises suggests that this attack, and the fact that Spann identifies Marxism with liberalism and individualism, have purely political motives, resulting from Spann's hostility toward liberalism.

"It is illogical," says Mises, "to deduce a similarity of the two from an opposition to both."[31] Let's put aside here the fact that Mises, in his turn, identifies social democracy with Marxism, and has not yet been persuaded that social democracy is completely harmless. But it is very characteristic that Mises aspires to make peace between democracy (liberalism) and fascism. We have partly observed and are still observing the similar process in Italy. Fascism, being purely a bourgeois movement, needs liberalism: scorpions for the workers, but liberalism for the bourgeoisie, since the bour-

29 [Mises, "Anti-Marxism," p. 84.—Ed.]

30 ["Spanna" is the Russian word for "teenage street gangs."—Ed.]

31 [Mises, "Anti-Marxism," p. 85.—Ed.]

geoisie needs liberalism for protectionism and the internationalism of the state.

Mises and Werner Sombart[32] are two aggressive warriors of "anti-Marxism." But Mises is not happy with Sombart. He considers Sombart, who was the first "to introduce Marx to German science," still to be a prisoner of Marx. It is very instructive that Mises talks about Sombart's hidden sympathies that one can find when reading between the lines. It happens to be that Sombart dreams about the Middle Ages and an agrarian state. He is the enemy of modern industrialism, the enemy of "railroads and factories, steel furnaces and machines, telegraph wires and motorcycles, gramophones and airplanes, cinematography and power stations, cast iron and aniline colors."[33] Mises gives this quote from Sombart, as an enumeration of what the socialist critics "have not yet once accused capitalism." It looks like cast iron and aniline colors didn't please Sombart. . . . It is wonderful that for Spann, the leader of nationalistic anti-Marxism, the social ideal also is "a return to the Middle Ages." This confession by Mises is very interesting. The state of affairs in Mises's camp is very sad; the "theorists" of German fascism are probably simply not very healthy people. And Mises reproaches Sombart for "a sickly weakness of nerves," in the inability to preserve spiritual stability even among gramophones and airplanes.

But Sombart and Spann are precisely those who advertise Teutonic strength and fortitude; Mises hits them at their weakest point. He hits them from the perspective of their own sergeant-major psychology, pointing to the fact that without steel furnaces and airplanes Germany will find itself helpless if confronted with the foreign enemy. Sombart is dreaming "pre-proletarian utopianism" with its "bucolic" character. Mises's response to him is that with the establishment of a bucolic agrarian state in our own time they should kiss goodbye any dream of domination. The conservatism

32 [Werner Sombart (1863–1941) was professor of political economy at the University of Breslau and, beginning in 1917, at the University of Berlin. While never labeling himself as a Marxist, in the 1890s and 1910s he strongly sympathized with Marx's critique of capitalist society. However, beginning in the 1920s, he became highly critical of Marx and Marxism for its positive outlook on the progress to industrial society. Sombart came to oppose what he considered the uniformity and ugliness of modern civilization. Instead, he looked back to the world before industrial development. By 1934, he had become a supporter of German National Socialism, endorsing the corporativist state, the Führer (or leader) principle, state intervention and planning of the economy, national autarky, and a partial reagrarianization of Germany. —Ed.]

33 [Mises, "Anti-Marxism," p. 86. —Ed.]

of Sombart and Spann reflects their retrograde ideal of a Prussian land-lord—the diehard; Mises "corrects" this ideal on behalf of the bourgeoisie, with its imperialistic tendencies.

Mises accuses his colleague Sombart that in his two-volume book of one thousand pages on *Proletarian Socialism* (1924) he never gives "a precise definition of the concept of socialism."[34] Sombart interprets the argument about socialism not as a discussion about "economic technology" but as an argument either for God or for Satan. According to Sombart, socialism wishes to throw the source of all the evil in the world, money, "into the rain," like the rings of Nibelungs.[35] Those pitiful phrases that can impress a young fascist student makes Mises reproach Sombart bitterly for the fact that he does not speak against socialism as a whole, but only against proletarian socialism, against Marxism. But Mises himself is also a follower of "national socialism."...This is too much of contradictions and confusions.

A little further on, Mises finds that Sombart admits that socialism is in accordance with the interests of the proletariat. The struggle against "proletarian socialism" appears to be a hopeless affair, and Sombart himself become an unconscious Marxist. This is what Mises, the keeper of anti-Marxian purity, asserts. Really, Sombart wants to overcome class conflict through ethics and religion; but in that case, according to Mises, Sombart is admitting that class conflict exists. . . . As a result, Sombart has to appeal to God, which is more of a confession than a statement of science, and thus, as a result, provides no proof. That is how Mises dethrones Sombart in order to retain the laurels for himself as the only actual "anti-Marxist" and theorist of fascism.

34 [Ibid., p. 87.—Ed.]
35 [This refers to Richard Wagner's (1813–83) opera cycle, *Der Ring des Nibelungen.*—Ed.]

INDEX

Note: Page numbers followed by *(n)* indicate material in footnotes.